KURT G. BLÜCHEL

GAME AND HUNTING

VOLUME 1

KÖNEMANN

© 1997 Könemann Verlagsgesellschaft mbH
Bonner Straße 126
D-50968 Köln

Design:	Peter Feierabend
Coordination:	Birgit Beyer, Peter Feierabend
Editing:	Ralph Fischer, Martin Gross,
	Sylvia Hecken, Martina Schlagenhaufer
Assistants:	Karl Georg Cadenbach, Lydia Wegener
Translation from	
the German:	Christine Bainbridge, Clive Norris,
	Martin Walters, Gordon Wells for Hart McLeod, Cambridge
Copy-editing:	Martin Walters for Hart McLeod, Cambridge
Typesetting:	Goodfellow & Egan, Cambridge
Production manager:	Detlev Schaper
Picture research:	Verlags-Service K. G. Hütten
Reproductions:	Imago Publishing Limited, Thame
Printed and bound by:	Neue Stalling, Oldenburg

Printed in Germany
ISBN 3-89508-471-9

GAME AND HUNTING

Contents

MESSAGE FROM THE PRESIDENT OF THE CONSEIL INTERNATIONAL DE LA CHASSE ET DE LA CONSERVATION DU GIBIER (CIC)

NICOLAS FRANCO

Hunting is firmly rooted in regional life and local culture all over Europe.

Originally, hunting represented an activity that was recognized and accepted by the majority of the population. Nowadays, however, huntsmen are obliged to justify their actions.

Under pressure from critics, contemporary hunting has had to introduce a comprehensive review of its traditional values, and is now obliged to create new hunting concepts and to develop a more positive image, which requires clarification.

The huntsman needs to be aware that the concept of nature's bounty has been superseded, and he must now consider his handling of wild animals in a new geographical situation. In this context, he should be aware of the different functions of the activity on which he spends time, energy, and money.

Hunting should, now more than ever before, oppose the changes in habitats and landscape which are so very harmful to nature conservation.

Fortunately, the fact that many endangered species of animal can only be protected with the co-operation of hunting, has now been widely established. The consideration of hunting in the context of nature conservation is, however, a recent development, which will require a great deal of intelligence and expertise.

Hunting has to present itself as an activity which helps to maintain the biological cycles of wild fauna, and which takes nature into consideration. This requires constant research into the development and dynamics of different populations, both within individual countries and along the whole migration chain.

Certainly the most important consideration is the need to define hunting more clearly, so that its rules can be accepted and therefore better upheld. The formulation of a new hunting ethic is the first step. This is best done in accordance with values that go back to the International Hunting Council (CIC).

In our modern, civilized world, hunting offers one of the few opportunities available to people to commune with nature, to return to the wild, leaving the stresses and strains of everyday life behind them. This is the true privilege of those who choose to hunt, and is a just reward for those who serve nature.

In what other context could hunting possibly exist?

MESSAGE FROM THE PRESIDENT OF THE FÉDÉRATION DES ASSOCIATIONS DE CHASSEURS DE L'UE (F.A.C.E)
PIERRE DAILLANT

As president of F.A.C.E, the federation of all the associations for the protection of hunting in the European Union, I gladly respond to the request to write an introductory message for a book which covers all aspects of hunting. The people who read this book will learn much about hunting traditions in the different countries which make up Europe.

Hunting is Man's oldest occupation, and has a long tradition in all human societies. It also has cultural importance, and hunting plays a central, indeed a vital role in the preservation of different habitats and species. The huntsman today is fully aware of his responsibility to preserve wildlife and its habitats, and contributes towards this in a variety of ways.

F.A.C.E too sees its main role, besides the representation and preservation of the interests of its 7 million huntsmen in the European Union, to be the development of hunting in accordance with the principle of 'wise use'. This principle, which demands the reasonable and sustainable use of natural resources, has been expressly recognized as an important instrument in the preservation of wildlife and wild habitats by the World Conservation Union (IUCN, formerly the International Union for the Conservation of Nature and Natural Resources)—a member of F.A.C.E.

Today's hunting practices have a specific economic significance. A study carried out for F.A.C.E. by the Institut National Agronomique (Paris, 1995) puts the expenditure on hunting in Europe at about 10 billion ECU (this includes, for example, money spent on measures for habitat protection). Also, about 100,000 jobs in Europe are directly or indirectly connected with hunting.

Unfortunately, hunting is still blamed for the decline of some species, particularly certain birds, although research makes it clear that other factors are actually responsible for these problems. Take the loss of habitats, for example. The conservation efforts of huntsmen are important. For this reason, F.A.C.E, together with Wetlands International and Ducks Unlimited Inc. (USA), created the European stamp for habitat preservation. From the proceeds of the annual sales of new editions of this stamp, and from limited-edition prints, more revenue was created for investing in the preservation of wildlife habitats.

F.A.C.E and Diana Jagdreisen have created the Diana Conservation Award (D.C.A.) and set up a 5,000 ECU prize, to be used for the discovery and instigation of ideas, initiatives, achievements and projects which represent hunting through the principle of sustainable and reasonable use, as a pragmatic instrument for the conservation of nature.

This book is an overview of the differences and similarities between European huntsmen and their hunting practices. It should help to dispel long held misunderstandings about hunting, and to replace these with understanding and tolerance. It gives me great pleasure that such a fine account of hunting has been made available to a wide audience through this publication.

HUNTER AND HUNTED

UWE LEIENDECKER

One need only watch a buzzard, talons outstretched, attacking its prey, to
realize that hunting and the use of weapons are not restricted to man.
But man has so perfected his weaponry that the balance is definitely tilted
in his direction.
In nature, however, where predator and prey have evolved over a long
period, the balance is much more even. Each advance in equipment or
strategy by the hunter is matched by an equivalent evolution of defensive
methods by the prey, preventing the extinction of either. Thus an attack
by a golden eagle on a group of chamois is by no means always
certain of success.

Leverets in the snow are vulnerable to attack by a bird of prey.

Human beings almost certainly evolved from ape-like ancestors in the forests of Africa over five million years ago, and underwent an important transition from mainly vegetarian woodland dwellers to hunters of the savanna, an almost unprecedented change with many consequences.

The success of this development is even more remarkable considering that, in body shape at least, our ancestors were not particularly well suited to this new lifestyle. A human, even running at top speed, would have been no contest for carnivores such as lions, leopards, wolves or hyenas.

Some other factors must then have been responsible for our success. Over the course of the next few million years we developed a kind of secret weapon, with the help of the evolution of our ever more complex primate brain. What we lacked in strength, speed and stamina we increasingly made up for in cunning. Soon the benefits of hunting in groups became apparent. Cooperation required effective communication. For proper communication, similar meanings had to be associated with similar sounds, and only thus could information be transmitted clearly to all group members. The development of weapons represented a further

Not every attack is successful, and even a golden eagle can fail to catch a leaping rabbit.

Goshawk attacking a hen pheasant. They usually ambush a flying bird from below.

Goshawk striking a typical pose to deliver the coup de grâce. Here the prey is a rabbit.
Left: Adult goshawk.

Rabbits seldom escape attack by a goshawk, even when they flee in zigzags.

13

advance, and the first weapon to appear was the simple hand-ax, followed by pit-traps and more elaborate hunting strategies. Eventually our ancestors could overpower animals several times heavier and more powerful than themselves and since that time no animal has been safe from man.

Early humans represented a new peak of evolution and enabled our species to spread almost throughout the world. Nowadays we do not have to compete against wild animals and we rest secure in the fact of our superiority. Nevertheless we can (and should) strive even harder now to be responsible and protective toward nature's own hunters and predators, for whom we have a particular fascination.

Such animals have after all succeeded right up to the present day in a world whose characteristics have fundamentally changed in just a few thousand years, and for that alone deserve our admiration and respect.

Hunting was without a doubt an important stepping stone to success in human evolution. Moreover, hunting, or at least weapons, existed long before there were people. It was nature, not people, that discovered the hunt. Hunting was thus an early and necessary result of evolution, and became moreover the driving force behind the

rapid increase in diversity of form and species which we see in nature today.

The first predators in search of prey were probably certain bacteria or similar unicellular organisms which developed in the primeval soup of the ancient oceans between four and six billion years ago. These probably began by feeding freely on organic material such as protein molecules. Eventually the stage arrived when all available resources had been used up and the early life forms confronted the first energy crisis. The only way around this involved the development of other feeding strategies. This marked the beginning of hunting, which could in itself have led to the relatively rapid extinction of all life, were it not for the 'discovery' by certain organisms of photosynthesis. They developed the facility to produce sugar from carbon dioxide and water using the sun's energy, mediated by the green pigment chlorophyll.

Using this energy-efficient method involving raw materials in abundant supply, these organisms were able to feed and reproduce with great success. These green creatures then became the preferred prey of many of the non-photosynthetic organisms. Most importantly, this development offered a path through the energy crisis, since the

Pages 14/15:
This lynx has surprised an Artic hare in its hideout. Like its close relative the brown hare it sits tight until the last second.

To warn off competitors (or in this case the photographer), this golden eagle is "mantling" its prey – a fox.

Golden eagles spot their prey either from soaring flight or from a high perch. Their eye sockets (far right) are arranged to give them a wide field of view.

25°

110°

They kill their prey by repeatedly opening and closing their sharp talons.

Even though it is as large as a goose, the golden eagle is a skilful hunter and usually catches its prey, however much the hare jinks and turns in its efforts to escape.

In nature most hunters are themselves hunted. As soon as this female sparrowhawk leaves her nest the young become easy prey to the beech marten (left).

Male sparrowhawk and prey. About half the size of a goshawk, he hunts mainly for sparrows and finches, amongst bushes and trees. The female is larger, and can take prey to the size of jays or pigeons.

green organisms could manufacture their own food and were able to reproduce faster. Life took a second great step forward.

Thus plants and animals developed, along with the basic principle: animals eat plants and animals eat animals. In rare cases plants also eat animals.

These basic food chains persist today—one animal lives as another dies—it is hunted, killed and eaten, overcome and driven out, in a survival of the fittest. This principle even operates within the brood of an eagle in its eyrie—the chick is driven away from the food by its siblings and often jostled and pushed until it goes over the edge of the nest and falls to its death.

Although conservationists and bird lovers, critics and opponents of hunting invoke a romantic image of nature and creation as a harmonious Garden of Eden, and contrast it to the destructiveness of human civilization, it cannot be overemphasized that this fine-sounding tune is nothing but sloppy sentimentalism. Nature involves and promotes forms of killing and exploitation which would be unimaginably cruel if we attempted to judge them on the basis of human ethics and our moral code. One only needs to think of parasitic

wasps which lay their eggs in their previously paralyzed prey so that the emerging wasp larvae can gradually eat their way through the living body of their host.

Apparent cuteness, exuberance and joie de vivre, feigned sluggishness, deceptive camouflage, enticing colors and seductive shapes conceal voracious jaws, deadly claws and crippling toxins. This is hardly a Garden of Eden. Animals live in constant fear of being eaten and fight for food and territory in order simply to survive and preserve their species in hot, cold and dry environments. Every creature involved in this competition has to obey certain rules.

With its beak full of insects, a chaffinch flies back to its nest. It could have saved itself the trouble because the young which it intended to feed have just been eaten by a squirrel. The squirrel is also unlucky: as it returns to its dray it falls victim to a pine marten. Just a few days later the pine marten meets its fate when it encounters a hungry eagle.

Apart from the eagle, all the creatures involved in this chain were both predators and prey. This is just one of countless similar examples from the

vast tapestry of nature, in which each living creature is just a tiny cog which nevertheless makes an
important, usually indispensable, contribution to
the smooth running of the mechanism as a whole.

For far too long we have viewed processes in
nature in terms of human moral and value concepts, we have classified creatures as pests or beneficial animals, categorized animals as predators
or prey and divided nature up into good and evil.
Although such notions are inappropriate, they
have survived tenaciously—sometimes with far-
reaching consequences.

Incapable of comprehending nature in its
entirety, we have persistently changed the world
and concentrated on isolated aspects by persecut-
ing and even exterminating certain species of animals and plants which actually caused far less
damage than was thought.

Our attitudes toward nature are gradually
changing thanks to awareness of modern ecology
and behavioral science and we are starting to look
at living creatures with fewer preconceived ideas.
They are all involved in an unending struggle for
existence and, despite frequent assumptions to the
contrary, it is often the creature that is best

adapted to its environment, in short the cleverer
creature, which survives, as opposed to the
strongest.

Predators have the same importance and right
to exist as do prey in this system. Human yard-
sticks such as 'good and evil' are alien to nature;
there are simply winners and losers. At first sight
the relationship between predators and prey may
appear cruel. Nevertheless, both have their
chances, and predators are not the enemy of their
prey. Prey is subject to the harsh pressure of natural selection, which plays an important part in
establishing an ecological balance.

Under natural conditions, predators are always
in the minority. For instance, there are always
more mice than mouse predators. If rodents
reproduce more successfully in years when there is
plenty of food, their predators also increase in
numbers because they in turn are able to rear
more young with the more plentiful supply of
food. If mouse predators proliferate, mice will
become scarcer, and the predators will have
destroyed an important part of the basis of their
existence. Usually things do not go this far
because, as a rule, they only catch the actual quan-

Their mortal enemy swoops down suddenly and
destroys the idyll – to eat and be eaten is one of
the oldest laws of nature.

21

tity of prey that they need in order to survive. When mice are plentiful, predators become fat, hunt less effectively and catch fewer mice. Very soon their numbers balance again. In accordance with this same principle, there is a proportional decrease in the number of predators in years which are bad for mice.

Mice and predators regulate each other's numbers reciprocally. Rodents make a decisive contribution to the food supply and survival of their predator species. In the final analysis the predators have the same effect because they prevent an excessive explosion in the mouse population which would in turn harm the mice. Mouse and predator therefore have a mutually beneficial relationship. The one cannot do without the other, a state of affairs which applies to all other natural predator/prey relationships. It must be remembered that a specific predator is not usually restricted to a specific prey and has other alternatives.

However, predators and prey do not make life easy for each other. They are constantly attempting to outsmart and trick each other; evolution has seen the development of extremely surprising and refined behaviors which will continue to evolve beyond current attack and defense strategies. Strategies are still being perfected, especially in the case of higher animals, and many mechanisms are almost automatic and instinctive. As always, there is an unrelenting arms race between predators and prey, but several strategies have proven particularly successful.

VERSATILITY ALWAYS PAYS

In terms of energy it is more cost-effective for a predator not to rely exclusively on a meat diet and to fall back on eating plants if necessary.

The fox is an example of such an omnivore. It eats whatever is available and food it can catch with little effort. It may surprise many experienced hunters, but it is the earthworm that occupies the number one position on the fox's daily menu rather than the stolen goose as claimed in many fairy tales. The fox can find earthworms relatively easily at twilight and at night. In addition, mice, which the fox can even find under a solid snow covering, and young birds which are not fully fledged, make up an important part of its diet, and if rabbits are on offer, the fox will not turn its nose up at them. The fox's diet is chiefly meat-based, but at certain times of the year, especially in the fall, plant food becomes more important, or even predominant. The fox is also taking

A male peregrine falcon displays with its wings spread out waiting for the return of its mate.

A female peregrine falcon feeding on its freshly killed prey.

When the peregrine falcon hunts at top speed hardly any prey is fast enough to escape it.

Peregrine falcon in juvenile plumage.

The peregrine falcon is the fastest of all hunters and achieves an attack speed of over 200 mph.

23

A hunting goshawk usually approaches flying prey (here a woodcock) from below, but strikes ground prey from above, of course.

A kestrel keeps a sharp lookout for prey in various ways: it can hover in the wind and remain almost stationary...

... or sit on a high perch. No suspicious movement up to 100 yards away will escape its keen eyes.

▷ A kestrel gives a mouse the so-called kiss of death: it breaks the mouse's neck in a single jerk.

an increasingly keen interest in trash from our kitchens, likes to tackle garbage cans in residential areas at night and wanders around landfill sites where there are many welcome tasty morsels to be found.

The badger, which is related to the marten, can hardly be classified as a true predator in the same sense as the polecat and weasel for example. The badger is a gatherer which eats anything that it can find during its nocturnal scouting trips or anything that it can dig up without too much effort. This includes earthworms, insect larvae, young rabbits, many plant species, including their roots—in short anything that is edible and which the badger finds tasty. The badger's counterpart, the wolverine or glutton which lives in the far north of Europe, mainly eats plants, small animals and carrion in the summer, but the snow and hunger of winter will drive it to kill lynx and weakened reindeer.

Brown bear are classified as carnivores in zoological terms, but are hardly predators in the true meaning of the word, and are similar opportunists. Roughly three quarters of their diet consists of plants. Insects form the bulk of their protein nourishment and they have a strong predilection for bees' nests. When brown bears plunder a bees'

nest they eat the honey and also tuck into the bee larvae. They also eat small mammals, carrion, game and, occasionally, domestic animals such as sheep. Nevertheless, they inflict far less damage on farmers than is often assumed. Despite the widely-held belief to the contrary, brown bears are not dangerous maneaters. Attacks are rare and usually only occur when a human makes a bear feel threatened. Most attacks are provoked and are therefore accidents caused by the victim's own negligence.

North American raccoons, which have become quite widespread in central Europe but are rarely seen, are even greater opportunists. These animals are active at dawn and dusk, are among the most perfectly adapted omnivores and are not dependent on any particular diet. Raccoons living in the wild are less hygienic than reputed: only captive raccoons wash their food before eating it.

A mute swan teaches a mallard drake that it has no business in its territory.

Illustration pages 28/29:
A mute swan is not to be trifled with. In the nesting season it will attack any animal or human that dares to approach its territory.

Patient Lurking Means a Full Stomach

The ambush or sit-and-wait technique which is found in many groups of animals is especially cost-effective in terms of energy for predators whose diet is predominantly or exclusively meat-based. This includes mantises among the insects and chameleons among the reptiles. Both of these freeze in a motionless posture and strike like lightning as soon as quarry comes within immediate range. Trappers use different tactics. These specialists include the ant-lions, whose larvae dig a funnel-shaped hole in dry sandy soil, usually in the vicinity of trails used by ants, and lie in wait at the bottom. As soon as an ant appears on the upper edge of the funnel it falls down into it. The larva, alerted by the grains of sand that roll down the slope of the hole, throws additional sand at its prey in order to prevent it escaping. If the ant drops to the bottom of the hole the ant-lion larva seizes it in its powerful jaws. Ambush predators include orb-web weavers such as the garden spider. It can catch up to 500 insects a day in its delicately woven silk web. It only needs one thing—a little luck.

All forms of ambush are more or less passive waiting strategies to catch prey. They are very successful but depend on chance in many respects. It is particularly important to choose a location which offers a good prospect of prey. Because life is not always quite so easy, many predators have to resort to active hunting. In addition, most predators have fast-acting digestive systems which demand a high food throughput and they therefore have to make kills relatively frequently. This applies in particular to small predators such as shrews or insect-hunting songbirds, which can die from starvation in a day or even less.

A blend of passive and active hunting is used, for instance, by the European wild cat. Like the domestic cat, it hunts primarily by ambushing and waiting in a specific location for hours on end. It only pays attention to quarry that is close enough for it to reach in just a few short bounds and which it is physically capable of overpowering. Its diet chiefly consists of small animals, especially mice, birds and fish which it catches in daylight, at dawn, dusk or night. When times are hard, in winters where there is heavy snow for instance, it becomes an active predator, makes extended forays and makes do with carrion, or occasionally slips into dovecotes, henhouses or rabbit hutches in order to grab an easy meal. It would never get involved in relatively long chases or pursuits.

The second European wild cat, the lynx, also does not hunt by chasing. It exploits the terrain to creep up on its preferred quarry—roe deer, chamois and weakened red deer, so that it can strike in a short dash over no more than 20 yards.

The splendidly colored drake's only option is to flee quickly in order to avoid the swan's pecks.

Because the lynx often fails, it likes to corner its prey in rugged mountainous terrain where it can leap down and grab them by making a huge pounce from a high vantage point. It is aware of the risk that the quarry will catch its scent early. It has often been observed that, unlike wolves and other canine species which generally attack upwind so that they are detected as late as possible, the lynx pays no attention to the wind direction when attempting an attack. For the lynx it seems that attacking from above is all-important. Cats use another tactic: they often alternate the extensive areas in which they hunt so that prey animals do not get used to their continuous presence, and in order to lessen the hunting pressure on prey. Quarry animals therefore only come across a lynx at relatively infrequent intervals and the lynx is therefore called an interval predator.

The behavior of the otter, which hunts almost exclusively in water, is slightly different: it always attempts to save as much energy as possible when searching for food, and initially scours the river banks in its home area for anything edible. Nevertheless, it also behaves like a genuine pursuit predator and can chase its prey for up to ten minutes. Its chances of success are admittedly not very high because it has to swim to the surface of the water in order to take a breath every 40 or 50 seconds during such highly demanding physical exertion.

Wild cat, lynx and otter exhibit two further traits of many predators, they claim territories for themselves and mark their borders to warn off members of their own species (e.g. by marking with urine). The size of a territory depends on many factors such as seasonal conditions, population density, the supply of food or the strength of the territory owner. The territory boundaries are not necessarily exclusive; adjacent territories may sometimes overlap in places and this is tolerated as a rule by neighbors. Usually it would be far too hard a task for territory owners to consistently defend a large territory—the brown bear, for instance, occupies a territory covering an area of roughly 25,000 acres (10,000 hectares). Serious fights usually only occur when the core area of a territory or a cave in which a bear lives is disputed.

Many predators are also characterized by a solitary lifestyle, and hunt chiefly to meet their own needs. Exceptions only occur in the breeding season and while young are being raised when the mother animal has to provide food for her offspring and prepare them by teaching them the skills they will require as predators in the future.

However, good neighborly relationships between females and males of many species have occasionally been observed: animals meet now and again or regularly on the boundaries of their territories, sniff at and greet each other, pause and 'chat' for a while before going their separate ways. Despite the competition for food which exists, predators do not exhibit a fundamentally hostile attitude. During the next breeding season there is a possibility that they will form a temporary partnership and mate because they already know each other well. A loose liaison of this type makes it significantly easier for predators to select a partner whereas excessive aggression or fights within a species can only compromise its survival.

Golden jackals, which are easily confused with foxes and which have now spread as far as Bulgaria, Hungary, Austria and former Yugoslavia, form long-lasting partnerships. They are monogamous and sometimes hunt in pairs or even in small packs of up to eight animals in Bulgaria, where they even bring down large hoofed game. Badgers, and raccoon dogs which have moved in from the East and now spread as far as France and Scandinavia, are able to live monogamously with a family structure because they mainly eat plants, insects and small animals.

HOW TO FIND WHAT YOU ARE LOOKING FOR

Hunting strategies are typical of active predators. They may vary greatly in type, but the pattern of hunting remains highly uniform. In principle, the hunt can be divided up into three phases: searching and finding, the approach and, finally, overpowering and killing the prey.

Among higher animals, both instinctive and learned behaviors play an important role. Animals often assimilate learned behaviors by watching and imitating older members of their species and siblings on a trial and error basis. They are also keen to practice, and young, inexperienced predators are far less successful than adults.

Bats locate their prey by ultrasound and are the undisputed champions when it comes to finding food. They emit high-frequency sounds that are reflected by solid objects and then picked up by the bat's ears. Even in total darkness, this gives bats a perfect image of their environment and they use this ultrasonic system to track down quarry with unerring accuracy. Shrews, dolphins and common seals also use echo-location.

Sharks, those terrifying hunters of the sea, have an excellent sense of smell. As soon as these graceful, fast swimmers scent blood in the water they are on the spot almost immediately and an unstoppable feeding frenzy may ensue which occasionally claims a human bather as a victim even though they were not necessarily the intended target of the attack. This sometimes happens in the case of the somewhat unjustly feared blue shark even though humans are not among its

The sparrowhawk's chances of success diminish if an attentive jay gives the forest inhabitants an early warning.

A sparrowhawk on patrol over its territory. It is particularly fond of small songbirds and the heavier female will even tackle a blackbird or magpie.

natural prey. Many shark species not only have an exceptionally good sense of smell, they also use an extremely sensitive electrical system to locate prey. They have special cells in their skin (ampullae of Lorencini) which allow them to search out even flatfish buried in the sand and other quarry by detecting the extremely faint electric fields which they radiate.

In contrast, many snakes detect their quarry by the heat which they give off. Crotalid snakes such as rattlesnakes, for example, have a special pit organ between their eyes and nose. Using this they can not only locate their prey in darkness, they can also use radiated heat to distinguish between potential quarry and attackers: a high level of heat radiation denotes a large animal and hence a possible enemy and the snake moves away to be on the safe side. On the other hand, less heat suggests a small animal and the snake investigates further. Measurements using special instruments have revealed that these snakes are capable of differentiating temperature differences as small as 0.003 °C.

Predators in the animal kingdom not only track down their prey using an excellent sense of smell or sensitive hearing, some predators also use their extremely sharp eyes. Under ideal lighting conditions, a golden eagle can spot a hare at a distance of nearly two miles and a peregrine falcon can see a pigeon at a range of five miles.

How to Get What One Has Earned...

Once a prey animal has been spotted, the predator must get to it as skillfully as possible. One tactic, with which we are familiar from the lynx, is to sneak up on it. The mighty polar bear, which is beautifully camouflaged by its white coat, is said to be an extremely cunning stalker. The Inuit claim that a polar bear can smell a seal from more than 20 miles. When a polar bear sees a seal basking on the ice, observers claim that it uses its head to slowly push a large chunk of ice in front of itself to provide cover. When it gets close enough it then uses its powerful paws to make a surprise strike. Other accomplished stalking experts include various cat species as well as canids and mustelids.

Swooping predators such as sparrowhawks, goshawks and falcons rely on speed, and attack their prey in flight. The peregrine falcon is reckoned to be the fastest predator of all and attacks at a top speed of over 200 mph. Under favorable conditions it is even capable of catching such agile fliers as swifts and swallows. Birds which specialize in catching fish, such as the osprey, are slower, and, as they stoop onto their prey they make allowance for the refraction of light by water because the actual position of the fish in the water is not where it appears to be.

A fieldfare with fluffed up feathers perching on a branch during a meal of berries.

This beech marten has spotted a tasty morsel.

... AND HOW TO FINISH IT OFF

Once the prey has been caught it must be over-powered. When large predators catch small prey this is no problem, the prey is simply swallowed, but prey which is large in comparison with the predator must be killed before it is eaten.

It is often assumed that higher vertebrates despatch their prey in a quick, painless and quite humane manner. If this view is so widely held it is probably due to the fact that most of us like to assuage our instinctive horror and pity. The short clinical bite to the throat given by felid, canid or mustelid is reckoned to be particularly 'humane' because it ensures rapid blood loss. This famous bite to the throat may well be the predator's intention because killing is just as exhausting a business as actual hunting. Nevertheless, it is more of an emergency solution and is undoubtedly far from pleasant for the prey, even though the creatures involved in this situation often behave in a strikingly calm manner. In reality such a bite is more a matter of slow suffocation. A bite to the back of the neck which breaks the neck is more effective for the predator because it produces a faster result. The weasel, for instance, usually first attempts a bite to the back of the neck, a throt-tling bite to the throat being used only if the prey is large. Strangulation can take up to 20 minutes. Owls also usually kill by a bite to the back of the neck, whereas many diurnal birds of prey have razor-sharp claws which are their main weapon and are used to stab the prey to death.

SURVIVAL DEMANDS INVENTIVENESS

Many predators are able to store provisions when food is very plentiful. Foxes and other canine species bury dead prey that they do not need to eat straight away and feed on the carcass later. The shrikes, although classified as songbirds, impale prey animals on thorns and other sharp objects. Moles keep a supply of 'live preserved food' for lean times by biting into the belly of earthworms at a specific point and storing them in this crippled condition, and martens incapacitate frogs by carefully biting them in the back of the neck. Many spiders do not kill immediately and merely paralyze their prey before wrapping it up and keeping it in store for hard times.

Group hunting can be no less successful than solitary hunting and a number of predators use this strategy. This can prove beneficial when, for

The beech marten does not let this opportunity slip. He needs to make two such catches for his daily rations.

35

The stoat's fur turns snow white in winter apart from the tip of its tail. It can overpower prey animals that are four or five times bigger than itself. Such prey includes little owl (1), brown hare (2), raccoon (3), partridge (4), rabbit (5) and Alpine marmot (6).

example, relatively small animals hunt larger animals when their greater numbers give them an advantage. Among European wild animals, the wolf is such a group hunter. Wolves live in packs of varying sizes in which there are strict hierarchies. Wolves also have a body language that gives them a distinctive ability to communicate and enables them to hunt in a coordinated fashion. The members of a pack know what the other members are doing while out hunting and can adjust their own behavior accordingly. They can also predict the probable reactions of quarry animals. Wolves usually hunt by a short chase, but they can also track their prey over considerable distances. One or two animals chase the prey and others direct the prey from the flanks. Eventually the animal is often driven towards an experienced older wolf which actually makes the kill. Without such coordination, discipline, and strength in numbers it would be impossible to attack relatively large prey. The wolf's diet is correspondingly varied. Inexperienced immature wolves or solitary old wolves usually have to make do with small rodents, whereas wolves in a pack take on quarry up to the size of an adult red deer or elk, a feat that requires at least four or five wolves who are experienced hunters. As well as sick and weakened animals, it is not uncommon for wolves to select healthy deer with large antlers because the

weight and size of their impressive antlers reduces their mobility and speed considerably compared with other members of their species. Wolves have also developed another tactic: they allow themselves to be chased and entice their quarry into an ambush. There were reports from the Baltic of a wolf walking calmly through a village and deliberately enticing domestic dogs – a prey animal of which the wolf is very fond. At the exit from the village the waiting members of the wolf pack gave the group of pursuing dogs an unexpected reception. Although this report exhibits several features of an apocryphal hunter's tale, it is quite believable that intelligent wolves could act in such a manner.

Other team hunters have good coordination skills and intelligence. Some pelicans form into semicircular lines of beaters and force shoals of fish into shallow waters where other birds can catch them in their beaks which they use like landing nets.

Dolphins live in smaller groups and act in a similar manner. When they spot a shoal of fish a proper round-up starts as these sea mammals leap out of the water and plunge back while making as much noise as possible. This not only alarms the fish, it also alerts members of their species in the immediate vicinity.

Other dolphins arrive quickly and take part in the hunt without any rivalry. The greater the

The stoat is one of the most versatile of predators. It can jump across a treacherous yard-wide ditch in a single leap.

Whether in its white winter coat or fawn-brown summer coat, the stoat is a gourmet and certainly appreciates a hen's egg.

When hunting a rabbit, the first attack is decisive – here an unwary rabbit receives a powerful bite to the back of the neck.

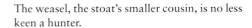
The weasel, the stoat's smaller cousin, is no less keen a hunter.

This tiny predator darts out from his hideout like lightning and seizes a vole as it scurries past.

▷ After the kill the prey is either eaten on the spot or dragged to the weasel's burrow to feed an often large family.

'Heads down in the water, tails up in the air' – mallard demonstrate how to dabble for food. This idyllic scene may not last long because danger lurks as soon as the ducks approach the banks where Reynard the fox often lies in wait for a plump duck.

The red fox makes a much more handsome impression in its long winter coat than in its summer coat. Its proverbial cunning helps this skilled predator catch even flying prey. The fox plays an important role as health inspector in forest and field by culling weaker animals.

When a new earth is needed early in the year, members of a fox family frequently encroach on each other's rights.

Two young foxes await the return of their mother. When she is raising her young, the vixen is constantly busy, searching for anything edible.

It does not matter whether the catch is a duck or a mouthful of mice, the main priority is to feed the hungry offspring.

A cock pheasant is an exceptional item on the untiring vixen's menu. The vixen is more often seen hunting mice.

As soon as she hears a mouse squeak, the vixen's ears locate it precisely and she attacks by leaping high into the air in a maneuver which is typical of a mousing fox.

47

▷ It is very rare for the brown bear to interrupt its hibernation and go in search of fresh prey.

◁ The wolf defends its prey, except against a higher-ranking member of its pack.

number of animals involved, the more successful the hunt. When neighboring schools of dolphins hunt collectively, they need only spend about half an hour to meet their daily food requirements. If they hunt in individual schools, they need to spend three hours on average.

WEAPONS AVAILABLE TO PREY

What weapons can prey use against their predators? Although hunting strategies differ widely, most predators share one common feature: they are highly adapted to their environment and as inconspicuous as possible. This is the only way of achieving any prospect of success. Prey animals also use the same tactic to remain unnoticed by their predators. Camouflage is therefore a widely encountered weapon in the struggle for survival. The white color of animals that live in year-round snow, the greens and browns of many of those inhabiting meadows and fields, are just a few examples. Other animals adapt to seasonal changes: stoat and ptarmigan have a brown summer plumage and a white winter plumage.

Where camouflage tricks such as this are not enough, running away is often the best way of escape, and prey animals are usually a match for and even superior to their predators in terms of speed and endurance. The well-camouflaged brown hare is an expert in this respect. If it is spotted by the sharp eyes of a flying bird of prey, the hare has usually also seen its predator. Initially it bravely sits tight in cover and waits motionless, hoping that the bird will lose sight of it. If the bird nevertheless stoops, the hare attempts to escape at the last minute by putting in a frantic sprint and rapid zig-zags to confuse its foe.

Living in a group is another form of self protection and one with a number of advantages. It is difficult for an attacker to concentrate on individual animals if they form dense swarms, as is the case with many midge species for instance. This increases a single individual's chance of survival considerably. In addition, many eyes and many noses can see and smell better. Deer, for example, have an excellent sense of smell and can detect the scent of a potential predator over long distances if the wind is favorable. One typical behavior of animals that live in herds is to keep close together when they start to flee in order to make it difficult for the predator to pick out an individual animal. The predator often only manages to pick out, separate and finally overpower young, old or sick animals that cannot keep pace.

Many animal species warn each other of attacks by giving off a specific odor. As soon as minnows, small fish of European streams, are

Two unequal contenders. As the photograph shows, the buzzard left the hungry robin alone.

attacked, they release an alarm substance that has not yet been chemically identified, which causes all the other members of the shoal to scatter. For days afterwards the fish avoid locations where they were attacked. The alarm substance therefore has a persistent effect and may make it very hard for a sedentary predator to hunt minnows for a certain period of time.

Running away is a common defense strategy but does not offer effective protection to many, especially slow-moving, animals. It is often simply an interim solution in order to reach a hiding place, for example a crack in a rock, heap of leaves or brushwood, cave or den which affords maximum protection against a predator.

Natural means of concealment are not safe enough for many animals. They build their own sometimes extensive, ingenious homes which not only protect them effectively against predators but also fulfil other functions: places where they can bring up their offspring in safety, store sufficient food and obtain protection against inclement weather. Animals such as mice, rabbit, foxes, badger and marmots are all accomplished builders.

The beaver is the most interesting and brilliant representative of animals which build. It makes lodges of different designs near the banks of lakes and rivers. The highest priority function fulfilled by these structures is to satisfy the beaver's need

to feel secure. The entrance to a lodge is always under water. In order to prevent unwanted changes in water level, the beaver constructs suitable dams, largely made of branches and twigs, in the expanse of water where it lives. In this way it creates a system of relatively small artificial lakes to ensure the water level remains as constant as possible. If repeated changes in water level occur despite this, especially undesirable drops in water level caused by natural or man-made events, the beaver begins to build extra dams. It builds new earth banks intended to prevent further drainage of water in front of its original dams. This urge to build structures for its protection condemned the beaver to extinction in large parts of Europe as it inevitably lost out in a conflict of interests with human water management and forestry needs. Even today many biologists who study wild animals are voicing concerns about the reintroduction of beavers (which has been successful in many places in Europe) because beavers could cause ecologically radical changes in vegetation along entire river landscapes if their populations were allowed to expand unchecked.

Some animals use a different strategy as an alternative to running away or building a home: they stand their ground and face their attacker. Various wild goats and their strong, brave relatives the musk-ox rely on this tactic. In the winter

◁ A buzzard caught in the act of hunting – a second later it was all over for the mouse.

A herd of chamois in a snow storm. Even alpine animals descend to lower altitudes in snowy winters.

when they gather in mixed herds and travel over relatively long distances, they form a circle in order to defend against attacks. If a pack of hungry wolves approaches, the snorting, bellowing bulls form a circle—an almost invincible wall of heavily built heads and dangerously sharp horns. The calves and pregnant females stay in the center of the circle where they are afforded effective protection. It is extremely rare for such a formation to be seriously attacked, most potential predators wisely giving up after a couple of skirmishes.

Taste Bad and Survive

One very different defense strategy is designed to reduce an animal's attractiveness as prey. Just as teeth and claws evolved into offensive weapons, many animals adopted corresponding defensive weapons which make them unattractive as prey. The hedgehog is a good example of this. When it senses danger it rolls up into a ball and its enemy is confronted with an all-over spiky coat consisting of up to 16,000 spines. This will quickly give an inexperienced young fox a bloody nose and teach it a lesson which it will not forget in the

future. When the remains of hedgehogs are found in the stomachs of foxes and badgers the hedgehogs were probably victims of road traffic accidents. Among creatures that live in the water, sticklebacks defend themselves with small erectile spines along their backs and sides. Contact with just a few of these is enough to ruin even an adult pike's appetite for sticklebacks.

Any animal that tastes unpleasant is also of no interest as prey. Cats often kill shrews but ignore them once they are dead, probably because of their foul taste. Unfortunately, shrews have not yet discovered any means of warning their predators that they are not a tasty meal and that they merely bear a passing physical resemblance to one.

Many moths are much more successful in this respect. They listen in on the high-frequency communications of bats and send them back a message at their own ultrasonic frequency: abort attack, I do not taste nice! (in bat language naturally). The bats avoid them if at all possible. This extremely ingenious acoustic warning system operates so well that some pleasant-tasting species also transmit at this wavelength and feed their attackers false information. Thoroughly tasty prey animals use this method to trick their potential predators and remain unscathed.

There are similar communication possibilities in the visual field. Especially among insects, there are numerous species which go through life wearing striking colors that are as conspicuous as possible rather than camouflaging themselves. They obviously want to be seen because this often indicates that there is something a bit unwholesome about them. Either they taste awful or they have other hidden, hazardous defensive weapons such as poisonous stings. In most cases predators learn by experience if they survive.

Yellow and black is a color combination which signals danger. Even humans have an almost instinctive reaction when they think of wasps and hornets and their painful and occasionally life-threatening stings. However, many totally harmless insects have also adopted the wasp look. These sheep in wolf's clothing include the hornet clearwing. This moth looks deceptively like a hornet at first sight but is totally harmless. Because of its color it is nevertheless respectfully avoided if a predator has previously had an unpleasant encounter with a wasp or hornet. This type of imitation is called mimicry and offers a form of collective protection to an entire group of widely differing animals.

Warning colors can be used to bluff in even more sophisticated ways. One example of this is the false eyes of many butterflies and their caterpillars which are actually pleasant tasting. They cunningly deceive enemies about their size and repel attackers who are frightened when they suddenly see these 'eyes' and immediately abandon their attack. The familiar peacock butterfly is one representative of these insects which disguise themselves for protection.

Finally, there are also active defense strategies where prey use almost unimaginable weapons. The hormone jet of the great diving beetle is one example of this. It produces large amounts of the vertebrate hormone cortexone in its abdomen, a substance which is of no direct use whatsoever to the beetle but, among other things, controls the metabolism of salt in fish. If a fish attacks a beetle thinking that it is a juicy snack, the beetle sprays this hormone into the water at high concentration. This renders the attacker completely unconscious, sometimes never to recover.

Animals also include marksmen among their ranks. One of the most sophisticated of these is the usually quite small bombardier beetle. It produces a complex chemical explosive in special glands in its abdomen and, if attacked, fires this accurately at its foe through two tubes, causing an audible explosion. It has been established that this is one of the many species using chemical

Red deer also gather in sheltered valleys at this inhospitable time of the year, where hunters help prevent starvation by providing feeding stations.

processes to produce hydrogen which reacts with oxygen in the air causing an explosion. This forms water which is heated up instantly and strikes the attacker as a hot blast of steam. Such a beetle can fire roughly ten times before it has to produce fresh ammunition. The explosions give off a slight smell of iodine.

Fieldfares—a kind of thrush—have recently developed projectile weapons of a different sort. In the mid 1970s fieldfares were observed, firstly in Sweden and then not long afterwards in Bavaria, ganging up together deliberately and pelting sitting birds of prey—goshawks, kestrels and, in particular, buzzards (all fieldfare predators)—with their droppings. The feathers of the raptors are sometimes so contaminated by such bombing raids that the victims can no longer fly and hunt and may even therefore be condemned to death by starvation. Roosting nocturnal predators may also be similarly attacked. Ornithologists later observed similar behavior in other regions although fieldfares in some areas seem to be unaware, as yet, of this type of precautionary defense measure. Many scientists do not exclude the possibility that such concerted actions are acts of retribution or preventive strikes.

Because there are no earlier reports of such behavior, we must assume that this harrying of predators by their prey is a recent invention. How these birds devised this exceptional defense strategy is still in doubt, and it is also unclear how knowledge of the strategy spreads. Observation and imitation are obvious explanations. Perhaps deliberate pelting with droppings developed from the milder form of mobbing where even relatively small songbirds fly along behind their predators, scolding them loudly and even physically attacking them on occasions, but without running any serious risk of injury. One thing is certain: if increasing numbers of fieldfares or other bird species discover the proven protective benefits of dung bombing, the future for their already endangered predators will be even bleaker.

Illustration page 54:
One man's meat is another man's poison – the lynx exploits the herds of game that move down into the valleys in snowy winters.

Illustration page 55:
A roe buck in velvet. This species, as well as sick, weak red deer and chamois, are all on the lynx's menu.

A carrion crow has stolen two eggs from the nest of a smaller bird species – photographic evidence that supports hunters' demands that crows should not be removed from the list of quarry species.

Nest robbers include jays and squirrels, which are a constant threat to many songbird species (a pair of long-tailed tits is shown above).

Musk-Oxen

Wolf

Musk-oxen on the tundra in northern Norway form a defensive wall to protect their young. This formation is strongly reminiscent of a circle of waggons in the Wild West. An attacking wolf pack (diagram) is usually unable to penetrate it.

A gray heron will wait motionless for a good hour if necessary before concluding its hunt successfully.

Here a lurking gray heron outsmarts an eel.

▷ ▷ Catching a frog is a comparatively easy task for this riverbank predator with its dagger-shaped beak.

61

The osprey sits on a high perch, and as soon as it spots a fish swimming close to the surface it plunges into the water.

The osprey allows for the fact that light is refracted by water in order to pinpoint and grab its prey.

When it arrives at the nest the young, almost fully fledged ospreys are waiting to be fed. The freshly caught fish is often still alive and is only killed just before it is fed to the chicks.

HUNTING THROUGH THE AGES

By Bernd E. Ergert

Hunting is a primeval aspect of life rather than a human invention. For several million years the diet of our presumably peace-loving ancient predecessors was predominantly vegetarian. In contrast, the arrival of *Homo erectus* almost two million years ago can be regarded as having a causal relationship with a high-protein meat diet. A hunter who was inferior in terms of speed and strength to the mightiest of the animals on which he preyed had to develop other abilities in order to be successful: boldness, cunning and inventiveness, communication and cooperation paved the long development path towards *Homo sapiens*. Tools and weapons marked the beginnings of human technology. As soon as the hunter became aware that to kill meant life, hunting became the focal point of ritual and magic.

In September 1991, tourists on the Hauslab mountain ridge in the Ötztaler Alps in Austria came across the brown, discolored body of a man half buried in the ice. At the time of the discovery, the corpse was assumed to be that of a victim of a skiing accident, but it eventually turned out to be the body of a man from the late Neolithic age. An ax head with its handle, remnants of clothing made of leather and intertwined grass, stone blades kept in a leather bag and, in particular, a wooden bow with a quiver full of arrows, suggested that the man in the ice had been a hunter equipped for hunting in the mountains.

In many respects this hunter—comparatively 'young' at 5,200 years old—matches the image that most people have of his kind: courageous, defying danger, intimately familiar with hunting skills and tracking game to ensure his own survival and that of his kin. But wildly romantic appearances can be deceptive. Our fearless hunter had actually been preceded by an important stage in human development which had taken place long before. Some 3,000 years earlier (in the Fertile Crescent on the northern fringe of the Arabian peninsula, some 3,000 years earlier still), humans stopped living as nomads and gradually adopted a more agricultural way of life.

Consequently, hunting had lost much of its original importance as a means of obtaining food.

Precisely what the man in the Ötztaler Alps was doing has not yet been established with any certainty. Was "Ötzi" a shaman trying to commune with the gods in the mountains? Was he a herdsman who was taken by surprise when the weather suddenly worsened? Perhaps he was some kind of mineralogist searching for copper deposits with which to make weapons?

Our human ancestors made the transition from animal to human intelligence by deliberately making weapons and tools. The hand that held a weapon was a vital prerequisite for successful hunting by *Homo erectus* in Africa two million years ago, and his steady upright gait finally left the hands free for hunting and other tasks. This upright gait also extended his field of vision and, equally importantly, it was thanks to eating meat and hunting that the human species was able to survive until environmental circumstances and its own development made farming and stockbreeding possible.

The oldest human fossil remains so far discovered in Europe were found in 1994 at Atapuerca in Spain and date from 780,000 years ago, (finds in the south of France prove the

Our human ancestors gradually evolved from herbivores into hunters and omnivores by scavenging dead animals. Hunting therefore played an important role in the process of human evolution. A scene such as this could have taken place anywhere in central Europe between 250,000 and 150,000 years ago.

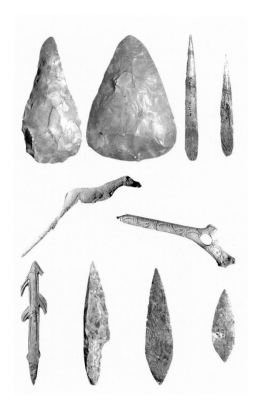

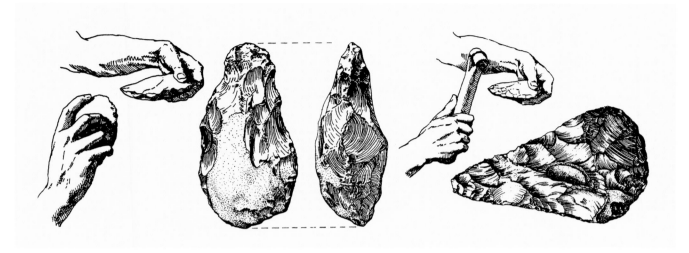

Finds of tools enable us to draw conclusions about cultural levels and also help with dating. Hand-axes (top left) are found up until roughly 42,000 years ago, and by the end of the Paleolithic period (some 12,000 years ago) there is already an abundance of different tool shapes, such as pointed bones, spears (only the ends are shown here), harpoons and blades.

The hand-ax, struck from a mother stone (top right), could be used to scrape, cut, stab and to make holes. Using a technique developed subsequently, the shape of a flake was carefully retouched using a napping stone or an implement made of organic material (bone or ivory).

Tracks, trails and other animal signs can be regarded as letters of the world's first alphabet. Hunters everywhere used the language of nature as a pattern for their own sign language.

existence of hominids in Europe a million years ago, while Italian, Czech and German finds are only slightly more recent).

The lower jaw of *Homo heidelbergensis* found in quarries near Heidelberg is dated at 500,000–600,000 years and finds from Boxgrove in southern England at 500,000 years.

The first general-purpose implement used by our tool-producing ancestors was the hand-ax, which usually had a circumferential cutting edge. The core implements, roughly worked stones, were superseded by so-called napped tools roughly 300,000 years ago. As well as the hand-ax, Neanderthals also used pointed flints and scrapers, and napped flints with retouched working edges that sometimes tapered to a point or were curved. The stiletto-like blade was an improved form of napped flint which, in the Magdalenian period, gave rise to many special tools during the last part of the Paleolithic age. Like art, the increased sophistication of stone implement technology seems to be closely linked to the arrival of Cro-Magnon man, a type of *Homo sapiens sapiens*, some 42,000 years ago.

In addition to stone tools, our hunter-gatherer ancestors used an implement when hunting which, as far as we know, is the oldest complex hunting weapon used by humans—the spear-thrower. This device artificially lengthens the thrower's arm, thus extending the acceleration distance, increasing throwing velocity and, consequently, the penetration power. The trailing end of the spear fits into the spear-thrower, and the hand of the throwing arm holds them close together and parallel. The movement for throwing the spear is as normal, but with the difference that the

implement prolongs the time during which force can be applied to the spear, thus producing the improvements described above.

One of the earliest cultural achievements of primitive man was undoubtedly the reliable interpretation of signs in his environment. Animals' tracks can be regarded as the letters of the oldest alphabet. Our ancestors had to be able to tell whether tracks had been left by a dangerous animal which would be better avoided, or by potential quarry which could be useful for the survival of the hunter and his group. They also needed to identify the condition of the animal: was it old and sick or was there the prospect of good meat and a thick coat? Was it a female with young or a lone male which was quite often not only stronger and faster but also more cunning and wary than the human hunter? In short, prehistoric man, as yet unfamiliar with agriculture and stockbreeding, had to learn to make very precise observations in order to make the right decisions and choose the course of action that offered the greatest chance of survival.

Nowadays such tracks would be unintelligible to most humans. The symbolic language of primitive hunting tribes is also a puzzle to us. For instance, how would we interpret the drawings shown on the left at the bottom of this page, which ethnologist Henri Lhote saw in 1950?

"One evening" writes the French scientist "I was sitting with a few Tuareg hunters in our camp. One of them traced a drawing in the desert sand. I asked the hunter what his puzzling figure meant. 'Look closely', he answered and pointed with his finger: 'The point in the middle is the camp fire round which we are gathered. The four

It will never be possible to give an absolutely definitive explanation of the significance of cave paintings and rock-drawings (a later example from the Gasulla Gorge near Ares del Maestre in Castellón, Eastern Spain, is shown here). It is generally assumed that the oldest caves, grottos and niches which contain representations of animals dating from the Paleolithic age were sacred places.

The depiction in art of animals that can be hunted is as old as art itself. The first finds were so amazing, and the expressiveness of the pictures and ornaments seemed so familiar, that modern forgery was suspected, especially since some artifacts were actually exposed as fakes. Most dubious finds were exposed at an anthropology conference in Constance in 1877.

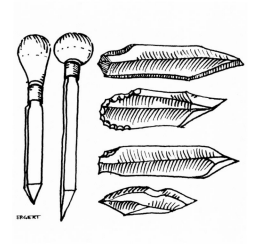

Chisel: this tool, very similar to the goldsmith's grave, was used to embellish antlers, bones and stone.

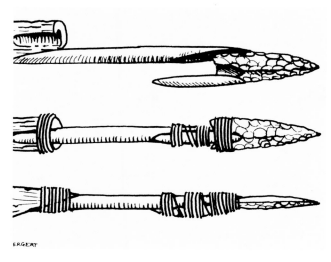

Experimental reconstruction of spearheads fitted on shafts (drawing by Bernd E. Ergert)

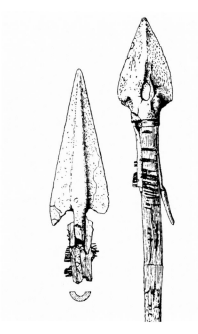

Two differently shaped arrowheads of types encountered roughly 32,000 years ago (right) or 20,000 years ago (left).

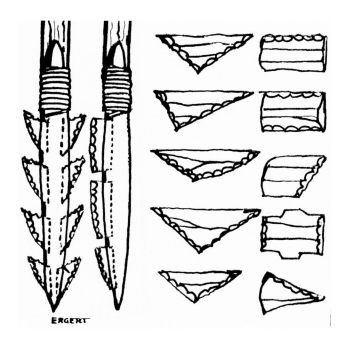

These very small objects (drawing based on a model) may have been used as quickly replaceable cutting teeth or as barbs on spear and arrowheads.

Two arrowheads in a decayed wooden quiver from the Bronze Age.

Over 100 caves with colorful pictures of game animals from the Stone Age are known, as well as thousands of individual works of art on stone, bone, antlers and ivory. The scratched drawing of a mammoth shown opposite, from the Magdalenian period, comes from near Kelheim in Bavaria; it measures about 4 inches (9.5 cm) across.

lines around it are us lying round the fire and each of us has his three dogs behind him.'"

The ground beneath our feet can be full of surprises, and throughout the world science is revealing new facts which correct or supplement our image of early people. One of these exciting finds is the recent discovery in Chauvet cave in the Ardèche valley in the South of France. Faced with these amazing images, there can be no doubt that nomadic European hunting tribes were producing paintings some 30,000 years ago, much earlier than those at Lascaux and Altamira. Far from being primitive, our Neolithic ancestors reveal themselves as sensitive beings with splendid artistic ability, who viewed the world of animals and all its mysteries with respect.

The Magdalenian period (named after the site of the La Madeleine find in the French department of the Dordogne) drew to a close at the end of the last Ice Age, roughly 12,000 years ago, at a time which witnessed the start of the postglacial climatic period, the Holocene, which has lasted until today. The landscape in Europe gradually changed. Initially, pine, poplar, birch and willow grew mainly in sheltered valley locations, but a landscape of general dense forest cover soon developed.

Humans still lived as hunter-gatherers and, because of the increasingly dense forest, they preferred to locate their settlements on river banks and at the edges of forests. This resulted in a change in hunting practices, because game which remained in the forest could be killed with less effort in the vicinity of settlements. The hunters were skilled in the use of weapons that killed game at a distance and the dog, the first domesticated animal, became an indispensable hunting assistant.

There is plenty of evidence to suggest that the wolf was domesticated during the Magdalenian period, and it must be more than a coincidence that the invention of the spear-thrower and bow and arrow also falls in this period. It is easy to postulate a causal link between the fact that a hit was not immediately fatal at longer ranges and the need to track wounded fleeing game with the aid of a canine hunting companion.

The oldest surviving European bow was discovered at Stellmoor near Hamburg. It dates from the end of the Ice Age, and is roughly 12,000 years old. Indeed, if the arrow in the picture of a horse at Lascaux can be interpreted as a real weapon rather than, as sometimes suspected, a symbol, this would be evidence of the existence of the bow and arrow at an even earlier date.

Is this figure, the so-called "Sorcerer" from the cave of the Three Brothers, Ariège, France, a hunter disguised for stalking or a shaman entreating the spirits to grant successful hunting? (drawing by B. Grosser, based on photographs).

The stylized geometrical representation of figures, in this case a hunter with a spear confronting a stag (Vogelaskos, Italo-geometric, early 7th century B.C.), appears to be an integral component of archetypal pictures and constantly reoccurs in various mutually independent cultures.

What do we know of the life of our Stone Age ancestors? The greatest problem with the scant information that we do have is the fact that only the strongest materials have been preserved (especially objects made of stone, antlers and ivory). Finds made of wood, bark, animal skin, linen or wool are extremely rare and only survive if they were preserved by chance in an airtight location.

In one of these rare strokes of luck, two quarrymen in the Neander valley (Neanderthal) near Düsseldorf stumbled across some bones in 1856. Thinking they were simply the remains of a cave-bear they initially threw them aside, but the quarry owner, who happened to be passing by, made them salvage the skeleton remains and reported the find to Johann Carl Fuhlrott (1804 through 1877), a teacher at the High School in Elberfeld, who was well known as a cave specialist and who is often wrongly cited as the finder. He was the first to realize the extreme age of this find, and the early people since known as Neanderthal Man thus found a place in the annals of human prehistory. Other experts dismissed the Neanderthal skull as a relic of a Mongolian Cossack, a Dutchman or a subnormal person. The true age of the remains was only recognized in 1901, almost a quarter of a century after Fuhlrott's death.

When we use the term "Neanderthals" today, we mean those primitive humans who lived approximately 300,000 through 42,000 years ago in a region that extended from Spain to Uzbekistan and from North Germany to Israel. We now know that, far from being clumsy, grunting cave dwellers, we would probably hardly notice a Neanderthal on a bus, provided he was wearing appropriate clothes. Their brains were almost as large as those of present-day humans. They are the oldest of our ancestors known to have had a highly developed social system and buried their dead with ceremony by providing them with food, tools and weapons and placing flowers in their graves. These were apparently the first humans who believed in life after death.

But were the Neanderthals really like us? Some geologists and paleontologists, including Wilfried Rosendahl from Darmstadt, have put forward the idea that Neanderthals maintained contacts with so-called modern humans, *Homo sapiens sapiens*, over a relatively long period of time and even interbred with them. This would make the Neanderthals one of the direct ancestors of Europeans. Rosendahl mentions certain physical features of Europeans, such as their relative hairiness, as evidence of this.

In hilly terrain or on the steep banks of the Rhine, descendants of the Neanderthals used a simple trick when hunting: they drove entire herds of animals, such as the wild horses shown here, straight over a precipice. Pits containing bones have been found in many places in Europe, such as the one near Solutré to the north of Lyon in France which contains the bones of an estimated 50,000 horses.

Mammoth bones were used to build solid structures. Two skulls with the ends of the tusks joined together formed the entrance. Finds in the Ukraine provide evidence of such construction methods for between 17,000 and 14,000 years ago.

As when hunting wild horses, hunters had to devise a method of catching these hairy giants because their primitive clubs and spears were totally inadequate to combat the fighting strength of a mammoth. They drove them into pit traps, onto thin ice or into a swamp and then lit fires.

Hunting the giant Irish deer, which often fought off an entire pack of wolves, was equally dangerous. In the end, the feature that had given this deer an advantage for thousands of years became its undoing: at the end of the Ice Age the forest became denser again and there was no room for this creature, with its sweeping antlers spanning almost twelve feet, and it soon became easy prey to its animal and human enemies.

Because remains of the giant deer were found mainly in Ireland, it was named the giant Irish deer. Would any modern hunter care to swap places with an Ice Age counterpart?

The inspiration for Dutch artist Rien Poortvliet's impressive pictures of the giant Irish deer came from a visit to the famous German Museum of Hunting and Fishing in Munich. As well as many other often highly unusual exhibits connected with hunting and fishing, the antlers of the giant deer are on show at the museum.

As proof that we have long misunderstood Neanderthal culture, he mentions, in addition to burial rites, social behavior which apparently included caring for the sick. Evidence of this is shown by finds of primitive humans who evidently sustained serious injury in their youth but despite this lived on to an age of roughly 40. Someone must have looked after them.

The find that came to light 12 miles (20 km) to the east of Düsseldorf in the tiny Feldhofer cave was the first evidence of the existence of the Ice Age humans, named *Homo sapiens neanderthalensis* after the place where they were discovered in the Neander valley between Düsseldorf and Elberfeld. This was not the oldest Neanderthal. Initially, little was known about him, and there was a tendency to underestimate his importance. Later excavations, for instance in Rheindahlen near Mönchengladbach, produced proof: "the primitive Rhinelanders" were not only extremely brave hunters, determined travelers and skillful craftsmen who were capable of meeting a certain demand for jewelry,

they apparently even played musical instruments. These may have been a kind of whirling instrument that alternately produced a high and a low buzzing sound when attached to a thong and swung in a circle through the air. Such instruments were used primarily as cult implements in recent history by the original inhabitants of Australia, Melanesia, Africa and South America. According to their traditions, this instrument was created by a mythical creature whose voice it represented.

Where Düsseldorf is now, some 50,000 years ago the Rhine snaked its way between steep hills through light woods of pine, birch and alder. Summers were sunny but cool, rarely rising above 50°F (10°C), even in August. At the time of the Neanderthal hunters, this region was under the influence of a continental climate. During the long, cold Ice Age period, huge quantities of water had been locked up by being frozen, and the sea level was some 330 feet (100 meters) lower than it is today. At this time, Britain was joined to the continent, and the Thames was a tributary of the Rhine.

The deadliest weapon of the Neanderthal was the spear. Later on, modern humans managed to improve its effectiveness still more with the aid of a relatively simple additional implement, the spear-thrower. This device, which provided added leverage and could be made from an antler, gave the hunter awesome striking power.

Our ancestors only learned to handle the bow and arrow at a relatively late stage. The earliest finds are approximately 12,000 years old, and it is therefore not assumed that Neanderthals had mastered this technology. Using such a weapon a skilled hunter could kill a roe deer at a range of over 50 yards.

Napping a flint and turning it into a hand-ax by removing one fragment at a time demanded a high level of skilled craftsmanship.

Part of an antler could be used to chip out fragments of flint.

Rien Poortvliet's imaginative scenes of everyday life bring alive a time that is unimaginably ancient. It is easy to understand how the children of Ice Age hunters learnt to handle a bow and arrow through play. Their arrows may not have had flint heads, but a sharpened wooden arrow was adequate to shoot a magpie.

Camouflage is all-important in hunting. Our Ice Age hunter ancestors also learned how to adapt themselves to the type of quarry that they were pursuing.

In order to close within spear range of a reindeer herd, hunters disguised themselves in appropriate skins and wore reindeer antlers on their heads.

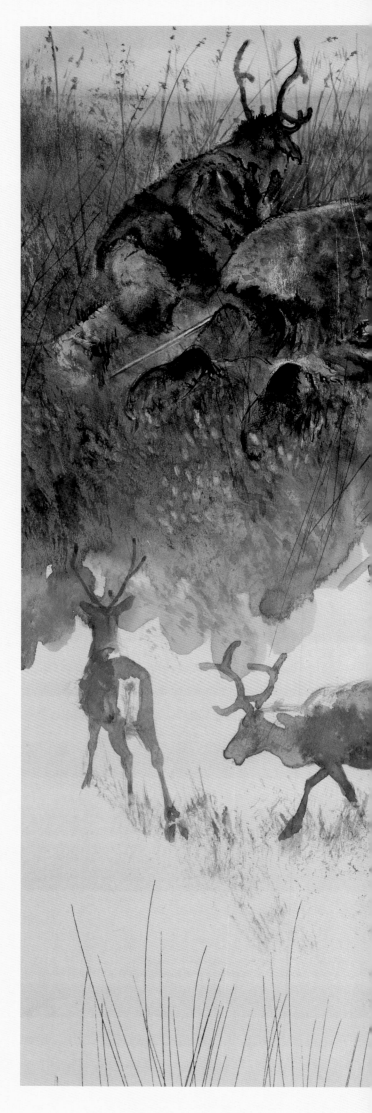

Anyone who was fortunate enough to acquire a flint would first inspect the unworked stone to assess its usability. As soon as the first blow was struck, a skilled Ice Age craftsman knew whether he would make a scraper, blade, chisel, boring tool, or arrow or spearheads.

Vegetation consisted chiefly of forests in the river valleys, sparse scrub on the mountains, grass on the high plains and prairie which stretched as far as the eye could see. The Rhine at Düsseldorf was then up to 550 yards (500 meters) wide in places, shallow and winding, and had many tributaries separated by gravel banks. It teemed with swans, geese, ducks and other waterfowl, and game hunters found sufficient animals here to hunt throughout the year.

Mammoth up to 13 feet (4 meters) tall and 16–20 feet (5–6 meters) long, weighing 4.5–5.5 tons, woolly rhinoceros 5 feet (1.5 meters) tall, 10 feet (3 meters) long, weighing over 2 tons, bison 7 feet (2 meters) tall, up to 11 feet (3.5 meters) long, weighing over 1 ton, aurochs up to 6 feet (1.85 meters) tall, up to 10 feet (3.1 meters) long, weighing over 1 ton, and wild horses grazed here. On average, every 30 humans shared this river landscape, as a kind of hunting-ground, with 50 mammoth, 10 woolly rhinoceros, 100 wild horses,

100 reindeer, 30 aurochs and 10 cave-bears. This hilly country, with its numerous limestone caves and rocky ledges, was just as attractive to the Neanderthals as an area for settlement as the wide prairie on the uplands of the Rhine basin.

Ice Age inhabitants of the Rhine region were sturdy, robust, about 5 feet (1.6 meters) tall on average and weighed around 165 pounds (75 kg). They lived in extended families of up to 30 people. Their life expectancy was scarcely more than 30 years, child mortality was very high, as is characteristic of prehistoric humans, and many women died young in childbirth. The men often died prematurely as well, as a result of injury after hunting accidents or infections. Anyone who reached the age of 60 was afflicted by arthritis, rheumatism and, probably, nutritional problems because human teeth were then largely worn out by the age of 30.

Neanderthals usually only built their camps for a limited period. They lived in a cave or under a sheltered ledge, but they also built huts on flat ground (one of these was discovered near Rheindahlen). We know that modern humans maintained additional camps which hunters used as bases on their far-flung forays. We do not yet know whether Neanderthals organized themselves in this way. Each group claimed their own territory, and only moved on once it had been overhunted.

One of the quarry animals for Neanderthals, who had not yet developed any speciality in hunting, was Przewalski's horse, the original wild horse and ancestor of domestic horses. In size and height it was reminiscent of a modern Norwegian pony and was surrounded and killed by lances with flint heads. Mammoths were probably killed by chasing them into deep pit traps.

Slaughtered animals were skillfully dismembered, and the meat roasted over a fire. Neanderthals may also have eaten the vitamin-rich vegetation in the stomach contents of the dead animal. The menu was rounded out by berries and roots.

They made spearheads and, possibly, needle-like tools from the bones so that they could make carefully scraped, cured and boiled skins of animals into desperately needed clothing by sewing, using thread made of sinews or gut. Neanderthals had to be able to produce everything which they needed for everyday life themselves. This certainly also included a great number of wooden implements which have not survived.

The way in which Neanderthals lived together shows clear signs of a social structure. Finds provide evidence that wounded members of the group were cared for, evidence of burial rites and, linked to the latter, possible notions of an afterlife. The motives behind a type of skull cult in which only the head was ceremoniously preserved—after it had been forcibly separated from the body—are still unclear. Skulls have been found with stones carefully arranged around the cranium as if the intention was to specially protect or emphasize the head.

We lose all trace of Neanderthals 42,000 years ago and what became of them is still a mystery. For a long time it was believed that they had died out before the arrival of modern humans. In the meantime, clear evidence has been found in the Near East that Neanderthals and Homo sapiens sapiens occasionally lived side by side. Further speculation on the fate of Neanderthals cannot exclude the possibility that they were wiped out by early modern humans or continued to develop into modern humans.

Once the shell of the hut had been completed by stacking up the bones of a dead big-game animal, the hut was covered with heavy animal skins and possibly finished with reindeer antlers.

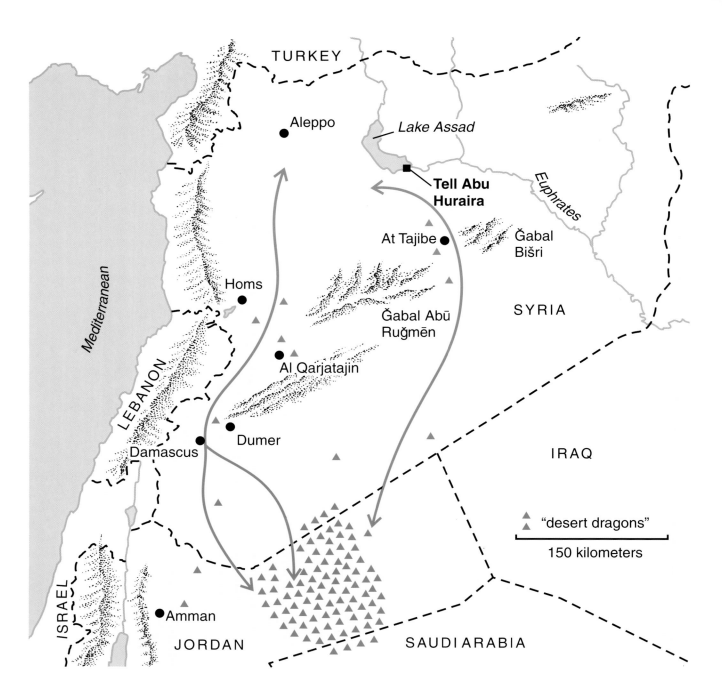

Gazelle migrations in Jordan and Syria are in a north-south direction. In late spring the herds move northwards to their breeding grounds, returning south toward the end of the summer. The eastern route ended at Tell Abu Huraira where the gazelles were hunted as they arrived in April and May.

The goitered gazelle (*Gazella subgutturosa*), also called the Persian Gazelle or Ahu, was the main quarry of hunters at Tell Abu Huraira. The male (below) grows to a height of 2 feet (60 cm) at the shoulder. This animal has been wiped out in Jordan and Syria by relentless hunting and is now mainly found in Central Asia (Turkmenistan).

A Neolithic Revolution
Hunter-Gatherers as Farmers
and Stockbreeders

A fundamental economic change which brought with it a different way of life occurred roughly 8,000 years ago in Central Europe. Our Neolithic ancestors grew cultivated plants, raised domesticated animals and became farmers and stockbreeders who clung to their land. Forests were cleared extensively along watercourses as well as on uplands, and this produced isolated clearings with relatively small settlements, surrounded by vast tracts of virgin forest. There were still no meadows, and cattle, goats and pigs were herded onto so-called forest pasture.

We believe that this revolutionary development began in the Fertile Crescent 10,000 or 11,000 years ago. The Neolithic revolution depended on ecological preconditions and was to have far-reaching ecological consequences: humans began to change their natural environment. No doubt

farmers living under Stone Age conditions continued hunting as before, as we can assume from the body found in the ice of the Ötztaler Alps. By the end of the Ice Age the natural habitat of most big quarry animals such as the mammoth had largely disappeared, but rivers and coastal regions offered new opportunities for fishing and hunting other aquatic animals once water levels had risen.

Excavations in Tell Abu Huraira near the Euphrates in Northern Syria have yielded evidence that hunting continued to make a significant contribution to human diet, even after the changeover to agriculture and the adoption of a more settled lifestyle. Even though crops had been cultivated for 1,000 years, the settlers there met their needs for animal protein by lying in wait for migrating gazelles early each summer. The animals were driven between walls that converged in a funnel shape into a kind of corral which was big enough to accommodate the entire herd comfortably. Analysis of the finds shows that the animals were slaughtered on the spot.

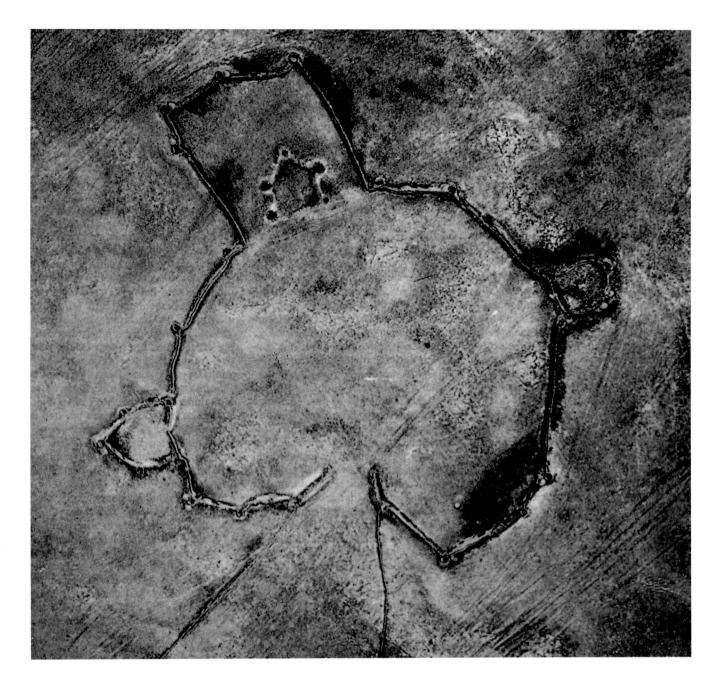

Pilot L.W.B. Rees called the structures which he discovered from his aircraft during mail flights between Cairo and Baghdad "desert dragons", and first described them in 1929 for the archeological journal "Antiquity". They are in fact facilities for catching and killing entire herds of gazelles and are found in Syria, Jordan, Saudi Arabia and in the desert regions on the Sinai Peninsula. The photo shows such an arrangement near Dumer, some 30 km northeast of Damascus. It was probably made of stone, and the gazelle were driven between walls that converged in a funnel shape (bottom) into the large enclosure where they were slaughtered.

Finds such as these give us a more detailed understanding of the slow acclimatization process which must have taken place. The find shows that one aspect of agriculture (in this case arable farming) may have become established much earlier than another (in this case the domestication of animals). In the transitional phase, hunting and gathering may well have continued alongside a rural economy and hunting may even have made a greater contribution toward supplying meat than did keeping animals.

The cradle and nursery of humans and their ancestors was in Africa, from where people probably migrated eastwards through the Middle East to Asia, Australia and America, with a westward population movement through the Middle East into Europe. This is one of the hypotheses that has been advanced in an attempt to explain a frequently observed north-south difference in cultural level. For instance, tribes living exclusively by hunting inhabited the north, where spears with stone heads were used for hunting wild boar and aurochs in Central Europe, whereas a sporting, formal type of hunting had already evolved in ancient Egypt. We have precise records which go back as far as the early days of Egyptian culture and it seems that hunting was a popular sport there among the upper social classes. Murals and extremely finely detailed works of art, together with hunting equipment found in graves, point towards elaborate hunting methods.

Waterfowl were hunted from boats on lakes and rivers using an S-shaped wooden missile, and trapping nets were used to catch ducks and geese. The net was attached to long poles which were suddenly raised in front of the low-flying birds and then immediately lowered once the quarry was entangled in the net. In addition to hunting waterfowl—the Egyptians were already using decoy ducks made of clay and feathers—hunting with a bow and arrow from a chariot was a popular pastime of the aristocracy. Hunting scenes show that antelopes, wild cattle and lions

While Neolithic hunting tribes in Europe were still leading a comparatively primitive life in the 3rd millennium B.C., the historical age was beginning in Egypt with the First Dynasty, the foundation of Memphis and hieroglyphs. The Egyptians practiced a formal type of hunting, and water fowl were hunted using an S-shaped wooden missile in 1500 B.C. They also used nets to catch ducks and geese.

The lord of the grave is standing in a small boat in the midst of a papyrus thicket. He is about to throw his boomerang-like missile into the approaching flock of birds. This Egyptian grave relief (circa 2250 B.C.) is part of a bird hunting scene.

85

A Sassanian prince hunting ibex and wild boar. Hunting motifs are not uncommon in this culture group (dish, gold-plated silver, 5th/6th century).

Ibex feature on many Achemenide works of art. On this magnificent embossed silver dish (Iran, 6th century B.C.) four ibex surround a gold rosette in the shape of a stylized sun. The ibex was a sun creature in the Achemenide iconography.

A group of seven wild boar with magnificent bristles, curly tails and heads lowered ready to attack decorate the lid of a Chalcidean mixing vessel for water and wine (circa 540 B.C.). Their tusks were originally white, as can be seen on some of the animals.

This archer and lion are from a plinth relief in the Western Palace of Prince Capara in Halaf (Guzana/Upper Mesopotamia). They date from the first half of the 9th century B.C.

Hunting a fox with dogs. The hunter in this Roman mosaic is armed only with a staff.

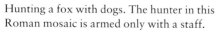

This hunting scene from a Roman floor mosaic (circa 150 A.D.), discovered in Westerhofen near Ingolstadt, shows a hunt for fieldfares, which are mentioned in old recipe books. A lime-twig was used, fixed to the tip of a length of bamboo rods that could be fitted together.

Killing an animal in its den was and still is considered unsportsmanlike, but perhaps this mounted hunter with his double-pronged lance only intends to put up the hare.

Natural-stone mosaic from Pella (Greece) showing a fallow deer hunt (circa 325 B.C.).

Artemis with bow, arrows and quiver and her hound going out to hunt (Syracuse, circa 215 B.C.).

Early Classical 4-drachma coin from Selinunt (Sicily), dated 460 B.C. The image shows Apollo and Artemis hunting from a quadriga.

A stater coin from Caulonia (Southern Italy), circa 400 B.C. A stater was originally twice a unit of weight, later becoming the highest-value coin of a set.

Ten-drachma coin from Acragas (Sicily), 411 B.C. showing two golden eagles feeding on a hare. The significance of the grasshopper on the right-hand edge of the coin is unclear.

This Roman mosaic from the middle empire period (circa 150 A.D.) shows an attacking wild boar which has already knocked down one hunter and put two others to flight.

were the preferred quarry. When it is the Pharaoh who fires the fatal arrow we are looking at something more than merely a genre-painting of a hunting adventure, we are experiencing the conflict between good and evil in ritualized form.

The Greeks and Romans were the first to describe hunting in detail. Xenophon's (circa 430–circa 354 B.C.) "Kynegetikos", which contains interesting facts about hunting hares, deer and wild boar, as well as details of dog breeding and training, is the oldest surviving hunting treatise. Almost as if explaining the origins of big game safaris, he tells of hunting exotic animals such as lions and leopards in foreign countries. However, Xenophon also emphasizes the educative role of hunting as a means of strengthening men for war, thus echoing the analogy between hunting and war which had been expressed earlier in Homeric epic poetry and which runs as an unbroken thread through the whole history of hunting.

Other famous ancient authors who expressed views on hunting include Plato, Cicero and Virgil. Flavius Arrianus (circa 95–175 A.D.), a pupil of Epictetus, Roman Consul and historian, whose style was influenced by the sober down-to-earth clarity of Xenophon on whom he modeled himself, writes knowledgeably on the best hunting methods and on dog breeding.

Seneca (4 B.C.–65 A.D.) writes about Roman hunting methods: "You may carry a throwing spear in the right hand and in the left hand a heavy oak lance with a broad blade. You should remain concealed in hiding, scare the animal into flight with shouting and remove the entrails with a curved knife after victory has been won."

As well as hunting for hares, red deer, wild boars, bears, wolves and foxes, ancient authors, like Xenophon before them, also mention that most royal quarry of all in North Africa and the Orient – the lion. Very few Romans would have been familiar with lions and tigers in the wild, but they had usually seen them as animals put on show in menageries. This form of entertainment originated from Mesopotamia, as did the practice of throwing common criminals, political prisoners and those of a different faith to wild animals.

The bloody spectacle of staged hunts and animal fights was usually played out in the amphitheatre. The Colosseum in Rome, the largest and most sophisticated of its kind, had an estimated capacity of between 50,000 and 73,000 spectators. The tiered seating could be shaded with awnings rigged like sails, and the arena could be transformed into a lake or stage set in which wild animals were hunted; 5,000 wild animals were killed during the 100-day opening ceremony of the Colosseum alone, on the orders of Emperor Titus (79–81 A.D.). The last of these animal set pieces (venationes) took place in 523 at the behest of one Consul Maximus.

"Then when the thundring *Jove* his Snow and showres
Are gathering by the Wintry houres;
Or hence, or thence, he drives with many a Hound
Wild Bores into his toyles pitch'd round:
Or straines on his small forke his subtill nets
For th'eating Thrush, or Pit-falls sets;
And snares the fearfull Hare, and new-come Crane,
And 'counts them sweet rewards so ta'en."

*Horace on hunting in the "Epodon liber",
Epode II, Country Joys (circa 29 B.C.),
translated by Ben Jonson.*

THE CHIVALROUS HUNT IN THE MIDDLE AGES

There had been secular hunting scenes in the ancient world when interest focused on humans and their sphere of activity, but they disappeared almost completely in early Christianity. Only extremely scarce finds from excavations and conclusions drawn from handed-down traditions in subsequent periods, analyzed using linguistic techniques, enable us to sketch out a picture of hunting before the Middle Ages.

No doubt hunting using hedges as barriers developed alongside drive hunting or hunting with hounds at a very early stage. Perhaps it can be regarded as the first distinctive feature of "German" hunting because, although it stretches back into ancient Germanic times, its significance lasted well into the late Middle Ages. Whereas game was driven into nets in the Mediterranean countries, hedges which had gaps in them through which game had to pass were planted in Central Europe. For driving hunts, snares or nets were set in these artificial game runs. Place and field names ending in "Hag" are a present day reminder of these often kilometer-long hedges consisting of dense undergrowth.

Trapping and bird-catching using nets and snares had a special place in early hunting practices. It is precisely in these activities, described in classical antiquity and continuing into the 19th century, where we need to make the distinction between trapping for economic reasons and real hunting.

In ancient times, bird-catching and fishing undoubtedly made a decisive contribution to the diet of a wide range of people, and large-scale netting was probably carried out as a profession. Bird-catching using static snares or collapsible limetwigs, for which there is extensive evidence in Art from ancient times onwards, can be classified as hunting. Where the Roman hunter used a limetwig to catch a game bird that had been frightened into a tree by a tame bird of prey, the Germanic peoples used the clapper trap.

This device for trapping small birds consisted of two close-fitting wooden slats that were manually operated by a pull cord. An explanation in Stephan Behlen's Forestry and Hunting Lexicon published in 1842 in Frankfurt am Main shows just how long this trap was in use: "Such traps are placed near holes in the hide with decoy birds alongside them. As soon as a bird lands on it the cord is quickly pulled, both the pieces of wood snap together and catch the bird by the feet, the trap is then quickly pulled into the hide, the bird is despatched and the trap put out again to catch another bird."

By the end of the Dark Ages (6th century A.D.), untouched forests were found only on land that was less suitable for agriculture, and in mountainous regions. The days of uncontrolled forest clearance were over by the end of the 14th century. Woodland was thus a rare commodity and was therefore worth protecting. It became increasingly economically important as a raw material and as a means of production for early industries (glass, salt or iron smelting) and for building towns.

Two miniatures from the Codex Mansse (circa 1330):
The left-hand picture shows minnesinger Kol von Nüssen practicing a form of falconry for small game in which a tame bird of prey, in this case a blue falcon, attracts other birds which mob it, in turn allowing the hunter to shoot at them with his crossbow. Two magpies and three jays with opened beaks are evidence of the din they are making. The picture on the right shows Austrian (?) minnesinger Pfeffel out angling. He is pulling the rod with the fish out of the water in an elegant sweep—but his lady companion seems to have his undivided attention.

Riding out to hunt; the picture for the month of August from the Breviarium Grimani, a Flemish book of hours circa 1510.

A growing population and a boom in towns in the high Middle Ages caused new types of environmental problems. Sovereigns and town councillors concentrated on containing the sources of pollution rather than on eliminating them. Tanneries and dye works were always located outside the town walls, there were sewerage systems and early forms of waste disposal, and pavements controlled the spread of dust and mud.

As early as the 6th and 7th centuries, unrestricted hunting was only possible on unclaimed land, that is lying outside the March. Only members of the March were permitted to hunt within the March and the first hunting and fishing laws came into existence.

Influential centres of power had formed since the 8th century with the concept of kingship. This led to reform of the legal situation that had previously prevailed at the expense of those members of the population that no longer had political influence. As more and more woodland fell victim to extensive clearance for settlements in the 8th century, the "high and mighty" placed specific tracts of previously ownerless woodland and common land under the jurisdiction of the king, reserving them exclusively for the ruler.

Hunting red deer with specially trained hounds became a social event and was positively celebrated. Once the animal had been killed it had to be gutted, skinned and dressed, with a portion of the entrails reserved for the hounds. The hunt also afforded an opportunity for other pleasures, a fact that is certainly not glossed over in this deer hunt scene from the Devonshire Hunting Tapestries (Arras or Tournai, circa 1445).

Rights could be transferred to other persons in the form of a fief. This brought about the separation of hunting rights and land ownership.

It was the Frankish kings who, as part of re-forestation, created the first hunting districts where hunting and specified types of forest exploitation were exclusively reserved for authorized persons but were prohibited for all others and punishable by harsh penalties. Foresters who had the job of looking after game as well as its habitat were employed to administer these areas.

From the 13th century onwards, noblemen and communities, as well as the royalty, acquired hunting rights that were part of the prerogatives and attributes of sovereignty belonging to the king or a prince. Such privileges were not confined to individual regions, but extended throughout the entire territory. These prerogatives dealt with those game species designated as "big game," especially red deer and wild boar, which were particularly highly prized and reserved for hunters from the higher nobility. "Small game" were left to the lesser nobility, and these included hares, foxes, various game birds and other animals.

In order to understand hunting in the Middle Ages and therefore hunting weapons, implements and works of art, it is essential to understand hunting techniques as well as the social system. The hunter's primary objective was to procure wild animals, either living or dead.

The usual three-part division applied to the Middle Ages also applies in terms of its weapons technology. The bow and, possibly, the spear-thrower may be considered the typical long-range weapons of the early Middle Ages (circa 500–1000). In addition, hunters carried a hunting spear, a throwing spear and a sword of a type similar to that used in battle.

In the high Middle Ages (circa 1000–1400), in addition to the bow, which remained a popular hunting weapon into the 17th century, hunters used the new and increasingly popular crossbow, with a stave made of wood or horn. The boar spear, also called a hog spear, was another useful weapon. This, like the hunting sword, had a bar to fend off a powerful animal such as a bear or wild boar. The expert handling of this weapon is described in an old hunting book: "A hunter who wishes to catch and stab a wild pig must stand so that he can dominate with the spear in the left hand and press vigorously with the right hand planting his feet so that the left thigh is below the left hand and the right thigh is firmly and solidly braced below the right hand and presses towards

Riding out to hunt with falcons. In the Middle Ages the art of falconry was a form of hunting reserved exclusively for higher nobility and the clergy.

Rabbits were regarded as small game and rabbiting was the domain of the lower nobility. The services of domesticated, specially-trained polecats (ferrets) have been used since the Middle Ages. They chase the rabbits out of their extensive underground warren into the open where they can be caught in nets. A Flemish tapestry (dated circa 1470) vividly records this form of hunting.

the pig." The major game species, in addition to the potentially aggressive wild boar, was red deer, with roe deer playing a less important role. Small game such as hares, badgers, martens, beavers and otters were also sought after quarry.

This basic hunting equipment had changed little by the late Middle Ages (circa 1400–1520).

Early crossbows were made of wood. Later on in the 13th century the stave was made by gluing many sheets of horn together and, finally, the crossbow was fitted with a steel stave that could be drawn by using a cogwheel mechanism. Using this weapon gave the hunter a longer range of fire but he had to cope with the fact that, in cold weather, the bow was liable to go off as it was being drawn. This was why Emperor Maximilian I (1459–1519) advised, in his "Private hunting book", that the steel stave only be used in summer.

Emperor Maximilian was one of the first people who sought to experience nature and measure sporting prowess by hunting. His passion for hunting should not lead us to overlook his efforts to care for and protect game. The German "White King", another document detailing courtly culture in the late Middle Ages, mentions the following

game species as worthy of protection: hares, marmots, wild pigs, chamois, ibex and deer.

Conservation increased game stocks significantly and game animals helped themselves to the peasants' already meagre crop yields, but peasants were not permitted to take any defense measures. Among other factors, the erosion of peasants' rights to use forest and meadow, and damage caused as a result of excessive conservation of hoofed game led to unrest toward the end of the Middle Ages, culminating in the various German peasant revolts.

The Renaissance Chase

Unmistakable structural changes in the landscape were already apparent by the end of the Middle Ages. A huge increase in demand for timber for house construction, shipbuilding, furniture, tools and heating due to the increasing number of town dwellers led to a noticeable encroachment on natural habitat. Destructive lumbering and, above all, advances in weaponry significantly reduced the chances of survival of game. Big game in particular, such as wild cattle (aurochs) and

Nowadays it is impossible to imagine how "holding" hunts, in which large numbers of animals were methodically driven into an enclosed area and bagged, could be reconciled with ethical hunting. The thinking behind this behavior is best understood by remembering that animals in those days were largely considered as mere objects, hardly living beings, and certainly not sentient creatures. (Chromolithograph from Deigné Delacourt, La chasse à la haie, Paris 1858).

Detail of boar hunt with hounds from the
Leopold altar by Rueland Frueauf the younger.

Pictures such as this illustrate the formal nature
of hunting. Leopold III, Margrave of Austria,
rides out to hunt with his wife Agnes (a boar
hunt with hounds, see Figure above). They ride
behind his hunters in full array at a measured
pace. This panel is part of the Leopold altar
(1505, a copy is shown here) by Rueland
Frueauf the younger, representing the legend of
the foundation of the Klosterneuburg Collegiate
Church near Vienna. This church was begun in
1114 after a vision of the Virgin Mary which
Leopold experienced on the occasion of this
boar hunt.

European Bison as well as elk and bear, began to feel the effects of human interference with nature.

Black powder had been used as a propellent in guns since the late 13th century. Powder factories to produce and refine gunpowder sprang up everywhere, for example in Augsburg in 1340, in Spandau in 1344 and in Liegnitz in 1348.

The conscientious huntsman appears to have subjected his powder to thorough, almost suicidal testing. F.E. Jester's work entitled "On small game" (Königsberg 1793) states that: "It (the powder) must have a cold, salty taste and not be crushed easily between the fingers but, when pinched hard it must leave no trace or only slight blackening on the fingers."

The paper mortar and ballistic pendulum were used to test the "expressive power of the powder." The "rack powder test" was also used. This consisted of a cylinder with a very close-fitting lid. When a precisely measured quantity of powder was exploded in the cylinder, the movement of the lid in opposition to the force exerted by a spring was transferred to a disk by means of a toothed rack, and the huntsman could then read off the "power" of his powder from graduations marked on the disk.

The refined form of hunting with hounds and cross-country hunting, riding to hounds in the 17th and 18th centuries, usually took place in a wood specially laid out for that purpose.

The many parks that have been preserved complete with their stands of old trees in the vicinity of stately homes are remnants of these areas used for court hunts. If any natural woods still remained in those days despite excessive exploitation of woodland, especially by intensive tree felling, the credit for this must go to proper forest management. This wonderful means of preserving woodland is called "the sustained yield method", in other words one must never fell more timber than the amount that is currently regrowing.

It was primarily the use of firearms that brought about a change in hunting ethics. Firearms for use in war had been familiar since the 14th century

The hunting coat of arms of Emperor Maximilian I.

The legend of the foundation of Polling Monastery near Weilheim also has its origin in hunting, as is recorded by the rood altar (circa 1450). Tassilo III, Duke of Bavaria (circa 741–794) was pursuing a hind when it suddenly stopped running, began to paw the ground and exposed a cross that was allegedly identical to that on the high altar in Polling.

Hunting deer and bear with hounds was a lordly distraction. This picture by Lucas Cranach the younger, dated circa 1540, shows Frederick the Wise, formerly the Regent of Charles V, at the foot of Torgau castle on the Elbe. The extent to which such a spectacle was carefully prepared is evident from the fact that only royal stags have been presented for the hunting party's enjoyment.

but hunters could only use firearms once the wheel-lock had been invented because matchlock guns were awkward to handle, making them unsuitable for hunting. The wheel-lock system is similar to that used in a lighter with a flint: a small toothed wheel linked to a wheel spring rubs against a piece of iron pyrites, thus producing sparks which ignite the powder charge.

This system, invented in Nuremberg in around 1520, remained in use on target and sporting guns into the 18th century.

As well as the large crossbow, a lightweight crossbow which fired a round projectile was used, especially for hunting birds. Artistic decoration on weapons became very popular in the Renaissance, and animals, plants, human figures and fabulous creatures were often represented as inlaid work using gold wire, ivory, mother-of-pearl, bone or horn.

Large reserves were established in order to ensure a plentiful supply of game which could be hunted by courts. Field or place names such as "deer park", "game meadow" or "deer meadow" are present-day reminders of these enclosed areas. Menageries which formed part of a princely household were another way of keeping game. Both native and exotic game were kept in Vienna, London, Versailles, Stockholm, Copenhagen and Dresden for staged hunts, in cages and arenas patterned on the Roman model.

Festive occasions in those days were planned and organized at an expense which is nowadays unimaginable and they afforded a welcome opportunity to show off one's prowess. Hunting was the preferred medium for these theatrical productions, which were always focused on the prince.

At the same time as riding to hounds, which was especially popular in France, so-called German hunting began to develop in Germany. Although cross-country deer hunting which sought to achieve the most perfect possible interplay between hound, horse and rider was still practiced, the effortless trapping of game in hedges and nets increasingly came to the fore.

Hunting with equipment such as nets and toils made it possible to achieve large bags, especially in the case of hoofed game (notably red deer and wild boar), and this technique was also used to catch wolves when necessary. Virtual plagues of wolves sometimes occurred, particularly where tracts of woodland adjoined each other. The wolf took a high toll of red deer and roe deer, nor did it spare livestock and domestic animals.

The population tried to protect itself against the wolf as a competitor for food by making wolf pit traps and snares. This cunning raider was so greatly feared that special prayers were said as the cattle were driven to pasture. If prayers, pitfalls, traps and shooting the wolf at specially laid carrion lures (a rotting carcass was used as bait) all failed, those in authority arranged special wolf hunts. Large nets were hung from securely anchored poles as soon as the wolves had been tracked and located. In winter the holes for the poles were made in the frozen ground using a hole borer. The wolves were then "held" by being driven into the semicircle with the nets in position. Then they were chased to and fro by peasants, shouting and beating drums, until they ran into the nets and were beaten to death by specially positioned guards.

Detail from frescoes (post 1385) from the hall of the knight's castle at Runkelstein near Bolzano. Maximilian I had them restored.

The horn is blown to proclaim the end of the boar hunt in the picture for the month of December from the "Très Riches Heures", the Duc de Berry's book of hours. The Limburg brothers are inspired by an Italian model in their choice of subject. The soaring towers of Vincennes castle where the Duke was born in 1340 can be seen in the background.

Duke Ludwig of Württemberg and his wife in the midst of a large hunting party. The picture provides detailed information about princely hunts at the end of the 16th century. Such scenes have seldom survived from this period. The sequence of a deer hunt is depicted in three parts: the hunt is still in full swing in the wooded countryside in the background; the hunters gathered in the middle part of the picture proclaim the end of the chase by blowing their horns; the skinning, dressing and removal of the deer are shown in the foreground.

Art, music and literature have been influenced by hunting in every age, but to widely differing extents. For instance, the spread of Christianity is associated with a decline in secular literature and secular art until the early Middle Ages. Pre-Christian texts and images were rejected as heathen, and early Christian art and literature had no more reason to deal with secular topics than had early medieval art and literature, because the church enjoyed a virtually exclusive monopoly on education in those days. Naturally, hunting topics were also affected by this form of church censorship. This state of affairs only changed with the consolidation of non-ecclesiastical power and the associated development of courtly culture.

Hunting literature gradually revived with the first written accounts of hunting techniques and hunting customs in verse form in medieval heroic epics such as the Spessart hunt in the Nibelungenlied, which was written in its final form in around 1200. Previously there is little information, and hunting lore, like literature, was probably handed down orally during those centuries. In Gottfried von Strassburg's verse epic entitled "Tristan" (circa 1210) we are told about huntsmanship according to the statutes of a guild that had its own language. The young Tristan shows an English hunting party how to gut, skin and cut up a deer properly, in the manner he had learned from the prince who taught him.

It seems that the first independent writings on the subject of hunting which are worthy of the term "essay" dealt with falconry, a fact which can perhaps be attributed to the crusaders' encounters with Oriental culture, in which this form of hunting was even more prestigious than at home. Thus the impetus which led Emperor Frederick II (1194–1250) to create the most important European manuscript on this subject, "De arte venandi cum avibus" (On the art of hunting with birds) is often linked to his involvement with the crusades. Frederick made use of his experience of falconry going back over 30 years and described all the falconer's jobs, hunting methods and cooperation with hounds as well as the distinctive characteristics and typical behavior of quarry animals. His own deluxe edition was divided into six books dealing with different topics, was lavishly illustrated and is said to have been as thick as two Books of Psalms. It fell into enemy hands in 1248, was mentioned in 1264/1265 and was then lost for ever.

Only text and miniatures have survived, and none of the known copies can be traced back

Frederick II—the falconer on the imperial throne.

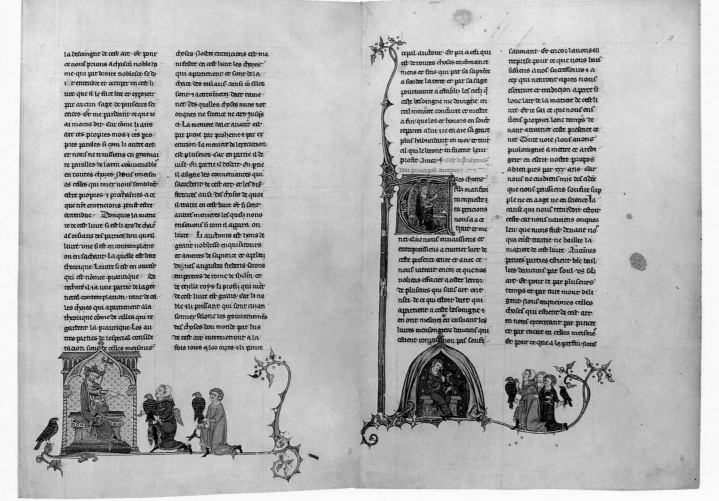

The magnificent original of Frederick II's falconry book which fell into enemy hands in 1248 went missing during the second half of the 13th century. The work nowadays so admired is a duplicate produced by order of Frederick's son Manfred. After King Manfred died in battle in 1266 fighting against Charles of Anjou, this manuscript turned up in France as booty. In around 1300 it came into the possession of Jehan de Dampierres, who ordered the translation that is shown here (folio 2r and folio 3r have been mounted.)

The first part of the falconry book describes the quarry animals for hawking as well as their various types of behavior. The self-defense strategies of individual birds are described here.

The second part of the manuscript is devoted to the correct way to handle falcons. Here the falconer learns what he must do if the bird becomes unsettled on its perch.

◁◁ A restive falcon is best soothed by showing it the "reward" (a plump morsel of meat). During the initial stages of training it is important that the bird sees both the falconer's face and the reward.

◁ King Manfred who expanded his father's text is shown on one of the first pages of the falconry book.

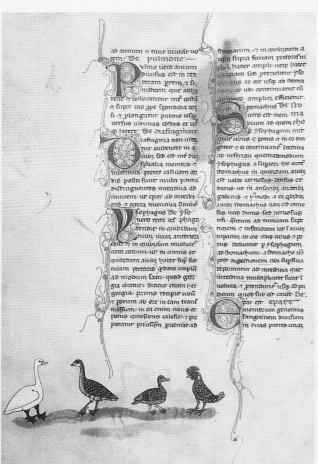

◁◁ No matter how informative the miniatures are, they cannot illustrate everything. From the text the aspiring falconer learns that the gullet of the swan (left) is convoluted rather than straight. White-fronted geese, wild ducks and chickens (to the right) are quoted as examples of birds which have a fleshy, tough gizzard.

◁ Big raptors are even capable of taking four-legged game, even sometimes a gazelle.

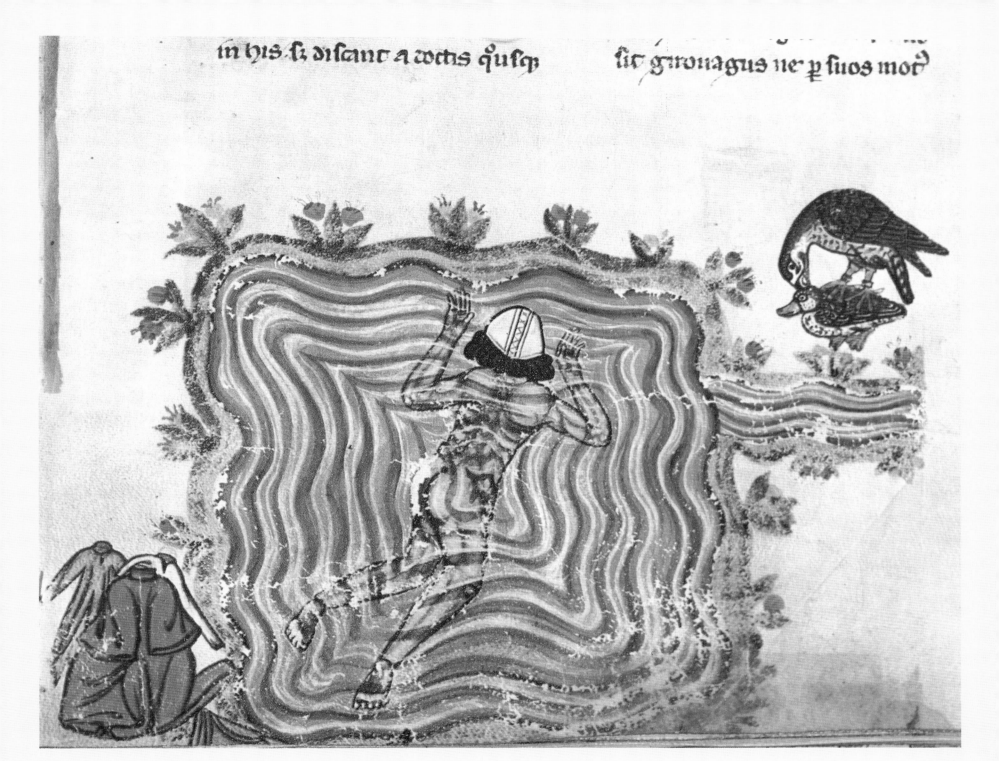

A falconer had to possess many skills if he
wanted to achieve mastery in his profession and
Frederick II obviously felt that swimming was
one of them. How else could one retrieve a
falcon that was starting to feed on its prey on
the other side of the water?

de plaisance en sa chasce plus q
en beste du monde par .v. raison
si ne treuet si petite chose. Ime
car tout lan sa chasce dure sens
riens esparguier. et de nulle
autre beste ne le fait. Et aussi
le peut on chaleier au uespre z
au matin. au uespre quant
sont releuees. au matin quat
sont alees au giste. et des autres
bestes non. car sil pluet au ma
tin vous aurez pour vne iournee
et des heures non. Lautre le q
ur et cerchier un lieure est trop

With his "Traité de la chasse," Count Gaston de Foix (Gaston Phoebus) a hunter who was both enthusiastic and well-to-do, produced a masterpiece of didactic hunting literature toward the end of the 14th century. He is one of the first people who dealt with the subject of hunting exclusively and comprehensively rather than simply picking out isolated aspects.

The miniatures on this page and the following double pages are taken from a copy produced around 1405, attributed to the studio which produced the Breviarium of Bedford.

One of the crucial requirements for really successful hunting is a well trained pack of hounds. They need constant expert attention in order to remain in top condition. Gaston Phoebus employed many trained attendants to care for his hounds.

directly to the original. The most splendid copy is that produced at the instigation of Frederick's son Manfred (1258–1266) for his own personal use; this conveys a good idea of the illustrations but reproduces the text in an abridged version with his own (marked up) additions.

The oldest essay on the hunting of red deer is probably "De arte bersandi", an informative introduction to the art of deerstalking written by a certain Guicennans in the first half of the 13th century.

"La chasse du cerf" (Deer hunting) dates from the second half of the 13th century. It is a work in verse form intended for teaching young hunters and deals with working with the lead hound in particular detail.

Around the year 1300, hunting literature witnessed a tendency for specialist literature to be written in one of the relevant national languages rather than in Latin. This meant that texts could only be circulated across national borders once they had been translated, but the number of readers grew despite this.

A rich, didactic hunting literature, of which many sometimes impressively illuminated manu-

scripts still survive, blossomed in France during the second half of the 14th century. "Livres du Roy Modus et de la Royne Ratio" by Henri de Ferières and the "Traité de la chasse" by Count Gaston Phoebus which both deal comprehensively with hunting, deserve special mention.

Gaston de Foix (1331–1391) nicknamed "Phoebus" because of his radiant appearance and long blond hair (or in order to make a reference to Apollo, the brother of Artemis, the Goddess of the Hunt), proved to be an expert authority on French hunting and his text left its mark on the hunting literature of successive generations. The number of surviving manuscripts (40) is unusually large and is also a testament to the fame of his book, as was its early translation into English and its increasingly lavish adornment. Gaston Phoebus was a passionate hunter and, with his mastery of all the important hunting weapons, explains how they are best used, and their hidden dangers.

He writes of the hog spear in the following terms: "As soon as the spearhead has penetrated the boar's body you must ram the shaft below the armpit and push it as hard as possible without ever letting go of the shaft. If the boar is stronger

Chapter LXXIII is devoted to various types of camouflage. One promising strategy is to hunt the game from a cart disguised with leaves and branches.

Gaston Phoebus advised his pupils to bag game in a noble and refined manner which would both afford good amusement and allow more animals to survive.

Catching hares in ripe corn requires little expense: simply a net and a few beaters to pull on each end of a rope strung with small bells.

This miniature and the next three concentrate on an eventful hunt for wild boar: the beast is driven into a pit through the only exit it can take...

... or the hunters select a suitable concealed stand at the edge of a glade and use the crossbow from cover because it has the longest range.

Unlike sows, male wild boar react more aggressively and turn to face the hunters' hounds and hog spears, in this case exposing the hunters to greater risk.

The wild boar is also a suitable quarry for riding to hounds, the hunter on horseback being permitted to carry a throwing spear or sword.

If one should tire of hunting one can also take wild boar in a trap by digging a pit, for example in its usual feeding place.

How to shoot hares in a grain field: the hare sits tight due to the presence of the dog, thinking that it is well concealed. It can then be shot from very close range.

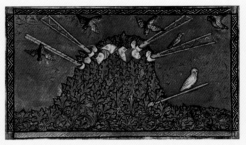

How to catch redwings from a hide: the picture shows a typical German device for catching birds, the clapper. As soon as a bird lands on it, the pull cord is used to snap the two slats together, thus trapping the bird by the feet.

Roy Modus instructing his pupils in falconry. Henri de Ferières' text on King Moderation and Queen Reason was written in the second half of the 14th century, and much acclaimed. The miniatures on this page originate from a manuscript dated 1379.

How to approach and shoot with the bow. The bow can be more powerful than that used when lying in wait in a concealed spot or on horseback, because it does not have to be held drawn for as long, the archer being closer to the game.

The social gathering of hunters at a pleasant spot in the woods is an important part of the hunt. Here they are eating and drinking as they wait for information on the location and quality of game before setting off for the hunt.

How to hunt a wild sow: because it does not attack in the same way as a boar, and flees without tiring, it can only be tackled by repeatedly setting fresh dogs on it.

Philip the Good, Duke of Burgundy, ordered the production of this copy of the "Livres du Roy Modus et de la Royne Ratio" in 1454 and had it illuminated by Jean Dreux.

Riding to hounds was a technique used for hunting wolves as well as red deer (above shows an unarmed hind hunt).

This rather less spectacular hare coursing scene offers an opportunity to admire the miniaturist's landscape perspective and bold, lively brush strokes.

Hunting otters could be very tricky because they are equally at home in water and on land. The best method was to stand on the bank of a stream and use the otter fork.

At the end of the chase the pack is given some of the innards as a reward, the liver being reserved for the owner of the hunting ground, whilst the tracking hound is rewarded with the deer's head.

The pack chases the deer by sight, while the tracking hounds remain on the leash. Before the hunt they pick out the deer and make sure that it does not escape the hunters during the chase.

Before the hunt the hunters wait for news from the scout. "Then they sit on the green grass to drink and eat. He who knows a good joke should tell it", recommends Roy Modus.

This hunter dressed in green sitting in the treetop is well camouflaged and watches the deer browsing peacefully below. Anyone wanting to hunt animals successfully should know as much as possible about their habits.

As well as hunting red deer, hunting wild boar was considered particularly enjoyable because of the very different way in which boars and sows behave.

Then as now, a picture of the hunter would be incomplete without a dog. Pursuit hunting would have been unthinkable without the support of hounds, specialized in performing different tasks.

than you are you must twist from side to side as well as you can without releasing the shaft until God gives you his help or other succor is nigh."

The "Livres du Roy Modus et de la Royne Ratio" by Henri de Ferières occupy a special position in hunting literature because their overall concept is more than that of simply a hunting text book; they afford instruction in behavior that is well pleasing to God. King Moderation and Queen Reason were put on the earth for this purpose. Where, in the first part of the Books (Le Livre de chasse or the Book of Hunting), the King explains to his pupils how to handle the bow and the various forms of hunting, this is done in order to incite humans to perform a meaningful activity that will help them to avoid the dire consequences of idleness. In interspersed allegorical passages, Queen Reason discusses animals from the moral viewpoint, thereby revealing many details of the spirit of the age in the mid 14th century. In the second part (Le Songe de pestilence; The plague dream), the author dreams of the lamenting of the royal couple over the wickedness of mankind. God then sends angels to investigate the facts and circumstances, Queen Reason makes accusations against Satan, and God punishes mankind with war and pestilence.

Hapsburg Maximilian I (1459–1519), Holy Roman Emperor after 1493, the "last knight" and a dauntless hunter, was a glittering figure in German-speaking countries. As a patron of the arts, he surrounded himself with artists who pro-

claimed his fame in works veiled in allegory. The "White King" is an interesting although historically unreliable autobiography of the Emperor which gives a precise account of his training to be a hunter and knight. The woodcuts are valuable in terms of the history of hunting and were produced by Hans Burgkmair (1473–1531) and Dürer's pupil Hans Springinklee (1512–1522 in Nuremberg). Maximilian I's hunting ability and knowledge of huntsmanship were recorded in the "Private hunting book".

The "Little falconry book" published in Augsburg by Anton Sorg is the first printed European hunting book. It can be traced back to a manuscript produced in the 14th century called the "Older German Hawk Tutor", the original of which has not survived. This book was reprinted several times.

The development and spread of book printing around the middle of the 15th century, which completely revolutionized literature in general (although it did not immediately supersede manuscript texts), had a similarly positive impact on hunting literature, which expanded steadily from this point on. The last example that should be mentioned here is Johann Conrad Aitinger's "Brief and simple report on bird-catching with snares" (1631) because the volatile history of its publication throws light on political unrest, and its subject illuminates social structures because bird-catching with snares was the form of hunting most favored by the population at large.

It is not just text that is didactic, pictures can be just as informative. Such pictures include the engravings of Johannes Stradanus (Jan van der Straet, 1523–1605) such as this "Bear hunt with hunting spears", 1578.

Maximilian I taking a chamois with his crossbow, accompanied by two hunters with spears. Hans Burgkmair created this illustration for the "White King" (1505–1516).

The illustrations in the "Private hunting book" of Maximilian I are by Jörg Kölderer (died 1540) who is mentioned as a court painter as early as 1500. Here we see a deer hunt using the crossbow. Maximilian's conservation of game, which is nowadays often (justifiably) mentioned with approval, was far from selfless and even ruthless as far as his peasants were concerned because they had hardly any opportunity to prevent the damage that the game caused to their fields and crops.

THE SPLENDOR OF PLEASURE HUNTS IN THE BAROQUE PERIOD

In 1731 the philosopher and mathematician Christian Wolff claimed that "The world behaves in the same manner as a clock mechanism", thus reflecting the prevailing view of life in the 17th and 18th centuries which was characterized by the belief that the earth operated like a clockwork mechanism in which the individual elements of nature were perfectly tuned to each other. In this cosmos animals were regarded as creatures that had no soul and no feelings.

Almost all western considerations of ethics either ignored animals or mentioned them only to expound that there was no obligation to treat them humanely. French philosopher René Descartes (1596–1650) viewed animals as mechanical like creatures with no sense of self, which were driven through life by instincts. He saw humans as the only beings that had both mind and body; in his opinion all things were either purely material or purely intellectual. Animals, since they consisted only of physical substance, were part of the material world and therefore had no feelings. Feelings presupposed a soul. If animals were to have a soul, they would have to be immortal like humans, and this seemed absurd. This belief, together with ideas which lingered on from the Old Testament, has determined the relationship between humans and animals through to modern times.

The fact that humans should subjugate nature was just as self-evident as that they should subjugate animals. Buoyed up by this claim to absolute power, the belief already expressed in ancient times that nature must be shaped by mankind reached a new high point in the parks and hunting grounds of the baroque period. Landscaped countryside was art and the term "artificial" was construed in a thoroughly positive sense. Artistic landscaping created extensive "artificial woods" criss-crossed by kilometers of ingeniously contrived networks of paths and rides as lines of view, with hunting lodges, summer houses or hunting blinds at points where they started, intersected or ended. Princely hunting took place in this architectural network based on geometrical patterns (as though in a spider's web) and, not uncommonly, was played out as part of court festivities. Countless paintings and engravings show that major formal hunts, often staged for state visits and weddings, were an indispensable part of court ceremony. Even rulers who were less interested in hunting were unable to escape the duty of staging such events, which were seen as appropriate to their standing.

Hunting culture in the baroque period is marked by these ambitious show hunts. The princes employed "huntsmen with knowledge of deer and forest" who had the job of ensuring that the artistically choreographed deployment of hounds and horses ran smoothly and that there was always an adequate supply of sufficiently high-quality game. When gentlemen of the higher nobility devoted themselves to the protection of extensive uninterrupted tracts of forest containing valuable stands of trees, some of which still exist today, they did this in order to create or preserve adequate habitat and sustenance for game, primarily red deer and wild boar, rather than for what we would nowadays call ecological reasons. This also ensured a supply of venison for the palace kitchens.

These ostentatious official hunting events combined an exclusive form of leisure entertainment with subtle propaganda in a most agreeable fashion because they afforded an opportunity to conspicuously parade one's wealth, power and status to guests and, naturally, to one's own subjects. At a time of absolutism, the state hunt gradually became a political institution aimed purely and simply at parading the power and prestige of the state at court. It continued to flourish for centuries in a scaled-down form and only gradually lost its significance toward the end of the 20th century. An extreme display of splendor is mandatory for this type of hunt, which was a prince's right and therefore a prince's duty.

In the area of firearms, a new ignition system, the so-called flintlock, was beginning to attract attention. The much simpler spring-bolt lock had come into use in Germany in the 16th century alongside the more complicated wheel-lock, but only gained wide acceptance in the 17th century. With this mechanism, which was generally fitted on the still widely used muzzle-loaders, the sparks were caused by impact rather than by friction as on the wheel-lock. A flint was screw-mounted in the jaws of the hammer, which was driven forward by the effect of spring tension, the flint struck a steel plate and the sparks dropped into the touch pan below. The fine gunpowder in the touch pan ignited and, through a small hole, exploded the powder charge, thus propelling the lead bullet out of the barrel.

Because loading the muzzle-loaders generally used in the 17th and 18th centuries was a tricky and time-consuming business, gunsmiths concentrated their attention on speeding up this loading process. Weapons were produced in which the butt and barrel were hinged and could be folded in order to insert a cartridge containing the charge and detonator. Experiments were also performed with air guns from which bullets were propelled by pulling the trigger, thus releasing compressed air contained in a reservoir rather than by using the explosive power of powder.

As well as expensive and sometimes ornately designed firearms, hunters in the baroque period

The inspiration for this page was a copperplate by Johann Elias Ridinger from the set entitled "Complete and thorough presentation of the most excellent hunting of Princes or nobility" (1729). The accompanying text explains how to choose a location for a water hunt where "A stream or river flows by a wood and makes a sharp turn" so that the deer can be driven along a prepared lane out of the wood straight into the water toward the gentlemen standing on a boat anchored in the stream; they wait until just their heads are visible before shooting.

carried a range of cutting weapons, among which the magnificently decorated double-edged hunting knife and also a hunting knife with a slightly curved blade were especially important. At the end of the chase the hunt master used the straight blade of the double-edged hunting knife to despatch the wounded deer.

This hunting method spread from France to the courts of Europe toward the end of the 17th century. It was a hunting art based on complicated rules that demanded considerable expenditure on huntsmen and hounds. In contrast to previously practiced hunting with dogs and "holding" hunts where the primary objective was the quantity of the game bag, this form of hunting involved a single animal, usually a deer. The particular attraction of this form of hunting lay in the frantic pursuit of the quarry by the pack and huntsmen on horseback, in its differentiation of other game, in the excitement of the search and in the finding the scent again after possibly losing it. Contemporaries criticized riding to hounds mainly because of the danger that a pursued red deer or wild boar

at bay could pose to the hunt master as he attempted to despatch it.

Other critics objected to the high cost, but this only rallied its defenders into action. One of these was Georg Friedrich Probst, the head groom at the court of the Duke of Saxe-Weimar, who wrote a short pamphlet in 1737 entitled: "Particular conversation concerning riding to hounds between Nimrod the first hunter and the world famous Huberto". At the end of the pamphlet Hubertus calculates that an average pack consisting of roughly 40–50 hounds plus a whipper-in and two kennelmen as well as the necessary horses could be maintained for less than 1,000 thalers a year. This expenditure would not even have to come from the purse of the owner of the hunt if each tenant "paid 16 groschen per 100 in proportion to his tenancy for hound money and fodder and gave half a bushel of grain and half a bushel of oats every month as can also be arranged for millers, innkeepers, stewards and executioners. No one will decline to give so little when they hear that it is used for the enjoyment of their sovereign, that

121

the yield from such a sum will be so considerable, that one may have a surplus far in excess of that claimed. Should such an Important Lord see fit sooner or later to reduce such hunting said monies could remain in effect and be used in other matters." So much for tax policy 1737 style.

The communication signals that were blown on the hunting horn were indispensable to the orderly running of this form of hunting. When the huntsmen caught sight of the deer chased by the hounds the "tally-ho" was blown to inform the hunting party how the chase was progressing. Once the deer finally faced the hounds, the horn sounded the call to the prince which marked the climax and the end of the chase. In his "Text book for huntsmen..." which was published in 1852 in Stuttgart and Tübingen, Georg Hartig describes this part of the chase vividly: "Then the huntsmen sound the call to the Prince whereupon the master of the hunt and the entire hunting party come rushing and the deer is despatched either by the master himself or by a person appointed to strike it with the double-edged hunting knife behind the shoulder-blade or in the left of the chest cavity or to shoot it in the head above the eyes. While this takes place the huntsmen draw their hunting knife

several inches from the sheath with their bare right hand, shout Halali! in unison and blow the fanfare proclaiming the kill."

This is followed by precise instructions on how to gut the deer and how the four legs are to be taken off before the deer is skinned, dressed and cut up, so that the skin is undamaged from the knee upwards. The skin was then slit so that the leg could be hung from the handle of the hunting knife. The right foreleg, decorated with a sprig of oak or conifer, belonged by right to the master of the hunt. The other legs, each decorated with a sprig, were presented to other participants in the chase in order of their rank.

Riding to hounds to catch wolves was accorded special prestige in France. It was a privilege enjoyed by the Vénerie Royale and the Grande Louveterie. The Louveterie (wolf-hunt) handled all aspects of measures to eradicate wolves and other pests. The masters of the wolf-hunt in a royal household were appointed by the Préfet for a period of three years (they were originally appointed by the King). It was their duty, at the request of peasants or parishes, to kill all animals that caused damage to crops.

Wolf hunting gradually became more organized and special hunting groups, so-called packs, were

On the occasion of the festivities marking the marriage of Duke Charles of Württemberg (1737–1793) with Elizabeth Friederike Sophia, born Margravine of Brandenburg-Bayreuth, on October 8 1748, this hunting spectacle was organized at Leonberg some 15 km west of Stuttgart. Jakob Wagner's colored copperplate records the lavishly staged spectacle. According to contemporary descriptions of the festivities, 800 red deer and wild boar were herded together weeks beforehand. Half of them had been killed by the time the end of the gory entertainment was proclaimed on the hunting horn, the rest having escaped.

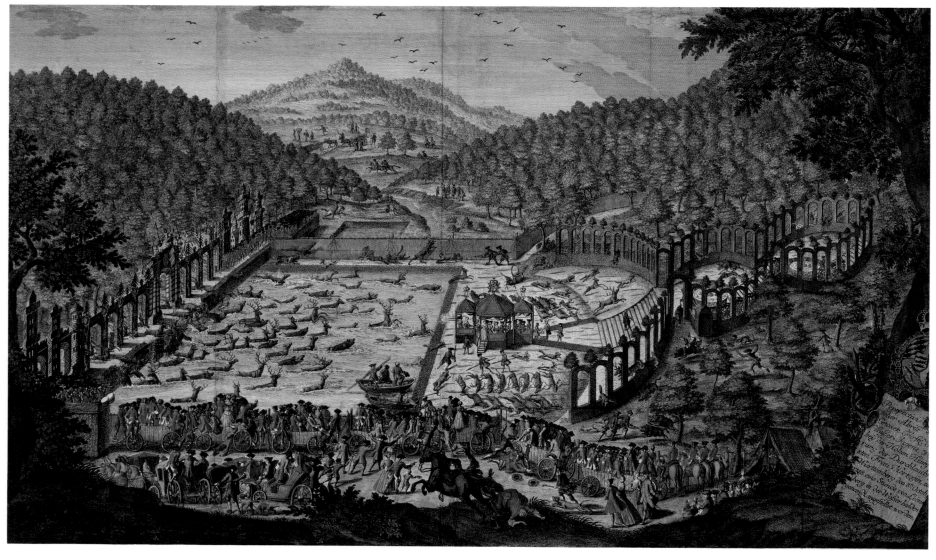

formed. Henry IV bought himself the first wolf pack set up by Andrésie. Louis XIV preferred to hunt wolf with the Duke of Vendôme's pack. Wolf hunts took place in Normandy, Poitou and Angoumois/Saintonge. The packs of the Count of Songeon (1774) and the Count of Fussey (1780) were the first of forty subsequent packs which concentrated exclusively on wolf hunting. An Association of Professional Wolf Hunters (Corps des Lieutenants de Louveterie) still exists today in France.

The escalating organizational efforts required for European courts to stage feudal hunting operations would have become unmanageable much sooner were it not for the employment of highly qualified specialist personnel who were responsible for the smooth running of hunts. It was the duty of these professional hunting associations, who had to perform an extremely wide variety of tasks and services, to make all the necessary plans for a successful hunt and implement them with the support of peasants assigned as unpaid laborers. "Holding" hunts which, alongside riding to hounds, enjoyed enormous popularity during the baroque period, demanded immense effort in terms of personnel, equipment and, above all, preparation time. The game for the great day had to be "held" in a wood surrounded by hedges, nets and special curtains or cloths known as toils and shewels.

In the Middle Ages, living hedges, usually consisting of hornbeam, were used to enclose the game for this style of hunting, and openings in the hedges could be closed off with snares and purse-shaped nets. This inflexible system of hedges was gradually superseded by moveable nets and high toils which Henri de Ferières and Gaston Phoebus (to whom we owe our gratitude for the most comprehensive information concerning medieval hunting techniques in France) had preferred even in the 14th century.

Although this hunting method was well known in ancient times and was practiced at almost all European courts, it was the German princes who developed such a marked preference for this otherwise inglorious form of hunting that the term "German hunting" began to gain currency in the mid 17th century. In these parts, sovereigns evidently obtained most enjoyment from hunting for the pot. They were apparently less inclined to physical exertion and sought to prove their personal competence and knightly virtues by achieving an impressively large bag.

High toils were used to contain the game. These were huge canvas strips some 5 ells high and 200 ells long (1 ell was a somewhat imprecise unit of length equal to 20–35 inches (50–90 cm); in Germany there were more than a hundred

Although it is possible to regard riding to hounds as exercise for riders, horses and hounds, the killing of animals herded together with no escape was simply decadent amusement for the bored nobility. The once popular pastime of fox tossing, in which foxes or other small animals were thrown into the air until they died, using a large piece of linen cloth or cords joined in a ladder-shaped arrangement, now seems particularly tasteless.

The unknown master who captured this "holding" deer hunt in the Neckar valley at Dilsberg near Neckargemünd for posterity in 1758 remembered to include in his picture an essential element of water hunts which was a source of particular enjoyment to even the most serene ladies and gentlemen according to contemporary accounts: the sudden plunging of the frightened animals into the water.

These sumptuous hunting events made greater demands on the organizational skills of hunt personnel than on the accuracy of the marksmen. Together with the following four illustrations, this series from (or based on) the famous Schwetzinger show hunts in the first half of the 18th century conveys a unique impression of a type of hunting difficult to comprehend from a modern standpoint.

For this slaughter of wild boar, foxes and hares, watched with great interest by the entire court, the stage in the background had a backcloth depicting a hilly terrain, offering the game an illusion of refuge.

Depending on their individual need to show off, the courtiers gained status by shooting their firearm from safe cover or by using their hog spear close to the bloody action.

"Amongst all other things, water hunts are a particular pleasure and delight as one can enjoy the sight of the hounds chasing the game into the water, (...) the rushing back and forth with the deer out of the water, then underneath the water, as are the hounds, diving like ducks and then swimming across the water after the deer."
(H.W. Döbel, Jäger-Practica, 1746).

Professional hunters and organizers of major hunts or festive hunts had constantly to dream up something new and sensational in terms of the artistic design of the "stage" for their hunting spectacle in order to meet the exacting demands of an Elector bent on parading a lifestyle appropriate to his dignity (and who, after the confusion of the War of the Palatinate Succession, wanted it to be documented that he was in charge).

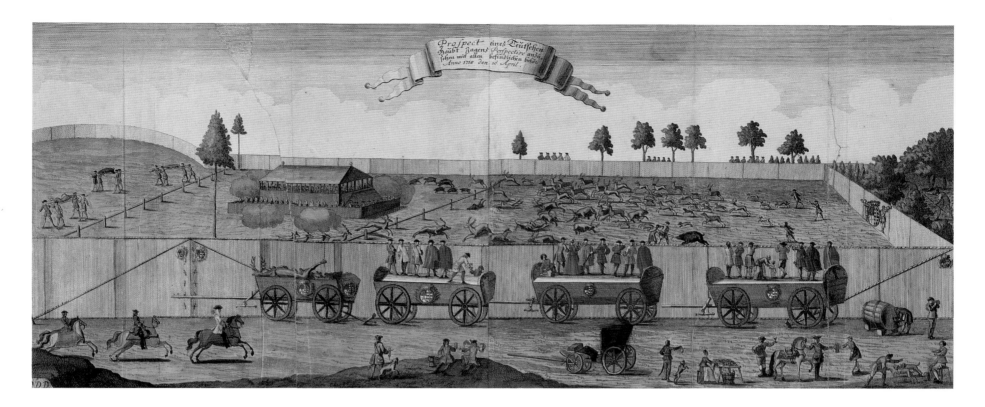

different forms of the ell in total).

Attached to the longer side of these sheets of canvas were rings through which hemp ropes were threaded—proper anchor cables with the strong upper rope some three inches thick. Once erected, the toil was supported by wooden poles, so-called forks, with two prongs at the top in which the top rope was placed. The lower rope was securely pegged down, with slanting guy ropes tied to short stakes on both sides of the top rope ensuring lateral stability. The actual toils were joined to each other by button flaps and were carried in wagons to the places where they were erected. The line of wagons then split up and slowly circled the area to be enclosed in opposite directions, the toils were thrown off each wagon at the proper place and erected by assistants.

If things were rushed because the hunters had already spied red deer or encircled wolves, it was possible to dispense with the long-winded business of setting up toils and to make do with simpler baffles or shewels. Heinrich Wilhelm Döbel (1699–1759) writes in the "Recently published hunting practices or the well-versed experienced hunter, including full instructions for all the science of hunting for both big and small game" (1746) that the preparations for such major hunts were very prolonged and could last up to five weeks. The first job was that of the scouts. These were dog handlers who went with their lead hounds to the edge of the woods in the morning in order to search for tracks so that they could report how many huntable and weak deer, adult animals and calves there were in each of the young forest stands. After assessing the game, the line of beaters was immediately placed in order to gradually drive the animals towards the spot chosen

for the hunt. When a drive stopped, a line of feather toils (pairs of feathers hung from a rope) was set up to prevent the game moving back.

This method was used day after day to drive more and more game closer and closer together, until the hunting area became so small that the shewels, nets and toils were sufficient to surround it completely. As long as the game was only ringed by shewels, there was always the risk of a breakout, especially at night, and the area enclosed therefore had to be watched around the clock. Camp fires smoked in a wide arc in the darkness of the night and hundreds of men lay resting on the soft leaves of the forest floor. When the "gear" was finally set up, a close eye had to be kept on the canvas and lines in order to tighten or slacken them depending on the weather (damp or dry). The hunt tailors and ropemakers had to remain in a permanent state of readiness so that they could repair equipment damaged by any game that broke out.

A three-part arena with drives, a chamber and a run was the focal point of this German hunting method. The arena was not excessively long, and was surrounded by high canvas toils. At its narrowest point the arena was split into the run and the chamber by the so-called cross sheet and the rear part led into the drive, partitioned off by a canvas or net. The game was eventually pushed into the drive from where it escaped into the chamber and, when the cross sheet was opened, into the run. A blind in the form of a small pavilion was erected for the sovereign, from where the approaching game could be shot comfortably without any inconvenience or risk to life or limb.

The coat of arms of the house of Saxony on the "equipment wagons" used to transport the rolls of canvas to the location of the "holding" hunt identifies this event as a court hunt of August II, known as "The Strong", the Elector of Saxony and King of Poland. The same etching, but not in color, was printed in 1719 in the specialist hunting book entitled "The complete German hunter" by Hanns Friedrich von Fleming, the Chief Forest Officer of the Electorate of Saxony.

When hunting bear or wild boar on foot, the hunter's most important and effective weapons were bear or hog spears which differed only in the thickness of their blades (Peter Paul Rubens, The Wild Boar Hunt, circa 1620).

The climax of the chase is reached when the pack corners the game.

This undated line drawing by Johann Elias Ridinger was probably produced as part of a set of 16 copperplates dealing with the chase. It shows riders, scouts and hounds just before the start of the hunt.

This copperplate, based on the style of a hunting tapestry by Peter Candid (Pieter de Witte, 1548–1628), gives a good impression of hunters' clothing and equipment.

◁ The scout and his hounds were responsible for finding the scent of suitable game (line drawing by Valentin Wagner, first half of 17th century).

The wolf is at bay and it is only a question of time before the huntsman delivers the coup de grâce (painting by Jules Bertrand Gélibert, 1898).

Johann Elias Ridinger (1698–1767) produced copperplates of all types of hunting and also this detailed picture of the many tools of the trade carried by a professional bird catcher (Sheet S of "The work of hunters and falconers," circa 1764).

Vogelfænger auf den Vogel-herd mit seinem geræthe siehend.   Oiseleur sur L'oiselerie tirant les filets.

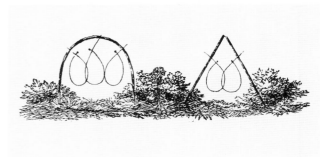

Bird trapping using nets and snares was the most popular type of hunting in earlier centuries, being the only form of hunting permitted for the lower social classes.

Wie der Wolff mit Stricken zu fangen.

La prise du Loup par moyen des filets.

"How to catch a wolf using nets", recorded in words and picture by Johann Elias Ridinger. Ridinger is considered Germany's most eminent chronicler of the history of hunting.

Certificate of apprenticeship issued for the young hunter Joseph Löw on July 13 1792 by Joseph Reichsgraf of and at Arco. This certificate, on paper with an attached seal, is generously embellished with watercolor decoration and figures.

A Silesian certificate of hunting apprenticeship from 1799 issued for the young hunter Johann Gottfried Sebastian from Gross-Vorwerk near Gross-Glogau. Parchment with watercolor hunting scenes. The seals of the issuers can be seen at the bottom.

RIDING TO HOUNDS, GERMAN HUNTING AND OTHER HUNTING SPECTACLES
By Karl Sälzle

Hunting on foot with hounds was almost the only form of hunting in Germany until late into the 17th century. The hounds that were used had to be faster than the hunted game so that the hunters following on foot could kill the game quickly without having to cover long distances. The hounds hunted by sight, and abandoned the chase as soon as they lost sight of the game. There was no stipulation concerning the size of the bag for such hunts—the aim was simply to make a kill, and a high bag was a source of satisfaction. Even when wild game was still a necessity of life, hunting with hounds German style was criticized by the French. From the standpoint of the pursued animal, riding to hounds is certainly no less unpleasant. Nevertheless, there is a crucial difference between the old style of hunt and riding to hounds. Whereas the former was a matter of achieving the largest possible bag, riding to hounds always involved just one animal, usually red deer or wild boar in Germany or hare or fox as well in France. In contrast to hunting with hounds on foot, riding to hounds meant that one had to use hounds that were slower than the game, following them by scent and tiring the hunted animal. Because such hunts took place chiefly in open countryside, often over long distances, they involved not insignificant risks to riders, horses and hounds as well as strenuous exertion. This was hunting for the sake of hunting, ingeniously devised to exploit the various qualities of pedigree hound blood-lines. Such hunting was always ostentatious and consumed vast amounts of money, entirely disproportionate to the meagre bag: a single deer, one wild boar, a paltry fox or miserable hare. This could no longer really be called hunting, it was more a sport for the property-owning class, especially the nobility.

One aspect of riding to hounds should not be overlooked: without skilled huntsmen and well trained servants, the hunt, which involved complicated rules, could scarcely have come into being. The lead hound, which was led by the scout on a leash as often seen in old pictures, was

Although wild boar and small game were hunted on horseback with hounds, in France and Germany deer were the preferred quarry for this type of hunting and are therefore often depicted in hunting scenes. (Vase with lid, manufactured in Berlin circa 1840; hunting bag, German, end of 17th century).

Johann Elias Ridinger, from the "Complete and thorough presentation of the most excellent hunting of princes or nobility" (1729).

Apart from the chase itself, the preliminary preparations, here the training of hounds for hunting on horseback, were also worthy of depiction as far as Ridinger was concerned.

entrusted with a crucial task. With the help of his dog, the scout had to inspect the game trails (deer paths and runs) that led to the wood and, on the basis of clues such as tracks and droppings, provide his master with precise details of the sex, age and number of points on antlers. After a number of deer had been found in this way, the master of the hunt determined those which were to be chased.

Once the deer selected for the chase had been confirmed again by the lead dog, often days later, hunters on horseback and hunters on foot with hounds were divided up and placed at relay points, those places where the deer had to pass. Each group of hunters had roughly 20 or 30 hounds. The master of the hunt and his entourage then rode off to the location of a deer and arranged themselves so that one or other of them would be bound to see the deer when it was flushed out. The animal was then tracked and approached by the hunters with the hounds. Only then did the actual chase commence, with the pack sometimes numbering 100 or more hounds. The chase was taken up by fresh hounds at the relay points, and continued on horseback and on foot through woods and fields, often into the night, to the sounds of shouts from the hunters and calls on the horns. The whippers-in directed the chase, and the hounds were frequently halted to allow others to catch up or because they had lost the scent. As soon as the deer was glimpsed again, the "tally-ho" call went up; roughly meaning "happy hunting". This type of hunting usually took place in flat, wooded countryside where a network of rides had been cut to allow faster riding and closer observation of the deer.

The horses were often changed so as not to tire them, and many horses were needed, up to 200 in the case of the larger hunts, which were sometimes quite protracted. The deer would often double back on itself, swim down a river over a long distance and join up with other deer. It was therefore sometimes really arduous to hunt it out, but in the end it would be bound to be picked up by the pack. Many deer were pursued to the death, particularly during later chases, or the hounds were trained to drive the deer rather than attacking it so that the chase lasted even longer. The cornered deer was almost invariably forced to face the hounds and the huntsmen following on horseback. In mortal fear of its life the deer could still be a dangerous opponent, and seriously injured or killed many a hound by stabbing it with its antlers.

The hounds were often held back and the call to the Prince was blown to allow him the honor of the kill. Nevertheless, killing the animal with a hunting knife was sometimes so risky that it was quite out of the question to expose the sovereign to this danger. In such cases the end of a chase, during which a noble animal had been pursued, often for hours or even days, in a proud sporting manner, occasionally degenerated into a dreadfully undignified spectacle. One of the huntsmen would sneak behind the deer to hamstring it (cut the tendons in its back legs) with the sharp double-edged hunting knife. Once the animal had been rendered defenceless in this way, the master of the hunt despatched it.

It cannot be denied that riding to hounds was a picture of feudal splendor, and this is borne out by many old paintings and prints. The flash of the blue or red uniforms trimmed with gold braid, the galloping of the horses and the baying of the pack of hounds, mingled with the various notes of the hunting horns must always have been a unique experience. For most princes it was all the more entertaining because it involved hardly any real physical exertion, let alone danger.

Heinrich Wilhelm Döbel writes that "The Lord can do as he please and also attend the chase in his carriage. For the work of directing the chase and keeping the hounds in order is the task of the huntsmen, whippers-in and scouts engaged for this purpose. Regardless whether the Prince and Lord rides along with the chase, he can be careful and has no need of chasing through thick and thin as do the huntsmen but need only remain nearby the chase so that he may hear and perceive the pleasing melodious sounds of the hounds, huntsmen and hunting horns. What an especially beautiful music it is and many devotees prefer it to the sound of the best glockenspiel; consider that 50, 60, 100 or even more hounds give chase, one having a higher voice, the other a lower voice and harmonize with each other as if it was music with descant, tenor, alto and bass, which loveliness is enhanced yet more by the shouts and hurrahs of the huntsmen and the blowing of the horns."

Similar sentiments are expressed in Gasse de la Bigne's poem written in 1359: "He who has only heard the baying of the hounds once will find it hard to desire any other paradise, and the sound of the hunting horn surpasses without doubt music of the angels."

Döbel continues: "In addition this (chase) is also a display of pomp for a Prince and great Lord the like of which the nobleman cannot imitate since it is not only costly to maintain the chase but it also calls for a fair district of land or woods on which one does not hunt alone and on which so much (game) is protected and raised in that one can hunt."

If even Döbel's justification of riding to hounds sounds fairly threadbare, we should not be surprised that this type of hunting found it hard to win acceptance in these parts and was soon debased into a fashionably staged show. Nothing demonstrates this state of affairs more clearly than a splendid hunt on the Starnberger lake in the Electorate of Bavaria in 1722.

Heinrich Wilhelm Döbel (1699–1759), the author of the "Newly published hunting practices or the well-versed, experienced hunter" (1746).

Huntsman on horseback, Meissen, 18th century.

Johann Elias Ridinger (1698–1767) handed down an accurate portrayal of the customs and manners of his time, and covered riding to hounds in particular depth in his pictures comprising more than 1,700 engravings. The illustrations show (from top to bottom): "The master of the hunt places the relays of horses and hounds", "The procession to the place where the deer hunt starts", "The entire pack of hounds arrives at the rendezvous", "The arrival of the Prince at the rendezvous".

Bohemian glass tankard, smoke-colored glass with enamel decoration, 17th century.

Johann Elias Ridinger depicted the chase in his day, which saw the huntsman as an actor in a predetermined play. The four engravings on this page show the decisive moments of a red deer hunt (from top to bottom): "The hunted deer is started by the stag hound", "The deer is at bay and drives off the hounds", "The deer is hamstrung", "The deer is attacked by the hounds and despatched".

A court hunting party chasing a powerful wild boar which a boar hound has just grabbed by the ear. There are two ladies on horseback on the left in the foreground, one of whom seems to be giving a commentary on the scene. The huntsman on foot in the centre is holding a pistol ready to fire (Southern Germany, circa 1750).

This detail from a painting by an unknown artist shows a huntswoman riding to hounds with her lance at the ready.

The Elector (Max Emanuel, 1679–1726), the Electress, the Princesses, the Elector of Cologne, the ladies-in-waiting and a large entourage boarded boats which took them to a part of the shore where the park bordered on rushes at the edge of the forest. The most high-ranking ladies and gentlemen boarded the Bucentauro, a magnificent boat closely modeled on the famous boat of the Venetian Doges, and the other guests boarded smaller boats. In the park an outlet had been set up so that the chased deer could be forced to break out through the exit and plunge into the lake.

A commentator reports as follows: "The Princes and their huntsmen, informed of the arrival of the Princesses on the boats by the firing of cannon, pursued the deer and forced it to break cover by the sound of the French horn. Twenty times or more it came to the shore and, frightened by the sight of the boats, retreated each time. Finally, chased by the hounds who were urged on by the huntsmen blowing their horns, it leapt into the water with the hounds swimming after it and surrounding it. It immediately dived under the water and was lost from view, but soon reappeared and was again pursued by the hounds. The more it defended itself the more it was attacked; this struggle lasted almost an hour and provided endless enjoyment. The horns sounded in turns during this time, the deer finally fought its last battle and the huntsmen proclaimed its death. Four gondolieri then seized the deer by the antlers and dragged it on board, where it immediately perished."

This account makes it clear that the chase was incidental, the main attraction being the court festivity.

A generation before Döbel, Hanns Friedrich von Fleming already objected fiercely to this type of hunt. He did so not out of compassion for animals, such a sentiment being unthinkable in the early 18th century, at a time when even some of the human population were regarded as objects rather than people. He simply pointed out that "Riding to hounds is a hazardous type of hunting and to describe it did not befit him as a German hunter or appear respectable." Elsewhere he says "That Sovereigns of noble birth have been the victims of countless accidents while hunting wild animals and that one should therefore have devised more convenient means whereby gentlemen could hunt game in greater safety." He is referring to the holding of game by enclosing it in high toils, "One of the most refined items of hunting equipment wherein the wild animals are surrounded and killed in various ways with enjoyment."

Fleming also defends hunting using toils against the reproaches of the French claim that "The Germans only practice bloodthirsty hunting. I leave it to any unbiased observer to judge whether or not our German hunting and enclosure with toils or hunting gear is a highly commendable invention whereby the high authorities of the land can kill the desired wild game with greater convenience from cover at their pleasure with greater comfort whether in their tender youth, when sick, when their body is afflicted by tiredness or even in their old age." Having repeated his opinions on the hazardous nature of riding to hounds he

Peter Paul Rubens, Wild Boar Hunt, circa 1615 (studio replica).

Mounted huntsman with hounds from the Nymphenburger hunt figures, Nymphenburg, circa 1760.

comes to the following conclusion: "I therefore believe, because of the many unfortunate fatalities suffered by the whippers-in, that the evil spirit must have devised it."

It was for a perhaps more noble reason that North German scholar Johann Georg Hamann (1730–1788), nicknamed the Magus from the North, objected to riding to hounds; in his case it really was sympathy with the creature chased to death that caused him to disseminate broadsheets for the benefit of mistreated game. Unfortunately, such exhortations were a waste of breath although, even in those days, there were royal persons to whom such cruelty to animals was deeply abhorrent.

Things became even worse when noble lords misused game as mere playthings at their whim. The hunt became the amusing entertainment of the court in the 17th century and, even more so, in the 18th century. The much-vaunted poetic charm of the hunt had already largely faded by then, and what little was left finally disappeared when the owner of the hunting ground and his guests took to shooting huge quantities of game that had been packed in together in an extremely small area with no chance of escape. As well as an exhibition of great splendor with vast quantities of game, these hunts placed great emphasis on decorating the run as extravagantly as possible and on the opulent furnishings of the blind or hide which was generally used as a shooting position and for the hunt breakfast. Because water hunts were so popular, artificial lakes were often created if there were no natural lakes. The royal persons of the day were little bothered by the immense cost involved because they felt that this was the price of a lifestyle appropriate to their standing, to be paid if they wished to be successful. There were also sufficient numbers of peasants on hand who could act as unpaid laborers.

Let us describe one of the most remarkable festivities of the 18th century in order to give an impression of the extent of this desire for ostentation: the magnificent four-day reception which Duke Joseph Friedrich of Saxe-Hildburghausen prepared for Emperor Francis I and Empress Maria Theresia (accompanied by some of their children) from 23 through 26 September 1754 in the palace courtyard of a domain which he owned near the March river (to the east of Vienna, where the March flows into the Danube).

This event was possibly one of the most lavish which was laid on during the long round of court festivities which took place in the 18th century. The program included concert symphonies and opera, lavish banquets and jolly outdoor picnics, an innocent water carousel and a charmingly arranged bacchanalian feast. Among other persons engaged, Metastasio was the librettist, Gluck the composer, Quaglio the stage designer, and the

The lead hound played a decisive role during the red deer chase.

famous female singers Tesi and Heinisch performed; this gives some idea of the high quality of the entertainment. Given such an outlay, no expense would be spared for the hunt, which was staged on the afternoon of the second day.

It took place on the banks of the March and no fewer than 800 deer were herded together, some of them from a considerable distance. There was a building in the form of a triumphal arch which was linked to the hills behind it by a bridge. The construction of this bridge alone required 2,000 double-sized posts. This building extended far out into the river, and the deer were to be hunted as they leapt from it into the deep water. The triumphal arch consisted of nine great arches on which three identical arches were constructed as an extra story; a statue of Diana stood in the middle, with trumpeters and timpanists stationed under both the arches to the sides. The shooting blind was erected on the opposite bank of the March and the elite hunting party arrived on boats inspired by the Venetian ship Bucentauro. Musicians in yellow and red masquerade costume, and female singers dressed as nymphs, delighted both the eye and ear.

As soon as the ladies and gentlemen reached the shooting blind the Duke gave the sign for the huntsmen to enter the woods. Hunting horns and French horns sounded above the shouts of the hunters, the curtain was raised and several hundred peasants, also dressed in red and yellow and carrying red and white flags with the coat of arms of Austria, mingled with the huntsmen emerging from the bushes and pursued a herd of deer down

the hill, onto the bridge, through the triumphal arch and into the waters of the March. It was the Duke's intention that the noblemen present should board the small boats and slay the deer in the March using the hunting spears trimmed with plumes of feathers that were provided on the boats. But then something occurred which can only be regarded as a bizarre event in the hunting history of those days: "Her Majesty, the Empress, whose pitying heart could not bear to see an animal harmed, not only did not permit the throwing of the spears, she herself did not shoot at the game nor suffer others so to do but rather wished that they should be given their freedom."

And so it was. However, it appears that the Empress who, like Frederick the Great, was an avowed opponent of the hunt, did not succeed in imposing any further restriction on the enthusiasm of the noble gentlemen, because another hunt which was organized in a quite unusual manner was arranged immediately after this memorable one. A specially constructed ornamental palace with several stories was used as a backdrop. "This was constructed in such a way that more than 1,000 hares, 100 or more foxes and in excess of 60 wild boars had to play their part. They first reached the top roof timbering which was built in the Italian style as a composition floor, then ran down the specially installed steps to the middle story, emerged from the windows and doors onto the gallery, ran down from there into the first story whence they then jumped out of the windows onto the wide staircase into the run. Many of these animals took the easy route but some, especially the first ones, jumped straight down

The festival of Diana near Bebenhausen in 1812 on the occasion of the 58th birthday of King Frederick I of Württemberg on November 6 after a copperplate by Johann Friedrich Wilhelm Müller, 1814. In just two hours the King and his entourage accounted for a total of 832 game animals. The preparations for the event lasted six weeks and 30 beaters drove the game in from the entire surrounding area. Fatalities also included an assistant forester who died of rabies and a carpenter who fell to his death during construction work.

from the top and immediately fell to their death."

The entertainment of fox tossing, which took place at the courts of princes at the end of the 17th century, was undoubtedly one of the most lamentable aberrations. It involved using so-called bruising nets to toss foxes into the air until they died. Linen straps approximately 9–10 ells long, or cords joined at intervals were used. Hares, wildcats, badgers, otters, martens, ferrets and young wild boar were tossed as well as foxes. Fox tossing was usually organized in castle courtyards to make it more convenient for the lady and gentlemen spectators. The entire "hunting ground" was lined with sand, because otherwise the fun would have been over all too quickly. It is no surprise that Fleming, who was always eager to flatter the aristocracy, was quite delighted when "The gentlemen and ladies dressed in green costume trimmed with gold and silver begin their noble work" but it is harder to conceive how even Döbel can express such enthusiasm concerning the "Delightful to behold Fox tossing" which took place in 1724 in Blankenberg. During such "hunts" hares were even fitted with collars made of stiff paper cut in the shape of various musical instruments and "Some of the hunters disguised as savages tramped around" the wretched beasts.

It appears that fox tossing was highly popular even earlier, especially at the court of Saxony. Gabriel Tzzschimmern's rare and, from a cultural historical viewpoint, highly interesting work entitled "The most serene assembly" published in 1680 in Nuremberg, describes the festivities in Dresden in the year 1678 and contains an illustration of this bizarre entertainment. 108 foxes and 20 badgers were tossed and, after all this noble enjoyment, "All the trumpeters sounded the call to table which was given on two trestles in the Church Room where the mountain singers and Elector's pipers were waiting etc." This noble "hunting" lost none of its popular appeal for three quarters of a century, which is perhaps hardly surprising if it is true that such "Noble princely enjoyment contents every man and brings forth such particular merry laughter whereby the heart of noble and princely persons and their ladies are eased and their health improved beyond measure".

Hunters in the 18th century also regarded animal fights inspired by the Roman model as proper hunting, and Fleming and Döbel called these "staged hunts". Even deer, which are exceptionally powerful, were used for these fights. The Duke of Cumberland pitted a deer against a tiger in 1764 in a fenced off part of Windsor Forest so that he could observe them fighting. The deer used its antlers to bravely repulse two attacks by the tiger and, when attacked for the third time, threw it off so violently that the tiger gave up; the Duke gave this deer its freedom and placed a wide silver

Gutting a slain deer. From the group of Nymphenburg hunt figures, Nymphenburg, circa 1760.

◁ Count Palatine Frederick IV had this collar of 12 brass-plate links placed on a red deer in 1609. In addition to the coat of arms of the Electorate of the Palatinate, the collar is engraved with the following words: Dear hunter let me live. The Elector gave me freedom 1609. Frederick Count Palatine Elector.

collar engraved with the story of the combat around its neck. It seems that such collars were customary from time to time because the Bavarian National Museum also contains such a brass bearing the words: "Dear hunter let me live. The Elector gave me freedom 1609" on its links. One of the end links bears the words "Frederick (IV) Count Palatine Elector", with the coat of arms of the Electorate of the Palatinate engraved on the other.

The Electors of Saxony and the Landgraves of Hesse had tame deer in their royal stables and liked to use them as draft animals on festive occasions. Court hunt painter Georg Adam Eger depicted such a team of six deer pulling a carriage decorated with seashells (a rider has to lead the team) in which Landgrave Ludwig VIII of Hesse-Darmstadt is sitting. This small painting is one of the exhibits in the Kranichstein hunting lodge.

In the major hunt procession held in Dresden in 1662 when Christian Ernst, the Margrave of Brandenberg-Bayreuth and Erdmuth Sophia, the electoral princess, celebrated their nuptials, the then Elector Johann George III, the instigator of the celebrations, appeared in his exalted person in the form of Diana riding on a white deer.

He was accompanied by the usual horde of mythological nymphs, satyrs and savages and the endless procession of hunters and bird catchers had with them a veritable zoo of animals, some of them free and others in boxes and chests: tigers and lions, polar bears and brown bears, wolves and lynxes, wild boars and hares, badgers and otters, martens and ferrets, squirrels and hamsters were all part of the colorful procession, plus hundreds of English hounds and boar hounds, not forgetting an impressive total of 139 horses.

There is a printed list of the guests at a masked deer hunt in Nymphenburg on March 1 1734. This pageant must have anticipated the colorful world of Bustelli who was then only eleven years old: in addition to most of the figures of the Commedia dell'arte such as harlequins, brighellas, pantalones, dottores, scaramouches, pulcinellas and pierrots, there were fools and clowns, Bavarian, Austrian and French peasants, apothecaries and schoolmasters, chimney sweeps and many others. Obviously, there had to be German and French huntsmen as well, and Dukes Ferdinand and Theodor played the former, with all the other roles being taken by nobles from the surrounding area and the Electorate of Cologne.

Although this hunt was not recorded in picture form, it is possible to make certain inferences concerning its progress from similar events and with the aid of a copperplate produced only a few years before. Here we see the deer leaping out of a leafy closed area into the run between two barriers, closed off by a net. The gentlemen are riding toward the deer outside the run. One can see that the deer have straps round their bodies which are attached to long cords or belts in order to prevent them breaking out. The stage setting is

a rectangular area with a pavilion and with an arch constructed on each side for the ladies and gentlemen, for trumpets and kettledrums, for the directors of the "tournament" and for the musicians. There is also an amphitheatre for the spectators. Lances, bows and arrows, pistols and hunting daggers were used, and the winners in the various disciplines were awarded expensive prizes.

Frankly, it would be impossible to treat noble quarry in a more deplorable fashion, and one can only be thankful that the dawning of a new age was slowly but surely to bring a sorry end to these horrors. The new age in question was the French Revolution, the first warning signs of which had hardly been noticed by German royalty. Only when the storm eventually broke and shook the centuries-old conviction that princes and nobles were all important and the people were nothing did the tastes of the German princes become somewhat plainer.

In addition, the financial resources of the nobility had been depleted and they were unable to continue hunting entertainments in the old style as a consequence of the Napoleonic Wars, the secularization of church properties and in many cases, their loss of sovereignty. Some hunting rights even had to be leased or sold to "reputable" citizens, referred to usually only as "individuals" in the official language of the time, and the days of extravagant hunts at court came to an end, as the sport of hunting transferred to the middle classes.

"Come! Here is a model for you French horn players/Hear how excellently this master plays:/No doubt you all long to possess his art/For the world has never seen his like before." Thus reads the caption of this illustration entitled "Hearing" which is one of a set of pictures showing the five senses.

Josef Schmitzberger (1851–1940), red deer escaping through the shewels.

The honorable gentlemen organize a picnic after a successful hunt.

Hunting becomes Middle Class

In the late 18th and early 19th centuries the Romantics declared that nature was a mysterious realm which had to be approached through feelings rather than via the intellect. Nature was no longer seen as rough, wild and unbridled, and hence an irresistible challenge to the relentless human will to create, but rather it had become something worthy of protection or restoration, and was perceived as an entity which existed in its own right and with its own dignity.

The Romantic understanding of nature scarcely conflicted with forestry interests, even though forest management had become a significant area of the economy. The forestry ideal at the end of the 18th century was homogeneous stands, whether broad-leaved or coniferous, because these promised the highest timber yields.

From that time onwards, forestry policy was determined by our knowledge of natural science and economics. Forestation using rational methods began in order to restore woodland that had been overexploited during previous centuries primarily by excessive logging and foraging as well as woodland grazing. This was a considerable achievement by foresters, but unfortunately resulted in extensive areas of monotonous spruce and pinewoods, with few broad-leaved trees.

The new spirit of the times following the French Revolution and Napoleonic Wars made itself felt in every area of life, and naturally also affected hunting which, under this influence, became increasingly middle class and less ostentatious. Hunting authors have identified the start of this new age. The main emphasis of hunting literature since the Middle Ages had been on specialized literature written for accomplished hunters and the nobility, but now it dealt with small-game hunting for citizens who were typically both hunting enthusiasts and dog lovers.

The attitudes of people towards animals also began to change, and enlightened thinkers began to accept the conscious sentience of animals as a fact. In an anonymous German pamphlet in 1780, attributed to Matthias Claudius (1740–1815), entitled "Letter from a chased deer to the Prince" (namely Landgrave Ludwig VIII of Hesse-Darmstadt), the animal speaks thus to its pursuer:

"Today I had the honor of being hunted by Your Serene Highness; I most humbly beg that you will graciously deign to spare me this in the future. If Your Serene Highness had only been hunted by hounds once you would not find my plea unreasonable. I lie here unable to raise my head and blood runs from by mouth and nostrils. How can Your Highness bring himself to hunt to death a wretched innocent animal that feeds on grass and plants? I would rather be shot dead and have an end to it there and then."

This new way of looking at animals and hunting as well as forestry management and agriculture was encouraged by increasingly influential authors of similar persuasion, and was also closely linked to other changes. An outward-looking thirst for knowledge—encouraged not least by political conditions that were felt to be intolerable—led to new insights into scientific and social relationships, and made people receptive to new solutions in the fields of technology, economics and politics. The "modern" person now saw nature all around him with more open eyes and tried to understand and respect it in terms of its own legitimacy.

This outward-looking, innovative mood encouraged the development of new technologies in general, and also gave impetus to weapons technology. In the early 19th century, the rifle and shotgun still used the French flintlock mechanism, an improved version of the spring-bolt, but the new percussion mechanism was a turning point in weapons technology. The percussion fuse, patented by the Scot Forsyth in 1807, dispensed with the need for a flint to produce sparks because the hammer, by striking a high-explosive mixture of mercury fulminate and potassium chlorate, produced the explosion. The first hunting weapons using this principle were produced in around 1820. The percussion cap was placed on a small tube with a bore (piston valve) linked to the powder chamber and ignited as it was struck by the hammer.

The invention of the cartridge which contained the detonator, powder and charge, completed the decisive final step toward the faster, more convenient and safer breechloader, although a few experiments had to be carried out before an appropriate method of detonating the cartridge was devised. Frenchman Casimir Lefaucheux produced a pin-fire cartridge that could be detonated in a breechloader with a hinged barrel.

Breechloading guns first started to supersede muzzle-loaders as hunting weapons when a cartridge, patented in Paris in 1855, which was essentially equivalent to a modern center-fire cartridge, made a completely new development possible.

Very soon after the introduction of the center-fire cartridge, hammer guns which were designed to use such cartridges gained wide acceptance and within a few years ousted the muzzle-loader and pin-fire cartridge. The hammer of these new weapons was smaller than those of percussion guns, and was designed to strike a firing pin into the center-fire cartridge.

At roughly the same time as this development, which primarily affected hunting weapons, especially shotguns, the repeating rifle, designed initially exclusively for military use, went into production. The invention of the hammer gun simplified life considerably for the user compared

The keen huntsman will want to surround himself with the objects of his passion, even at home. Alsace manufacturer Zuber & Co. in Rixheim marketed this panoramic tapestry called "Hunting country" after designs by J.J. Deltil in 1831, thus continuing a tradition that had started with medieval tapestries. Both these tapestry fragments are from the "Wild Boar Hunt".

with the muzzle-loader. An invention was patented in 1871 whereby opening the bolt simultaneously cocked an internal hammer, thus eliminating the need even to cock the weapon. This was succeeded by a variety of inventions, the best of which have been incorporated into modern sporting guns.

In contrast to the new techniques used in breechloader systems with hinged barrels which have been manufactured since the mid 19th century and where further development continued into modern times, the tradition of decorating weapons has persisted well into the 20th century. The simple engraved intertwined vines, flowers and animal motifs which were so popular during the Biedermeier period (1815–1848) can still be found today on modern hunting weapons.

Hunting in Europe took a completely new direction after the middle of the 19th century. For example, in the new legal situation following the revolutions of 1848/49 in Germany, farmers who had come to oppose hunting began to destroy any wild animals that appeared on their land. One can hardly blame them for this because they had been forced to endure the tyranny of the royal hunting prerogative, which guaranteed princes almost un-checked hunting sovereignty throughout the land but prohibited the farmers, on pain of harsh punishment, from protecting the very basis of their livelihood against the incursions of rapidly increasing numbers of overprotected game animals. The link between hunting rights and land rights was finally ratified in 1850, but the exercise of hunting rights was made dependent on a specific minimum estate size. This made it possible to avoid the risk of many game species being wiped out completely, given the fact that large sections of the population were interested in hunting.

Munich court painter Wilhelm von Kobell, famed for his pictures of animals and battles, painted "The Hare course" (circa 1795) at a time when he was influenced by English sporting prints, although the English usually hunted foxes when riding to hounds.

"LET NO ONE DARE TO STEAL GAME FROM OUR FORESTS ..."
By Walter Norden

"The hunter spoke to the King and spoke thus unto Gilgamesh: O Master, thou slayest the fierce forester in the Cedar wood, with thine hand killest thou the Lions in the mountains and the mighty bull ..." So reads the first poaching story known to us, as written down by the Sumerians in cuneiform writing 5,000 years ago.

Theft of game has always been a very special category of offense against property. Charles the Great decreed as follows in 802 in the Capitularia: "29. Let no one dare to steal game from our forests, a deed which we have prohibited several times (...). Any person who has committed theft of game shall pay the penalty and no mitigating circumstance shall be taken into consideration..."

Theft of game was not yet punishable by the death penalty, although punishment usually involved cutting off the offender's right hand.

However, just a few hundred years later the penalties for poaching had become even more savage. Counsellor of the Consistory N. Rephan relates the following facts in his book entitled "Esau venator" in 1621 concerning an unprecedented act of brutality: the Archbishop of Salzburg, Michael von Khienpurg, ordered a peasant who had hidden a wounded deer that died on his fields to be "Sewn into the deerskin and told that if he could outrun the hounds, like the deer, he would be free. Khienpurg attended the execution and organized a chase in the market square, had the wretched man sewn into the deerskin brought forward, blew the hunting horn himself, had the English hounds set loose whereupon they, taking the wretched man for a wild animal, mauled and tore him to pieces as the tyrant gazed on with enjoyment."

Modern poachers, sometimes otherwise respectable people, usually carry out their activities from a car using a carbine with a silencer and a torch.

The Bavarian "Hiesel", whose real name was Matthias Klostermeyer, was the most infamous leader of a poaching gang. This shady character is surrounded by numerous stories and legends in which he became a kind of Robin Hood or Rinaldo Rinaldini of the Alps. In reality, Klostermeyer's stealing did have a social aspect; the oppression under which country people suffered meant that the poacher, who lived in a state of potential war with the hated authorities, enjoyed the backing and support of the farmers.

In 1767 the then thirty-year-old Klostermeyer, who already had one conviction for poaching, gathered a small gang together and traveled throughout Bavaria with them, poaching and stealing as he went. The gang was extremely well armed and engaged its pursuers, consisting ultimately of several squads of soldiers, in full-scale combat. There was more to their crimes however than simple theft of game; more than one

▷ The meticulously kept diary of a poacher who could easily have been convicted because of his scrupulously accurate bookkeeping.

▷ Double portrait of the Bavarian "Hiesel", a rustic painting from 1776 commemorating his capture in Osterzell in 1771.

In reality poaching was less romantic than its reputation. The prospect of harsh penalties for a misdemeanor that really should have been a petty offense drove poachers to increasingly reckless behavior in their conflict with gamekeepers.

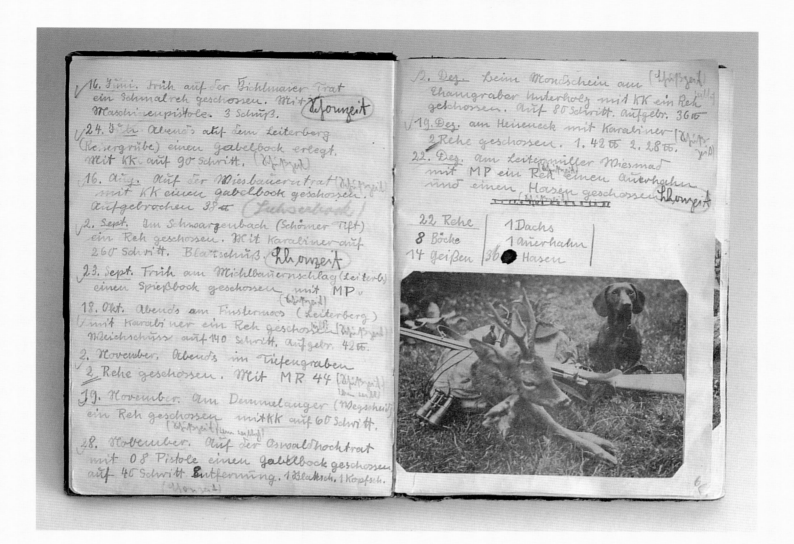

16. Juni. Früh auf der Fichlmaier Trat ein Schmalreh geschossen. Mit Maschinenpistole. 3 Schuß. (Schonzeit)

24. Juli. Abends auf dem Leiterberg (Reisergrube) einen Gabelbock erlegt. Mit KK auf 90 Schritt. (Schonzeit)

16. Aug. Auf der Wiesbauerntrat mit KK einen Gabelbock geschossen. Aufgebrochen 38℔ (Fehlerbock)

2. Sept. Am Schwarzenbach (Schönner Tift) ein Reh geschossen. Mit Karabiner auf 260 Schritt. Blattschuß. Schonzeit

23. Sept. Früh am Michlbauernschlag (Leiterb.) einen Spießbock geschossen. Mit MP. (Schonzeit)

18. Okt. Abends am Finstermoos (Leiterberg) mit Karabiner ein Reh geschossen. Weichschuß auf 140 Schritt. aufgebr. 42℔.

2. November. Abends im Tiefengraben 2 Rehe geschossen. Mit MR 44.

19. November. Am Demmelanger (Wegscheid) ein Reh geschossen. mit KK auf 60 Schritt.

28. November. Auf der Osswaldhochtrat mit 08 Pistole einen Gabelbock geschossen auf 45 Schritt Entfernung. 1 Blattsch. 1 Kopfsch.

2. Dez. Beim Mondschein am Chamgraber Unterholz mit KK ein Reh geschossen. Auf 80 Schritt. aufgebr. 36℔

19. Dez. am Heiseneck mit Karabiner 2 Rehe geschossen. 1. 42℔ 2. 28℔.

22. Dez. Am Leitenmüller Wiesmad mit MP ein Reh einen Auerhahn und einen Hasen geschossen Schonzeit

22 Rehe	1 Dachs
8 Böcke	1 Auerhahn
14 Geißen	36 Hasen

Bayr. Hiessel
Gefangennahme
in Osterzell
� 1771 �

Ich bin der
Fürst der
Wälder
und kenne
ist ungleich
so weit der
Himmel blau
ist so weit geht
auch mein Reich,
das Wild auf
weiter Erde ist keins
Eigentum darum las
ich mich nicht hintern und
und war es nicht Ganerbschaft dran

Man brannte voll be-
gier dem Wunder
wenn zusehen,
Soldaten, Jäger
konnten nicht
widerstehn.
Kein Haus
war auf dem
Sande kein
Haus wohl
in der Stadt
wo nicht der
Tiefel
prangte
a einem
schönen Platz

hundred robberies, murders and attacks were attributed to the Bavarian Hiesel. His boldest exploit was to attack, plunder and burn down the district office in Teferdingen. Warned by farmers who gave him shelter, he repeatedly managed to elude his pursuers. On January 14 1771 his gang was finally tracked down and massacred; the Bavarian "Hiesel" himself was slowly garroted, beheaded and quartered.

It should be noted that the offense of poaching had only existed since the ruling class began to claim exceptional hunting privileges. As far as the hunting activities of poachers are concerned, the records prove that the level of such crimes has dropped since the end of the 18th century as the living standards of the rural population improved.

*"I am the prince of the forests
and truly without peer
my kingdom stretches
as far as the sky is blue,
and game throughout the earth
is no man's property
I therefore do not stint myself
and he who does not shoot is a fool.
They burned with real longing
to see the miracle-worker
for the soldiers and the hunters
cannot withstand him.
There is no house in the country
and no house in the town where the "Hiesel"
did not reside splendidly
in some fine place."*

Poem on the double portrait of the Bavarian "Hiesel" (illustration at bottom of page 145).

Matthias Klostermeyer, nicknamed the Bavarian "Hiesel", with his apprentice and large dog which never left his side, in a contemporary engraving by Joseph Erasmus Belling.

146

Transport des Matthias Klostermayrs, oder Bayerischen Hießels und seiner Bande von Wildprätschützen, in das gemeinschaftliche Zuchthauß zu Buchloe, nachdeme solche den 14. Januarii 1771. auf Befehl der Hochfürstl. Augsburgischen Regierung zu Dillingen, in dem Wirthshause zu Osterzell, ohnfern Kaufbeuren, von 54. Grenadiers, 10. Jägern und 4. Amtknechten, unter Commando des Herrn Premier-Lieutenants Schedel, überfallen, nach einer 4. stündig-hartnäckigen Gegenwehr 2. todtgeschossen, und die übrigen 8. biß auf den Buben blessiret worden. Nach selbst eingenommenem Augenscheine zu Osterzell entworfen, nebst einer gedruckten Nachricht von dem ganzen Verlauf. Augsburg, zu finden bey Lorenz Rugendas, in der Capuciner-Gasse.

This engraving by Lorenz Rugendas conveys a vivid impression of the dramatic capture of the Bavarian "Hiesel" (lying on the sledge) and his band.

It must have been more than just a passionate love of hunting which prompted poachers to risk life and limb, as in this hazardous climb, to bring an illegally shot animal home without being caught.

Any convicted poacher who was only shackled and forced to wear deer antlers on his back could consider himself lucky. From the end of the Middle Ages the customary penalties were mutilation and even death.

The return of the hunters (1859) as seen by François Gabriel Guillaume Lepaulle still gives a festive impression. The location might well have been selected by Roy Modus, the fictional allegoric hunting tutor: "Then they choose a beautiful, pleasant out-of-the-way spot where the hunters meet after returning from their labors..."

Not all traditional types of hunting disappeared in France after the Revolution of 1789. Hunting with packs of hounds survived, even amid political unrest and radical changes, and the initially much-criticized customs of the upper classes were readily adopted by the revolutionaries and their successors. The fact that the hunting tales handed down to us from the Revolutionary years manifest a hunting passion which sometimes verges on fanaticism can be regarded as an expression of the spirit of the age.

Louis d'Orléans tells how, amidst the confusion of the Revolution, he pursued a deer right up to the barricades in Paris where he finally brought it to bay. He was probably the member of the Royal family who was secretly conspiring with the Revolutionaries. Paul Barras (1755– 1829), Robespierre's opponent and later President of the Convention, then Member of the Directory until it was overthrown by Napoleon, is said to have employed a black man as his whipper-in and hunted in the company of exquisitely beautiful ladies.

Hunting survived, though often in a debased form. Napoleon (1769–1821) dressed in green for the chase but always wore his legendary gray

waistcoat underneath. His pack consisted of 70 Anglo-Norman hounds. Nevertheless, the Emperor was regarded as only a mediocre huntsman. He imported deer from Germany in order to replenish game stocks which had been drastically reduced by poaching during the years of the Revolution. When we are told that he tended to hunt on royal hunting grounds, we can conclude that these lands must have survived without being split up, despite the trend of the times. They also survived the Restoration and subsequent rulers, who were all supporters of hunting except Louis XVIII (1814–1824), who, although he hunted out of a sense of duty, took no real pleasure in so doing, according to his own confidential admissions.

England is another country with a long tradition of equestrian hunting. Flavius Arrianus (circa 95 – circa 180), an important hunting writer in classical times, is said to have obtained grayhounds, dogs that hunt by sight, from England. Hunting in England must have been very similar to that in France for a long time because, despite their difference, the French Chasse à courre and English Hunting have similar rules.

One of these rules is that the scent of only a single specific animal is to be followed.

Two illustrations from a set of hunting scenes, etched as a mezzotint engraving after drawings by Tobias Heinrich Thomann von Hagelstein (1700–1764). Both the "Ibex hunt" (top) and "Chamois hunt" depict an unpleasant aspect of a hunting technique employed at the time: the hunters carry long pikes with a separately mounted sickle-shaped cutter which is used to cut the tendons in the hind legs of the animal as it flees into the rocks.

As soon as "simple folk" hunt, hunting changes, as do the depictions of it. A painting such as the "Gray partridge shoot" (circa 1850) by an unknown German artist records the change that was taking place; the observer is simply chancing upon a private Sunday pleasure rather than witnessing a seignorial presence.

Even though hunting rights were not exclusively reserved for the nobility, this did not mean that everyone could shoot anything they liked. This deer hunt is obviously illegal, and the enforcers of the upper classes are already on the scene.

Changes in the countryside at the start of industrialization were decisive for the later development of hunting in England. The economic success of sheep farming, which formed the basis of the world-famous English textile industry, had inevitably led to increasingly large areas of pasture with packets of land divided up by walls, ditches, hedges and fences producing an increasing number of natural obstacles in the landscape. The demand for timber for shipbuilding and, later, for pit-props and other industrial uses, drastically reduced the amount of woodland, and the grazing of felled areas discouraged afforestation. By 1890, 70 percent of the surface area of the British Isles consisted of pasture, grassland, fallow land and moorland.

Many parts of England had become ideal countryside for hunting on horseback and, thanks to the many obstacles, extremely demanding in sporting terms. This is confirmed, for instance, in the travel writings of Hermann Fürst von Pückler-Muskau (who financed his expensive gardens with the income from his writings): "We can hardly conceive of the type of riding which takes place here. Although most fields are surrounded by walls up to six feet high alternating either with dry stone walls or neat walls built using lime mortar, other fields are bounded by so-called ditches—solid earth banks made of clay and field stones five to seven feet high and tapering to a point at the top with a trench on the other side or even on both sides—the riders regard them as no obstacle whatsoever in taking their line. I have already described the exceptional manner in which the horses here jump … ."

As the woodland shrank, so the stocks of red deer also inevitably dwindled, until there were only a few herds, mostly on the royal deer reserves in Somerset and Devon.

The lack of forests and red deer meant that the packs had to adapt, and hunting the fox with hounds became predominant. Hare coursing, either with beagles or harriers, is also popular and takes place on foot in England.

The clothes of the huntsmen indicate that hunting in England, in contrast to France, is not part of the tradition of splendid baroque festivities. Nevertheless, the image of hunting has been deter-

Badger diggers listening for the sound of their quarry in his sett (Friedrich Karl Joseph Simmler, By the badger's hole, 1834).

In addition to hunting pictures where nobody is shooting, there are others such as these where the shots come thick, whether the subject be hares in winter or snipe in autumn.

mined by tradition, from the comparatively plain but elegant red ("pink") huntsman's jacket or riding tails through to the tall boots, knee-band, top hat, riding hat or, after it became fashionable in the reign of Queen Victoria (1837–1901), the bowler.

Communication in the field in England is achieved by giving direction signs holding the hat in the hand, by calling or using the short straight hunting horn which can only be coaxed into producing a single-pitch note and is only used by the huntsmen.

The House of Hanover occupies a special position in the later history of hunting and, to a certain extent, forms a bridge not only between England and Germany but also between the ostentatious hunts during the baroque age and the

drag hunts of modern times. In a drag hunt the hounds follow a scent laid down by a front runner, the drag layer. The skin of a fox or similar animal soaked in a solution and dragged from the end of a rope was originally used, and explains how this non-violent version of riding to hounds received its name. Nowadays the scent, in the form of diluted herring pickle, turpentine or aniseed, is trickled from rubber bottles, which the drag layer carries behind his saddle. Drag hunting is the only form of hunting on horseback which is practiced in Germany, where the pursuit of live animals on horseback is prohibited by law.

Surprisingly, the so-called Old Hanoverian pack is sometimes described as a French pack in the annals in the 17th and 18th centuries, although

Elector Georg Ludwig ascended the English throne in 1714 as George I and ruled the Electorate and England in personal union from London. Another ruler from the House of Hanover, Georg Wilhelm who ruled over Celle, prohibited "holding" hunts in his area of influence in 1665, thus giving significant impetus to hunting on horseback in the woods around Göhrde, an area covering some 85 square miles (220 sq. km).

The famous Old Hanoverian pack which, in its heyday, consisted of more than 400 hounds, dwindled during the Napoleonic occupation when French soldiers almost exterminated the game population of Göhrde, leaving only 15 animals, although this population recovered to 40 within four years. In order to save the pack, officers of the Cambridge Dragoons stationed in Celle and local farmers founded the Celle-Walsroder Hunt Association which continued to exist until Prussia annexed Hanover in 1866.

Royal hunting privileges were abolished after the 1848 Revolution, and hunting rights reverted to landowners. A new era began for German horseback hunters and for all German horsemen and horsewomen. The foundation of the Prussian Military Riding Academy in Berlin after the struggles for independence was a start: riding which even in Frederick the Great's time was considered crucially important for military training, was to be fully integrated into the training of soldiers. From then on until 1945, hunting on horseback was mandatory for all mounted elements of the army because of the perceived benefits for both rider and horse.

In Hanover, to where the Royal Prussian Military Academy had been relocated from Schwedt on the Oder, people were well aware of the value of such instruction. According to Cavalry Captain Kurt von Keudell, who died in 1887 and who translated George John Whyte-Melville's well-known remembrances of a horseman from English and grew prosperous from his own stories: "The start of hunting on horseback in Hanover coincides with the period after 1866 and the Cavalry Captain at the time, von Rosenberg, correctly identified the potential value of combining riding to hounds and show riding for the Military Academy which had been transferred to Hanover. The later General von Rosenberg took on responsibility for leasing the shooting ground, and created the first pack of hounds.

His Majesty Kaiser Wilhelm I was gracious enough to incorporate this creation permanently

Game bags after the Revolution in 1848 became increasingly small, the forests and fields having been almost "shot out".

Maximilian Bernhard Count of Arco-Zinneberg, an artist who hunted or a hunter who was keenly interested in the arts, produced this breathtaking illustration of the capture of an eagle in Rohrmoos in 1860 based on a real event. In order to prevent the eaglet, whose parents Arco had killed, from certain death by starvation, he used three ladders tied together to climb up to the eyrie in order to save the bird.

into the Military Academy for the benefit of the army and order the allocation of funds for its continued upkeep. However, the benefits which riding to hounds offered for the training of officers were correctly spotted by the Directors of the Officers' School and this first brainchild of General von Rosenberg was supported accordingly year after year." Rosenberg is reported to have had a saying that an ounce of cross-country riding is worth more than a ton of theory. Once again we see the unbroken thread, mentioned earlier, which connects hunting and riding.

The ethics of hunting as well as hunting technology changed after the decline of the court hunt and the associated decrease in game, especially hoofed game. The more accessible to wide sections of the population hunting became, the greater became the desire to keep and collect parts of animals as trophies. Deer antlers were customarily used as a simple room decoration from the 16th century onwards, and the deer did not necessarily need to have been bagged by the owner of the house. The trophy then began to become an object of desire as a permanent souvenir of precious hunting memories. It is not unknown for roe deer and red deer antlers, chamois horns and boar tusks to sow discord between hunters and non-hunters. But the worth of a trophy really is dubious when the souvenir becomes the ultimate purpose of the hunt.

The last bear in Bavaria was shot on October 24 1835 near Ruhpolding. The dead bear and the marksman were led into the village in a triumphal procession. Heinrich Bürkel recorded this memorable event for posterity in his picture (1840).

A successful day's hunting comes to an end, and the hunters are content with a relatively small bag.

Mountain hunters resting in wild craggy country: these are stout fellows at rest amongst the rocks, at home with each other and at one with the massive mountains. This hunting picture is certainly not free from clichés.

Emil and Benno Adam, the Pardubitzer Hunt, circa 1870

The picture shows:
1 Groom
2 Groom
3 Huntsman Stevens
4 Countess M. Chotek
5 Princess H. Rohan (on the left in the carriage)
6 Whip Jirutek
7 Mrs Schawel
8 Mr Schawel
9 Prince Franz of Liechtenstein
10 Prince Louis of Liechtenstein
11 Count Fr. K. Kinsky
12 Count Rud. Kinsky
13 Count N. Pejácsevich GM
14 Prince M. Fürstenberg
15 Princess L. Fürstenberg
16 Prince Benjamin Rohan
17 Prince J. Arenberg
18 Count E. Wrbna
19 Princess M. Kinsky

20 Prince Ferdinand Kinsky
21 Count J. Waldstein
22 Prince R. Liechtenstein
23 Count G. Stockau
24 Master Prince E. Thurn und Taxis
25 Prince V Auersperg
26 Prince A. Liechtenstein
27 Princess Croy-Nugent
28 Princess F. Arenberg
29 Coachman
30 Prince E. Fürstenberg
31 Prince K. Liechtenstein
32 Prince Holstein
33 Prince L. Arenberg
34 Countess Z. Fürstenberg
35 Prince L. Rohan
36 Count E. Clam-Gallas
37 Count A. Kaunitz
38 Prince A. Windischgraetz
39 Count J. Sternberg
40 Princess R. Hohenlohe
41 Count Sals

42 Count S. Khevenhüller
43 Baron H. Wiedersperg
44 Baptist Pollinger (master's equerry)
45 Prince L. Croy
46 Prince Öttingen Wallerstein
47 Duke F. Waldstein
48 Duke R. Chotek
49 Count G. Fürstenberg
50 Conte Veit
51 R. Reynolds
52 Emil Adam

Emil and Benno Adam, the Lippspringer Hunt, 1871
The picture shows:
1 Duke Adolf von Nassau
2 Duchess, née Princess of Anhalt
3 Clemens August Imperial Count of Westphalia
4 Berta Baroness Preen
5 Herr von Unger
6 Huntsman Strange
7 Whip Tate
8 Coachman
9 Benno Adam
10 Baroness von Breidbach-Bürresheim
11 Max (Duke's equerry)
12 Friedrich Baron of Breitbach (senior equerry)
13 Noak (forest ranger)
14 Count Levin Wolff Metternich Gracht
15 Baron von Ketteler
16 Count Max, Holnstein
17 Duke Rudolf Croy-Dülmen
18 Count Max Wolff Metternich Gracht
19 France Egon Count of Fürstenberg
20 Baroness Therese von Breidbach-Bürresheim
21 Count Philipp Castell
22 Herr Franz von Olfers
23 Count Fritz Wolff Metternich, Vinsebeck
24 Count Ferdinand Wolff Metternich Gracht
25 Duchess Isabella Wolff Metternich Gracht
26 Prince Alex Croy
27 Prince Alexander Croy
28 Henry Booth (Duke's equerry)
29 Baron Ignaz Landsberg-Steinfurth
30 Prince Philipp Croy
31 Prince Alfred Salm Anholt
32 Count Ferdinand Merveldt
33 Josef Imperial Count of Westphalia
34 Elisabeth Countess of Westphalia, Princess Alexander Croy
35 Count Fritz of Westphalia
36 Hound handler

Although hunting ceased to be the exclusive privilege of the nobility after the French Revolution and, increasingly, in Germany after the period from 1815 to the March Revolution of 1848, the nobility still preferred their own company and even the new aristocracy found it difficult to infiltrate so-called High Society because this style of hunting remained an expensive pastime. Lists of those involved in the meets of the Lippspringer and Pardubitz hunts clearly show that a minor title was a minimum requirement to gain acceptance. How long one had had the title or the reason why it was bestowed was not quite so important.

Julius von Blaas
The Pardubitzer Hunt, 1903
The picture shows:
1   Prince Otto Windischgraetz
2   Prince Max Egon Fürstenberg
3   Princess Irma Fürstenberg Schönborn
4   Count Gottfried Clam Marinic
5   Count Clam-Gallas
6   General von Balthasar
7   Prince Ferdinand Kinsky
8   Count Friedrich Larisch
9   Prince Franz Auersperg
10 Princess Gabrielle Taxis Kinsky
11 Countess Marie Kinsky Wilczek
12 Count Rudolf Ferdinand Kinsky
13 Prince Gottfried Hohenlohe Langenburg
14 Princess Marie Auersperg

15 Count Carl Kinsky
16 Baron Felix Aehrenthal
17 Count Luis Trauttmansdorff
18 Count Ferdinand Kinsky
19 Prince Vinzenz Auersperg
20 Prince Elia Parma
21 Prince Alois Schönburg
22 Count Ottokar Westphalia
23 Countess Mini Kinsky
24 Princess Christiane Auersperg
25 Count Hans Larisch
26 Princess Wilhelmine Auersperg Kinsky
27 Prince Gottfried Hohenlohe Schillingsfürst
28 Count Ottokar Czernin
29 Baron Parish
30 Countess Marie Czernin Kinsky
31 Prince Carl Windischgraetz
32 Count Erwin Nostitz
33 Count Theobald Czernin
34 Count Heinrich Clam Marinic
35 Hereditary Prince Hans Heinrich von Pless
36 Hereditary Princess Daisy von Pless
37 Countess Fanny Sternberg
38 Count Heinrich Larisch, junior
39 Count Leopold Sternberg
40 Prince Miguel von Braganca
41 Count Carl Trauttmansdorff
42 Count Moritz Fries
43 Rudolf Wiener von Welten
44 Captain of Horse Pollek
45 Charles Peck (huntsman)
46 Burisch (whip)
47 Count Heinrich Larisch (His Excellence the Master)
48 Major Krausler
49 Herr von Mahlmann
50 Captain of Horse Prince Alois Liechtenstein
51 Count Nicolaus Desfours

Die guten Freunde.
Von Moritz v. Schwind.

In the broadsheet entitled "Good friends", from a series in the "Münchener Bilderbogen", Moritz von Schwind (1804–1871) debates the topic of gullible trust in satirical fashion. In extreme cases it can lead one to mourn for the death of a person under whose rule one has experienced nothing but suffering; the illustration shows the funeral procession of animals who are burying their hunter.

August Franz Schelvers (1805–1844) shows just how tough a keen hunter's life can be in his chromolithograph entitled "Mishap during the duck shoot".

▷ Four old hands who no doubt know a trick or two: Friedrich Wilhelm Wörz, farmer and parish councillor, Ludwig Heinrich Pflugfelder, master carpenter, Friedrich Wilhelm Pflugfelder, innkeeper, Friedrich Wilhelm Kuder, nicknamed the Fish Baron. When this photograph was taken in 1895 these four hunters lived in Neckargartach, south-west Germany.

THE ART OF FALCONRY

HORST NIESTERS

No other form of hunting has been held in such high regard over the centuries as falconry, and to have a noble falcon perched on the fist became a symbol of persons of rank. Those convinced of their own importance—or who wanted to convince others of it—had themselves depicted with falcons in oil paintings, metal-engravings, or woven in wool (as on a Munich figured tapestry dating from 1615).
Falconry reached its peak around the time of the crusades. The Holy Roman Emperor Frederick II of Hohenstaufen (1194–1250) was a highly individual crusader who produced the famous benchmark manuscript "De arte venandi cum avibus" ("The art of hunting with birds," see illustration above), a work still relevant to falconers throughout the world.

Falconry is one of the oldest forms of hunting known to man, and mummified falcons have even been found in the tombs of Pharaohs of ancient Egypt. Even if they were worshiped as deities and not used as hunting birds, this still implies that falcons were already considered as something quite special at that time.

In many countries—chiefly in the Arab world—these noble birds are still considered status symbols; indeed they are the quintessence of beauty, speed and audacity. In parts of Europe and America the majestic eagle has been adopted for coats-of-arms, and is symbolic too of strength, courage and dominance.

The idea of hunting with trained birds of prey allegedly originated around 3,500 years ago among the hunting peoples of the central Asian steppe. In the open plains birds of prey were much more useful "hunting equipment" than any weapon known to man at that time. Sculptures and later written accounts are a testimony to the golden age of hunting with birds of prey in Turkey, China and Tartary. In the late 13th century, Marco Polo wrote an account of the great Kublai Khan, who would spend March of each year with 10,000 falconers and bird-catchers of Khanbalik (Beijing) hunting small game—wolves, foxes and hares—in the extensive plains of his country using golden eagles.

The Mongols are also supposed to have been the first deliberately to use whole cornfields as a lure for potential prey for falconry. The Arabs hunted gazelles and antelopes with saker falcons, whilst in Europe herons and geese were hunted with gyrfalcons, ducks and chickens with peregrine falcons, and hares and rabbits with golden eagles.

In wooded terrain a hunting party would usually prefer to take goshawks, the only birds of prey capable of taking moving prey either on the wing or on the ground while in the forest.

Falconry in Europe was mentioned for the first time in 330 A.D. by Julius Firmicus Maternus of Sicily, but was adopted neither by the Greeks nor later by the Romans, who caught birds with lime-twigs, as depicted in numerous Greco-Roman sculptures.

While falconry was initially pursued as a means of livelihood, it was developed to an art form in Western Europe during the time of the Crusades. Following a white falcon on a noble horse was considered one of the most exclusive privileges of the nobility. Soon after that the falcon was introduced into medieval French and German lyric love poetry as an erotic symbol.

Mummified Horus falcon from the tomb of a Pharaoh.

In his book on falconry from the fourth decade of the 13th century Frederick II omitted nothing. Here he describes how to feed a falcon by holding out small pieces of meat on a board, or how to prepare a sort of scrambled egg mixture for it if there is a shortage of meat.

This picture for the month of August from the Duc de Berry's "Très Riches Heures" (illustrated by the Limburg brothers around 1415) depicts an elegant party of falconers out riding. The man accompanying them carries a long pole with which he "beats the bushes" to put up birds.

The technical skill of Arabian falconers was such that even at full gallop they could carry three falcons simultaneously (the third one being presumably up in the sky). Eugène Fromentin sketched this print in 1863 for the December edition of "Magazin Pittoresque".

Above right: This miniature from the Manes lyric poetry manuscript (around 1330) is dedicated to Kunz von Rosenheim who encounters a reaper in a cornfield while hunting with falcons. Her gloves reveal her true rank; thus, in this case, falconry is meant as a symbol of courtly love.

This Persian silk embroidery shows a falconer with a white goshawk which at that time was extremely valuable. Goshawks were used in falconry even before falcons.

A contemporary drawing of a Mongolian falconer with a white goshawk.

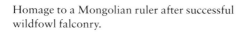

Homage to a Mongolian ruler after successful wildfowl falconry.

In the lower circular panel the lady is carrying a tame falcon on her hand as a sign of her noble birth, but also as a symbol of courtly love. (Enamel jewel box, Limoges, 13th century)

The same ambiguous display of noble hunting is the focus of this romanticized illustration (from a copy by Charles Aubry) in a textbook on falconry from the 19th century. Top right, Aubry reproduces ideas from Henri de Ferières' "Livres du Roy Modus et de la Royne Ratio" (1379).

Depiction of falconry (1578) by the Flemish-born Giovanni Stradanus (1523–1605), whose adopted city was Florence.

This miniature from a 15th century manuscript shows the Knight di Capodilista with his falcon on his bandaged hand.

The delightful detail of the laboriously draped garment worn by the female rider reproduced by Daniel Rabel (around 1578–1637) seems eminently unsuitable for the pursuit of falconry, but reveals Rabel as the creator of fashion plates.

The subject of expert bonding with these easily agitated hunting birds has occupied authors and illustrators over the centuries.

To spare the bird unnecessary agitation it is hooded, a procedure which, initially, is rather stressful for the bird. Frederick II, therefore, in his falcon book advises practicing the hooding procedure in a darkened room, and gives instructions on how the hood should be held.

The ornithological knowledge that Frederick II compiled was not copied wholesale from other books, but based on his own observations. Here he deals with birds with differently shaped necks, linking them with habitat and feeding behavior.

A frightened falcon can be calmed down by the falconer turning his face away, or by offering the bird a tidbit (a meaty leg of fowl). Frederick II's falconers wore distinctive clothing and headgear with which the birds could familiarize themselves.

François Desportes (1661–1743), French artist to the court, allowed himself artistic freedom for this painting of gyrfalcons, which depicts a densely packed group of seven hunting falcons. In actual fact, falcons would never sit so closely together, either in the wild or as trained birds.

The stories of Bajessid I, Ottoman Sultan and ardent falconer, give us some idea of the value of falcons in the Middle Ages. After winning the battle of Nikopolis (1396), the victorious Sultan apparently refused to authorize the release of a few captured prisoners belonging to the French nobility, because the ransom offered in the name of Charles VI, amounting to 200,000 ducats, six horse-loads of scarlet cloth (a very highly-prized woollen fabric which was elastic because of the way it was twisted) and priceless tapestries from Arras, seemingly failed to attract him. It was not until he was offered 30 falcons that he finally relented and the deal was clinched.

There is, however, no-one as closely associated with the history of falconry as the Hohenstaufen Frederick II (1194–1250), grandson of Emperor Frederick I (Barbarossa), King of Sicily (1198), Germany (1212 and 1215) and Jerusalem (1225/1229). In 1220 he was crowned Emperor in Rome.

On the occasion of his coronation as German King in Aachen in 1215, young Frederick pledged to the Pope that he would undertake a crusade, a promise that he delayed for twelve years. It was not until the Holy Father inflicted excommunication on him that the Emperor set out. After he had taken control of Jerusalem without bloodshed (at the negotiating table instead of on the battlefield), he consequently had personally to crown himself King in the church of the Holy Sepulchre. In his meetings with Sultan al-Kamil and Emir Fuhr ed-Din, during which he negotiated privileges for the Christian pilgrims at the holy places of Jerusalem, Bethlehem and Nazareth, Frederick's insights into Islamic culture, his knowledge of Arabic and his personal philosophy stood him in good stead. After 200 years of repeated warlike exchanges he had brought about peace between the Orient and the Occident (at least until 1244).

Frederick's fondness of nature has given us the most comprehensive and significant work so far on falconry and ornithology, entitled "De arte venandi cum avibus" (The art of hunting with birds). The priceless "édition de luxe" in the Emperor's

The ardent falconer Archbishop-Elector Clemens August of Cologne —here depicted as a small boy with his tutor—lived in Falkenlust, near Brühl, 250 years ago.

Hooded falcons are depicted on many of the over 6,000 hand-painted Dutch tiles in the stairwell of Falkenlust. The hoods bear the Elector's monogram.

▷ Three magnificent hoods decorated with the feathers of prey species. Above left a calming hood. This design was used for newly captured wild falcons right to the beginning of our present century.

▷▷ Icelandic gyrfalcon tethered by jesses and surrounded by falconry equipment. The metal plate in the center was placed on a heron which had been attacked, but not killed, and then released again. It displayed a registration number, which supplied information should the bird be caught again.

handwriting was stolen during Frederick's siege of Parma in 1248 by those imprisoned there, who began their premeditated attack at the precise moment that the Emperor and his son Manfred had gone hunting with falcons, accompanied by a large entourage.

Manfred, later King of Sicily, practiced falconry with the same passion as his father, and we have him to thank for the production of a magnificent new edition, with a reconstruction of a part of the text, following the same pattern as his father for the layout, and expanded with his own observations. This priceless manuscript is today housed in the Biblioteca Vaticana in Rome.

The manuscript is illustrated with over 500 pictures of birds, representing 80 different species. Manfred's endeavor to continue his father's work is clearly recognizable.

Frederick II recorded the comings and goings of migratory birds with scientific accuracy, even describing the different heights at which they flew, and the frequency and speed of their wing strokes.

The example of bustard hunting demonstrates that the Emperor conducted scrupulous ornithological research. He describes how it tries to put off its attacker by spraying it with droppings, or keeps the enemy at a distance by puffing itself up, or making other threatening gestures. In his well-informed notes, Frederick specifically points out that any vigorous, rapid or sudden movement should be avoided at all costs when working with falcons, as it can hamper successful bonding with humans—a fact as fundamental today, some 750 years later.

The Emperor's falconers wore distinguishing headgear, the shape and color giving information about their respective tasks. Caps were worn by those falconers who were responsible for feeding and attaching the jesses, and these people spent their time predominantly inside the Emperor's palace. Falconers who worked in the open air, however, wore pointed hats which were much easier to put on and take off frequently; often necessary when handling the birds.

It was not only the falconers who wore protective headgear; Frederick's birds also wore hoods. The Emperor became familiar with this essential item—which helps calm the birds—much used in the Orient, and employed this method alongside the more customary method still in use at the time. This consisted of raising the lower eyelids of the birds using a thin piece of thread.

There are also accounts on falconry from later centuries. Margrave Karl Wilhelm Friedrich of Brandenburg, for example, kept a falconry logbook from 1730 through 1755, from which it can be deduced that he successfully hunted 34,429 items of game. The Wittelsbach Clemens August, Archbishop-Elector of Cologne, indulged in falconry with similar lavishness at about the same time. It is him we have to thank for magnificent buildings like Augustusburg palace in Brühl near Cologne and the neighbouring Falkenlust hunting lodge (the name means "falcon-pleasure". Clemens August invested his not inconsiderable wealth in the pursuit of his passion, and his falconers, for example, were worth at least three times as much to him as were his ministers.

Richard Bloem (died 1705)
illustrates hunting with
falcons for pheasant,
partridge, duck and heron in
these four scenes (clockwise
from top left).

German playing card, the "trump falcon knave"; painted piece from an Upper Rhine game around 1440.

The Augsburg hunting chronicler Johann Elias Ridinger (1698–1767) wrote the following about this illustration: "Because autumn is the best time for hunting the heron with birds, / The falconer makes the necessary preparations, / And to this end keeps the retrievers at the ready for when the time comes, / And wind, water and spaniel too".

This plate by H. Schlegel and A.H. Verster van Wulverhorst from the "Traité de Fauconnerie", published in France in 1853 shows three magnificent plumed hoods (top left, top right and bottom center), two calming hoods (bottom left and right) for placing on newly caught wild falcons, a feathered lure for retrieving hunting falcons (top center) and two falconer's bags.

Hunting with falcons at the Birdhouse near the Green House, recorded by Peter Jacob Horemans. In the foreground the hunting party have gathered in the Palace Park outside Munich. The centre of the picture shows the Elector, Prince Karl Albrecht (1697–1745) and his wife, Princess Maria Amalie (with a falcon on her hand).

Approximately one hundred years later (1844–1853) two Dutchmen, senior chief forester Verster van Wulverhorst, chief inspector of hunting and fishing in Southern Holland, and Dr Schlegel, director of the natural history museum in Leiden, compiled the historical falcon book entitled "Traité de Fauconnerie". This complete work outlines the high skill of falconry in Europe and specifically focuses on the Netherlands.

It is known from old records that three falconer families lived in Arendonk (Holland) in the 14th century, and by the 15th century there were 36 professional falconers mentioned there—an indication of the increasing popularity of falconry.

The founding of the Royal Loo Hawking Club under the presidency of Prince Alexander of the

Netherlands, and the fact that there were ideal conditions for heron falconry in Het Loo and in the surrounding area of Soenen, transformed Holland into a highly desirable hunting region. Moreover, the surrounding area of Valkenswaard was on a migration route for peregrine falcons, which could then be caught there and trained for numerous royal dynasties in Europe.

Prince Alexander's professional falconer, Adriaan Mollen, was also held in high esteem here. He not only had a brilliant reputation as a sympathetic falconer, but was equally famous for his technical skill as a maker of falconry equipment. The equipment he produced—bells (small round bells which birds wear round their legs), falcon bags and his artistic falcon hoods—were highly desirable in professional circles.

Jan van Noordt (1620–1676), a page with a hunting falcon.

After the death of Prince Alexander, the respectable club, to which many high-profile figures from the nobility at the time had belonged, disintegrated. Even Adriaan Mollen was dismissed, although he received a small pension from the King for his loyal service. In 1854 Europe's last professional falconer, Karel Mollen, son of Adriaan Mollen, was born in Valkenswaard. He still learned the craft of hand-producing equipment according to old traditions. Both father and son caught migrating falcons right to the end, and supplied these to the English and French aristocratic dynasties.

Karel Mollen died in Valkenswaard in 1936 at the age of 82. In 1925 he had supplied probably what was the last falconry equipment to Renz Waller, who had been the co-founder of the German Order of Falconers in 1923. Waller was my teacher and above all else it is him I have to thank for imparting countless facts to me on the subject of this noble cultural pursuit. His many years of experience in bonding with birds of prey have been set down in a book which even today is acknowledged as an authority on the subject, as well as in numerous prize-winning paintings and drawings.

In 1942 Renz Waller achieved a global first by successfully breeding peregrine falcons in captivity—a milestone in the history of modern falconry. He was able to prove that falcons bred in captivity hunt just as well as those caught in the wild. There has been a fundamental transformation of this noble sport in other ways too.

Whereas hunting with falcons was previously reserved exclusively for high-born aristocrats—and in the Arab world this is still the case—today it is possible for "ordinary people" to take up the sport of falconry.

In the second half of the 18th century considerable wealth was still required, for example, to catch 150 Icelandic gyrfalcons; in one case, at least 58 oxen and 156 sheep had to be procured to feed the catchers and helpers! No wonder only grand-dukes could afford such an expensive hobby.

Which birds of prey is it possible to hunt with? We make a distinction between the lower-flying hawks—goshawk and sparrowhawk—and the falcons, which tend to fly higher. The main falcons involved are peregrine, found throughout the world in over 20 subspecies, lagger, lanner, and the majestic gyrfalcon. Nowadays, successful breeding of eagles, hawks and falcons means that falconers can also support wild bird populations with birds bred in captivity; indeed many falconers have contributed to the safeguarding of wild peregrine falcon stocks. Thus the wildlife reservation which I manage in Hellenthal (Eifel), which has one of the largest bird of prey sanctuaries in Europe, has in the last 20 years promoted programs, free of charge, for the conservation of wildlife, supported by captive breeding.

One should distinguish falconry from flight displays by larger birds of prey such as powerful eagles, soaring up to 2,000 meters in favorable

▷ An unknown Italian miniaturist from the 15th century imparts an almost sacred moment to his portrayal of hunting for herons and ducks with falcons. The falcon at the top center edge of the picture, about to attack a heron, is highlighted with rays. It strikes its prey with its back to the sun.

▷ ▷ The falcon is used and understood as a symbol of sovereignty even in portraits of children, for example, in Jean de Saint-Igny's (around 1598–1647) lavish portrait of the youthful Louis XIV and equally in Jan van Noordt's modest painting of an unknown boy (top).

Gray gyrfalcon by Renz Waller around 1935.

Renz Waller (1895–1979) founded the German Order of Falconry in 1923. Apart from falconry he was passionately fond of art, and the paintings and drawings on this spread are by him.

Two peregrine falcons make a joint attack on a gray heron which is trying to shake off its attackers with wild flying maneuvers. This hunting strategy, whereby one bird distracts the prey while the other strikes at the right moment, would have been taught to both falcons in arduous training sessions.

Immediately after an attack by a white gyrfalcon, the most valuable falcon of all, ...

The well-rehearsed tactics have worked once again. The comparatively heavy gray heron is first of all rammed as it nose-dives; then it is attacked for a second and third time, after which it falls headlong to the ground. Not until it has landed can it become, with its bill, a source of danger again to the pursuing peregrines.

... the fatally wounded raven spirals to the ground. Renz Waller received innumerable international awards for his dramatic impressions of an old majestic form of hunting.

A magnificent ornate hood of silver and gold, with the cheeks of lapis lazuli, the rear straps of sodalite, and the plume (tuft of feathers) of rock-crystal. Falconer's gloves of 18-carat gold support the smooth granite baseplate.

This magnificent ornate hood was crafted from solid silver.

179

Johann Elias Ridinger (1698–1767), hunting geese with goshawk, colored copperplate engraving.

Johann Elias Ridinger, hunting hares with goshawk, colored copperplate engraving.

This painting by Johann Heinrich Tischbein the Elder (1722–1789) is of his patron Frederick II, Count of Hesse-Kassel, out hunting herons with falcons.

These two paintings and the main one on the opposite page form part of a series of hunting scenes, which Johann Heinrich Tischbein the Elder was commissioned to do by the Count. The picture on the far right is evidence of the protection which the Count conferred on the herons which were so indispensable for his enjoyment of hunting; they had adequate opportunities for nesting and any disturbances were kept to a minimum during the breeding season.

warm up-currents of air and then returning obediently onto the hand of the trainer, or by falcons swooping down, arrow-like, from the sky at up to 250 kilometers per hour, to the lure. These people may also be falconers who for the most part own hunting and falconry licenses, but such displays have little relevance to real falconry.

However, by no means all birds of prey are suitable for falconry. Unsuitable species include white-tailed, tawny, steppe and bataleur eagles; vultures; kites; harriers; kestrel; hobby, and honey, rough-legged and common European buzzards. By contrast, the American red-tailed hawk (a *Buteo* buzzard) is eminently suitable for hunting rabbits and hares. It has the courage and temperament of the goshawk, and is unusual in that it can hunt and strike its moving prey, in short bursts, both on the ground or on the wing, even in wooded terrain.

Trust and bonding between falcon and falconer develops as a result of frequent hard work and the supply of good food. All important is contact with the falconer which strengthens the bond of trust between man and bird, and real training cannot begin until the bird of prey has lost his fear of the falconer.

It is important that the bird of prey being trained is fed a diet corresponding to the prey it must later attack. Therefore, during practice the hawk is flown onto the pelt of a rabbit or hare, with the reward being rabbit or hare meat. For falcons being trained on wildfowl the lure is used. This consists of a bunch of feathers of the type of

bird being hunted, to which is attached a long cord and a piece of meat, which is swung round and round. Only in the last phase of training is the falcon then presented with a real, albeit dead bird, such as a pheasant. A few head-feathers are plucked, so that later, when attacking its prey, the falcon will concentrate firstly on the head, thus killing its prey quickly and safely.

Falcons generally kill with their beaks, whereas eagles and hawks tend to kill with their talons. Moreover, a falcon should not be introduced to the idea of gorging (feeding) on the breast of a pheasant—roast pheasant minus the breast does not taste half as good to the falconer! It is possible to hunt successfully in wooded terrain with hawks, which have good acceleration over short distances, but falcons need wider, open spaces.

One of the finest types of falconry involves a bird working jointly with a well-trained pointer (dog). A good team consisting of falconer, dog and bird, is so well coordinated that the moment the dog "points" to a pheasant or gray partridge, the falcon already knows that its prey is about to fly. Then everything happens at lightning speed. The prey flies upwards, the falcon swoops down from the sky at approximately 170 mph, attacks the prey, does a loop and returns once again to the prey in frantic flight.

It should be added that the falcon does not retrieve the prey for the falconer, as for example does the hunting dog. Instead, the falconer must make for the kill and take the bird off its prey. Frequently a falcon strikes its prey to the ground

Some of the falconer's equipment: heron lure by Karel Mollen (top left), Mollen falcon bag, falconer's glove, jess straps (center bottom), jess leash (center), long Mollen jess (top), two pairs of falcon bells, two falcon hoods by Mollen and a hunting horn.

Karel Mollen, the most famous Dutch falconer of modern times with his British friend George Oxer.

Belgian (or Dutch?) hunting party hunting herons with falcons in the presence of His Royal Highness Prince Alexander of the Netherlands.

Hunting for herons with falcons with King William III (on horse wearing long riding boots) and P. Bekker, who is bending over the heron.

Ornate Indian hood, silk embroidery with pearls and gold brocade.

Indian hood for a peregrine falcon

Dutch hood for a peregrine falcon

Arab hood for a female saker falcon

Arab hood for a sakret (male saker falcon)

Dutch hood for a lanner falcon

Dutch hood for a gyrfalcon

Dutch hood for a gyrfalcon of the Elector Archbishop Clemens August

Mollen hood for a tiercel (male) gyrfalcon

Mollen hood for a gyrfalcon

Mollen hood for a peregrine falcon

Indian hood for a lagger falcon

Mollen hood for a merlin

Mollen hood for a peregrine falcon

Indian hood for a tiercel lagger falcon

Indian hood for a "Red Empress" peregrine falcon

Mollen hood for a tiercel gyrfalcon

Ceremonial Austrian hood for a prairie falcon

Dutch hood for a lanner falcon

Dutch hood for a sakret

Ornate Indian hood for a "Black Empress" peregrine falcon

Arab hood (gilded) for a saker falcon

French hood for a tiercel peregrine falcon

English hood for a tiercel "Alphanet" falcon

Belgian hood for a tiercel gyrfalcon

Dutch hood for a goshawk

French hood for a sakret

Belgian hood for a gyrfalcon

Dutch hood for a peregrine falcon

Dutch hood for a golden eagle

Spanish hood for a Bonelli's eagle

English hood, Arab shape, for a saker falcon

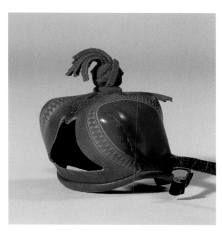

English hood, Indian shape, for a tiercel gyrfalcon

A brown hare runs in vain for its life.
The next moment the hunt is over.

This goshawk has succeeded and has a freshly-slain pheasant between its sharp talons.

In this collision between goshawk and pheasant, the latter will come off worst.

at a fairly long distance and may have already started to gorge itself before the falconer arrives on the scene.

Training an eagle can be more problematic, since it can react aggressively if the falconer makes a false move, and under certain circumstances can inflict serious injuries. Any abrupt movement, a reaction not understood, or the sudden removal of the prey, can lead to the bird rejecting the falconer or even attacking him.

For training an adult wild bird or a young bird which has been reared by its parents, it is initially necessary to subdue the wild characteristics. Training requires an even more marked sensitivity, and such birds are particularly well-suited for breeding programs which originate with artificial insemination. This technique is used for preference for breeding hybrids, using two different species which, however, are genetically compatible. Examples are gyrfalcon and peregrine, gyrfalcon and saker, saker and peregrine and lanner and lagger. As with horses and dogs, it is possible, given a great deal of patience, to breed hybrid individuals with excellent characteristics. One species of bird can contribute courage, strength and size, the other speed, stamina and resistance, not to mention beauty.

Although this scene happens at top speed the hare is not fast enough and will not be able to escape the eagle much longer.

Here the outcome of the hunt is as yet uncertain. With each swerve the brown hare evades attack by the eagle. But one swerve will be his last.

Hunting fever in the eyes of a trained golden eagle.

Goshawk on the falconer's fist.

The emblem of the German Order of Falconry was designed by Renz Waller on the occasion of its founding in 1923.

Captions to pages 192 & 193
A trained goshawk on a hunting flight through its territory. When it suddenly spots its prey, it launches its final attack as if shot from a bow.

The dog waits impatiently for his turn.

The dramatic end for a brown hare; it can no longer escape from the grip of the experienced old goshawk.

Not every attack is successful. This rabbit leaps vertically into the air in mortal terror and the goshawk misses it.

This golden eagle on the fist of his master has just killed a fox – prey too large for a falcon.

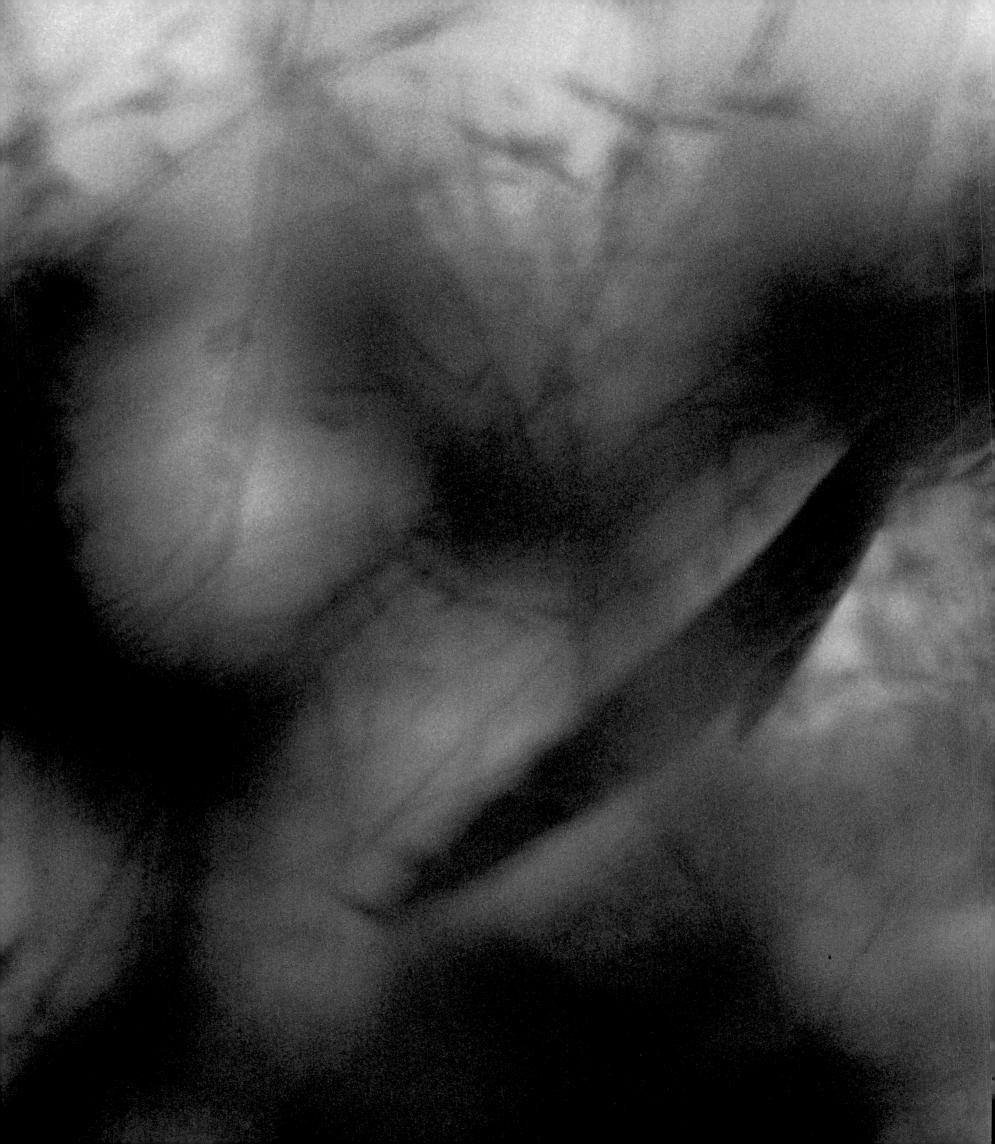

HUNTING IN ART

BERND E. ERGERT

There are cave painters of the Paleolithic, and there are court artists of the baroque. They have little in common, and yet their worlds meet when it comes to the subject of hunting. For the one group it is hunting itself which provides their livelihood, while the other group earn their living by creating an image of hunting. And yet the art which emerges from their hands remains the same, though aspiration and form of expression may change. Whereas we can only speculate about the function and significance of cave painting, the task of baroque art is clear—its purpose is to exalt the power and prestige of its patrons. To this end it cannot be too lavish, as we see from the famous Weissenfels hunting goblet (right) by Johann Melchior Dinglinger, commissioned by Augustus the Strong, or Melchior Mair's clockwork model (above), created for Christian II of Saxony, in which the characters roll their eyes and shoot arrows from bows.

When, early in 1995, the French Minister of Culture opened Grotte Chauvet to the public, a new chapter opened in the history of art and of hunting. Since then, the quantity of artistic representations of animals has become even more impressive; ranging from the peculiarly lifelike Stone Age cave paintings to the impressionistic animal drawings of Joseph Beuys. Indeed, perhaps modern representations are more like the early ones than many would suspect, so that one might say the wheel has almost turned full circle.

Since animals are older than mankind, they are necessarily the oldest companions of man. From the very beginning of our cultural history they have been dangerous as enemies, attached to us as partners, useful as helpers, necessary as a source of food, and welcome as the hunter's quarry. At times their sacrifice was supposed to make the gods merciful, and at times they were regarded as the bearers or even the embodiment of divine qualities. The relationship of man to animal has remained ambivalent to this day.

Today we believe that the evolution of man took about three and a half million years, in the course of which the plant-eating tree-dweller became the hunter, walking upright and making tools. Over hundreds of thousands of years, he progressed from occasionally snatching small animals to carefully planned hunting. Apparently, it was the switch to a mainly meat-based diet—which ultimately meant hunting—together with the mastery of fire, that were the decisive factors in man's evolution.

The beginnings of art lie so far back in the past that there would be little purpose in an approach from the perspective of our contemporary under-

standing of art. There is a need, then, for an open definition of the concept of 'art' which can be constantly correlated with the artistic evidence.

Some of this evidence of *Homo erectus* is already available: in the Thuringian Basin, for example, alongside the remains of hunted animals, bone artefacts with simple but deliberate markings, have been found, dated at around 400,000 years. If we assume that this decorative work is the expression of the emotions and imagination, they bear witness to a highly developed power of abstraction, and demonstrate the ability of these early hunters to relate to their environment, and to formulate and exchange both ideas and perceptions of nature in symbolic form.

In 1874, two small works of art, allegedly part of a large find near the German–Swiss border, were put on display. These were subsequently shown to be forgeries, with the result that experts in the field began to regard artefacts 10,000 years old or more with understandable suspicion. True, at a congress of anthropologists in Constance in 1877, this suspicion was largely dispelled, but sufficient doubt remained to question the authenticity of the rock paintings of Altamira, which were discovered in Northern Spain in 1879 and which are some of the most important works of European cave art. It was only the discovery of more caves containing rock paintings in the early 20th century that furnished the proof that these paintings were indeed of Stone Age origin.

At an early stage, Abbé Breuil (1877–1961), the doyen of researchers into the Paleolithic art of Southern France and Northern Spain, reflected deeply on the content, form and purpose of this cave art. He it is who is responsible for attributing

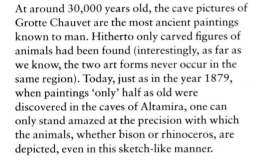

At around 30,000 years old, the cave pictures of Grotte Chauvet are the most ancient paintings known to man. Hitherto only carved figures of animals had been found (interestingly, as far as we know, the two art forms never occur in the same region). Today, just as in the year 1879, when paintings 'only' half as old were discovered in the caves of Altamira, one can only stand amazed at the precision with which the animals, whether bison or rhinoceros, are depicted, even in this sketch-like manner.

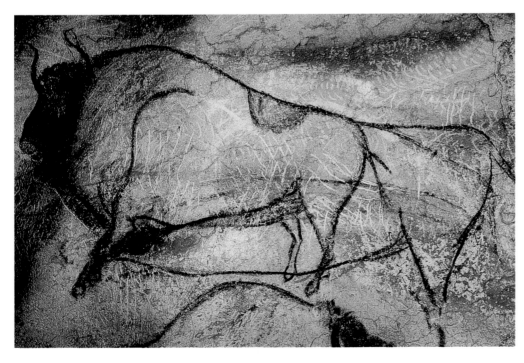

Franco-Cantabrian art to the two cultures which bear the names of the sites where the art works were found: the Aurignacian-Perigordian (between 30,000 and 20,000 years ago) and the Solutrean-Magdalenian (between 20,000 and 12,000 years ago).

At first it was customary to regard Ice Age art merely as an expression of hunting magic, but recent Paleolithic research in the fields of ethnology and the philosophy of religion have, since the middle of the present century, opened up new ways of looking at it. The Paleolithic animal pictures, which are either engravings or paintings in single or multiple colors, using paint made from manganese earth (black) or ocher (various shades of red), leave no room for doubt that they are also representations of real life.

Some of these pictures speak with moving directness of actual hunting experiences. One of them (in the shaft of the cave of paintings in Lascaux, Southern France) shows the violent death of a hunter. The animal too is fatally wounded, its intestines spilling out. The bird-like head of the prostrate man has been seen as a symbol of the transition from this life to the hereafter. According to another interpretation the picture represents a scene of invocation. In fact, however, it is not crucial to know in detail what is portrayed here; far more significant is the fact that an action which is evidently highly complex is being portrayed, and how this is done.

The creators of these early works of art, the most remarkable of which include small animal sculptures, objects made of bone, ivory, antlers and jet (black lignite, rich in bitumen), were hunters and gatherers. Dependent as they were on the climatic zone and period, their way of life was primarily determined by the seasonal rhythms of the migrating animals on which they depended for food.

Almost no motif of cave art has given rise to as much speculation as this hunting scene from Lascaux, which dates back some 15,000 years. What is so puzzling is not only the head of the prostrate man or the bird on a stick close to him, but also the striking stylistic difference in the depiction of animal and human. Even the dots scattered about the picture have inspired imaginative interpretations.

THE OLDEST ART GALLERY IN THE WORLD
GROTTE CHAUVET IN THE ARDÈCHE VALLEY

The most recent Stone Age find in Europe has revealed the oldest paintings known to man. They were created around 30,000 years ago, and their expressive force, as well as their state of preservation, have been acclaimed worldwide as a sensation in the field of prehistoric archeology. Nothing since the discovery of the cave paintings in Altamira in Spain between 1869 and 1879, and in Lascaux in France in 1940, has aroused as much interest and admiration as the wealth of pictures in Grotte Chauvet. What really excited the scientists was the result of the tests to determine the age of the pictures. By the use of color pigment analyses, scientists were able to prove that the pictures are about twice as old as the celebrated paintings of Lascaux, which were preserved on the rock for posterity some 15,000 years ago.

The function and meaning of the many paintings on the calcareous limestone walls of Grotte Chauvet will continue to puzzle researchers and speleologists for a long time to come. But even if we never succeed in fathoming their meaning, the very existence of these pictures demonstrates that our forefathers of 30,000 years ago were more like us than we had hitherto imagined. And if, in spite of the numerous other artefacts that have been found, it is primarily the pictures which impress us, this is simply further proof of the fundamental importance that pictures have for our perception.

On the evening of December 18 1994, the French cave explorers Eliette Brunel Deschamps, Jean-Marie Chauvet and Christian Hillaire reached a previously undiscovered cave and found themselves in the oldest gallery in the world, Grotte Chauvet, which is now regarded as possibly the most important piece of evidence of Stone Age culture in existence. Altogether the explorers counted no fewer than 267 animals depicted on the walls of the 535-yard-long limestone cave: horses, and herds of reindeer, lions and bison, mammoths and fighting woolly rhinoceroses—an impressive array of the larger fauna of the Ice Age savannahs of Europe. Situated at the foot of a rocky slope of the Ardèche gorge in the South of France, Grotte Chauvet is at the heart of an area which the three successful speleologists have been combing for years for traces of our prehistoric hunter-gatherer ancestors.

The explorers themselves describe their sensational discovery thus:

"Suddenly the light of the torch falls on a huge black frieze, which extends for about 12 meters along the left wall. Again we catch our breath, and in silence shine our torches over the walls. Then we simply explode with a mixture of laughter, tears and cheering. At first we are overcome with a feeling of giddiness. But then what a sight meets our gaze! There are countless animals:

Under this mountain the cave known as Grotte Chauvet lies hidden. It has been closed by the French Government in order to protect the priceless art treasures in this recently discovered system of caves from being put at risk by visitors. These treasures could suffer irreparable damage from light, humidity, temperature variation, and of course malicious damage and theft.

a dozen lions or lionesses (they have no mane), rhinoceroses, bison, mammoths, a reindeer, most of them facing towards the exit. (...) We are particularly struck by a curious small mammoth, almost a mythical beast. Also by a glorious bison with a slightly wavy mane, the horns shown from the front, the head in profile, the mouth slightly open. It is covered in scratches. To the right, on a rocky ledge in the arch of the ceiling, Daniel discovers a figure with the head of a bison and the body of a man, which seems to be watching over the gigantic frieze like a 'magician'. Red lines, which in some places are discernible beneath the black ones, suggest the pictures may have been painted over.

We are amazed at the perfection of the execution in this frieze too. One of the lions seems to dominate the herd of animals with his piercing gaze. His head is drawn in a deeper black. A horse in a niche of the rock strikes a theatrical pose. Bison heads are arranged one above the other like hunting trophies. A rhinoceros appears to have several horns, giving the impression of motion. The natural relief of the rock has been used to perfection, as, for example, where, on a small ledge, the head of a bison has been drawn from the front, whilst the body can be found in profile on the rock wall further back, as if the animal is turning its gaze toward us.

Then, on the floor, we see something which looks to us like ibex tracks, and we go no further, as the entire floor of the cave is now covered with animal tracks. Back in front of the frieze, we open the bottle of champagne that Daniel has thoughtfully brought along, and pause before this masterpiece, lost in contemplation. We are happy that our friends are with us at the discovery of this new frieze, one of the finest in the entire cave.

Back at the great frieze of horses we notice more imprints at the base of the wall. The outline of two human hands is clearly visible in a thin strip of clay. The palms of the hands are clearly recognizable and are more deeply imprinted than the fingers, which are harder to discern. Perhaps it is the hand of one of the artists? The sight of these fragile imprints, which have been preserved over the millennia, is profoundly moving for all of us. As we return to the entrance, we clamber on to fallen boulders which tower up to our left. Behind them, in a hollow, we can make out a red deer. Crawling on all fours, we reach the entrance of a tiny, orange-colored rock chamber scarcely a meter high. At the far end of this small hollow space, which is protected by a curtain of golden stalactites, we can recognize three bears following one after the other. We go no further, as here too the floor is covered with the bones of bears."

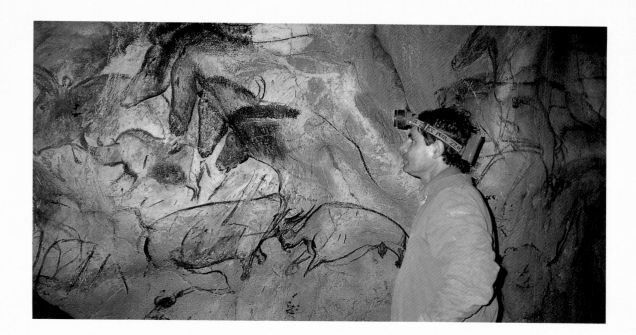

On the evening of December 18 1994, three French cave explorers squeezed through the narrow clay passage of a rocky shaft and soon afterwards were rewarded with the sight of the oldest known picture gallery on earth. They are (from top to bottom) Jean-Marie Chauvet, after whom the cave has since been named, and his two friends Eliette Brunel Deschamps and Christian Hillaire.

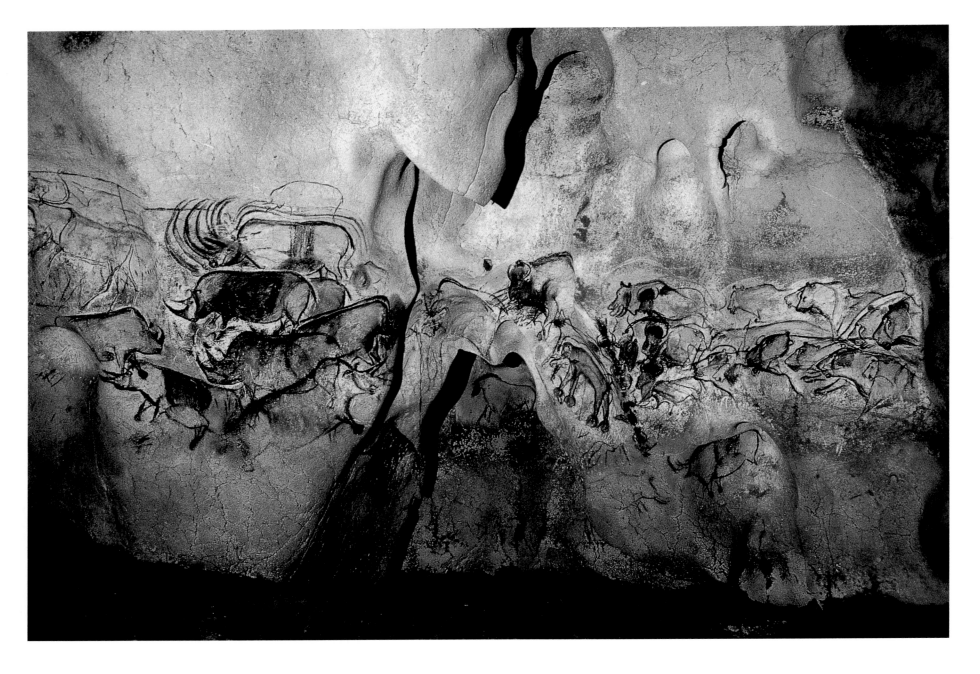

The lion panel in the rear hall of the 535-yard-long Grotte Chauvet shows a pride of lions (with bison, rhinoceroses, and a small mammoth amongst them), and a herd of rhinoceroses at the side of a niche in the rock. To the human observer the way many of the figures overlap conveys the impression of motion.

With the end of the last Ice Age about 12,000 years ago the landscape of Europe gradually changed again. Scattered, sparse woods in sheltered spots gave way, in the course of time, to dense forests of deciduous and coniferous trees. The most suitable areas for human settlement were now increasingly the river banks and the fringes of the forests. The forests were rich in game to be hunted, so that it was no longer necessary to travel long distances in pursuit of migrating herds to obtain food. Hand in hand with man's settled way of life went the cultivation of crops and animal husbandry. Only as the hunted animal gradually ceased to represent almost the sole food source did the hunter-gatherer become the true hunter.

This transition from the acquisitive to the productive type of economy can be detected in art as well, for in both conception and composition the rock pictures now differ from older illustrations. A glance at Eastern Spanish or North African examples makes this clear. Unlike the Paleolithic paintings in the caves of the Franco-

Cantabrian region, they are more scenic in character, and place greater emphasis on man.

Thus, in the rock drawings of Eastern Spain, there are more humans than animals. Men in knee-breeches appear, wearing belts and loin-cloths, with their shoulders covered and with feathers in their hair, headdresses or caps. Many men are bearded and wear jewelry. We see women in widely flared skirts, with naked torsos, leather aprons and, like the men, wearing jewelry on their arms and legs. There are illustrations of men at work, hunting with bow and arrow, running and fighting with their own kind, wounded and fallen.

Frequently the representation of people is true to life, as in the Cueva Saltadora in the Valltorta Gorge; it may, however, be deliberately distorted, with legs that are either long and thin or short and fat. Often human forms are severely minimalized; one can sense the tendency towards those schematic or abstract forms which are soon to dominate the art of rock painting.

All the pictures of this phase in Spain are two-dimensional in style and appear as silhouettes, as the outline is simply filled in with red or black coloring. The former linear style is intensified to form highly expressive silhouettes, and it survives in still more starkly reduced form in, amongst other places, the geometric style of the Bronze Age rock pictures of Scandinavia.

Alongside polychrome rock paintings, the post-Paleolithic peoples of North Africa have also left pictorial art created by a different technique. Thousands of pictures in stone found in Egypt, Libya, Tunisia and Morocco are not painted, but carved or engraved in outline on steep rock faces, the rock floor of a valley or in boulders. There we see dramatic representations of the long since extinct wild buffalo, elephants, giraffes, ostriches, rhinoceroses, as well as domesticated animals such as camels, oxen and horses; a constant theme remains, that of man engaged in hunting or fighting.

The precise dating of the North African paintings created over a long period of time is not easy. The best examples begin to appear at about the same time as those of Eastern Spain, which are between 10,000 and 12,000 years old. However, an approximate chronology can only be established with the aid of the animal pictures. Thus the keeping of livestock was only possible during the moist phase of the Sahara, which lasted from about 5000 B.C. to the second half of the third millennium B.C. Horses are only known to have existed in the Sahara from 2000 B.C. at the earliest.

Camels were only introduced, as domesticated animals, in the reign of Alexander the Great, so pictures of these animals can only date from the most recent centuries of the pre-Christian era.

From the point of view of type and style, representations of animals, whether painted, engraved or carved, follow on from those of the Neolithic Age, and doubtless the same can be said of their significance. Animals were a constituent part of the natural environment, and an attempt was made to convey with particular force both their relationship with and their difference from man. Many of these paintings and engravings may have cult or ritualistic interpretations, whilst the numerous scenes of hunting and fighting may very well be seen as pictures recording an event, votive pictures or illustrations of myths or ballads.

Between 3500 and 3000 B.C., the urban culture of the Sumerians grew up between the rivers Tigris and Euphrates, and a little later came the Egyptian civilization, with its god-kings. For almost 3,000 years these Mesopotamian and Egyptian cultures, which often cross-fertilized each other, were the pillars of the known world, until the Greeks took over the leading role around the middle of the first millennium before Christ.

It was the fertile soil, a result of the cyclical deposits from the rivers, that made these ancient cultures possible in the first place, and which also created the conditions for the profusion of game

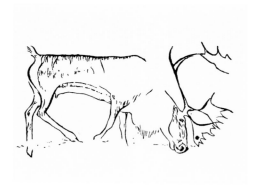

This picture of a magnificent stag is in the cave at Lascaux.

This c. 10,000–12,000-year-old engraving on a baton, found in Kesslerloch cave, near Thayngen in Switzerland, shows a rutting reindeer.

The reindeer panel in Hillaire Hall, Grotte Chauvet. In the flickering light of the torches the play of shadows on the uneven stone walls may have influenced the shape of the animal drawings.

The famous standing bison on the ceiling of the Altamira cave in Northern Spain shows how the artist has tried to represent the solid dimensions of the animal's body by the use of lighter and darker shades.

202

in this region. "In those days I killed fifty wild oxen and captured eight on the other side of the Euphrates. I killed thirty elephants in the mountains. I slew two hundred and fifty-seven mighty wild bulls in the struggle (...). By the stretching out of my hand and by the courage of my heart I captured fifteen strong lions from the mountains and forests." With these words King Assurnasirpal II (883–852 B.C.) boasts of his heroic deeds and has them depicted on the walls of his palaces.

The portrayal of royal hunts is one of the principal themes in Assyrian relief art. The glorification of the victorious ruler naturally takes centre-stage, and perhaps for this reason the animal is depicted with almost shocking realism. A graphic example is the hunting relief from the North Palace of Assurbanipal in Ninive (approx. 650 B.C.), with its picture of a fatally wounded lioness. Pierced by three arrows, the animal raises itself up on its front paws, though the rear part of its body has sunk to the ground.

Presumably all these hunting and animal pictures are more than mere accounts of the hunt, but are closely linked with the myth that demonic powers manifest themselves in the form of certain animals, such as the serpent, the lion or the bull, whilst the creative gods usually appear in human form. After the victory of the creative gods, some of the demons in animal form become emblems of the victors, or are used to proclaim a message. As composite hybrid creatures having both animal and human form they have an important part to play in numerous Assyrian murals and reliefs or they act as impressive palace and temple guards.

Animals have also left their mark on the culture of ancient Egypt over a period of almost 3,000 years. Animals and hybrid creatures comprising both animal and man are the commonest manifestations of the world of the Egyptian gods. We meet them as reliefs and on murals, as statues and cult figures of the great shrines, as votive figurines, on graves, seals and amulets, on house altars and in hieroglyphics.

On the fertile flood plain of the Nile, a great diversity of species was able to develop. This ensured plenty of variety for the court hunting parties, as shown in numerous murals and reliefs

This bronze standard (used for ritual purposes) from a prince's tomb near Alaca Höyük in Turkey is about 5,000 years old, whereas the Schirndorf clay vessel of the Hallstatt culture is only about half as old. When objects which are so different in origin, period, material and function, depict the same animal, it is clearly outstandingly important, and there are many such examples. With its speed of movement, elegance, and, last but not least, its mighty antlers, the deer has the right qualities to be a symbolic figure, though what is represented may vary. The shaman, Acteon suffering his punishment, the Celtic stag-god and the defeated, yet victorious Christ; have all appeared in the form of a stag.

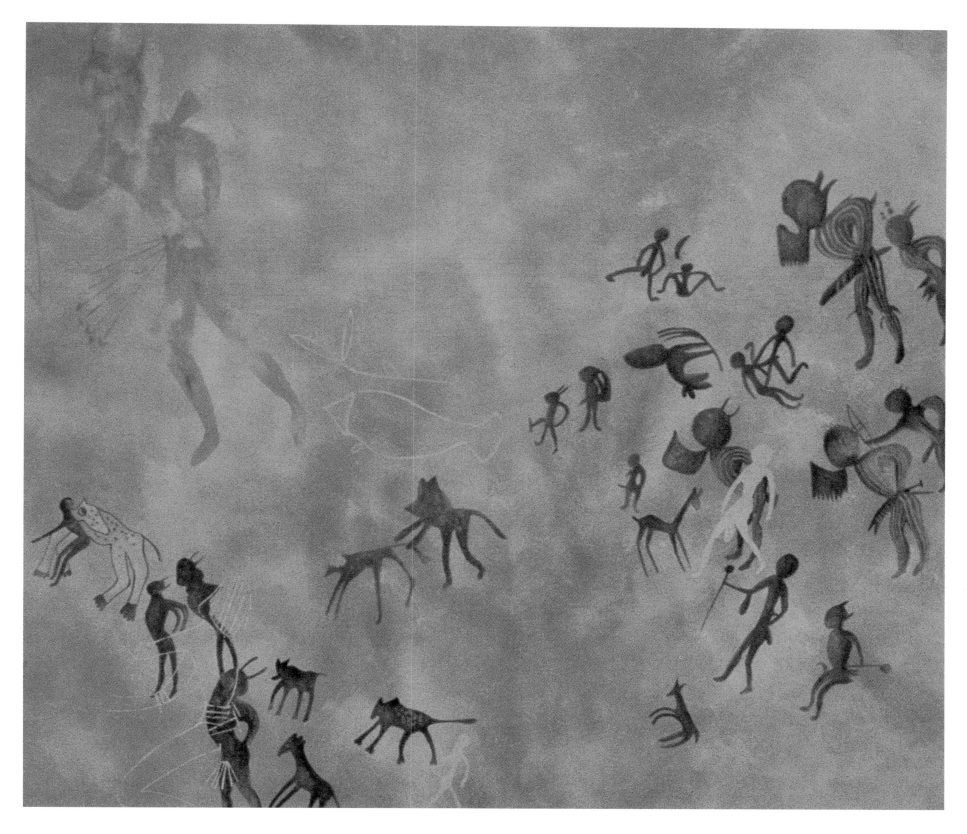

in the burial chambers of the Pharaohs and high officials. In the neighboring desert areas lion, gazelles, antelopes, ostrich and giraffe were hunted. The most ancient hunting picture in the Eastern Mediterranean dates from the predynastic period around 3000 B.C.; it is a cosmetic palette of grey slate with the relief decoration showing a royal lion hunt (this item is now in the Louvre, Paris).

Egyptologists today see these hunting pictures not so much as genre paintings of a hunting adventure, but rather as a conflict between good and evil. This applies especially to those depicting the Pharaohs. The three levels of the hunt—desert (wild animals), water (fish and hippopotamus) and air (birds)—were inhospitable to man; he could not survive in them. Beings which lived outside the human sphere of existence could thus easily be felt to be embodiments of threatening forces. These were not necessarily demons and magicians, they could just as easily be enemies from this world. Thus birds were hunted "because they were Nubians". So, in killing a certain animal the hunter overcame a particular enemy. With its apparently superior abilities, to swim, to fly or to travel at great speed, the animal was a symbol of the conquest of death, and came to represent hope for the afterlife.

These rock pictures already include portrayals of human activities.

Bronze statuette of a boar from Lindau on Lake Constance, Latène culture (450–415 BC).

Mammoth and wild horse; ivory carvings from Vogelherd Cave in the Lone Valley (c. 30,000 years old).

Dying lioness, hunting relief (detail) from the Northern Palace of Assurbanipal, Niniveh, about 650 B.C.

Lion struck by an arrow as it leaps, hunting relief (detail) from the Northern Palace of Assurbanipal, Nineveh, about 650 B.C.

The depictions of animals on these pages were done over a period of about 28,000 years, during which time hunting evolved from being a necessity for survival to a 'pastime'. The Neolithic ivory carvings could have been amulets designed to bring success in hunting the animal in question. The hunter would have been carrying the magic charm on his person at the crucial moment. The bronze figure would perhaps have been in the nature of a burial gift, since a hunting charm was not strictly necessary in a society of successful cattle-breeders. The ivory figures sought to cast a spell over the animal portrayed in order to make it more easy prey for the hunter, and the Assyrian relief suggests that the act of killing itself had a magical significance.

The West has long been more strongly influenced by the spirit of Greek and Roman antiquity than by the cultures beyond the Mediterranean. The arts which arose in the land of the Greeks thousands of years ago continue to exert an influence right up to the present day, in philosophy, literature, painting, sculpture and music. The Greeks' image of the gods is close to man, and differs from that of the oriental cultures, even though remnants of earlier zoomorphic concepts may persist, in the form of hybrid creatures or those that change their shape. Thus even amongst the Homeric and post-Homeric Greeks we find gods appearing in animal form, for example Artemis, the goddess of nature and the hunt.

Without man's knowledge, a god or demon may appear in animal form—providing material for the countless tales of metamorphosis which are the stock-in-trade of ancient literature and have survived in the most varied forms through the Middle Ages and the Renaissance to the present day. Yet not only do gods transform themselves into animals, they also have the power to transform men, whether to punish them, rescue them from their pursuers, reward them or raise them to a higher plane.

The hunt in all its variations, from bird-catching to the lion hunt, became established in mythology and became a favorite theme of contemporary artists. About 800 B.C., Homer writes: "Odysseus hurls himself on the boar/But it quickly turns/And rends him in the loins." Xenophon (c. 430–c. 354 B.C.), to whom the hunting book "Kynegetikos" has been attributed, stresses that the boar hunt puts both the hound and the hunter in mortal danger. The most famous instance was the hunting of the Calydonian boar, related by Homer in the Iliad, which Artemis, angered by the failure of King Oineus of Etolia to make sacrifices to her, had sent to lay waste his fields. Only Prince Meleager, aided by the bold huntress Atalante, was finally able to kill the monster.

The motif of the Calydonian hunt was for a long time a favorite subject for art. From the 7th century B.C. it is found in vase painting with black figures; then from the beginning of the 6th century B.C. in what is known as the red-figure style, in which the figures are formed from spaces in the black background. By the advent of Christianity it was losing significance, and in the Middle Ages it fell into oblivion, though in the Renaissance it was revived, along with the general rediscovery of Antiquity. This was followed by treatments of the subject by Primaticcio, Tibaldi, Rubens, Poussin and others.

The goddess of hunting is surrounded by a veritable complex of myths. When the hunter Acteon observes her bathing, she punishes him by turning him into a stag, which is then torn to pieces by his own hounds. And when Artemis, mistress of nature and the unspoiled wilderness, who demands the oath of chastity from her companions, discovers that her nymph Callisto is pregnant, the angry goddess transforms the unfortunate nymph into a bear. Zeus, who had seduced her, takes pity on her and transports her to the heavens where she becomes the constellation of the Great Bear.

At an early stage Artemis came to Italy, by way of the Greeks, the Illyrians and the Etruscans. There she soon merged with the native Diana, the glittering, luminous goddess of the night, and the pair formed a single entity. The mistress of the animals as we know her from Asia Minor, who was also responsible for fertility and bountiful harvests, became the goddess of the hunt. With the Roman legions she migrated to the Imperial provinces, where she was a goddess in a society estranged from nature and which had nothing in common with the animal.

The Romans had, it is true, adopted hunting as a sport from the Greeks and the Celts, but they acquired an increasing taste for comfort and easy living. Nevertheless, exciting hunting scenes are to be found on stone reliefs and sarcophagi, as frescos and as ivory carvings, on the Roman pottery known as Terra Sigillata, and on costly table decorations of bronze, silver and glass. The floor mosaics to be found in palaces, the villas of wealthy patricians and the thermal baths of late Roman Antiquity, are particularly attractive.

These detailed pictures tell the story of hunting with beaters, hounds and trappers, who set out to kill many species of wild animal, ranging from the hare to the mighty bear, or to capture them for the games in the Roman circus.

With the decline of the civilization of ancient Rome and the Roman emperors' growing passion for sumptuous display, the hunt became an ever more costly spectacle. Emperor Aurelius entered the Circus Maximus in Rome in a silver chariot drawn by four white deer, and the bloodthirsty Emperor Caligula had a hundred four-horse chariots drive up, the last two of which, however, were drawn by four camels and four elephants. Following this, in the Circus Maximus, the 'hunters' could indulge the passion which their forefathers had pursued out of necessity: they massacred wild beasts such as deer, crocodiles, lions, bears and elephants before the eyes of the crowds of enthusiastic onlookers.

One of the oldest Christian legends is that of Placidus, one of Emperor Trajan's generals, who was converted when the crucified Christ appeared to him between the antlers of a stag, saying "Placidus, why do you persecute me, who seeks your salvation?" After his baptism he was named Eustace, and suffered severe trials, losing rank, possessions, wife and sons. The mortal remains of St Eustace, who became the patron saint of hunting, lie in San Eustachio in Rome, and the Church celebrates his memory on September 20.

At the latest from 1444, when the Order of St Hubert was founded by the Duke of Jülich-Berg, the vision of the stag (part of the vitas of several saints) became part of the legend of St Hubert. The vision of the stag is a subject artists have frequently returned to.

The early Middle Ages saw the spread of Christianity, the rise of the Islamic world and the formation of the Carolingian Empire ruled over by Charlemagne, the first Western Roman Emperor since ancient times. From his Empire, France, Germany and Italy were later to emerge. It was a turbulent epoch, in which different cultures were at times in competition and at other times cross-fertilized each other, resulting in a range of different artistic styles. The tension between the Christian West and the Islamic world, for instance, proved stimulating for the arts.

The chief source of our knowledge of this period is literature. In "Tristan", Gottfried von Strassburg gives a detailed picture of courtly hunting customs and represents the noble Tristan as particularly expert in cutting the deer into pieces. In the heroic romances surrounding King Arthur we can read of the hunting of the white stag and the fierce boar, which sounds like fantasy but is described with great realism. One of the finest legends to revolve around the medieval hunt is the verse minstrel-epic "Guingamour" by Marie de France, a 12th century Norman poetess. Guingamour, hunting the dangerous white wild boar in the forest, gets caught up in a magical adventure. When he decides to continue the hunt after three days, he finds that 300 years have actually elapsed.

The Basle tapestry (c. 1500 A.D.) depicts four allegorical animals, facing each other in pairs. The (incompletely preserved) animal on the left is identifiable with the help of a very similar tapestry as an elephant(!). The captions express Christian ideas, but even without the accompanying words each of the animals is known to be allegorically linked with Christ from its behavior as a hunted beast. Because the elephant allegedly has no knee-joints, it is said to lean against the trunk of a sloping tree to sleep. The hunter need only prepare this tree in such a way that the elephant falls over when it leans against it; as it cannot now get up again it is at the mercy of the hunter. The animal cannot be rescued by its adult fellow creatures – only by a baby elephant (Christ). It is said of the lion that it obliterated its traces with its tail as soon as it scented the hunters, just as Christ hid his divine origins by means of his incarnation. The unicorn could only be vanquished with the aid of the virgin, into whose womb it jumped, as Christ entered the body of the Virgin Mary. The metaphor of the stag harried by the hounds as an image of the suffering of Christ has been referred to in sermons since the 14th century.

DIANA – TRIBUTE TO THE ALMOST FORGOTTEN GODDESS OF HUNTING
Sigrid Schwenk

St Hubert is often confused with St Eustace (shown here), a convert Roman general. Both are credited with having seen a vision of a stag with a crucifix hovering between its antlers, though in the case of Hubert the first written evidence only dates back to the 12th century. (Pisanello, The Vision of St Eustace, around 1436)

⊳ Diana as people liked to imagine her in the baroque age: lightly clothed, but wearing costly jewels, she hastens through the woods with her dogs, carrying her bow and selecting an arrow. Her quarry is the stag below in the clearing, but her glance is directed almost provocatively at the viewer.

The attentive visitor to baroque palaces will sooner or later meet the figure of a graceful young woman—either as a sculpture, in paintings on the ceilings or walls, or on tapestries. She is usually portrayed with quiver, bow and arrow, or with her spear in her hand, and is rarely without her hounds. She is sometimes together with her companions, but often she wanders through the woods alone. Her hair is usually adorned with an ornament in the shape of a crescent. She is Diana, the goddess of hunting.

For the kings and princes who built these palaces, as well as for the artists who decorated them, Diana was obviously the personification of the hunt, the goddess who protected hunters and hunted animals alike. But there came a time when she had to step aside. If you ask a huntsman to name the patron saint of hunting, German huntsmen at least will name Saint Hubert, for he is the only one they recognize as their patron, it is he whom they revere and on whose saint's day, November 3, special Hubert hunts take place, Hubert masses are said and Hubert ceremonies held.

Diana is usually thought of as a kind of lucky mascot. "Many hunters know", writes Paul-Joachim Hopp in "The Magic Conscience" (1973), "that they can have good and bad runs of luck in shooting. It is as though Diana was guiding them in person, when for a time they seem able to solve the most difficult tasks. Success breeds success..." The Diana of today is a good luck goddess, generous but unreliable, pretty but temperamental, lovable but with no practical significance for hunting. Recent research has revealed that this was not always the case. The goddess who began life in ancient times was once at the very center of hunting – not only amongst the gentry, but also for professional huntsmen and foresters.

As many people know from their schooldays, Diana was the Roman equivalent of the Greek goddess Artemis, who originated from the Minoan culture of Crete, and ruled over the animals and the fish. In addition she was able to bring blessing or destruction upon mankind by sending either a bountiful harvest or a famine.

At least since the Homeric period, that is the 8th century B.C., the picture of Artemis is clear. She is the daughter of Zeus and Leto, sister of Apollo, born on Delos. As queen of the animals she is predestined to be the goddess of hunting, an activity very popular in the society described by Homer. From the 7th century B.C. virginity seems to be an indispensable attribute, and from the 5th century B.C. she comes more and more to play the part of the goddess of the moon—as the female

equivalent of her twin brother Apollo, the god of light. (From the 6th century B.C., Apollo had become established as the sun god alongside the older Helios, whilst she took over the role of moon goddess, formerly played by Selene, the sister of Helios).

The cult of Artemis reached Italy by three routes. The principal one was via the Greek cities of the South, that is via Magna Graecia, then via the Illyrians in the North-East and thirdly via the Etruscans. As early as 500 B.C. Diana (whose name derives from 'diviana,' the luminous) can be found in Italy in the form of Artemis and with all the symbols associated with Artemis; her main characteristic already being that she watches over the hunt. By taking over cults that already existed she soon became firmly established in the new regions, and continued as an object of popular veneration, in various guises, but chiefly as the goddess of the forest and fields, despite fierce opposition from the Church. Not until the Middle Ages did the Catholic Church succeed in vilifying Diana as a demonic woman who practiced the black arts by night in the forest with like-minded companions. In the Renaissance she re-emerged in her original classical divine form, and enjoyed the veneration of hunters.

Without doubt it is a universal phenomenon that man calls upon God, either directly or through an intermediary, whenever he needs help or is striving after a particular goal. The sphere of hunting is no exception. In the past every social group has sought out a 'helper in need', a deity or intermediary to whom it can make requests or give thanks. (We are not referring simply to the 14 'auxiliary saints' of Catholic theology.) This applies to peasants and shepherds, warriors and members of the various estates, and of course to huntsmen.

Between the 15th century and the present, social upheavals and legal changes have occurred in the hunting community, that is, those authorized to hunt and actively involved in hunting, and these events need to be taken into consideration before anything definite can be said about Diana. Four periods can be defined: the first one from the middle of the 15th century through about 1680, a second from around 1680 through 1850, the third from 1850 through 1950, and a fourth from 1950 to the present. In the first period Diana belongs exclusively to the world of the aristocracy; in the second period she became accepted by the whole hunting community; in the third she almost completely ceases to have any significance for hunting, and in the fourth she has relinquished her position entirely in favor of Saint Hubert (at least in German-speaking countries).

St Hubert's vision of the stag is referred to in many places. Right up to the end of the 19th century gun casings were decorated with patterns like this one.

This picture of Diana out hunting, by an unknown artist of the school of Fontainebleau (around 1550/1560), is thought to be modeled on Diane de Poitiers, the mistress of Henry II. Again, the look in her eyes suggests that her quarry is not to be found in the picture.

In the first period those who engaged in the hunt were the aristocracy and the huntsmen in its service. These two social groups were quite distinct in manner of life and level of education, with scarcely anything in common outside of hunting. The one group were the product of courtly culture, and the other group were craftsmen. The latter group, which was far more numerous, probably had little interest in Diana right up to the second half of the 17th century. Their world was that of hunting calls and of the huntsman's sayings, the origins of which can be traced back to the 14th century, but which were dying out by about 1700. Hunting calls were the means by which they communicated. It was not until after 1600 that the special hunters' language evolved. None of these hunting calls or sayings mentions Diana, although there must have been plenty of occasions when help was needed.

It is also interesting to note that Martin Strasser von Kollnitz, at that time the most important German-language writer on hunting, never once mentions Diana in his "Book Concerning Every Kind of Hunting ..." (1624). And this was a man whose knowledge of hunting and the hunting customs of his age was second to none. This confirms the impression that in the 16th and early 17th centuries Diana, as goddess of hunting, existed only for members of the aristocracy. Thanks to the humanists they had rediscovered the Greco-Roman gods and goddesses, and had employed painters and sculptors to produce images of Diana for their mansions, images which together epitomize the Renaissance view of the goddess.

Of course, developments in art cannot give us a true picture of the actual experience of hunters, and yet we know that the new beginnings of the cult of Diana go back to the end of the 15th and the beginning of the 16th centuries. The evidence for this is found in a book which should be seen as part of hunting literature, although traditionally it has not been so regarded. The book in question is "Ludus Diane" by Conrad Celtis (1459–1508), a Shrovetide gift from the Poet Laureate to his lord, Emperor Maximilian I, in 1501. It is a mythological festival drama with music and dancing, in which the goddess Diana greets the Emperor Maximilian as "venator maximus", or mighty hunter. Conrad Celtis, the distinguished humanist, who had already published a large number of writings, reworked the material about Diana into this drama, sometimes referred to as the first opera.

Diana also appears elsewhere in the literature of this period. Ovid's "Metamorphoses" was particularly admired in the Renaissance, and the meeting between Diana and Acteon, recounted in Book III, was familiar to every educated person of the time. This is where Diana punishes Acteon, who has defiled her virginity by catching sight of her when naked, by turning him into a stag, whereupon he is torn to pieces by his own hounds.

All this demonstrates that up to the second half of the 17th century Diana is important to educated humanists and the aristocracy, but probably almost unknown outside these circles.

This is to change fundamentally toward the end of the 17th century. Diana becomes the patroness of all hunters, which is to say, not only of the members of the aristocracy authorized to hunt, but increasingly also of professional hunters, and finally all those concerned with hunting in any way. Thus it is she who decides on the success or failure of the hunt. As her admirers see it, she herself is a participant in the hunt, and is herself the fate which determines its outcome, for she alone controls the course of the hunt in all its phases; this is true for hunters and hunted, men and animals alike. She affords her protection both to the hunter and to his prey, being completely at one with nature. To call upon the goddess is to call upon fate to deal kindly with you.

The second period, from 1680 through 1850, is dominated by Diana. Johann Täntzer, a professional hunter, calls his three-volume didactic work, published in Copenhagen (first edition 1681, second edition 1734), "Diana's Great and Small Hunting Secrets". Each volume opens with a copperplate engraving of the goddess, together with a poem emphasizing the importance of Diana for all aspects of hunting, including hunting accessories and the hounds.

A large number of books bearing the name of Diana appear in the following years. In 1696 "Diana's Great and Small Hunting Delights" is published in Augsburg—it is actually just a translation into German of François Fortin's "Ruses innocentes", which was published 36 years earlier in France, and renamed by the translator to accord better with the spirit of the age. In the year 1749, Magnoalt Ziegelbauer, writing under the pseudonym Venantius Diana, published his amusing "Royal and Imperial Hunting Tales", and six years later a new literary genre, the hunting journal, made its appearance, with the publication of "Diana, a Pleasant and Useful Entertainment for Huntsmen and Those who Love the Hunt". In similar vein there followed from 1797 through 1816 the four-volume work "Diana, or a Popular Treatise for the Extension and Correction of the Lore of Nature, Woodlands and Hunting". The editor was the distinguished hunting author Johann Matthäus Bechstein.

Diana festivals were also nothing unusual at this time. In 1813, Friedrich von Matthison reports on "The Bebenhausen Diana Festival." People liked to link song collections with the

style which was imported from France about 1680. Their patron saint was Hubert. All the rest looked to Diana.

Not only the titles, but also the frontispieces demonstrate this. Thus in Stisser's "Forest and Hunting History of the Germans" (published 1737) Diana is shown in the picture as presenting the book to Frederick William I. And Gottfried von Moser, in his "Forest Archive for the Extension of the Science of Forestry and Hunting" (1788), had the idea of beginning each volume with an emblem on the title page. The first volume bore the image of Silvanus, who was seen as the god and protector of forestry. The second volume began with the picture of Diana, since the journal's primary interest was in forestry, with hunting in second place.

From the Renaissance onward, the growing importance of Diana in the minds of German professional hunters and foresters remained unnoticed by scholars for a long period. Similarly we have only recently become aware of the important role played by the hunting poem between 1790 and 1850. People tried to recapture the hunting experience in poetic form, and anyone who was active as a writer tried his hand at poetry too. So it comes as no surprise to learn that Diana is frequently mentioned when the poet is tackling topics such as, for example, the experience of nature, or the relationship between man and beast. One example of this is the great hunting writer Carl Emil Diezel, whose book "The Hunting of Smaller Game" has been through 32 editions and is still regarded as a standard work. Until 1979, when on the 200th anniversary of his birth a collection of his poems was published, few were aware that Diezel, who was renowned for his textbook of hunting, had also distinguished himself in the field of lyric poetry.

Most of these poems were written between 1806 and 1808, in Diezel's youth, but he continued to be inspired by Diana until a very advanced age. He was fascinated by her, she assisted and protected him, she was his good fairy, she protected the game and provided the hunter's quarry. Münchhausen, Bunsen and many others, whose names have since lost the lustre and resonance they once had, constantly call upon the goddess. One such is Ludwig von Wildungen, the leading member of the circle of German hunting poets around the beginning of the 19th century, whose popular little poem begins: "Strive! Diana will not be mocked with impunity!"

Words like these were in keeping with the spirit of the times. When in 1830 Duke Heinrich of Württemberg wrote a report on the course of the rutting season for the "General Forestry and Hunting Journal" he proudly announced the successful killing of an eighteen-point stag, finishing

"Diana bathing" (1704) is another masterpiece by Johann Melchior Dinglinger at the court of Augustus the Strong. For the first time he was working with his fellow-artist Balthasar Permoser, who created the figurative decoration for the Dresden Zwinger. The motif of Diana bathing goes back to Greek mythology: Artemis, surprised by Acteon while bathing, takes revenge by turning the hunter into prey, thus delivering him to certain death.

name of Diana. In 1829 "Diana's Guide to Hunting, a Pocket-Book for Hunters, Foresters and Hunting Enthusiasts" came out, and in 1836 a collection of hunting poetry, edited by one Theodor Theuss of Weimar, was published. The title was "Diana – Song-Book for all Foresters and Hunters".

This series of titles, which could easily be extended, shows that in the 18th and the first quarter of the 19th centuries German hunters regarded Diana as the patroness of the hunt, apart from those in some courts who went in for hunting with horses and hounds, the parforce

St Hubert has proved to be a successful rival, and it is noteworthy that a Catholic bishop has supplanted the dubious pagan goddess, chaste though she might be. Oddly enough, the earliest accounts of the legend of Saint Hubert make no mention of him being a passionately keen hunter or that the stag with the crucifix appeared to him. They do, however, relate that Hubert banned the hunters of the Ardennes from sacrificing the first victim of the hunt to Diana. (Georg Lorenz Gaap II, silver relief with vision of the stag, Augsburg, around 1710)

with the words "for which I kiss the hands and feet of the beautiful Diana".

An indication of the high esteem in which Diana was held amongst professional hunters and foresters as patroness of the hunt, of the hunter and of game, is shown particularly clearly in an apprenticeship certificate which a nobleman, Joseph Count von und zu Arco, presented to a hunter who had qualified in deer-hunting and forestry on July 23 1792. This document, which is now in the German Museum of Hunting and Fishing in Munich, is beautifully printed, has a seal attached to it and, like many of the apprenticeship certificates of that time, is decorated with a number of attractive miniature water-colors. A small medallion on the left shows the torso of Acteon with antlers on his head, while the one on the right has a picture of Diana adorned with a crescent moon.

Diana's place in the affections of German hunters seemed secure. And yet from 1830 there are signs that a change could be under way, and that Saint Hubert, hitherto honored only by the relatively few devotees of horse-and-hounds (or parforce) hunting, could be about to extend the range of his influence. As we have seen, it was a common custom of huntsmen to celebrate Diana festivals. Wilhelm Bornemann, the Royal Prussian Director of the General Lottery, and Knight of the Order of the Red Eagle, published a book in 1827 entitled "Paintings of Nature and Hunting together with a Commentary on Natural History and the History of Hunting". He aimed to found a hunting association with a view to directing the social activities of hunters into more ordered paths, not least to expand what he felt to be huntsmen's scanty scientific knowledge by means of "training courses" and public lectures. On December 5 1827, to promote the foundation of such a hunting association, Bornemann organized a Diana festival in Berlin, which was evidently a great success and which inspired him to compose a poem with the plain title "Protocol of the Diana Festival of December 5 1827. The poem (which is in rhyming verse in the original German) includes the surprising lines:

The child must learn to crawl before it walks.
The festival will be baptized "Diana".
Then when the child can walk in grown-up manner
It soon will give a certain indication
That "Hubert" is its name of confirmation.

So Bornemann started with a Diana festival, but assumed that the hunters would change it to a St

Hubert festival—a sign that Diana could no longer retain her pre-eminence over Saint Hubert.

In the third period, between 1850 and the end of the Second World War, both Diana and her "rival", Hubert, who had been gaining ground on her during the first half of the 19th century, largely faded from the picture. The changed social structure of the hunting community after 1848, the new currents of thought, rationalism, technological progress, the ever growing importance of science, the approach towards industrialization and everything associated with it—this was not fertile soil for salvation figures like Diana or Hubert. No one actually turned against them, but neither did anyone turn to them. November 3, the feast of St Hubert, was a favorite day for a shoot, and on a wild boar hunt, as we read in contemporary accounts, occasionally a cheer was raised, but the cheer was for both Hubert and Diana, in order not to give offence to either of them.

The fourth and final period, the present age, began in West Germany shortly after the war with the re-establishment of hunting rights in the Federal Republic and is characterized by a marked rehabilitation of the figure of St Hubert, following the example of France. Apart from a few literary book titles in which she figures, Diana seems to have been finally deserted by practicing German hunters, although—who knows?—as times change she may one day regain her former glory.

Although St Hubert spared the stag on that memorable Good Friday he became the patron saint of parforce hunters. They are supposed to see every stag they hunt as a symbol of Christ, but perhaps they only do so on Good Friday.

Acteon, the hunter, oversteps the mark, and punishment by the chaste Artemis will be severe. The sight that cost him his life poses no such threat for the modern observer. Indeed, myths like these offered a welcome opportunity to portray the female nude – allowing the patron to delight in the unclothed figures while at the same time displaying his interest in culture. (Jacob Jordaens, "Diana and Acteon", c. 1640)

On most other days of the year this scene would represent a court hunting party, but on May 1 it was the custom (of pagan origin) to pick the first greenery in the forest. (Picture for the month of May from the Grimani Breviary, around 1510)

▷ A charivari is supposed not only to adorn the wearer, but also to protect from sickness and danger. The piece displayed has rarity value, as some of the trophies come from what are now protected species. They are (clockwise): beaver tooth, lynx claw, horn of the pudu-pudu (the smallest species of deer in the world), walrus tooth, Bonelli's eagle bill, wolf tooth, red deer tooth, claw of peregrine falcon, stoat head, marmot tooth, capercaillie claw, fox carnassial, sea otter tooth, Altai maral deer tooth, seal tooth, wapiti tooth, golden eagle claw, horn of young roebuck.

It is an essential feature of myths and legends that they cluster around actual events or objects about whose origins nothing is known, as man seeks an explanation. If the object in question has anything to do with woods or fields and if persons of high standing are involved, then it is not uncommon for hunting to have a place in these writings. This is why so many legends concerning the founding of a church or monastery are linked with the hunting adventures of individual rulers. Artists in later periods have picked these up and

their works have helped to keep them alive to the present day.

A good example is provided by the building activities of the Bavarian Duke Tassilo III, who, although dependent on the Frankish Carolingians, was able to exercise sovereign rule over his dukedom from 757. According to the foundation legend of Polling Monastery south of Weilheim in Upper Bavaria, Tassilo was out hunting one day when he witnessed a hind, oblivious to the pursuing hounds, scraping away in the ground and

Huntsman in traditional garb: Maximilian Bernhard, Count of Arco-Zinneberg (1811–1885).

uncovering a buried cross. This is said to be the very cross, covered in horse-hide and then decorated, which is today preserved in the high altar at Polling monastery.

The foundation of two further monasteries, Wessobrunn in the west and Kremsmünster in the east of his territory, is closely associated with Tassilo; he regarded these chiefly as fortresses to keep the peace and secure his borders.

According to the foundation legend which is told by Bernardus Moricus, the early 14th century Kremsmünster historian, the church was erected over the grave of Gunther, the son of the founder, who was fatally wounded by a wild boar near the Gundraeich Spring. The inspiration for the building is said to have been a stag with lighted candles in its antlers, which appeared to Tassilo. On the slab over the tomb of Gunther, which dates from shortly before 1304, the young son of the Duke is shown lying side by side with the boar that fatally wounded him, his faithful hunting dog at his feet. As a sign of his princely rank, his sword has been placed in his hand, but his hand grasps the hunting horn. The boar and the dog in the coat of

arms of the monastery also recall the circumstances of the founding.

According to the legend of the founding of Wessobrunn, the young Duke Tassilo had been hunting wild boar in Rottwald Forest in the year 753 when a Jacob's ladder appeared to him in a dream, at the top of which St Peter was celebrating high mass. At the foot of the ladder water was flowing from three springs in the form of a cross, forming a well. The next day his servant Wezzo led him to just such a well. Tassilo interpreted this as a sign from heaven that he should found a monastery, and that it should be dedicated to Peter, the prince of apostles.

The first duty of early medieval artists was to serve God. Initially, both animals and hunters were only displayed in the less conspicuous places: the sculptural decoration of a church, or as book illustrations depicting demons and mythical beasts which served as warnings of the Evil One.

One of the first and most delightful examples of a courtly hunt with an actual geographical location and real persons is found in the Book of Hours entitled "Très riches heures" of Duke Jean de Berry.

The age of the muzzle-loader is also the age of the powder-horn. These were fashioned from such varied materials and in so many shapes that they were bound to become popular and much sought-after collectors' items. This German example from the 17th century is made from the end of a cow's horn, and has silver mountings with decorative figures. It has an interesting shaker in the shape of a deer's head, which can be closed by means of a stylized bird resembling an elongated duck.

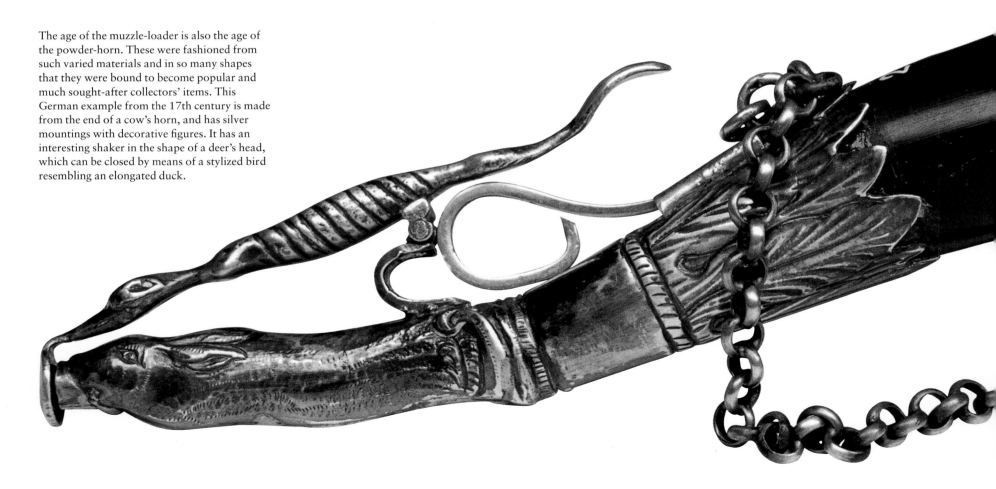

The picture for the month of December (Sagittarius) shows a wild boar hunt in a clearing in the ducal forest of Vincennes. It is therefore no coincidence that in the background the towers of the castle where Jean de Berry was born in 1340 are visible. The group of dogs savaging the wild boar is almost identical to the drawing of a wild boar hunt by Giovannino de Grassis of around 1400. It is not known how the motif reached the Limburg brothers, the artists responsible for the Book of Hours, but it was probably by means of a model book, that is, closely guarded pattern sheets, such as were commonly used in the Middle Ages (and indeed right up to the 18th century) in artists' workshops.

The December theme of hunting, like the rest of the illustrations in the calendar of the "Very Rich Book of Hours", is part of a long tradition. Thus the picture page of a Salzburg manuscript collection of the early 9th century devoted to the work of each month shows for the months of November and December a boar being attacked by a hunter armed with a spear, whilst another is holding a sword.

From the 12th and 13th centuries on, in almost all territories, hunting law was written down in deeds, laws and regulations. In this way hunting became an exclusive and increasingly strictly controlled sport of a small upper class with at least a minimum of education, and in time a specialized literature of hunting evolved. Some of the shorter texts from the late 12th century are primarily of veterinary interest; more relevant to the history of hunting are the 13th century sources, including Frederick II's falcon book. Other variants of hunting are dealt with in "De arte bersandi" (On the Art of Stalking) or the song of praise to the deer hunt "La chasse du cerf". In the second half of the 14th century, Henri de Ferières wrote his "Livres du Roy Modus et de la Royne Ratio", in which he has King Moderation and Queen Reason teach, amongst other things, the art of hunting, and in this way describes the hunting customs and methods of his time.

No self-respecting hunter would be seen without a tuft of chamois hair in his hat. This splendid chamois tuft reflects the prowess of its wearer.

"My Clothes are Green as Green can be ..."
Walter Norden

It is not only architecture or the visual and applied arts which express the style of an age; perhaps even more than this, man's outward appearance has become a pointer to the spirit of the age, as changing fashions reflect status, position and attitude.

"The apparel oft proclaims the man"—or the hunter. And it can also do a lot for the self-esteem. Countless youngsters dream of being fur-trappers and hunters. And it doesn't have to be the Wild West or a scene from the Jungle Book—the familiar woodland will serve equally well, because the romance of adventure depends less on the right geographical setting than on wearing the right gear. The gray-green loden coat still speaks to us of forests and fields; it is a reassuring symbol of the simple rural life.

What constituted correct dress for the hunt depended on who was hunting and for what purpose, for the status accorded to hunting in a particular period determined whether the outfit should be practical or appropriate to one's status.

The difference could clearly be seen in the case of the courtly parforce (horse-and-hound) hunt. Here the huntsman responsible for cutting up the dead animal wore fashionable long wide sleeves as befitted his courtly status; but this detail of fashion soon became a test of his dexterity. He was seen to be particularly skillful if he could carry out his task, using the regulation cuts, confidently and cleanly, without getting his sleeves messy. In contrast to this, hunting as a purely physical activity required something more practical:

"You shall wear gray and green clothing, partly gray, partly green", recommends Maximilian I (1459–1519) in his "Private Hunting-Book". "You shall at all times have two pairs of shoes; if you go into the mountains in the snow and your shoes get wet, you can take out the dry ones. The shoes shall have rims so that no stones can get in. You shall also have woollen socks with you. A small hat covered with taffeta for when it is very hot. Otherwise a small gray hat with a turned-up brim and a strap so that the wind does not blow it off."

A true Scotsman always hunts in a kilt, or so the artist who designed this tapestry believed. (Supraporte, 1st half of 19th century)

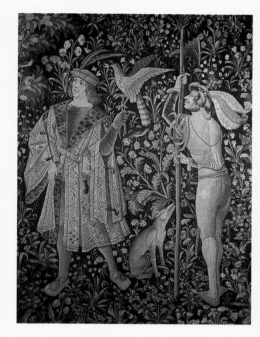

The noble lord in this French tapestry "Departure for the Hunt" is determined to dress according to his rank, however impractical this might be. (From the series "The Princely Life", late 15th century)

This young huntsman, from a French tapestry of embossed and painted leather (Avignon, c. 1700) is perhaps also more concerned about his appearance than about success in the hunt.

Little need be added to Maximilian's five-hundred-year-old hints. Nor to the old adage:
New hat and new cloak,
No good for hunting folk.
Today's hunters, too, prefer old, well-worn garments when out on a shoot, however meticulous their turn-out in everyday life. If the huntsman cannot avoid wearing new items of clothing they will very soon get rumpled and grubby, much to the chagrin of those who gave him them.

▷ German riding boots (end of 17th century) with bucket-top. The leather flap around the instep is preserved in only one of the boots. The spur straps were fastened with a buckle above the flap.

On the question of the hunter's camouflage, Friedrich von Gagern tells the following story about a hunter in his area called Skutnik, whose hunting skill was unrivaled and who always managed to bag the oldest and strongest bucks: "In the summer he would go stalking dressed in a linen cloak bleached to a dazzling whiteness. When questioned about this he replied laconically: 'The deer think I'm a stone!'"

In a letter dated February 14 1720 from Bamberg, written in his own hand to his nephew Friedrich Karl, Elector Lothar Franz von Schönborn describes his hunting outfit. He was evidently able to protect himself "thoroughly" from the winter cold and the wind, though doubtless at the cost of some restriction on his freedom of movement. The passage in question reads:

"I have been in good health so far, God be thanked, and do not go out, except when the weather is fine, and then I try to protect myself thoroughly from the cold and wind; I will now describe my hunting outfit just to satisfy the curiosity of the Imperial Vice Chancellor. Firstly I have a bearskin on my chair; this I take with me to sit or stand on later in the forest.

Secondly I wrap six thicknesses of towelling around my leg, over this a pair of knitted stockings, over these I wear stockings all of fur, over these a pair of fur boots and above the knee a pair of fur leg-warmers going half the length of the thigh.

Over the vest a good otterskin body-warmer on the chest, over that a lined clean linen jerkin, over this a jerkin of soft wild skins lined with flannel and over this a jerkin of lynx skins; and just to add the finishing touch an overcoat if I need it.

On my head a paper hood, over that a thick wig and over this a good otterskin hood covering the ears in the style of the Head Gamekeeper.

If the young gentleman can remember this set of clothes, then he should be able to recognize an ambassador from Lapland or Siberia at the Imperial court, for he will know the details of his dress from his uncle. Now enough of this winter and the hunting masquerade!"

Apart from the "overcoat" for especially cold days, the rest of the actual top clothing, consisting of trousers, hunting jacket, belt and gloves are not mentioned, in spite of the highly detailed description of the Elector's hunting outfit. The reason could be that "the Imperial Vice Chancellor", as the Elector and Imperial Chancellor jokingly calls his favorite nephew in the letter, would be quite familiar with the standard hunting dress worn by his uncle. This would undoubtedly have included a hunting knife for giving the coup de grâce. The Elector also failed to inform him what other equally elaborate (and just as interesting) arrangements he proposed to make to protect his most sensitive parts.

Evidently the Elector did not take part in the English type of hunt on horseback, as in that case

▷ German riding boot (2nd half of 18th century) made from strong oxhide. For the flap and the bucket-top the more durable flesh side of the hide has been used.

Huntress with three-cornered hat, around 1740

Noble hunter with bag and whippet, ivory miniature, 18th century

Nobleman as hunter with dog, around 1750

Paolo Veronese (1528–1588), self-portrait in hunting dress

Jan Wildens (1586–1653), winter landscape with hunter

Elector Max II Emanuel of Bavaria (1697–1776) in full ceremonial hunting dress

"Allgemeine Moden-Zeitung" (fashion journal), 1837

Thomas Gainsborough (1727–1788), Mr and Mrs Robert Andrews, around 1749

Dress of hunters' assistants, from "Allgemeine Moden-Zeitung," 1850

Modern Diana, from "Harper's Bazaar Italia," 1983

"Journal des Dames et des Modes," 1836

"Huntsman," around 1960

"Art Gout Beauté," 1928

"Style," 1922

French Hunter, around 1835

"La Pêche" (Fishing), from a series of French humorous picture postcards, 1911

"Costumes Parisiens," 1912

"Le retour de la chasse", from "Modes et Manières d'Aujourd'hui", 1913

"Petit Courrier des Dames" (Ladies' Post), 1849

"Costumes Parisiens," 1835

French poacher in peasant costume, around 1835

"Allgemeine Moden-Zeitung," 1848

Bavarian Hunter in costume of Miesbach, wearing "bottle-stopper" hat, 1850

"Allgemeine Moden-Zeitung," around 1825

"Le Voleur," around 1840

"Modes de Paris," 1833

Hunter with "Cordillera" hood, "La Mode," 1828

"Le Voleur," 1840

Tyrolean hunters, 1870, after Kretschmer, German National Costumes

Tyrolean Riflemen, 1870, after Kretschmer, German National Costumes

"Schnellpost der Moden" (Express Fashion Post), 1835

Hunter with hat in old German style, from "Allgemeine Moden-Zeitung," 1837

Hunters from Styria, 1870, after Kretschmer, German National Costumes

Hunters from Styria, 1870, after Kretschmer, German National Costumes

Fish-seller, around 1760

Corsican hunter with hooded jacket, around 1835

"Modes de Paris," 1836

Hunters in traditional costume in front of a mountain hut with Alpine herdswomen

"Musée des Modes," 1849

"Departure for the Hunt," from "Gazette du Bon Ton," 1912

Fashion plate, around 1850

"Allgemeine Moden-Zeitung,"
around 1850

Court Official and Hunter, from "Allgemeine
Moden-Zeitung," around 1843

Hunter, dressed in the American style,
from "Allgemeine Moden-Zeitung," 1841

"Allgemeine Moden-Zeitung," 1843

Hunting fashions from "Le Voleur"

"Le Progrès," 1885

"Le Progrès," 1885

Bavarian hunter with "bottle-stopper" hat

"Revue de la Mode," 1881

Hunters, dressed in the American style,
from "Allgemeine Moden-Zeitung," 1848

"Modes de Paris," 1836

"Le Progrès," 1849

"Simplicissimus" (satirical magazine),
1906

President of France hunting,
from "Je sais tout," 1913

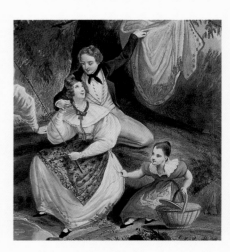

"La Pêche," fashionable hunting party
fishing, around 1830; aquatint

Modern Diana, from "Harper's Bazaar Italia," 1983

"For the bulletin of Fashion, New York", from "Le Progrès," 1869

Game-bird hunter, fashion plate, around 1850

"Des Modes Françaises Journal des Tailleurs," around 1880

"English Fashions," from "Allgemeine Moden-Zeitung," around 1860

"Modes de Paris," 1874

"Allgemeine Moden-Zeitung," 1863

Hunters in an expressionist forest, from "Style," 1922

"Allgemeine Moden-Zeitung," around 1850

"Allgemeine Moden-Zeitung," around 1840

"Les Modes Françaises Journal des Tailleurs," 1884

"Allgemeine Moden-Zeitung," around 1870

1502

"The Hunters in the Snow" (1565) by Pieter Brueghel the Elder is one of a sequence of large-format seasonal pictures. These hunters are returning from a hunt which was not for sport but a necessity. Their meagre bag is a scrawny fox. An ironic detail at the margin of the picture is the inn-sign: "The Stag".

Albrechts Dürer's watercolor of a hare (1502) is one of the best-known animal pictures in Germany. The hare was classed as lower game, which the lower nobility were permitted to hunt. When Dürer's watercolor was painted all was well with the world of hunting, but in the course of the 16th century critical voices were heard, even from among the hunting community, though they had little effect. In George Turbervile's hunting primer "The Noble Art of Venerie or Hunting" a hare voices its protest in the following words: "Are human hearts so unfeeling now that they enjoy seeing an animal in its own blood? A poor defenseless thing, a harmless worm that never does anyone any harm? If that is so I thank my Creator that he created me as an animal and not as a man."

riding habit rather than hunting dress would have been called for and would have been fitting for his station in life.

Perhaps the most important description of French hunting conditions in the 14th century, and one which can be applied to other courts in Europe, is the manuscript of Gaston Phoebus. "Three things I have enjoyed all my life more than any other", begins his "Traité de la chasse", "weaponry, love and hunting." The esteem in which this hunting book is held even today, rests as much as anything on the beautiful miniatures which illustrate many of the approximately 40 known transcripts. In the year 1391, Gaston III, Count of Foix and Béarn, who, because of his striking appearance had been given (or given himself) the nickname of Phoebus (the Radiant One), died while carousing after a bear hunt at the age of sixty.

A few years later this French textbook of hunting was translated into English by Edward Duke of York, who had been imprisoned for conspiracy against the King since 1406. Entitled "The Master of Game" the manuscript was finished by 1410. As Henry IV's Master of Game, the translator was thoroughly familiar with hunting matters in England, so in his version hare hunting, as the favorite English hunt, was given prominence, rather than the red deer hunt.

Two important technical advances, the woodcut and the invention of printing, revolutionized art in the late Middle Ages. In the following centuries a great number of instructional books on hunting and hunting registers were published. Clearly the rulers felt the need to record their hunting methods and hunting triumphs in representative works, to provide them with magnificent illustrations and have them reproduced.

Emperor Maximilian I (1459–1519), who gloried in the name of "Arch Hunting Master" or "Mighty Hunter", also wrote on hunting matters. The most illustrious artists of the time were employed in the illustration and layout of his books. Lucas Cranach the Elder drew the wild animals for the margins of the Emperor's prayer-book, and Albrecht Dürer, too, contributed impressive works. The woodcuts in "The White King" (Weisskunig) are by Hans Burgkmair and Hans Springinklee, and the colored miniatures in the Hunting and Fishing Book are the work of the Innsbruck artist Jörg Kölderer.

In the eyes of bibliophiles, Germany's greatest 16th century masterpiece is the luxury print of the first edition of "Theuerdank" of 1517, with its 118 woodcuts by Hans Burgkmair, Hans Schäufelein and Leonhard Beck. This verse epic, which deals with the hunt amongst other topics, depicts significant episodes from the life of the Emperor and pays tribute to his triumphs over adversity in the style of medieval heroic legends. On Maximilian's instructions Hans Schönsperger in Augsburg printed 40 superior copies for the closest friends of the Emperor, using specially created type. About 300 superb copies were

Jan Weenix (1640–1719) is famous for his hunting still lifes in the evening twilight. The subject of this picture is falconry.

packed in chests to be given away as presents in order to ensure his lasting fame after his death.

After the devastating plagues in Western Europe a new joie de vivre found expression, and a more open way of looking at men and animals led to a changed conception of art in the spirit of the princely courts of Upper Italy, with their secular orientation. The study of nature became a necessity for art, and artists like Pisanello (1395 through 1455) succeeded in transferring the animal image of Gothic art to the freer animal studies of the Renaissance. This new manner of contemplating animated nature influenced and changed art north of the Alps too.

The animal studies of Albrecht Dürer (1471–1528) are thus the expression of an understanding of nature which had been changed by the Italian Renaissance. "For in truth art is in nature, and he who can draw it out has it," wrote Dürer in 1528 in his esthetic discourse on the proportions of the human body. Dürer was also inspired to tackle the genre of the hunting still life by the work of the Venetian Jacopo de Barbari (who died between 1511 and 1515), who had taken up this classical genre and introduced it into the art of the modern world. Within his animal studies the theme of birds that have been killed and of birds' wings play a major part. Thus Dürer's "Dead Duck" (around 1502) as well as the bird still lifes of Lucas Cranach the Elder (1472–1553) and his workshop have been influenced by the works of

Barbari. The latter was engaged by Emperor Maximilian I as court painter in Nuremberg, then from 1503 through 1505 he was in the service of Elector Frederick the Wise of Saxony and collaborated closely with Cranach.

An important chapter in the history of hunting art was written by the Dutch and the Flemish. One of the finest representatives of Flemish art was Peter Paul Rubens (1577–1640), whose early hunting scenes are mostly located in the Hellenistic or Roman ambience of North Africa and Asia Minor. In these he incorporates the savage fights staged between exotic animals or with hunters. Amongst the sources for his hunting pictures were engravings by Tempesta and Stradanus. Jan van der Straet (1523–1605) was born in Bruges, but moved to Florence in 1550, where he took the name of Giovanni Stradano or Johannes Stradanus. He has secured a place in Italian art history (he is known by the Latin form of his name) by virtue of his drawings of all the game animals of his time, the accuracy of which was a testimony to his powers of observation. He also depicted hunting methods, equipment and articles of clothing.

Soon it was not only members of the aristocracy who came forward as patrons and collectors of art; well-to-do citizens also treated themselves to the luxury of pictures on their walls. So as to be able to satisfy the demand, many workshops employed a system of division of labor, each member of the team being responsible for the elements in which he was most competent.

The finest example of this method of working is the 30-year-long collaborative work of Frans Snyders (1579–1657) on the paintings of Rubens. Snyders, a talented painter of animals and flowers, had decided early in his career to concentrate on pictures of larders and on still lifes on the hunting theme. Rubens valued him particularly highly on account of his high level of skill in reproducing the fur and feathers of the game. Unlike Rubens' works, where man has the pre-eminent place, Snyders shows only the hunted game in his pictures. His preference is for hunts of wild boar, deer, wolf and bear hunts. His central theme is the drama of the chase and the beast at bay surrounded by the pack of hounds, a type of hunting picture which retained its popularity right up to the 19th century.

The political significance of the hunt reached its zenith in the age of Absolutism, when the power and prestige of the state was judged in part on the degree of ostentatious wealth the court displayed. It was natural, therefore, that the hunt would call for the most sumptuous show of splendor possible.

French hunting art, then, flourished to some extent thanks to the love of display typical of absolutist monarchs. Thus François Desportes (1661–1743) gave up his portrait painting and, as "peintre de la venerie" painted the packs of hounds and the hunts of Louis XIV and Louis XV. Desportes had done his apprenticeship with the Flemish painter Nicasius Bernaerts, who in turn

This hunting still life by Jean Baptiste Oudry (1686–1755) has certain elements of the classical still life, including the draped cloth, and the cat, which has noticed something outside the picture.

had been a pupil of Snyders. At the peak of his fame, which extended far beyond France, Desportes gave increasing prominence in his animal paintings to decorative elements like silverware, textiles, flowers and fruits. Later he devoted himself entirely to the still life.

Desportes was succeeded as hunting painter at the court of Louis XV by Jean-Baptiste Oudry (1686–1755), whose hunting pictures and animal still lifes were highly prized by his contemporaries, especially by the European aristocracy from countries such as France and Scandinavia, and including the Duke of Mecklenburg. Oudry's artistic career took him from being a simple sign painter and drawing teacher at Pont Notre Dame to his acceptance into the Académie Royale, and finally to the court of Versailles, where Oudry moved his studio in 1726. In order to draw hunting pictures, portraits of dogs and tapestries in a lifelike manner, Oudry accompanied Louis XV on the hunt.

The graphic artist and copper engraver Johann Elias Ridinger, who portrayed the customs of the hunt in Germany, was the outstanding hunt artist of his time. Born in Ulm in 1698, his first position after qualifying was with Johannes Flach and another Augsburg painter and gilder, but this dependent activity never satisfied him. His first

attempts to paint horses and animals in nature in his own way "according to his natural instinct" were given encouragement by an invitation from Count Metternich in Regensburg. In this study visit to Regensburg Ridinger acquired a thorough grounding in "the school of riding and hunting". As Thienemann wrote in 1856, after three years Ridinger returned to Augsburg for good and became the most famous painter of his time of "animals of every kind, in strength and weariness, in speed and slowness, in rest and flight, in fear and cunning, in rutting and heat, in anger, fury and rage, in pain and mortal fear". In 1759 Johann Elias Ridinger was appointed Director of the Academy of Painting in Augsburg, where he died in 1767. His sons Martin Elias (around 1730–1780) and Johann Jakob (around 1736–1784), who were both copper engravers and their father's collaborators, continued the graphic work of their father after his death.

To the aristocracy nothing seemed so clearly willed by God as the ordering of social estates and man's absolute dominion over nature. Dominion over animals is clearly expressed in the pageantry and splendor of the hunts.

True, the carefully staged hunting spectacles which rulers expected from each other were designed to impress, yet the killing of animals (and

At the beginning of the 18th century the princes and the aristocracy still clung to their hunting pursuits. They often had the wealth to surround themselves with costly objets d'art, and their obsession with hunting was such that these objects often had a hunting theme, like the table clock with St Hubert (far left) which Heinrich Köhler made in 1720 for August the Strong (the mechanism is by Johann Gottlieb Graupner). The Meissen covered vase with handles bearing ladies' heads and painted hunting scenes of the "Saxon Switzerland" (c. 1735) is the work of Johann Joachim Kändler.

in the enclosed hunts, which were particularly popular in Germany, the number dispatched could run to several hundred) undoubtedly gave pleasure to most of the participants. And since it was customary to regard animals not as living creatures but as soulless machines, they saw no reason to question their pleasure.

In the 17th and 18th centuries there was a widespread view that the world functioned like clockwork, an idea that was supported by important mathematical and scientific discoveries, and was itself favorable to further research. From the beginning of the 16th century there had been isolated protests against hunting and also calls for the protection of animals (not necessarily the same thing). Erasmus of Rotterdam in his "Praise of Folly" (1511), Thomas More in "Utopia" (1516), Cyriacus Spangenberg in "The Hunting Devil" (1560) and Montaigne in the essay "On Cruelty" (1580) had spoken out strongly, but the protests had little effect. Shakespeare too expressed himself critically on the hunt, using it as a metaphor for repression in "As You Like It" (1599), for murder in "Julius Caesar" (1599) or for rape in "Titus Andronicus" (1593). The times when hunting could serve as a symbol for erotic love, as in courtly love poetry, were past.

These aristocratic hunting pleasures were often staged in the baroque-style park, some of the features of which were designed for this purpose. For the practice of the hunt, whether this was "enclosed" (the game was driven into a fenced-off shooting area where the prince and his party were waiting) or par force (the hunting of an individual animal with horses and hounds), lengthy paths were needed. These were laid out like forest paths, could be several miles long, and radiated out from a raised hunting pavilion. A system of interconnecting paths, which also cut off the animals' escape routes, enabled the riders to move around the park easily.

Alongside elaborate systems like these, in which the paths were of course kept clean and raked over to make it easier for the horses to run, the hunt-crazy princes of the baroque period also commissioned the construction of substantial hunting lodges, whose dimensions and artistic decoration put many a royal palace in the shade. Sometimes these buildings, with their extensive hunting grounds, actually became the nucleus of state capitals.

The finest example of this in Germany is the city of Karlsruhe, which came into being towards the end of the late baroque period on the site of just such a hunting ground. In 1715 the charismatic Margrave Karl-Wilhelm von Baden-Durlach laid the foundation stone for his hunting seat, working to his own plans, in the circular clearing

This gold-plated silver diplay dish of beaten metal (c. 1612) by Elias Geyer shows a relief of a stag hunt.

in the middle of a star-shaped layout, in which 32 paths radiated out from the centre. The hunting lodge became first the secondary and then the principal princely seat, and attracted further settlement around it. Before long, together with its rapidly growing new town, it came to dominate old Durlach, which had been shaped by the Middle Ages and the Renaissance. Today Durlach is a relatively modest suburb of the city of Karlsruhe.

The basic idea of the "fan-shaped city" has been preserved to this day. It grew up only in the southern half of the star-shaped system, which was designed with geographical precision, whilst the northern half of the circular grounds, with its park, zoological gardens, pheasantry, adjoining hunting park and garden, canals, and historic hunting pavilions in the midst of tranquil woods – all remained completely untouched. The structure of a baroque hunting ground is still alive here, as it now forms part of the center of a modern city.

The people of those times did not seek some pristine experience of nature, for they regarded nature as their stage, and the wild animals as a kind of toy. In keeping with their function as a royal hunt or showcase for court ceremonial these extravagant hunting events were recorded for

posterity in a variety of forms by artists. But the magnificent hunts of the baroque did more than provide the spur for art, they were themselves works of art which unfolded according to fixed rules.

An essential feature of the Great Hunt, which was chiefly deerhunting, was the Parforce Horn, or Great Hunting Horn. This instrument, essential for the hunts of the 17th and 18th centuries, is also known as the Forest Horn, Trompète or Cor des Chasses, Corno da Caccia or French Horn. This instrument, which made its appearance in the middle of the 17th century, was used to attract attention during a hunt, for fanfares and for making music; it was not only played by professional musicians but also by masters of the hunt and by noble guests. Particularly worthy of mention here is the Marquis of Dampierre, master of the hunt to Louis XV. He is said to have been an extremely talented performer on the hunting horn and also composed a number of pieces for horn. He is also regarded as the father of the french horn, which is today one of the established instruments of every brass band and symphony orchestra. The large-diameter single-coil hunting horn has been named after him.

English foxhunting paintings focus primarily on horse and rider—the kill is rarely shown. "The Oakley Hunt" by Henry Alkens (1785–1851) is no exception. The horses gallop along with their legs stretched out, to give the impression of speed. It was not until 1878 that the photographer Edward Muybridge was able to prove, with the aid of phase photography of a galloping horse, that this rocking-horse posture is impossible. As the photographic experiment makes clear, the true picture of a galloping horse is conveyed by the legs meeting under the center of the body.

It was Franz Anton Spork (1662–1738) who made the greatest contribution to the popularity of the Great Hunting Horn in German speaking countries. In common with many gentlemen of that time he spent some years in his youth at the court of Louis XIV. While there he became such a devotee of court hunts and particularly of the Trompe de Chasse used on them, that on his return to his native Bohemia he dispatched two of his huntsmen to Versailles for training in horn playing. When they returned to Germany they became the first teachers of this art, which thanks to its use in hunting spread rapidly and was cultivated at many royal courts.

Whereas in the baroque the prestige of a rigid class society had been the driving force behind hunting and had found expression in the works of artists, this was to change at the beginning of the 19th century as the effects of the Enlightenment and of Romanticism began to be felt. Although the modern age in the true sense, as art historians understand it, did not commence until the end of the 19th century, its roots reached back to the middle of the 18th century when the first "free" artists—those that had been liberated from the ties of church and court—became established in middle-class society. The general political dissatisfaction led also to a great thirst for knowledge, and the publication of the first volumes of the French "Encyclopédie", by d'Alembert and Diderot, which began to come out in 1751, may be seen as an early expression of the spirit of the Enlightenment.

The English could afford to look on continental developments with more equanimity. In the 18th century English painting gained an international reputation. Artists like Thomas Gainsborough (1727–1788) learned to express in their portraits a combination of British reserve, a fitting degree of ostentation and a Romantic closeness to nature. Together with the society portrait, landscape painting acquired particular importance. Hunt painting, which takes first place in British "Sporting Art", offered the opportunity to link these two genres in a meaningful way.

One of the most admired and best known exponents of this genre (abroad as well as in England), was George Stubbs (1724–1806), although his preference was clearly for the pure horse portrait, and he would have been happy to dispense entirely with the portrayal of the human figure. A picture such as "The Grosvenor Hunt" (1762), with its many human figures, is an exception in a number of other ways too, since it not only shows the stag hunt, which had become a rarity, but also depicts the final stage of the hunt when the stag is savaged by the pack of hounds.

If, like Ben Marshall (1767–1835) or James Ward (1769–1859), they were not simply

George Stubbs' "Pointer" (1760/1768) is the perfect dog portrait. Posture and gait speak of the watchfulness of this highly individual animal.

producing static portraits of noble personages on horseback, surrounded by a few waiting dogs, the English painters of the hunting genre concentrated on portraying the activity of riding at full gallop over the fields and hedges of the rolling hills of the English countryside. Since the extensive clearances of the 18th century had led to a depletion of the red deer population, most of the riding to hounds was in pursuit of the fox, although the quarry rarely appears in the pictures. Originally the victor had the right to the fox's brush, which he personally cut off (a procedure known as brushing), and this was a theme which enjoyed a spell of popularity in painting.

As interest in hunting pictures was far more plentiful than the money to buy them, the popular motifs were very soon being graphically reproduced, at first as copper engravings and later as steel engravings. At the same time, prints were produced for plates. The best known and most prolific creator of these hunting motifs was Henry Alken (1785–1851). In many of his prints he observes the riding skills of his contemporaries with a twinkle in his eye. In the 100 years or so in which the English hunting engraving enjoyed the wholehearted favor of the public (until it was superseded by color lithography and photography) more than 150 well-known engravers helped some 60 painters of sporting and hunting themes to achieve respect, fame and good sales.

The 19th century was characterized by a profusion of different styles. The "bourgeois" period was defined by the Classicism which reached its peak around 1780. Toward the end of the 18th century various forms of sensibility and a closer affinity with nature began to prepare the ground for Romanticism as a reaction to Classicism, and in this turn finally gave way to the staid German Biedermeier movement.

Biedermeier Man liked to research and explore his environment, and the hunt provided him with a welcome opportunity to do this. Those who were not or did not wish to be hunters collected beetles or butterflies or tended their herbarium. Respectable citizens now began to collect hunting trophies, and, in the case of objects such as claws, teeth and small bones, ostentatiously wore them on their watch chains (and perhaps secretly hoped they would bring them luck).

Some of the oldest pieces of jewelry known to man, Grandeln (the gleaming, velvety-white canine teeth from the upper jaw of the red deer), became the most popular items of hunting jewelry in the German-speaking countries. Mounted in gold or silver they used to be given by hunters to their ladies as small love tokens. Right up to the present century they have been used as amulets and talismans.

Two huntresses from the "Nymphenburg Hunt" (Nymphenburg, c. 1760).

◁◁ Northern Bohemian hunting goblet (c. 1835) with surrounding frieze of a wild boar; matt glass engraving on amber stained glass

◁ Bohemian goblet (c. 1835) and wine glasses (c. 1850) with ruby background; matt glass engraving with decorative scenes of deer in wooded landscape.

▷ This gold mounting on the single volume of the Gospel of the Order of St Hubert shows the vision of the stag, surrounded by the Chain of the Order and the entwined initials "CP" (for Carl Philipp of the Palatinate) and surmounted by the Electoral Coronet (1727).

237

Talismans and Trophies – Deer Teeth and Diana

Bernd E. Ergert and Martinus Martin

The desire for self-adornment is probably as old as humanity, and our hunting and gathering forefathers were no strangers to it.

Ice Age people hunted not only reindeer and wild horses but also big game like mammoths and woolly rhinoceroses, mainly for food. In addition, the animals supplied furs to make weatherproof clothing, and bones to fashion into tools and weapons. And there is another by-product of the hunted animal that is too often forgotten, for the pleasure which our Ice Age ancestors took in adornment and trophies was probably no less than ours. The teeth of the arctic fox, which were strung together to form long chains, must have been especially sought after. In Sungir, east of Moscow, the graves of a man of about 60 and two children were found. With the bodies, which had been buried some 28,000 years earlier, was a belt consisting of 240 fox teeth. The old man had been sent on his last journey with 3,000 beads of mammoth ivory, and the children on theirs with 5,000. If only all the skins of tundra hares or arctic foxes they must have worn had survived, what a magnificent sight the old Stone Age hunters would have presented. As it is, all the paleontologists have at their disposal to build up a picture of life in the Stone Age are bones and stones.

Alongside the teeth of arctic foxes and the ivory of mammoths' tusks the canine teeth of deer were highly prized by the people of the Stone Age.

The blunt canine teeth in the upper jaw of the red deer are the mark of a hunter's success, and therefore greatly valued as trophies. When mounted in silver or gold they are amongst the most highly prized of all hunting jewelry. They must also have had a particular significance for our ancestors from the old Stone Age. These teeth were so much in demand that people even began to carve copies of them from mammoth ivory. In contrast to the mammoth or the reindeer the red deer was a rather rare species during the Ice Age. In the tundra, which covered almost the entire land mass at that time, only the river valleys were wooded, providing red deer with only a restricted habitat. And it is not only in our own day that scarce commodities rise in value.

Perhaps our ancestors saw a deeper meaning in deer's teeth beyond that of hunting trophies. Two of them placed together bear an unmistakable likeness to female breasts. In Dolní Vestonice and neighbouring Pavlov (Moravia, Gravettian period, between 27,000 and 20,000 years ago), some remarkable ornamental pendants were excavated. These small ornaments of mammoth ivory have a

Finds from Dolní Vestonice – on the left a pendant of mammoth ivory in the shape of female breasts, and in the center a stylized female figure – alongside two modern stag's teeth mounted in silver. This juxtaposition clearly shows the formal similarity between the ancient and the modern.

▷ In about 1900 Kaiser Wilhelm II presented his consort Auguste Victoria with this piece of hunting jewelry, consisting of stag's teeth, rubies, emeralds and diamonds.

The ample contours of this 25,000-year-old Venus of Willendorf suggests the existence of a fertility cult or the belief in a mother goddess.

In cave painting the reindeer and red deer hunt is well documented. This is a fairly recent example of a rock drawing near Alpera in south-eastern Spain.

Position of the canine tooth in the upper jaw.

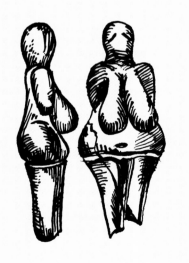

This figurine of a woman also comes from Dolní Vestonice. In contrast to the limestone Willendorf Venus it is fashioned out of clay.

striking resemblance to two deer teeth laid side by side.

The common life of men and women towards the end of the Old Stone Age must have differed starkly from that of a modern family. Taking as our starting point an ethnological comparison with primitive people (such as the Inuit San), who have retained the life of hunters and gatherers to the present day, we can make the assumption that the structure of Ice Age society was egalitarian. Tasks were divided up between men and women chiefly according to ability, without social distinctions. Each person gave of his or her best, on equal terms, working for the survival of the family. The numerous paleolithic figures of women and the many female symbols even suggest a dominant role for the mother. Thus as early as 1861, Johann Jakob Bachofen, a legal historian and classical scholar, developed the theory of the matriarchy and maternal law.

Something which cannot be entirely separated from the idea of a primeval mother figure, and which is thus perhaps older than commonly supposed, is the veneration of the goddess Diana as "patron saint" of hunting.

In pre-Christian times Diana was not only the goddess of the woods and of hunting, but also the mother of all creatures. In Greece, sacrifices were made to her under the name of Artemis, with shrines in Ephesus and Nemi. In ancient times, in order to emphasize her role as mother of all creatures, she was represented as having multiple breasts. In the Roman pantheon Diana was the "Queen of Heaven". To the Gauls of the 5th century she was still the highest divinity, and they worshiped her in the symbolic form of a branch cut from a tree. In the dark days of the medieval Inquisition Diana was the quintessence of heretical paganism. Anyone who worshipped or paid homage to her was most cruelly punished by the Church. Yet in spite of exorcisms and the burning of witches at the stake, faith in Diana was never entirely stamped out.

The cult of Diana and the canine teeth of the deer—these are deeply rooted cultural relics representing perhaps the last vestiges of a way of life long past. Long before the emergence of *Homo sapiens sapiens* in Europe some 42,000 years ago, modern man (modern in the anatomical sense) subsisted by hunting and gathering. Only about 10,000 years ago did the introduction of farming and animal husbandry lead to a lasting revolution in man's way of life. Today it is almost impossible for us to visualize the daily life or the mind-set of Ice Age hunters, and the people of the old Stone Age will remain mysterious to us. Our way of life and thinking are simply too far removed from theirs. But anyone who chooses to wear two of them as personal adornment should be aware that they are carrying around more than just the canine teeth of a red deer.

The French wall-hanging "The Hunt at Compiègne" (the section shown here is the departure for the hunt) is in Friedrichsmoor, the hunting lodge in the Lewitz region built in 1780 for Frederick of Mecklenburg-Schwerin. It was printed by Jaquemart and Bernard in Paris in 1815, after a design by Carle Vernet.

The art of the early modern period is characterized by the contrast between the traditional business of the art of the academies on the one hand, and the avantgarde on the other, with its tendency to break up into factions. Independently of the views of artists, themes such as "animals" or "hunting" remained important in Classicism, Romanticism, Historicism, Symbolism, Realism and Naturalism. By Naturalism is meant the most consistent portrayal of reality, something which is often loosely thought of as Realism; the latter, however, refers more to themes drawn from everyday life and emphasizes the truthfulness of the subject matter.

The man responsible for this new "ism", one which can even cause confusion amongst art historians, is Gustave Courbet (1819–1877). When in 1855, during the World Exhibition in Paris, he set up his own pavilion in the Avenue de Montaigne in protest against the rejection of some of his pictures by the jury, he brought with him a sign bearing the words "Le Réalisme. G. Courbet. Exhibition de 40 tableaux de son oeuvre". This unusual action alone reveals the independence of mind of the artist. Courbet had early broken with his teachers and from then on taught himself. From 1844, more and more of his pictures were admitted to the Paris "Salon", where they had a mixed reception—appreciation by some but rejection out of hand by those who found them ugly or too socially critical. Abroad, too, Courbet soon made a name for himself, with exhibitions in Brussels (1851), Munich (1851) and Frankfurt (1852 and 1854).

On his next visit to Frankfurt, from September 1858 through February 1859, Courbet, who was a keen hunter, had his greatest hunting adventure. In a letter to his friend Castagnary he wrote: "On New Year's Eve (...) while hunting in the mountains of Germany I killed a giant 13-year-old 12-point stag (...) with the two finest shots of my life." There were to be problems with this stag, as a wealthy Frankfurt industrialist disputed Courbet's claim to have shot it, but the hunting party supported the guest from France and in the end all disagreements were washed away in some 700 glasses of Bavarian beer.

Another outstanding French 19th century painter is Eugène Delacroix (1798–1863). At the World Exhibition of 1855 in Paris, while Courbet was again having problems with the jury, Delacroix was at the peak of his fame, exhibiting 35 works. He was regarded as the greatest French Romanticist, and at the same time was perhaps the most significant animal painter of the century. In terms of painting, French Romanticism was quite different from the German variety. The difference between the "animal" French and the "esoteric" German Romanticism is exemplified by a comparison between the work of Delacroix with that of Caspar David Friedrich, who never includes animals in his pictures. Delacroix is by no means famous for his European hunting pictures. A "Still-Life with Lobsters" (1827; Paris, Louvre) shows a composition consisting of the said lobsters, a rabbit, a jay and a pheasant, in the setting of an English landscape; in the background one can just make out the small and insignificant hunting party. The most significant element here is not the theme but the coloring. The reason why Delacroix is important in this context is primarily his incomparable way of portraying horse and rider in motion, and also his impressive scenes of exotic animals in combat.

Whereas German Biedermeier painting and Realism were rich in animal painters and poor in true hunting art, in the second half of the 19th century there was a new enthusiasm for paintings on the theme of hunting. The newly self-confident middle classes began to take up hunting as a leisure pursuit, and were economically in a position to purchase works of art as well. The hunting financier could afford to hang hunting pictures on the walls of his drawing-room.

Carl Friedrich Deiker (1836–1892) and Christian Kröner (1838–1911), both of the Düsseldorf School, were masters of this new hunting art. Even though in the realms of the "serious art" of the 19th century hunting was something of a poor relation, Wilhelm Leibl (1884–1900) must be mentioned at this juncture. Leibl, who was a keen hunter and a superb marksman was one of the leading representatives of German Realism. He gathered a group of like-minded artists around him, including Trübner, Thoma and Sperrl, for whom nature meant truth and authenticity. He found it amongst peasants, hunters, and in the experience of hunting in Upper Bavaria. "Here in the country, among children of nature, I can paint naturally," he wrote to his mother. The next generation of painters would be Expressionists, who did not aim to hold the mirror up to nature but to create images of the soul through art. To them Leibl would probably have said: "We should paint Man as he is, then his soul will be revealed."

Man—the citizen, the hunter—, as he felt and saw himself, was principally reflected in the genre

Whilst opinion in France remained divided regarding his painting, Gustave Courbet was officially honored by both Belgium and Germany. His picture "The Mort" was shown together with six other paintings at the international art exhibition in the Munich Glass Palace in 1869. It depicts the final stage of a hunt.

picture. Here hunting became a favorite theme and through painting became a literary theme too.

One of the first illustrators of hunting literature was the professional hunter Max Haider (1803–1873). Although he began by teaching himself, King Ludwig I of Bavaria granted him permission to continue his studies at the Academy at his expense. As illustrator of the periodicals Fliegende Blätter and Münchener Bilderbogen, he left many entertaining depictions of hunting in Germany since the 1848 Revolution.

Alongside periodicals and illustrated magazines another medium became popular and was much in demand for collectors, namely the picture postcard. About a decade after the publication of the first illustrated postcard in the 1890s, postcards with hunting themes made their appearance. There were reproductions of paintings, drawings and photographs of hunting scenes, hunting weapons, furnishings and utensils, famous personalities dressed for the hunt or actually hunting, items from hunting exhibitions, scientific collections and museums, monuments and ornaments.

Around the turn of the century, art postcards came into fashion. Reproductions of works by great painters like Courbet, Dürer, Holbein the Younger, Rembrandt and Rubens were popular. Far more common, however, were hunting scenes and animal pictures by painters such as Boucher, Delacroix, Jirsik, Liljefors, Neogrády, Ooms, Pausinger, Ridinger, Siskin, Snyders, Vos and Weenix. There were also pen drawings, engravings and watercolors specifically for reproduction on picture postcards; it was not unusual for these to be by artists well known and admired in hunting circles, including Beroldinger, Dall'Armi, F. Hines, R. A. Jaumann, Hofmann, Elsa Dehme, Julius Richter, G. Wolters, C. Zimmermann and Edit Zsolt. Many other artists, using pseudonyms or anonymously, also supplied work for reproduction.

The picture postcard reproductions from drawings, watercolors and later photographs were at first produced in monochrome, and later in

In Courbet's "Hunt Breakfast" (1858) the hunt is over, and a thrilling chase is reduced to a still life of the bag, the hunting equipment and the hounds. The hunters (with Courbet himself in the center) turn their attention to other pleasures.

polychrome by lithography, gravure or letterpress. In a few cases copper engravings were used. There are even a few examples of hand-painted and hand-drawn cards, photographs, relief prints, cards with feathers stuck on to make birds, or even cards made of metal.

Illustrators and painters found employment chiefly in graphic reproduction for supplements in hunting periodicals like Deutscher Jäger. It was here that they were able to present their work to a wider audience. They all built on the foundation which had been laid by the skill of the 19th century painters of the schools of hunting, animal and genre painting. In this way they preserved the heritage of this painting and developed it further into the 20th century. The grave economic situation after the First World War brought this development to a halt. The new styles turned away completely from illustrative and narrative painting, and there was no longer any connection between hunting pictures and the art of the salon. The ascendancy of photography opened up new paths for Naturalism and Realism.

At this juncture mention must be made of the architect and poster artist Ludwig Hohlwein (1874–1949). By way of book illustration, ceramics, graphics, watercolors and tempera painting he arrived at commercial art and poster art. His bold and eye-catching hunting scenes were frequently published in the hunting press. In 1923 he took part in a collective exhibition in New York. In spite of his modern, almost photographic, technique, he succeeded in preserving conventional images and subject matter, an achievement which

has made him the model for the hunting artists of today, especially the watercolorists.

During the National Socialist period hunting art, not surprisingly, flourished once more, as although it appeared harmless enough it could be harnessed for propaganda purposes, with the hunted animal representing the conquered enemy.

The economic recovery which followed the end of the Second World War proved fertile soil for hunting art. At the first great hunting exhibition in 1954 it was mainly artists of the pre-war generation that exhibited their works and so prepared the way for a new generation of hunting artists.

Manfred Schatz, born in 1925 in Bad Stepenitz am Oderhaff, is one of the new animal and hunting painters. Numerous exhibitions of his work have been held and he has been honored many times. At the international art exhibition of 1975 in Toronto, the biggest of its kind in the world, he was voted the world's finest painter of wild animals. Only what is essential for the artist is emphasized; everything else fades into the background, while remaining a vital part of the picture.

Whatever the current style, late 20th century animal art bears testimony to the lasting significance of this theme. Its fundamental feature is a turning to nature, and thus to what Franz Marc, as early as 1914, called "the animal's unspoiled love of life".

Since the twenties, various student hunting fraternities have existed alongside the classical student fraternities. The hunting fraternities in Germany and Austria wear a colored sash and most of them also a colored cap. Color-wearing fraternities exchange tags (Zipfel) on ceremonial occasions. The (larger) beer tag is presented to the "beer freshman" by his "beer father", who is given the smaller wine tag in exchange. In this way a lifelong relationship ("beer family") is founded. The fraternity assembly (Convent) awards honorary tags (here in the form of beer tags) or badges for special merit. The bunch of tags was once fastened to the pocket watch, then to the Biertaler (see picture left), and today they are fastened to the tag clasp. The tags often have a deer's tooth (Grandel) or other piece of jewelry attached to them. The tags include an engraving on precious metal (the badge) showing the monogram or coat of arms of the fraternity.

HUNTING LODGES – THEIR SPLENDOR AND GLORY

HEIDI WEIDNER-WEIDEN

From the late Middle Ages, the great hunts of kings and princes became ever
more spectacular and triumphal, and today we find it hard to understand the
curious and bizarre developments in the "noble art of venerie" that ensued in
the centuries which followed. But when contemplating the innocuous and
idyllic picture of a hunt at the Dianaburg lodge in Hesse, painted around 1760
by Georg Adam Eger, it is once again brought home to us that in the
unchallenged feudal world of the time different values prevailed.
However, if it had not been for the aristocracy's unbridled passion for the hunt
we should undoubtedly have been deprived of part of our cultural heritage.
For throughout Europe hunting lodges and summer palaces were being built
and furnished by their owners on a lavish scale. Even if they were merely
pursuing their own pleasures, they wished, indeed they felt obliged, to provide
a fitting ambience for their elevated station in life. One of the finest baroque
examples of a feudal "summer resort" was developed by Augustus the Strong
(right), the Saxon Elector and King of Poland, at Schloss Moritzburg
not far from Dresden.

247

Between cultivated flowerbeds and neatly clipped box hedges, expensively dressed ladies dance with their gallant gentlemen to the strains of baroque music. No sooner is the dance ended than a carriage drawn by white horses approaches. Flunkies officiously hasten to open the carriage door and the Margrave now deigns to appear, and with great dignity accepts the homage of his subjects. Then follow the ministers and generals and a conspicuous group of servants attired in green: the falconers. Their task is to entertain the Margrave, to lift his spirits and set his pulse racing.

This is no nostalgic vision of past glories, but a historical pageant organized by an astute tourist board. These "Rococo Games" take place today around the former Water Palace of Ansbach and call to mind the magnificence of the period of princely rule, especially that of the Margrave Karl Wilhelm Friedrich von Brandenburg-Ansbach (1712–1757), who, not without reason, was known as the Wild Margrave. His passionate love of the hunt, and especially his predilection for falconry, is said to have been the cause of his financial ruin.

According to historical sources, such ruination was by no means a rare occurrence in the days of the Wild Margrave. In the 18th century any prince of renown was expected to be addicted to the hunt and to indulge his passion with a degree of lavish expenditure that exceeded all reasonable bounds.

The Hohenstaufen Emperor Frederick II (1194–1250), well known to all hawking enthusiasts as the Imperial Falconer, was happiest when at Gravina, his hunting lodge in Apulia. Here he trained not only falcons, dogs, horses and even leopards and bears to hunt, but also maintained a breeding establishment for falcons and a zoo. It was here too that he wrote his celebrated mono-graph "De arte venandi cum avibus" (On the art of hunting with birds), which is still an acknowledged classic. His heraldic bird was an eagle grasping a hare in its talons, which can still be seen in the Eagle's Niche of Ursino Castle in Catania, Sicily. This majestic stone-carved bird of prey is chillingly naturalistic and possesses a powerful symbolic force.

Frederick's hunting lodge at Castel del Monte in Apulia, built in 1240, must be counted as one of the masterpieces of secular architecture of the Western world. This octagonal building is inspired by Charlemagne's Palatine Chapel in Aachen, where Frederick was crowned German King for the second time in 1215. In his "Wanderings in Italy" (written between 1856 and 1877) Ferdinand Gregorovius described it thus: "The people call it the Belvedere or balcony of Apulia, dominating the vast plain as it does, and visible from far away. It might be better named the crown of Apulia, for like the coping on a wall this saffron lodge crowns that hill. It appeared to me like the diadem of the Hohenstaufen Empire, crowning the glorious land, when it glowed purple and gold in the evening sun."

In 1519, in the Sologne region, some 60 miles south-west of Paris, King François I commenced work on his "hunting lodge" at Chambord. This most magnificent and most celebrated of all the 120 châteaux of the Loire is set back from the river on a broad clearing within a forested area 13,600 acres (5,500 hectares) in size, enclosed by a 20-mile-long wall. Although unfinished, it is undoubtedly one of the most imposing palaces in the world, with its 440 rooms and 365 chimneys and, alongside Versailles and Mont-St-Michel, is considered to be amongst the three most famous examples of French architecture.

The margraves, electors and kings, who in the 17th and 18th centuries understood perfectly how to combine state duties with pleasure, have come back to life as tourist attractions.

GRANDE CHASSE DONNÉE AU BAERENSÉE PRÈS DE STUTTGARD, EN PRESENCE DE ... S. A. I. Mgr LE GRAND DUC DE TOUTES LES RUSSIES & . & . & . au mois d'Octob. 1782.

Dediée à Son Altesse Sérénissime Monseigneur le Prince de Nassau Comte de Saarbruk &. &. Lieut. Gal des Armées ... Du Roi et Colonel Propriétaire de deux Régiments, Che des Ordres du Merite Militaire de l'Elephant et de S. Hubert

State visits were welcome opportunities to display the full panoply of the hunt. This baroque aquatic spectacle was staged in October 1782 near Stuttgart in honor of an eminent Russian guest.

The center of the complex of buildings is a large rectangular donjon, the living quarters of the medieval fortress, with four corner turrets. At the center of the three story donjon is the extraordinary double-helix staircase, whose two sets of stairs are built in such a way that a person ascending would never meet anyone descending. It is said to have been built according to plans drawn up by Leonardo da Vinci, who died in Amboise in the year construction commenced. On each floor the staircase opens up to four rooms, before finally emerging into the impressive roof terrace, which looks more like a miniature city, with its complex web of gables, chimneys, turrets, bays and niches. You can stroll about at these lofty heights and enjoy the view over the forest. François I is said to have used it for many a fantastic ball, and Louis XIV had Molière stage his plays here.

The luxurious life-style for which palaces like Chambord were indispensable can scarcely be imagined today. Thus chronicles record that François I was followed to his country retreat by a train of twelve thousand horses; furthermore, 27 women of the greatest beauty and elegance were constantly at his side.

Probably nowhere in the world do so many hunting lodges stand so close together as in the valley of the Loire. A particular gem is Château Gien, built towards the end of the 15th century by Anne of Beaujeu, the daughter of Louis XI. The château and the little town, famous beyond France's borders for its faience, is the first in the series of feudal buildings along the Loire. Situated in the midst of the hunting grounds so much prized by the French kings, Château Gien today houses a museum of hunting and falconry with a unique collection of magnificent trophies and costly hunting weapons from earlier centuries.

Just a few miles from Chambord lies the hunting lodge of Cheverny, which was built in the 17th century in the middle of glorious wooded country. This estate, which is still in private ownership today, is home to an interesting collection of trophies, and the owner keeps a famous pack of 80 hounds.

Hunting played a special ceremonial role in the absolutist philosophy of baroque princes, and so it occupied the central place in all entertainments. No expense was spared to make the setting for the hunt as magnificent and opulent as possible. The

249

Chambord was originally surrounded by an extensive enclosed game reserve. It may therefore be termed a hunting lodge, even though it is so vast, with its 440 rooms, and was unfinished. It was built by François I in 1519, and was the scene of fantastic revelry. By order of Louis XIV, Molière's plays were performed here.

251

ruler who enjoyed undisputed pre-eminence in his age, in hunting matters too, was King Louis XIV of France, who, with good reason, was known by the sobriquet of "Sun King". Almost without exception the European princely and royal houses followed his lead in courtly procedures.

This European ruling elite, which was to become increasingly vain and corrupt, was aped by even the pettiest of princelings, who attempted where they could to assume even more privileges than their illustrious idols and did everything in their power to equal and even surpass them in every possible way. Thus the hunting lodge became a status symbol, and anyone with any self respect felt he had to have one of his own. Wherever princes indulged their passion for hunting they built hunting lodges and grand edifices befitting their station in life as they saw it, siting them outside the cities, where game was plentiful and close at hand.

The hunting lodge, as a building, was adapted to the needs of its particular age. In the Middle

Hunting scene on a Meissen plate.

Painting on a Meissen vase with cover (approx. 1735). The hunting scenes are set in the so-called "Saxon Switzerland" (near Dresden).

Plates with oriental-style hunting motifs from the collection of the Saxon Electors

The slain stag is given the ceremonial fanfare in the presence of the hunting nobility, standing on the terrace in front of their lodge. (Polished mirror picture, South German, second half of 18th century)

Falkenlust near Brühl, the hunting lodge of Clemens August, Elector and Archbishop of Cologne, cost more than 600,000 thalers.

Ages it was a kind of fortress for living in, surrounded by thick ramparts, in the middle of wooded areas where game was plentiful, as, for example, Grünwald near Munich. The Renaissance princes, on the other hand, demanded quite different standards of comfort for their hunting residences. And as if they believed they had to justify the lavish expenditure to their subjects they had farms placed next to the luxurious living accommodation for the sake of appearances, hoping thereby to deflect any accusation of extravagance. These princely farms functioned so well that their products often achieved a high reputation for quality. Before long the hunting lodge had undergone a transformation from the medievel fortress to a kind of suburban villa, which was based on Mediterranean models like the Veneto villas of the Venetian nobility.

Considering the rules of ownership it is striking that many hunting lodges were made over to women. This custom had a practical purpose, the thinking behind it being that after the decease of the ruling consort the hunting lodge could serve very well as a residence for his widow, who would now be living modestly without a lavish court household. Amalienburg in the Nymphenburg Schlosspark in Munich is a classic example. Elector Karl Albrecht, a son of Max Emanuel, who was later to become Emperor Charles VII (1726–1745), had it built for his consort Maria Amalie by Jean François Cuvilliés in the years between

1734 and 1739, not least because the Princess, to secure the succession, had consented to undergo the rigors of a pregnancy in spite of having reached what in those days was considered the advanced age of 32.

The few rooms were designed for intimate social gatherings with members of the hunting party. For like Karl Albrecht, the Elector's consort was also passionately fond of hunting. The plump figure of Maria Amalie, however, would not have borne much resemblance to the somewhat disrespectful image that the hunters like to cherish of Diana the goddess of hunting, especially as she was not too fussy about her appearance. "She is a very good shot whether aiming at a target or at the game", it was said of her, "and she often goes up to her knees in the swamp when hunting. She is always to be seen on hunts dressed in men's green clothing and wearing a small white wig. On one occasion, although carrying a child at the time, she was taken on a hunt in a carriage, which, however, twice overturned and threw her. But when the coachman still managed to get her to the killing of the stag in time, she insisted on giving him the customary gold coin and would not let him be punished. She loves the dogs dearly, which is all too obvious when one sees what they have done to the red damask of the wall hangings and the beds at Nymphenburg. The little English whippets are her favorites."

THE MAN WHO CANNOT DOWN HIS BEER, I'LL NOT ABIDE HIS PRESENCE HERE
Christine Vielhaber

"Let us fish and hunt merrily/as in times gone by..." With these words King James, in Theodor Fontane's ballad "Archibald Douglas" sounds the happy ending. Now he will ride back to Linlithgow with his former steward, Count Archibald, where the pair of them will indulge their aristocratic passion—hunting. "Away, away to the merry chase", as the folksong has it, but it refers only to the privilege of the princes, which lasted right until the 19th century, of taking part, with their noble friends, in innumerable hunts of various types, whether battue, with hounds or parforce.

Of course there are plenty of historical sources that give us all the information we need about the merry goings-on in forest and on heathland; for instance, almost all the diary entries of Louis XVI of France are about the hunt, and there are paintings and engravings which have left us a rather idealized portrait of the ladies and gentlemen of the nobility lavishing care and attention on the countryside.

But alongside this there are some extremely valuable and fragile documents which show another aspect of hunting customs in a vivid, graphic and realistic style. "The man who cannot down his beer, I'll not abide his presence here." These are the words on a drinking vessel for huntsmen, dated 1600; one of the earliest drinking glasses

depicting hunting scenes. It is in many ways a revealing gem of the glassmaker's art, for we learn not only how hunting was carried on in that age, but also how the hunting fraternity celebrated their social gatherings. Furthermore, the manner and style of the depiction, and the material itself, bear witness to the skilled handicraft of the time.

The term "Luntz" is mentioned in the two-line inscription around the ten-inch-high tankard: "'Luntz' is what I have been named/Amongst the tipplers I am famed/The man who cannot down his beer/I'll not abide his presence here/Friends with him I cannot be/Who will not drain a glass with me."

The light green glass is elaborately decorated with colored enamel painting. The central section of the narrow, cylindrical glass, which like the ring at the base is mounted with pinched horizontal bands, shows a hunting scene with bears, foxes and hares, driven by two huntsmen and their dogs towards a prepared net. This medieval "net trap" forms a continuous ornamental frieze around the sides of many of these glasses. In many cases it runs all round the glass as the principal motif, as is shown by, amongst many other examples, an elaborately painted Upper Franconian hunting tankard (c. 1679). The base ring has a design similar to the "Luntz" example; the

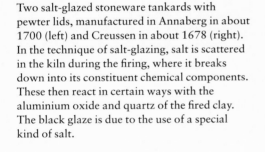

Two salt-glazed stoneware tankards with pewter lids, manufactured in Annaberg in about 1700 (left) and Creussen in about 1678 (right). In the technique of salt-glazing, salt is scattered in the kiln during the firing, where it breaks down into its constituent chemical components. These then react in certain ways with the aluminium oxide and quartz of the fired clay. The black glaze is due to the use of a special kind of salt.

bottom of the tankard is also recessed, but the cylndrical sides narrow slightly toward the base. The game is being driven into the net by leaping dogs. Stylized clumps of grass and trees form a complete surrounding landscape. On the lower edge stands a hunter, heartily blowing his horn.

The dress of this hunter makes clear his social status, for throughout the Middle Ages in almost all European countries the hunt was the privilege of the royal princes, who in turn conferred hunting rights on the less privileged nobility. The skills required for hunting, such as physical control and weapon handling, as well as the knightly virtues of courage, strength and endurance, could all be transferred to the art of war. Together with the armed conflict in which they were frequently called upon to engage, and the pleasures of the dance and the table, hunting was one of the favorite pursuits of the aristocracy.

Until well into the 19th century hunting remained a privilege of courtly society and the upper estates, and in only a few regions were peasants permitted to take part in small game hunting. In general their only contact with their masters' exclusive leisure pursuit consisted of being liable at any time and often for days at a time for compulsory hunt duties, when they had to act as beaters or drive the game into the hunting enclosures.

The countless hunting lodges, which were mainly erected during the baroque period, are witness to the popularity and the status of the noble art of hunting, although this took on forms which would make the modern hunter shudder. Interest was not focused solely on the hunting itself, but equally and perhaps predominantly on the accompanying social events. The proof of this lies not only in the elegantly and comfortably furnished lodges, but also in the quantities of stoneware, porcelain and glass that were ordered from the glassworks and factories by the masters of the hunt for the festivities that followed the hunt. The wine clearly flowed freely, and orgies of eating and drinking were an inseparable part of the total hunting experience.

Moreover—and for this too ceramic products provide the evidence—the hunt provided a welcome opportunity for secret dalliance. "Rendezvous During the Hunt" is the meaningful title given to a sculpture of a pair of porcelain figures designed by Johann Joachim Kändler, which was made around 1744 in the Meissen factory. Under a tree with finely drawn leaves sit a pair of lovers, gazing affectionately at each other. The lady, whose cheeky little hat with the dangling ribbons is perched loosely on her head, is wearing a bright yellow summer dress that is billowing out and seems to rustle when you so much as look at it. It is smothered with large Indian flowers in bloom, a favorite motif of all porcelain decorators, not just from Meissen. With the fingers of her right hand she holds her hunting rifle in a decidedly casual manner. With her left in a graceful gesture she hands the gentleman a bouquet of flowers. He returns the compliment by handing her a freshly killed partridge. At their feet lies a dead hare, looking decorative amongst the blossoms and the leaves of the plinth.

A model from the Ludwigsburg factory, created around 1765, is further graphic proof that deer-stalking could very well be combined with

As hunting motifs are so commonly found on drinking vessels it is a fair assumption that a true aim was not considered incompatible with liquid refreshment—the important thing being to get these in the right order! These examples of cylindrical tankards with pewter mountings date from the second half of the 18th century.

amorous pursuits, and here too the couple are undoubtedly sharing more than just hunting experiences. The model is thought to be the work of Johann Christoph Haselmeyer. Again the loving couple sit in the shade of a tree, which this time is more gnarled and whose branches form grotesque shapes. The admirer inclines his head down to her, and she raises her face expectantly towards him—one kind of hunting which can certainly end in tears but need not be fatal! The young man is clearly a successful hunter, as demonstrated by his two dogs, the gun which hangs loosely at his side, and the deer he has killed, the latter forming a vivid, natural border to one side of the little group. Nevertheless the meaning of this hunting scene goes beyond that of its obvious significance as a picture of the mores of the age to embrace allegory as well, visually relating the hunter's quarry to the realm of amorous pursuit.

As well as the concrete, allegorical, dramatic or romantic motifs from hunting life, there were the amusing and humorous ones. An example of this is the hunting goblet made by Kändler for Clemens August of Cologne. Not a single one of the authentic originals from 1741 (there are also imitations, which were produced between 1924 and 1926 in Meissen and are still being produced today) bears the coat of arms of the Elector, and yet it is beyond dispute that Kändler was commissioned by the Westphalian Estates in Münster to model this goblet for Clemens August. A note still exists, which states that in July 1741 the model was "molded and crafted" according to a drawing, and in September was "corrected and somewhat altered so that it could not become warped or bent in the fire." The goblet was intended for Falkenlust, the Elector's small hunting lodge, where, as the name suggests, he pursued the sport of falconry, for which the broad meadows beside the Rhine were an ideal setting.

However, the small, private lodge was not just a meeting place for hunting parties. It was also the venue for confidential political negotiations and, as the figures from the hunting scenes unmistakably hinted, amorous encounters as well. The Elector is thought to have retreated to Falkenlust almost every evening with two or three of his closest confidantes.

With regard to the hunting goblet, the motif is based on a true episode which occurred in the year 1739 at a royal hunt. A stag, pursued by hounds, fled in great distress on to the roof of a sheepfold. This incident must have made a lasting impression on the Elector, for we know that in 1749 he commissioned the Paris court goldsmith Jacques III Roettiers to make a ceremonial silver centerpiece which showed the killing of a stag on the roof of a hut. Clemens August had merely recounted the celebrated hut roof episode, whereupon Roettiers designed an entire hunting scenario, complete with four candelabras in the shape of oak trees. The object is a splendid Meissen porcelain lidded goblet. Fragments of the original lid have been preserved and are now in Schloss Brühl. On a notched plinth grows a gnarled oak tree, the top of which supports an elaborately fashioned cup. A whipper-in dressed in riding habit leans against a tree and blows his horn, with a skinned stag at his feet. The cup is decorated with a heraldic cartouche in relief on the front and rear, and is closed with a lid. The lovingly modeled pack of hounds hurl themselves furiously on the wild creature, which has been afforded little protection from the low roof of the small hut and is rearing up with the last of its strength. At this point the drama of the hunt situation verges on the tragicomic, and all the artist's skill is called for to express the emotions adequately.

In miniatures, hunting is also portrayed dramatically, but in a different manner. An eight-inch-high cylindrical tankard, made in about 1735/1736 in Meissen, shows the final moments of a royal stag, in a picture surrounding the vessel. The painting is by Adam Friedrich von Löwenfinck, who in 1727, at the age of thirteen, began his career as an apprentice painter in the famous factory and achieved renown through his expressive portrayals of fabulous beasts. He developed his own subtle and unmistakable version of chinoiserie, a style which was highly popular at that time. Following the example of Meissen, the style soon had numerous imitators, all of whom applied the successful formula: take a handful of comical Chinese figures and some fantastic flora and fauna, and add the occasional baldachin or other piece of exotic architecture.

Löwenfinck, on the other hand, composed a highly picturesque, vivid hunting scene with expansive figures, which he placed in an imaginative, colorful and rugged landscape, composed of various Asiatic and European elements.

It was particularly common for cylindrical tankards to be decorated with hunting motifs. Porcelain was seldom used, as the "white gold" was rare and expensive and its use was almost exclusively the privilege of the nobility. It was more common to find hunting scenes on the more widely available faience. In addition to hunting services and pie dishes, individual pieces like pear-shaped and cylindrical tankards or jugs with hunting scenes were extremely popular, especially as presents.

From the factory of Schrezheim comes a cylindrical tankard dated 1802, which is decorated with variegated underglaze paintwork. A large

Joke vessels of all kinds—whether the contents were difficult to get at or only too easy—were extremely popular amongst hard-drinking groups of friends. This glass with a stag on top of it (17th century) was completely useless if you put it to your lips and tipped it up. The only effective method was to suck hard.

This Bohemian drinking glass with its expansive scene of a battue hunt using nets is typical of many others of its kind from the late 16th and early 17th centuries. The ornamental band running around it creates a decorative spiral effect. These glasses had a capacity of several liters.

rocaille (sea-shell) cartouche, the most popular and characteristic stylistic feature of the rococo, portrays a stag against the background of a naturalistic landscape. "Donated by a Catholic Guild of Tailors/ To mark the 150-year jubilee of the inn." This object, which has all the hallmarks of the rococo style, is not a hunting scene in the true sense. The stag, a noble beast from the native woodlands, has now become an acceptable motif for middle-class domestic art.

The cult of friendship which soon began to flourish in the Biedermeier period brought with it an abundance of memorial and dedicated tankards. The ladies, however, had other preferences, and it was not long before the individual cup for the display cabinet began its triumphal march. From the Royal Porcelain factory in Berlin comes

an example of these cups, also with a stag picture of the still-life type. It is a cup in the shape of a bell-jar, which was created between 1800 and 1805 on the model of the Greek Cyathos ladle. The squat egg-shape with the lip turned inwards and the looped handle is considered to be the Berlin factory's most successful design. On its outer side the model shows a stag in the middle of a wooded river landscape. The shallow saucer displays two miniaturized versions of the cup motif on its banner. This example demonstrates that, quite apart from the hunt, animals in their own right have established their place on glass and pottery.

And there is more! Both of these materials had always been both modeled and blown. In the 17th century especially there was a fashion for picture puzzles and joke drinking vessels. A particularly unusual example is a 17th century conical-shaped tumbler of clear glass. Above the pinched base-ring the conical vessel is decorated with a rhomboid-shaped net of criss-crossing thread, the idea for which may have come from the net trap mentioned earlier. In the interior of the vessel there is a glass column with a drinking-tube fitted over it, crowned by a royal stag of hollow glass. From the base-ring to the antlers this glass measures about 10 inches (25.7 cm). The special feature is the stag's open mouth, through which the liquid has to be sucked. Vessels of this kind were not merely designed as gifts or as an amusing talking point after the meal. They also served as a reminder of the consequences of swallowing high-proof spirits too hastily.

It was not long before ornamentally cut and polished glass superseded the decorative enamel painting which had been predominant until then, but was now employed mainly for cheaper items for everyday use. The exceptions are the Schwarzlot (black stain) glasses, especially those by Schaper. The delicacy and artistic quality of this firing technique, which involves working with black and brown coloring only, and which, like glass cutting, was developed in the important art center of Nuremberg in the 17th century, is in a class of its own. Experts say that it bears the same relationship to conventional enamel painting as a miniature does to a crudely colored woodcut.

One of Johann Schaper's masterpieces (Nuremberg region, c. 1665) is a drinking-glass with ball-type base, decorated with Schwarzlot painting. The beauty of the execution of the wooded landscape, which surrounds the sides of the glass like a diorama, and the impression of depth conveyed in spite of the transparency of the glass, have an ennobling effect on the artist's portrayal of the staghunt. From the Nuremberg school of Georg Schwanhardt comes another glass with ball-type base: Schwanhardt was a master of the art of glass cutting with the wheel and of drawing and stippling with a sharpened diamond. The 4½ inch (11.6 cm) tall glass shows on its outer side a picture of a bear hunt meticulously cut with the wheel. Unlike the airy, almost sketchy yet dynamic hunting scene on the Schaper glass, this one, cut in opaque glass, appears tougher and more realistic, but at the same time tells a story more effectively. The well-known motif of hunting and being hunted is here seen from the animal's point of view. The fox surely stole the goose, as in so many tales, before falling into the clutches of the bear, who now in turn has fallen victim to the hounds and the beaters, ending up as a trophy of the noble lord.

From the Höchst factory comes a highly naturalistic and fearsome faience boar's head. The upper and lower jaw together form a covered tureen, which is placed on a stand, the base painted with oak leaves and a flying stag beetle. The fine gradations of the on-glaze muffle-kiln colors are the work of Johann Zeschinge. The tureen dates from about 1750, and is one of innumerable examples of the ever more extravagantly designed baroque table ornaments. As well as being useful, this kind of article was a highly decorative ornament for the table, evidence of a cultivated life-style. It is self-evident that members of the nobility who were in the fortunate position of being able to entertain their hunting guests in such style in their lodges also possessed a suitable table service for every social occasion.

Gradually, as art and culture filtered down to the middle classes, these gems of craftsmanship began to make their appearance in the showcases and collections of knick-knacks of middle-class homes.

At the beginning of the 20th century Max Esser and Paul Scheurich once again made a successful attempt to breathe the spirit of their age into these animal and genre subjects. In 1923 Esser sculpted his "Mandarin Duck" for the Meissen factory, and Scheurich created his "Hunter and Huntress" (1911/1912) for the Schwarzenburg studios. Unity of form and the dynamics of figures in motion, combined with economical decoration, are the expression of a modern artistic language, and even the refined figures by Scheurich, whose roots are certainly in the tradition of rococo sculpture, show a high degree of modern artistic conception in their treatment of the body, and in their characterization.

The porcelain sculptures of Gunther Richard Granget are undoubtedly amongst the greatest achievements of contemporary portrayals of the hunt. His "American Wild Turkey" is part of a series of ten groups of birds of hard-paste porcelain with "biscuit painting", that is, enamel painting on unglazed, fired porcelain. The series was based on studies carried out with the painter

and ornithologist John A. Ruthven. The delicate equilibrium of the figure of the turkey is itself a technical achievement of the highest order. The meticulous realism is also masterly, from the meadows in flower by way of the moldering tree stump, down to the smallest feather.

Hunting motifs have long since made their appearance as transfers on drinking glasses and crockery and are popular for use in the second home or country cottage. And the pie dish in the shape of a pig can be found in the household goods department of every self-respecting store. In an age when works of art can be reproduced by technical means these objects have once and for all lost the character of works of art, which makes the demand for the small masterpieces of glass and porcelain from past ages all the greater.

This so-called "Cup of Welcome" from Schloss Moritzburg (Bohemian or Saxon, 1602) shows the Danish coat of arms and the Saxon Electoral coat of arms below a hunting frieze with a drinking motto. It was probably offered to guests at wedding receptions. It could also be used to drink the health of hunters or to drink to the killing of the game—provided it was held in the left hand.

An indispensable part of the interior furnishing of a hunting lodge, alongside the pictures of the hounds, the hawks, the deer and the wild boars, were family portraits.

The large portrait of Maria Amalie's pack leader, Caesar, is an example of the value which was placed on these expensive dogs. Her husband, too, was constantly accompanied by dogs. For his favorite dogs he had bunks placed in the private rooms of his hunting lodges for them to sleep in, his favorite dog even having a regular place beside his bed.

As much trouble was taken with the dogs as with everything that could in any way contribute to the success of the hunt. In 1737, Georg Friedrich Probst, Chief Whipper-In to His Highness the Duke of Saxe-Weimar, in his "Special Conversation on the Hunt between Nimrod, First of the Hunters, and the World Famous Huberto", published a detailed description of how dogs should be looked after at a hunting lodge: "The kennels should be situated behind the dwelling house, furnished according to the size of the pack and built so that the dogs are always kept dry. Here belong lanterns, plank beds, fireplace, some tin funnels introduced through the roof for feeding roast meat to the dogs, a rope of plaited straw to tether the dogs, and a water butt on three legs, fairly high up (...) There must also be a spacious dog-pound. Adjoining the main kennels there must also be a separate kennel and a small pound for the puppies. In addition there should be a kitchen and a feeding compound. The bitches must not be forgotten: there should be a small kennel for the bitches on heat, and bitches feeding their young need a kennel to themselves."

Specially trained hunting hounds were extremely expensive, and the pack leader could easily be worth as much as an entire team of horses. Hawks for falconry were even more expensive. Anyone who was addicted to this sport needed to have virtually unlimited means at his disposal if he were not to run the risk of being bankrupted by his hobby.

The Elector's wife also indulged in the luxury of falconry, and it was not unusual for the Amalienburg lodge to be the setting for sumptuous falconry festivities. It was also very convenient to shoot at birds from the roof of the little hunting pavilion, which was designed for just this purpose.

If Amalienburg provided the perfect setting for "small-scale events with a few close friends", Nymphenburg was better suited to the more lavish, grand events. Much entertainment was provided, for example, by the so-called tournaments, in which red and fallow Deer were driven into fenced-off paths and were made to run the gauntlet of lances, spears, daggers and pistols.

Ever since the Middle Ages, hunting had been a privilege which was firmly in the hands of those who exercised power, and that meant the nobility. Within the ranks of the nobility, a kind of ranking order developed, for not everyone was permitted to hunt the same animals. Peasants, for example, were prohibited from hunting, on pain of harsh punishment, and economic necessity was seldom allowed as an extenuating circumstance. The only form of hunting not covered by the ban was bird-catching (although even here the nobility reserved the more interesting birds for themselves).

Those who were (or claimed to be) of sufficiently noble birth were allowed to hunt almost

▷ Neuhausen hunting lodge, near what was then a village just outside the gates of Munich, was one of the more modest hunting residences. Around the year 1770, 100 staghounds, 40 gamedogs and 20 pack leaders were kept here. The building, which has since been demolished, stood at what is now Rotkreuzplatz. (C. Adam Kunz, Neuhausen Hunt Museum, 1898)

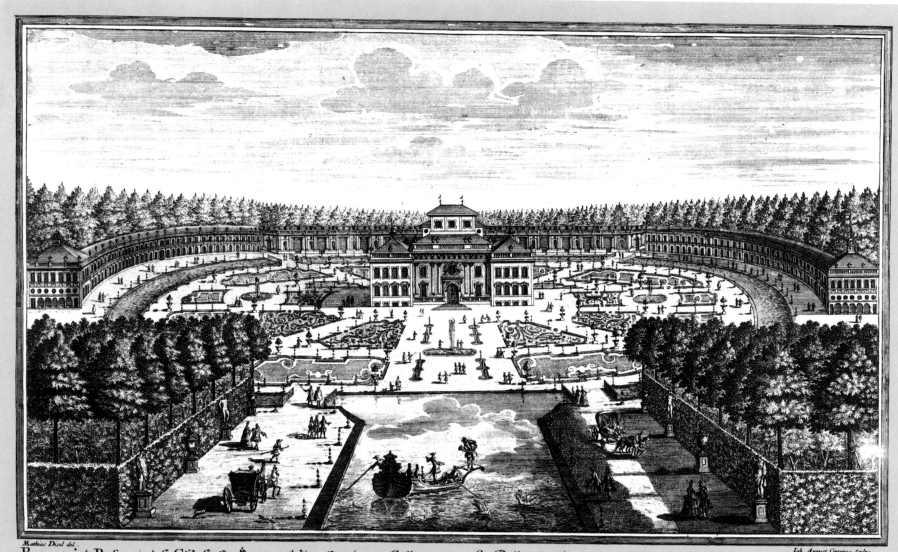

Mathias Disel del.

Prospect und Perspectiv deß Churfürst. Gartengebäude, samt denen Gallerien, parterres und Canal in Lustheim, wie selbes von Schleisheim anzusehen.

Cum Priv. Sac. Cæs. Majest.

Joh. August Corvinus Sculps.

Le Pallais du jardin en perspective avec les galleries, parterres et Canal de Lustheim, du coté de Schleisheim.

Ieremias Wolff excud. Aug. Vind

33.

anything, and there were many who made full use of this birthright. In parallel to the untrammeled power exercised by absolutist and feudalist rulers in the late 17th and early 18th centuries, hunting increasingly became a courtly social game, involving grotesque masked and fancy-dress balls.

In 1662 the Elector of Saxony organized a great hunt in fancy dress, at which he himself appeared as Diana. The rest of the hunting party was accompanied by a procession of caged animals, including dogs, bears, otters and squirrels. Two bagpipers completed the bizarre show. It was also thought amusing to dress up the animals themselves before shooting them down. Or, following the tradition of ancient Rome, lions, tigers, panthers and other beasts were set to fight against each other. No spectacle was considered too degrading.

It was customary for Their Highnesses to send each other invitations to the hunt. In this way neighbourly and at times even dynastic relations were cultivated, for in court circles women were involved in the hunt from an early age, and were sometimes even trained to hunt, just like the men.

In the 18th century hunting lodges were no longer built with an adjoining chapel, and a generation earlier they had given up their farms, which had provided the economic justification for their existence. Thus, for instance, the monastery of Schleissheim outside the gates of Munich was replaced by a summer palace for the Elector. The isolated hunting lodge in the centre of a "star" of woodland paths became the dominant symbol of the period.

◁ In numerous palace courtyards "hunting" provided welcome sport. Particularly popular was foxtossing, in which live animals (sometimes dozens at a time) were repeatedly flung into the air until they miserably perished.

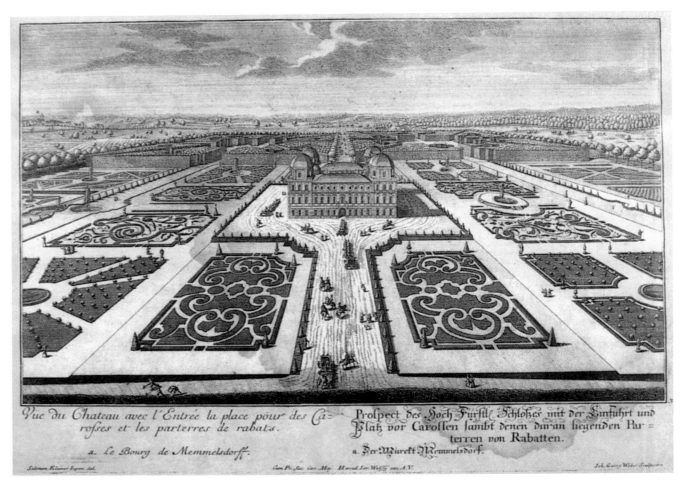

Vue du Chateau avec l'Entrée la place pour des Carosses et les parterres de rabats.

Prospect des Hoch Fürstl. Schloßes mit der Einfuhrt und Platz vor Carossen sambt denen daran liegenden Parterren von Rabatten.

a. Le Bourg de Memmelsdorff.

a. Der Marckt Memmelsdorf.

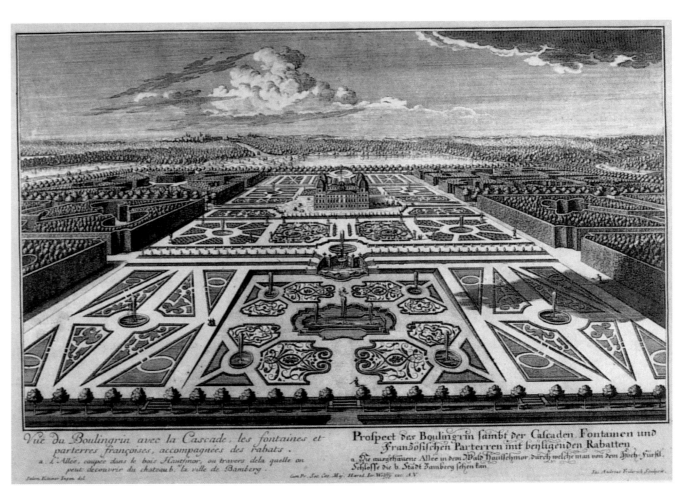

Vue du Boulingrin avec la Cascade, les fontaines et parterres françoises, accompagnées des rabats.
a. l'Allée, coupée dans le bois Hauttmor, ou travers dela quelle on peut decouvrir du chateau b. la ville de Bamberg.

Prospect der Boulingrin sambt der Cascaden Fontainen und Französischen Parterren mit beyligenden Rabatten.
a. Die außgehauene Allee in dem Wald Hauttschmor durch welche man von dem Hoch Fürstl. Schlosse die b. Stadt Bamberg sehen kan.

Chunrat (Konrad) von Altstetten, having returned from falconry, is tenderly greeted by his lady. With its warmth of feeling this miniature is one of the most touching in the Manessische Liederhandschrift (approx. 1330).

▷ In the 17th century, and even more in the 18th, buildings tended to be sited in flat, lowland locations, where there was more room for expansion, rather than on a picturesque mountain top or in a romantic river valley. Thus the Seehof hunting lodge was built outside the gates of Bamberg, under the direction of Antonio Petrini, work beginning in 1687. From 1693 until his death in 1729, Lothar Franz von Schönborn devoted himself to the development of the gardens. When Salomon Kleiner produced the engraving shown here, the fountains, an essential status symbol for royal gardens, had not yet been constructed, as the necessary water pipes were not laid until the second half of the 18th century.

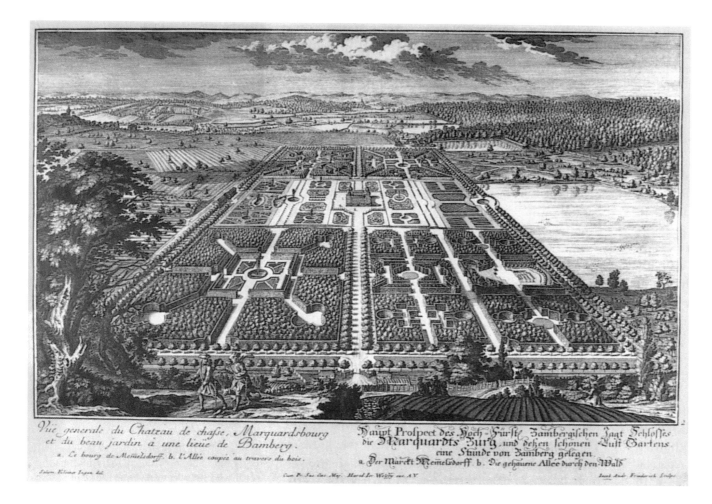

Vüe generale du Chateau de chasse, Marquardsbourg
et du beau jardin à une lieüe de Bamberg.

a. Le bourg de Memelsdorff. b. l'Allee coupée au travers du bois.

Jolam Eliaam Jugen del.

Cum Pr. Sac Cæs. May. Mard. Le Wolff exc. A.V.

Haupt Prospect des Hoch-Fürstl. Bambergischen Jagt Schlosses
die Marquardts Burg, und dessen schönen Lust Gartens.
eine Stunde von Bamberg gelegen.
a. Der Marckt Memelsdorff. b. Die gehaume Allee durch den Wald.

Joach. And. Friederich Sculp.

The falcon and the lure used to entice it back are
prominent features in this multi-faceted picture
of Wilhelm von Heinzenburg being handed a
message concerning a tryst with a lady.
(Manessische Liederhandschrift, approx. 1330)

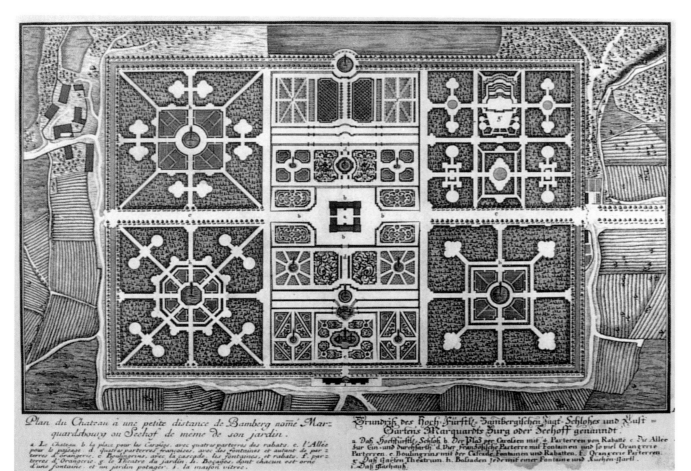

Plan du Chateau à une petite distance de Bamberg nomé Marquardsbourg ou Seehof de même de son jardin.

a. Le chateau b. la place pour les Caroses, avec quatre parteres des rabats. c. l'Allée
pour le passage d. quatre parterres françaises, avec des fontaines et autant de par 2
teres d'orangerie. e Boulingrins, avec la cascade, les fontaines, et rabats. f. par 2
teres d'Orangerie. g le Theatre du jardin. h. Bocages, dont chacun est-orné
d'une fontaine. et un jardin potager. i. la maison vitrée.

Grundriß des hoch-Fürstl. Bambergischen Jagt-Schloßes und Lust=
Gartens Marquardts Burg oder Seehoff genañdt.

a. Daß Hochfürstl. Schloß. b. Der Plaz per Carosen mit. 4. Parterren von Rabatté c. Die Allee
zur Ein-und Durchfarht. d. Vier französische Parterre mit Fontainen und so viel Orangerie
Parterren. e. Boulingrins mit der Cascade, Fontainen und Rabatten. f. Orangerie Parterren.
g. Daß garten Theatrum. h. Boßaden jede mit einer Fontaine und Küchen-Gartl.
i. Daß Glashauß.

The great feudal courts of the 12th century, and later the absolutist courts, kept open certain routes by which women could challenge the dominance of men. Hunting was one of these. Emperor Maximilian's first wife, Maria of Burgundy, shared his passion for hunting. While hawking one day she fell so awkwardly from her horse that she died shortly afterwards.

Accidents like these had to be avoided at all costs, the privileged hunters being considered too important to be allowed to risk life and limb. In order to protect them effectively all possible dangers were eliminated from the start. At the end of a hunt the hunted animal would be so severely mutilated that when the master of the hunt arrived to administer the coup de grâce it was completely defenceless. And in the case of the "enclosed hunt", where the game was driven into a fenced-in area from which it could not escape, victory was assured for the royal hunters, who slaughtered dozens, or even hundreds, of the animals from the safety of their hunting refuge.

At one of these courtly entertainments, hosted by Joseph Friedrich zu Sachsen-Hildburghausen at his lodge on the River March in Lower Austria, to which Empress Maria Theresia together with her family and retinue were invited, the hunt degenerated into such a bloodbath that, at the request of the Empress, the game (accounts mention some 800 deer) were released again. After the peasants had driven the game toward the river, into which they were supposed to jump, the terrified herd broke through the cordon and injured not only the other animals but the beaters too.

Essential components of these festivities were the exquisite feasts, exuberant carousing and whatever else tickled the fancy of the hunting party. So the extravagant display of the hunts was followed by sumptuous banquets for which no expense was spared. Some of these banquets went on for days, even weeks.

Many of the hunting lodges, large and small, that were constructed at that time are now much in demand as tourist attractions. In that they are still showpieces devoted to leisure pursuits, they retain a comparable function even in today's changed society.

The hunting grounds of the lodges were usually laid out as paths in the form of a star, as in the classical examples of Amalienburg in Munich or the Residence of the Margraves of Baden in Karlsruhe, which was expressly designed as a hunting lodge. The purpose of this design was that the hunters should never lose their way, as they could always get their bearings from the lodge. Moreover the game could be driven towards the central point of the network of paths, where the master of the hunt and his party would be waiting with their guns.

A noble falcon, a costly wig and expensive lace make up the portrait of a ruler. The faces on such portraits are interchangeable.

Schloss Übigau near Dresden was built between 1724 and 1726 according to plans by Johann Friedrich Eosander von Göthe for Field Marshall Count Fleming, but in the very year of its completion it was acquired by August the Strong. (Copper engraving by Johann Caspar Ulinger)

The decorative figures on the lid of this Meissen hunting vase (1739) are by Johann Joachim Kändler and Johann Friedrich Eberlein.

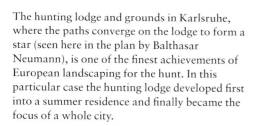

The hunting lodge and grounds in Karlsruhe, where the paths converge on the lodge to form a star (seen here in the plan by Balthasar Neumann), is one of the finest achievements of European landscaping for the hunt. In this particular case the hunting lodge developed first into a summer residence and finally became the focus of a whole city.

When water hunts came into fashion work on a set of that kind could require a dam, to form an artificial lake. Many of these spectacular shows have been preserved in the form of paintings or engravings, enabling us to form a clear picture of what took place. A popular element of these theatrical hunts was an architectural set similar to an ancient theater. The animals were simply driven through it or over ramps, causing them to plunge in spectacular fashion into the water. A bandstand was an essential part of the proceedings, as the royal hunt was set in motion with a fanfare and a roll of drums. It is worth studying these pictures carefully, for on close inspection many of their details are so fantastic that there must be a suspicion that they represent wishful thinking on the part of one or other of the less affluent masters of the hunt.

Most of the hunting lodges had arsenals attached to them, like, for example, that of the Prince Bishops of Bamberg or Kranichstein near Darmstadt. Here adequate supplies of all the equipment needed for hunting on a grand scale were stored.

The hunting lodge was also the right place to house the collections of trophies. The trophies consisted not only of especially powerful and healthy animals, but also of the diseased and abnormal, which if anything were even more sought after. Thus it is not unusual to find miracle chambers or freak cabinets in hunting lodges. At the court of the Salzburg Prince Archbishop there was even an ibex pharmacy, where liver, heart and other offal from the valuable animal were processed as medicines. The specialty of ibex medicine was the miracle-working bezoar stone (a little ball of solidified hairs, fibres etc, from the stomach of these animals), which was believed to relieve all kinds of aches and pains.

Mighty trophies of healthy animals are without doubt the pride of the hunter, but what really arouse the passion of the collector are antlers and horns that are misshapen or abnormal. The masters of the hunt in the past, especially in the baroque period, developed a keen interest in rare, bizarre objects, and built them up into collections.

Abnormalities in antlers are rarely hereditary, but are almost always caused by accidents at the time when the antlers are growing, the velvet period, or, more rarely, result from a hormone disorder leading to irregular growth. Such disorders can occur in all species of deer, but because roe deer are the commonest European species the abnormalities occurring in them form the bulk of most of the freak collections.

One of the most striking abnormalities is undoubtedly the wig antlers, resulting from a malfunction in the growth of the antlers. The cause is an injury to the testicles, the effect of which is that although the animal scrapes the velvet off its antlers, they do not stop growing as they should. Ultimately the antlers grow to such a size over the head that the animal can no longer see, and dies.

If the deer injures the young antler branches before these are fully grown, the tissue of the branches, which follows a regular growth pattern, becomes seriously disturbed, and bizarre antler shapes can result. These may include: more points than usual, split branches, or an unusual shape to the branches and points. Damage to the young antler branches is the commonest cause of antler abnormality.

In red deer and roebuck, the antlers are sometimes so twisted that they resemble corkscrews. The cause of this is almost always a disorder of the metabolism resulting from infestation of the stomach or gut by parasitic worms.

A deer can have extra branches if, instead of having just two bases from which the antler branches grow, it possesses one or more additional bases with branches growing from them. This is a result of injuries to the periosteum of the head at the time of first antler formation.

Serious and long-term injuries to the leg generally affect the growth of the branch of the antlers diagonally opposite the injured leg. Thus a fracture of the right hind leg can lead to a crippled left antler branch.

Deer with no antlers at all, which are however just as fertile as those with antlers, are known (in Germany) as "monks" or "bald heads", and in Scotland as "hummels" (from humble). This very rare abnormality probably comes from under-

Schloss Moritzburg, near Dresden, also houses a famous collection of trophies and freaks within its walls.

"This 2-year-old colorful wild boar was shot in the year 1797 in the Aertzen Forest of Schloss Hühne. Dedicated to Forestry Inspector Kuntze by his obedient servant and nephew Kuntze, Lieutenant. Hanover, July 24, 1797." The trophy itself was replaced by the picture and the inscription—which leaves certain questions unanswered.

The growth of these wig-antlers is the result of hormonal disturbance. This picture of the unfortunate roebuck bears the inscription: "In the year 1791, on Jan. 23, this roebuck was taken alive in the Pheasant Garden here in Moritzburg, by Forester Weislang from Tiemen."

nourishment of the embryo, and is not hereditary.

A relatively common deformation of the antlers in the roebuck is the condition whereby, instead of a regular set of antlers, whether with six points, two or none at all, he grows only two tiny knobs. Recent research has shown that the cause of this deformity is social stress, which may be due to overcrowding among roebuck or to repeated disturbance of the animals.

Alongside such monstrous and therefore interesting antler abnormalities, the baroque freak collections exhibited other wildlife curiosities. A common phenomenon to be witnessed by hunters was the spotted wild boar. The origin of such faulty coloration is easy to explain. Up to the end

of the last century, pigs, as well as cows, sheep, and goats, were driven out into the woods to feed, and hybridization between domestic and wild pigs could not be ruled out.

Of more doubtful authenticity is another freak of nature often numbered among abnormal phenomena, namely the hare with antlers, which has made its ghostly presence felt in natural history and hunting literature for centuries.

In his book "A Hunter Talks" (1799), Wilhelm von Heppe says: "I must confess to having seen an amazing kind of hare, which was shot by a forester in my employ, Balthasar Heyder, in the Hollenberg hunting ground. This hare was a strong buck, and had two small horns on its head

von dem Kopffe und monstrosen Gehörne des Rehbocks in der Animalien-Galerie zu Dresden, welchen Keyssler in s. Fortsetzung neuester Reisen, Hannover 1741. 4to. S. 1067. und in d'Ausgabe v. 1751. 4to. (mihi S. 1308.) beschrieben und abgebildet hat.

Der Bock ward castrirt, legte 4 Wochen darauf sein erstes Geweih ab, und an Statt, daß geschnittene Böcke nicht wieder aufsetzen, bekam dieser das abgebildete Gehörn, welches ihm immer blieb, und von keiner so festen Materie war, wie anderes Gehörn. Seine Aus-dünstung, Geruch p. muß sich ganz geändert haben, den Statt daß er nun den Geißen nachließ, zog er viele Rehböcke nach sich, welche ihm bis auf den Hof folgten.

This strange spotted stag was taken in 1726, and shortly afterwards engraved and described by Johann Elias Ridinger.

These few lines of description refer to the roebuck with wig antlers (bottom right).

Ridinger apparently regarded the existence of the hare with antlers as proven. But perhaps he simply did not wish to cast doubt on something of which his patrons were convinced.

This roebuck grew a permanent set of wig antlers following castration. The illustration and description is by J. G. Keyssler in the second volume of his "Recent Journeys" (1751) in the Dresden Gallery of Abnormalities.

Even in the encyclopedic standard work by Buffon (1749–1804) we find hares with antlers.

This illustration of a bizarre abnormality of the antlers of a roebuck (1589) is by Hans Hoffmann, of the school of Dürer.

between its ears. When the forester cut it open in my presence, it was found to have, like a female, four young inside it, which would have been born within eight days. Thereupon we examined it closely but could not find the least indication that this hare had been a hermaphrodite, merely that it had teats which were full of milk."

Again, in the "General and Specialized Natural History" (1749–1804) by the great French scientist Georges Louis Leclerc, Count of Buffon, we read: "From time to time nature, contrary to its own laws, brings forth horned bitches, does and hens, so why not also hares with horns or antlers?"

The Augsburg copper engraver and painter Johann Elias Ridinger (1698–1767), normally

well known for the accuracy of his pictures, also contributed to the currency of the legend with a copper engraving showing two hares with antlers drawn "from life", although both of them had already been shot, and the one on the right already stuffed.

In 1817, after close examination of the stuffed animals, reports and other supposed evidence, Head Forester Franz von Wildungen pronounced what could be the last word on this phenomenon: "So there is supposed to be such a thing as a hare with horns!/What? Could such creatures really exist?/I have never seen one on four legs, my friend;/But you can see plenty on two!"

Augustus the Strong had the Renaissance edifice of his predecessor Elector Moritz, which had already been enlarged several times, extended to form a great baroque palace. (Johann Alexander Thiele, Schloss Moritzburg with Hunting Party, 1733)

For their hunting lodges the princes insisted on engaging the top architects of their time. For example, Johann Philipp Franz von Schönborn, after his election as Prince Bishop of Würzburg and Duke of Franconia (September 18, 1719) commissioned the leading engineer Balthasar Neumann as city master builder and architect responsible for numerous hunting lodges on the Main and upper Rhine. Well-known lodges and estates, such as those at Würzburg, Schwetzingen and Bamberg, were constructed under his direction.

Elector Clemens August, a son of the Bavarian Elector Max Emanuel and brother of Karl Albrecht, engaged the Münster Architect Johann Conrad Schlaun for his hunting lodge Clemenswerth in the Hümmling hills, and for Falkenlust hunting lodge in Augustusburg Park near Brühl he obtained the services of the Munich court architect Jean François Cuvilliés. While still working on Falkenlust, Cuvilliés received the commission to build the Amalienburg hunting lodge in Nymphenburg Park for Maria Amalie, the sister-in-law of Clemens August.

For both lodge and park at Augustusburg, Clemens August provided his own plans. Similarly, Augustus the Strong, King of Poland and Elector of Saxony, produced his own sketches for extensions and alterations to the hunting lodge (which was also a summer palace) of Moritzburg.

When it came to the pleasures of the royal hunt, Augustus the Strong was undoubtedly the most talented and ambitious maître de plaisir. For a large proportion of his four years as Elector of Saxony and King of Poland (from 1697), Frederick Augustus I (King Augustus II) was not really present in any of his kingdoms but spent his time in a dream world, the fantasies of which he was only able to realize thanks to his immense wealth. As a man of unusual bulk (at least 286 pounds), who enjoyed performing feats of strength and relished combat with dangerous wild animals, he lived life to the full. He indulged in the most outlandish and bizarre hobbies, thus demonstrating his absolute authority as well as his refusal to conform to trivial, petty bourgeois expectations.

If Augustus the Strong could find no enemy to conquer on the battlefield he sought out the toughest and most doughty opponents for duels wherever he could find them. If he could think of no other outlet for his almost limitless strength, he showed off his martial talents on ceremonial occasions by performing as a bull- or bear-tamer. Thus at the wedding of the Habsburg Emperor Joseph II in Augsburg he caused great excitement when he pitted himself against a frenzied bear, which stood head and shoulders above him, striking off its head with two mighty blows of his sword.

In the extensive grounds of his palace in Dresden he would get his servants to let wild boars loose on him, and then amuse himself and his people by killing them single-handedly. On one occasion he hurled his heavy hunting spear and missed; but when the fearsome beast lunged at him a second time he leapt to one side, despite his bulky figure, seized the enraged animal by one of its hind legs and dispatched it with a well-aimed thrust of his hunting-knife.

There are endless stories of Augustus's physical strength, and they are still being told today. When it came to bending iron bars the Elector could outdo the strongest blacksmith. Once, when his horse had lost its shoe, he instructed the nearest village blacksmith to prepare a new one. To test it Augustus picked it up and promptly broke it in two. Thereupon he tossed the startled blacksmith a silver coin for a new horseshoe. Not wishing to admit defeat, however, the man crushed the coin in his hand like a piece of paper. The story goes that the Elector thereupon laughingly gave him a gold coin, thus purchasing perhaps the most expensive horseshoe in history.

Augustus used to enjoy riding through the cobbled streets of Dresden at full gallop, with the reins between his teeth, carrying under each arm a street urchin he had picked up as he passed by. It was no wonder he became known as Augustus the Strong. To the educated nobility of his empire, who, as the custom was, liked to celebrate his deeds with poems and ballads rich in allegorical, mythological and historical allusions, he was the "Saxon Hercules".

However, Augustus did not only excel as a champion duellist in the arena, he also took pleasure in ceremonial processions, receptions in the country, ladies' chariot racing, and balletic displays by exotically dressed noblemen on horseback. In pursuit of the same pleasure principle he furnished his palaces with magnificent treasures, which swallowed up vast sums and did nothing but reflect his extravagant fantasies. Many of these costly treasures were the work of the court goldsmith Johann Melchior Dinglinger (1664–1731), a Swabian from Biberach on the Riss in Württemberg, who worked for Augustus from 1698. With his artistry he strove to give expression to the vivid imagination of his patron.

Augustus lived out his dreams, and Dinglinger gave them artistic form in gold, silver and

The Moritzburg hunting lodge, near Dresden, today.

The unknown artist who recorded this water hunt at Moritzburg hunting lodge in the early 18th century has left us a good picture of how an "enclosed hunt" was organized and carried out, and of the risks involved.

Hunter on horseback, Meissen, 17th century.

On January 12, 1656, this wild boar hunt took place in the Boar Garden at Moritzburg. As it states exact dates and gives lists of participants the picture is in the nature of a historical document.

The head of this leaping stag with coral antlers is removable, revealing it to be a drinking vessel. (German, early 17th century, gilded silver)

precious stones. Since Dresden's ruler liked his surroundings to reflect the world of the gods of Greek and Roman antiquity, Dinglinger specialized in the creation of art objects which represented figures from classical mythology.

One of his most splendid pieces was the "Bath of Diana", a subject which would have particularly delighted Augustus, who had a reputation as a lady-killer. Possibly the costly vessel was also an allusion to one of the King's amorous adventures in one of his hunting lodges, when, wearing the costume of Pan, he was introduced to a new lover by a lady of the court disguised as Diana. It was not enough for Augustus the Strong to make a conquest of a lady, he had to lead her into his romantic dream world with some kind of ceremony. He treated the treasures of his court goldsmith Dinglinger in a somewhat similar manner. He had the state treasure chamber extended to form the Grüne Gewölbe (Green Vaults), which is

now world famous, where behind securely locked doors and walls six foot thick he could live out his fantasies in the style of the Arabian Nights.

It is hardly surprising that a man like Augustus the Strong could not be satisfied with merely being Elector. He was determined, by whatever means, to become a king. His opportunity came when in 1696 the Polish King John III Sobieski died, and as Poland was an elective monarchy, the King being chosen by the nobility, the succession was uncertain. The new king accordingly had to be elected by the higher nobility, and Augustus succeeded in convincing the majority of the Polish nobles that he, a Saxon, was the best man to occupy the vacant throne of Poland.

This political and strategic coup enabled Augustus, the Elector and General, as well as Dresden playboy and strongman, to enter the ranks of the ruling houses of Europe, and achieve undreamt-of triumphs. Many a power-seeker will

The famous trophy collection in the Great Banqueting Hall of Schloss Moritzburg, Dresden.

Trousse de chasse belonging to Augustus the Strong, known as the Emerald Set, consisting of: one hunting-knife with agate handle (9 emeralds, 81 diamonds, including 7 of the finest quality, for the hunting-knife belt); one dagger (90 emeralds, 200 diamonds), all by Johann Friedrich Dinglinger; the Order of the Golden Fleece (3 emeralds, 73 diamonds, 1732/33); the Order of the Polish White Eagle (16 emeralds; J. A. Jordan, 1746); one ornament for a hat-brim (4 emeralds, 67 diamonds, before 1722), one hat-clasp (8 emeralds, 8 diamonds), two belt-buckles (16 emeralds, 16 diamonds); also: 7 emeralds in gold mountings (various); 2 shirt-buttons, 1 neck button for a shirt, 1 walking stick knob, 16 coat buttons.

have taken fresh hope from the example of Augustus the Strong: the Saxons were convinced Protestants, and their land was the cradle of the Reformation, whilst the Poles were amongst the most devout Catholics in Europe. With the insuperable barriers of language and customs dividing them, the two nations seemed to have nothing in common, not to mention the fact that they did not even have a common border at that time. But to the unstoppable Prince this was just one more dream to fulfil, and somehow he managed to satisfy all sides, including both his Saxon subjects and the Polish aristocracy. True, the followers of Luther in Dresden did not take kindly to their Elector converting to Catholicism, but in the end they had to bow to the superior statesmanship of their Prince.

Furthermore, it is to this unusual switch of denominational allegiance by both court and people of Saxony that we owe one of the most magnificent compositions in the history of church music: in 1733, the year of Augustus the Strong's death, Johann Sebastian Bach (1685–1750), cantor of the Church of St Thomas in Leipzig, submitted to the Dresden court the "Kyrie" and "Gloria" from his Mass in B minor, which he had

written for the Catholic court orchestra, and requested a prädicat (an official position), as restrictions had been placed upon him in Leipzig. Thereupon Bach was appointed as court composer.

As King of Poland, Augustus reigned over a state that was twenty times as big as his home country of Saxony. It extended from the Oder to the Dnepr and from the Baltic almost to the Black Sea. In many respects the two countries complemented each other economically, but with his extravagant spending habits the dual ruler soon found himself in financial difficulty, despite his inherited wealth.

So Augustus could not have been more pleased when along came a man who claimed to be able to turn lead into gold. Of course, such a man was far too valuable a subject to be allowed to walk around freely, so Augustus simply had the man arrested. He was Johann Friedrich Böttger or Böttiger, an alchemist who had fled from Prussia to Dresden. The miracle-worker was now expected to demonstrate his secret art behind prison walls in Dresden. As King of Poland and Elector of Saxony, Augustus the Strong was powerful enough to deprive a man of his liberty in this way with impunity.

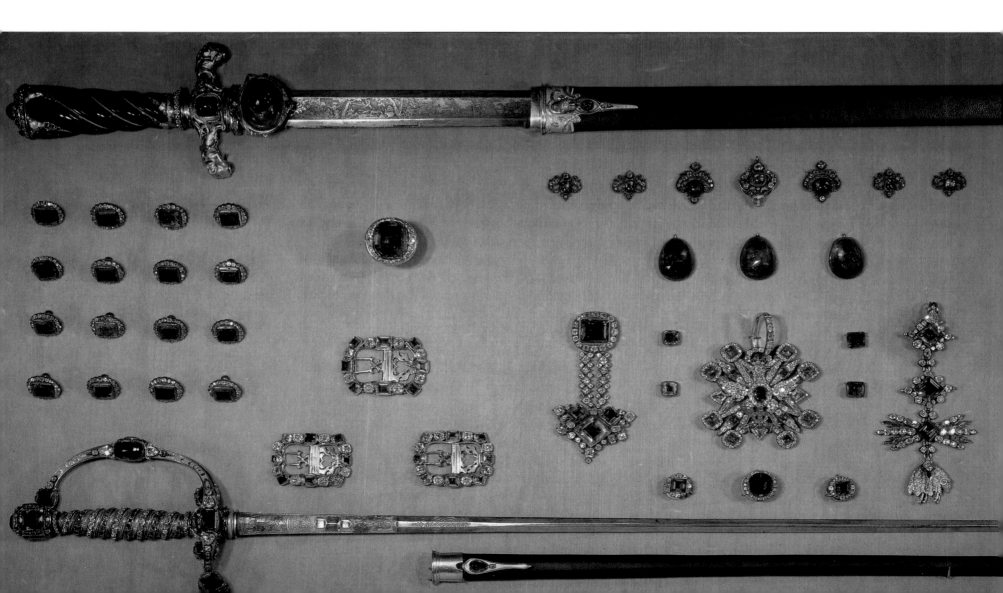

Soon, however, it turned out that the prisoner was nothing but a failed pharmacist's assistant and did not have the first idea of how to make gold; to a degree, however, the gamble did pay off, as after a few years the Prussian prisoner succeeded in manufacturing the so-called "white gold". Such were the curious circumstances which led to the foundation of the world-famous State Porcelain Factory, the first in Europe, in the small town of Meissen just a few miles from Dresden. In 1710 the factory commenced work and for its first nine years was under the direction of Böttger. In the early years production was mainly of Chinese porcelain.

Today we have lost the art of "composing symbioses of light from orbiting suns, radiant stars and glittering sheaves". We hear with amazement of the "fiery architecture and luminous lettering with which the baroque masters of pyrotechnics inscribed on the night sky". The art of fireworks, which the Saxon Elector also frequently employed to help to consolidate his power and to enhance his reputation in Europe, is today almost forgotten, like so many of the arts which occupied a respected place in the range of art-forms that flourished in the baroque period.

All that has remained is a small number of those magnificent hunting lodges, which through all the political changes have preserved their particular character. The majority are open to the public, including Augustus's favorite hunting lodge Moritzburg, just outside Dresden, or Augustusburg, near Brühl, which the German Federal Government uses for official functions. The hunting lodge of Kranichstein near Darmstadt, Amalienburg in Munich and the Springe hunting lodge in Lower Saxony, where the German Emperor used to spend his holidays, are also open to the public. Less well known is Schloss Veitshöchheim near Würzburg, well worth a visit for its rococo gardens, which have been preserved unchanged to the present day. Very few examples of this historic style of garden have survived the dominant "English garden" movement of the 18th century.

Many of the old hunting lodges have shared the fate of the gardens and have gradually fallen into decay, been destroyed, or undergone alterations, to the point where they are no longer recognizable. What remains is the more or less happy reminder of a time which was undoubtedly of great importance for the history of hunting—even if the hunter of today finds the manner in which it was carried out in those days unacceptable, if understandable.

Set of hunting accessories of Augustus the Strong, known as the Cornelian (or quartz) Set, including:
one large hunting-knife (327 diamonds);
one small hunting-knife and whip;
the Order of the Golden Fleece;
a watch with chatelaine (right), a round snuff-box with globe (90 diamonds), an oval snuff-box (104 diamonds) and a long etui (gold wire, 78 diamonds);
one rosary;
a total of 7 clasps and clips of various sizes.
(all from the Dinglinger studio, 1718–1728)

Fashions change, but the falcon has remained a prestigious object, whether at the time of the Hohenstaufen Emperor Frederick II or of the copper-engraver Jost Amman. (Left: illustration to "De arte venandi cum avibus," from the 1240s. Right: Noble on horseback with falcon, colored woodcut, 1578)

Das Churfürstliche Schloß Starenberg am Würmsee.

Under Elector Ferdinand Maria (1651–1679) the Starnberg hunting lodge and its adjoining lake were the scene of sumptuous receptions, the centerpiece being the magnificent ship Bucentauro, built on the Venetian model. (Copper engraving by Michael Wening, 1701)

▷ Everything with which a noble lord or lady surrounded themselves had to be luxurious, even if it was only a snuff-box. For the hunt, of course, it was essential to have one with a suitable subject. Here it is Acteon surprising Artemis and her nymphs while they are bathing.

The hunting lodge Kranichstein, near Darmstadt, was built by Jakob Kesselhut between 1571 and 1579 for George I of Hesse-Darmstadt and extended by Landgrave Ludwig VIII. Today it houses a hunting museum.

The pièce de résistance of a hunting lodge and the pride of virtually every hunter is a well stocked collection of trophies. The hunter will put a good deal of effort and expense into securing the prize of a trophy.

▷ The celebrated coach and six stags of the Landgrave Ludwig VIII of Hesse-Darmstadt (1691–1768). The artist is Georg Adam Eger.

HUNTING WEAPONRY

Once, at the dawn of human history, man "cast the first stone", and with this deliberate deed both tools and weapons came into being. No doubt it was not long before our ancestors were using sharpened sticks to kill game in order to survive. Thousands of years passed, during which club and spear, boomerang and sling and bow and arrow gradually increased the power of man over the animals (and over his less well armed fellow humans). The more civilized man became, the more effective became his weapons, and even the most powerful animals had virtually no chance against the sharp metal point of the boar-spear (right) or of escaping the range of the crossbow (above). Eventually, with the invention of firearms, wild animals were completely at the mercy of man.

This silhouette of a 10,000-year-old Iberian hunter from a rock painting in the Valltorta Gorge is reminiscent of contemporary archers in Africa. He is wearing neither belt nor quiver, and is holding the remaining arrows in his hand with the shaft of the bow.

Animals are usually equipped with exactly the weapons of attack or defense which they need for the preservation of their species. However, this was not true of our evolutionary ancestors. At some point their habitat underwent a change, and they adapted accordingly. They ceased to be pure herbivores and became omnivores, and if they were not to rely on the odd piece of carrion that they happened to come across they were forced actively to hunt animals, even though they had not been endowed by nature with the appropriate claws, carnassial teeth or muscles.

If they had had to rely on the tools and weapons they found about them in nature, and had not succeeded in developing them for specific purposes, they would have been unable to adapt to the changed circumstances and would probably have died out long ago. Primitive though their first weapons may seem to us, they are nevertheless the product of an astonishing mental feat; no animal had yet achieved anything like it.

Alongside the purposeful application of weapons—such as sharpened sticks or flintstones sharpened to a point by carving them on both sides—it was largely the skill of the individual hunter that determined whether he emerged triumphant from his encounter with a wild animal. This is also why a weapon such as a simple catapult, in the hands of a hunter and warrior from the Balearics or from Etruria for example, had sufficient force to kill an animal in full career, or shatter a shield.

It is thanks to their skill that many an Australian aboriginal or Egyptian, even today, is able to employ the boomerang (which was already being used in prehistoric times) as an effective hunting weapon; he uses it to kill not only birds in flight, but fleeing wild animals too. The Inuit, who go hunting in temperatures of 40 degrees below zero, have the capacity to squat motionless for hours on the ice, with a harpoon in their raised hand, waiting for a seal to approach. In sweltering temperatures of over 100 °F (40 °C), the Peuhl hunters south-east of Lake Iro wait patiently, spear at the ready, without moving, behind a thorn bush, if need be for a whole day and night, until Cape Deer or antelope pass by, searching for water. Even from a distance of over 20 yards they rarely fail to hit their target with deadly accuracy. Skill, stamina, and above all constant practice, have enabled these hunters to become artists in the business of death.

The era of silent weapons lasted about half a million years. Up to the 15th century, when the first firearms appeared in Europe, hunters had to make do with a relatively small selection of weapons and instruments for hunting. Thanks to the generally consistent behavior of the game, hunters were able over the generations to develop effective methods of operating, and to learn the tricks of the trade, some of which continued to be practiced even after the advent of long-range firearms.

Thus the practice of driving the game towards the edge of a precipice, common among the Old Stone Age hunters of Solutré in France, continued in many mountain regions until well into the 16th century. Another method, that of driving the game on to covered pits hidden by hedges, wickerwork, nets and cloths, was employed from at least the Quaternary period right up to the 18th century in Central Europe, and this kind of hunting is still favored by many primitive peoples to this day. In the United States they still hunt big game with bows and arrows, just as the native American Indians did for thousands of years, and in France and England the sport of archery is still popular, with hunting-style associations attracting several thousand participants. In the lagoons of Venice, bows and arrows were used to shoot water game as late as the 18th century, as was the custom in Europe 10,000 years earlier.

The invention of the bow and arrow shifted the balance decisively in favor of man. As a hunting device, the bow not only had a long range, it was, in the true sense of the word, a penetrating weapon. In the Middle Ages, arrows are said to have carried for some 550 yards (500 m), and a good archer was expected to be able to pierce a two-inch (5 cm) thick oak board from a distance of over 200 yards (200 m).

The climax of medieval weapons technology was reached when the use of the crossbow became widespread in the 12th century, the Chinese having been credited with its invention. The

If the arrows which appear to have struck this bison (from a cave painting in Niaux) were to be taken as representations of a specific weapon, rather than as an indication of how and from what direction the beast has been (or should be) attacked, then pictures like these would provide evidence that the bow and arrow already existed 15,000 years ago. No such weapon dating from this period has yet been found.

In his struggle for survival against wild beasts man needed any weapon he could get, to complement his bare hands and his physical strength. He must have quickly realized that success or failure in the hunt depended not least on the weapon's reach, and that in close combat with an animal he would be sure to come off worse if he allowed it to come within arm's length. Thus he fashioned wooden shafts of sharpened flintstone (right) for his spearheads. The Bronze Age weapons for throwing, stabbing and cutting shown here (above) were effective only when attached to the "extended arm".

heyday of the new weapon soon passed, however, for the Second Lateran Council resolved to ban it —the crossbow having proved all too deadly, both in war and in its peacetime use for hunting. In 1215 the ban was renewed by Pope Innocent III, though it was widely disregarded.

The dispute regarding the crossbow had a political background. The nobility, whose lofty principles of knightly combat did not permit the use of this "sniper's weapon", suddenly found themselves confronted by a middle class with a highly effective weapon at its disposal and which was not hampered by traditional notions of knightly virtue.

For hunting purposes the nobleman found it easier to accept the crossbow. In his treatise "De arte bersandi" (On the Art of Stalking) from the first half of the 13th century, Guicennans gives some tips on the use of the crossbow: "Crossbowmen should wear jerkin, hat and hood of a similar color to the trees, so that they are not noticed by the game when they stand by the trees. They should take a quiver containing five arrows and three spears with them, the arrows to shoot the game, and the spears to defend themselves if it should be necessary. If there is no war going on in the area, they should also take two bolts with them to shoot at birds." For safety reasons, a crossbow should never be drawn on the road, but always at the side of the road, and kept ready to shoot only when in the area to be hunted.

The crossbow of that period had been technically perfected to the extent that firearms, which had by now made their appearance, were unable to displace them for a long time.

Historians of the hunt like to describe the period from the Thirty Years' War until the French Revolution as the golden age of hunting. Never before in history, and at no time since, has so much money been spent on costly hunting equipment. Even if the true principles of the chase fell by the wayside, it is hard resist the fascination that emanates from the works of art and architecture created in the service of the hunt.

The ostentatious extravagance beloved of absolutist princes led to the construction of countless hunting lodges, which were filled with works of art until they resembled Aladdin's Caves.

The visual arts benefited from exemplary patronage; sculpture was either on the theme of religion, or depicted allegories of war and hunting, and hunting jargon became acceptable in polite society.

The products of weapons technology from that period are amongst the finest and technically perfect that have ever been created in this field, and the orders that were placed for elaborate engravings and other ironwork for the decoration of the rifles, spears, swords and hunting-knives guaranteed a living for many craft workshops.

To judge by the position of the missiles in this rhinoceros (from a cave painting found in La Colombière, near Poncin), we can deduce that it was killed while lying down. This would have enabled the old Stone Age hunters to strike the vulnerable softer parts of their prey.

This caboclo, a descendant of South American Indians and Portuguese, is no ordinary archer. As the swarm of frigate-birds is beyond the range of a normal handheld bow, the Brazilian natives invented a stronger bow which could only be drawn with the aid of the legs. (Drawn by J.-B. Debret, 1815/1831)

"One could wish that not every bungler, shoe-shine boy and apprentice clerk were at liberty to use the hunting sword (Hirschfänger in German), and that this noble symbol of the hunter were not so abused." Heinrich Wilhelm Döbel (1699–1759), in his "The Latest Hunting Practices or the Well-Trained and Experienced Hunter" (1746), does not mince his words when it comes to the fashionable excesses of his time. In the end, however, these only illustrate the fact that no other European hunting blade has experienced such a comprehensive cultural and artistic development as the hunting sword.

Bladed weapons are commonly divided into those with shafts and those with hilts. Until the end of the Middle Ages, weapons used on the field of battle and those used for hunting were very similar, and it is only with the appearance and spread of firearms in the Renaissance that we need to differentiate between weapons of war and those used for hunting. The early muzzle-loaders were awkward to operate, and took the hunter too long to prepare for shooting.

Amongst shafted weapons, the javelin was the leading distance weapon, until it was replaced by the bow and arrow. The spear was used right up to the 19th century for hunting bear, lynx, chamois and especially wild boar. The blade,

sharpened on both edges, and the head were fitted over a mature hardwood shaft (about 7 feet in length) and fastened with nails, with narrow iron bands serving to secure the head. A small lug, set at right-angles to the blade, prevented the weapon from penetrating too deeply into the body of the animal. Strips of leather bound round the shaft in different ways ensured a good grip. The blades were etched or the heads decorated and the bindings also showed some attempt at ornamentation.

By contrast, the development of hilted weapons was more complicated, perhaps because a weapon worn in direct contact with the body inevitably reveals something about the standing, power and character of its bearer. A hunting weapon could, after all, perfectly well be used for personal protection and was likely to be needed.

The 8th century Germanic scramasax (from the Latin secare) is perhaps the starting point of this development. It was both a weapon and a tool, and was long used by the peasants' militia. Pictures by Bruegel and Dürer show it in considerable detail. It is only moderately long, sharpened on one side only, with a simple cross guard and a rudimentary point for stabbing. The asymmetrical hilt is covered with horn or wood veneer, and the pommel is usually in the shape of a bird's head, rather like a bayonet.

The range and force of a javelin can be maximized by means of the javelin sling. This instrument, which was made out of antlers, is known to have been employed about 12000 B.C.

Bow and arrow are silent weapons, so huntsmen can attack and kill deer from behind cover without disturbance. Here, a scene from the Aeneid is depicted by Heinrich von Veldeke (c. 1230), in which Ascanius slays the tame Stag of Silvia. "Wounded, the deer straight away fled to its familiar home,/ staggered groaning to its stable, and, covered in blood, uttered a lament,/ as though it were pleading, which sounded throughout the house", as Virgil has it. The innocent wild creature, struck by the hunter's arrow, is here taken as a metaphor for the sufferings of love.

When pursuing wolf, lynx, bear or wild boar, the most important and effective weapons for the hunter on foot were the bear- or boar-spear. The two-edged forged blade, with the head, was fitted on to the 7-foot-long mature hardwood shaft and secured with nails. There is little doubt that the spears shown here, dating from the 16th and 17th centuries, were all well used. When examined as a group the different kinds of decoration on the shafts can be compared.

Two German ceremonial boar-spears
Left: the open-work blade and the edged head are decoratively etched, and the shaft covered with velvet (17th century).
Right: blade and head are decoratively etched and gilded.

These three scenes from the floor mosaic of a Roman villa (around 250 A.D.) illustrate the handling of the hunting-spear. Every Roman dreamt of visiting the Colosseum to see the games for himself, but the further away from Rome he lived the less chance he had of ever actually doing so. Gladiatorial combat with wild beasts was a particularly popular spectacle. In the pictures on this page gladiators are fighting with a bear (above), a wild boar (center), and a leopard (below).

For a long time the crossbow was superior to firearms in every respect. It was not only almost silent and therefore did not cause the game to panic, but was also very easy to handle. At the same time the missile which it fired, the bolt, had considerable penetrating force. These two crossbows are richly embellished, the upper one (mid-17th century) showing dogs in pursuit of a fox, and the lower one with staghunting motifs.

The quiver was worn either on the back or on the belt. In the baroque it seems to have become a luxury item, at least as far as hunting is concerned. This richly decorated Turkish quiver for bow and arrows is from the 17th century.

This elaborately worked German steel crossbow (mid-17th century) is a particularly splendid example. It is strengthened with rope binding and decorated with woollen pompoms, and the shaft exhibits superb decoration.

This dagger with the polychrome figurine handle is the work of Christoph Weidlitz, Augsburg, from the mid-16th century.

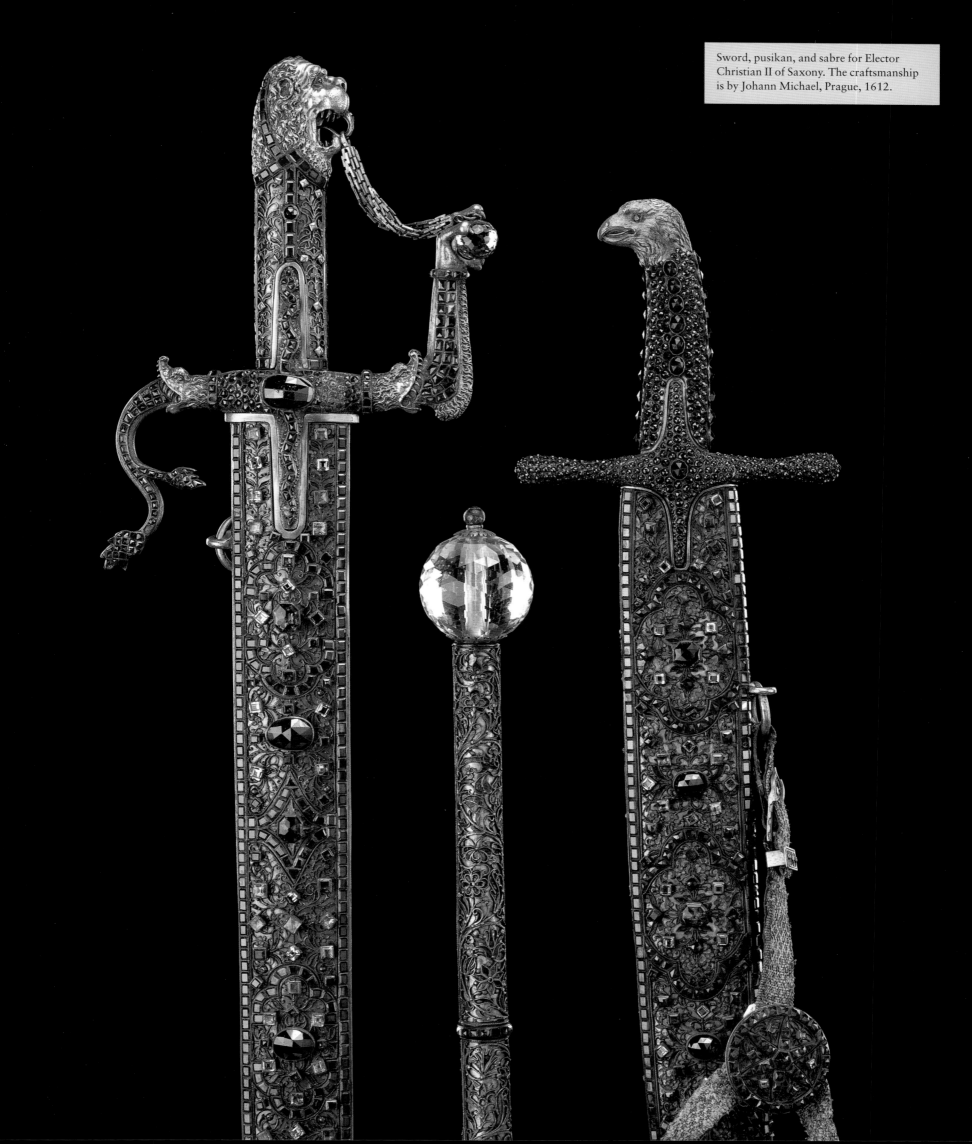

Sword, pusikan, and sabre for Elector Christian II of Saxony. The craftsmanship is by Johann Michael, Prague, 1612.

ICITVR INTER AQVAS, PATVLIS DEFENDERE CAMPIS
CVRRENDO POTERAT SE FERA, NANDO NEQVIT.

July's picture of the month (detail) from the Wittelsbach Series, a series of monthly pictures crafted in 1612 in the factory of Hans van der Biest, from sketches by Peter Candid.

▷ Turquoise trousse for Elector Christian II of Saxony, consisting of long hunting sword, set of knives and hunting sword. They are the work of Gabriel Gipfel, Dresden, 1606.

Illustrations on pages 292 and 293:
Pommel, s-shaped curved parrying guard, and handguard of the hunting sword (left) are generously studded with turquoise stones. Both the handguard of the long hunting sword (right) and the metal trim on the scabbard are embellished with small animal figures.

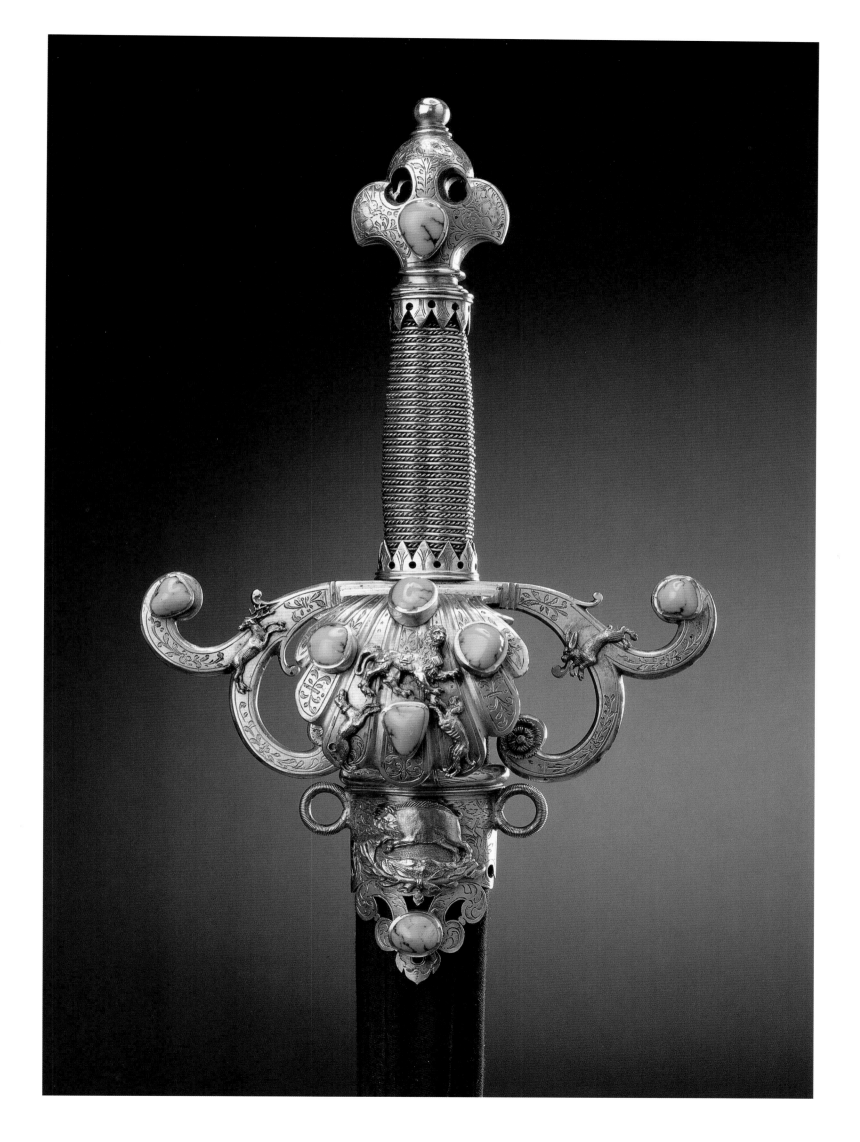

In 15th century Burgundy and, soon after, all over Europe, it became fashionable to use the long hunting sword. These swords were used for hunting boar from the saddle, but could also be used from a kneeling position against a charging boar. Typical features of these weapons are their broad points and the transverse lug.

Toward the middle of the 17th century the characteristic shape of the hunting sword developed. It had a straight blade, sharpened on both sides only at the tip, with cross guard or knuckle bow, a curved or straight parrying guard and a guard plate—also called the shell because of its shape. The hunting sword was also a status symbol. The hunting apprentice received his first one on his release, and hunting and forestry officials could be distinguished by the design of their hunting swords and their manner of wearing them.

Swords with cross guards and slightly curved blades were used by hunters of lower game. The instrument used to cut up the game was worn on the right, and mostly by the youngest hunter, whose junior status required him to undertake this somewhat messy job.

Finally, a curious ritual: three blows with the flat of the hunting sword, administered to the backside of hunters or guests of either sex "who had committed a faux pas in their use of hunting jargon or in some other way: which is a jolly punishment on the noble hunt".

HUNTING WITH FIREARMS

A healthy skepticism, the desire to cling to the familiar, and the hunter's instinct only to harvest that which will be replenished, hampered the development of hunting firearms and caused devotees of the chase to keep the instruments of war at arm's length. Long distance accuracy is a skill entirely in keeping with the ethos of the hunter, and the quick reactions of the marksman are much admired. It is therefore hardly surprising that the esthetic aspect of firearms should have been emphasized, so that many have become representative of the highest levels of the art and culture of their age and equally so, the ordinary weapons of everyday use.

The first firearm used in hunting was the 15th century match-lock gun. This involved a simple method of causing gunpowder to explode, but it was time-consuming and not too successful. Nevertheless, the mechanism continued to be used until the 17th century, although by 1517 the technically more advanced wheel-lock had been invented, probably by a clockmaker. A milled-edged wheel was wound up and then released, so that it struck a piece of iron pyrites, causing sparks to fly into the priming pan, which set light to the fine black priming powder, the flame from which passed through the touch hole to ignite the actual, coarser, powder charge. This weapon, too, was only usable against stationary game.

Guns such as this German match-lock musket (c. 1600), with its richly engraved inlaid work of ivory and mother-of-pearl, simply used gunpowder, consisting of saltpetre, charcoal and sulphur, to create an explosion. They were not only unwieldy, but they could not compete with the bow or the crossbow for effectiveness. These "thunder-guns" posed very little danger to game.

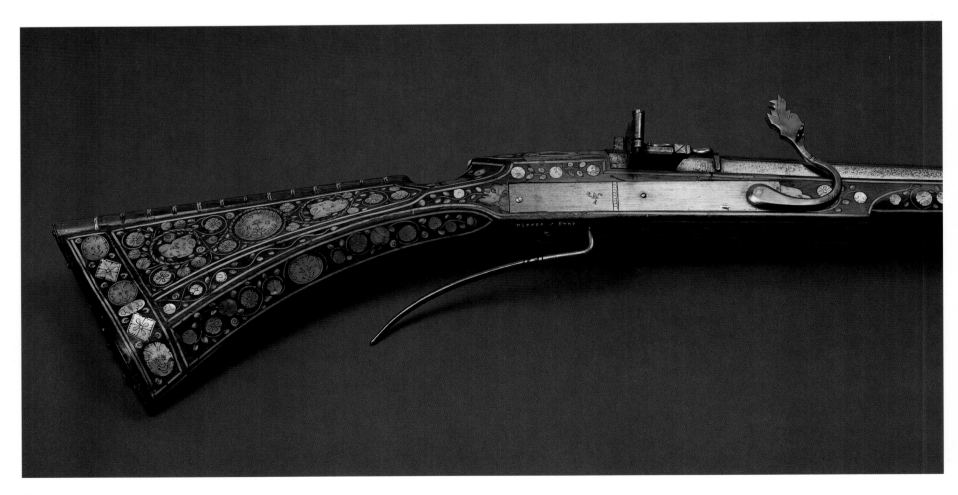

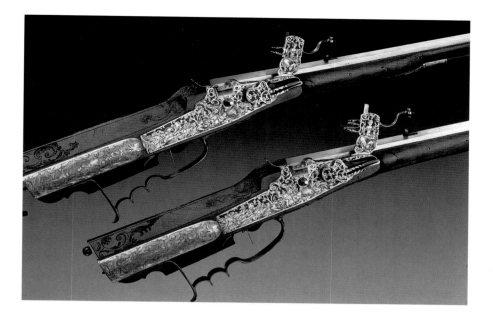

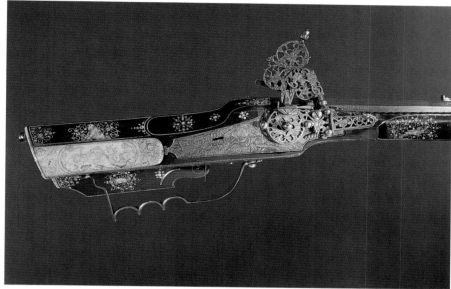

Wheel-lock rifles, Franz Joseph Mahr, Prague, around 1760 (see also page 304).

Wheel-lock rifle, around 1640, inlaid with engraved ivory.

Wheel-lock rifle from Dessau (Saxony), dated 1731, signed Johan Ertman Schinzel.

The invention of the wheel-lock rifle was the turning-point for hunting firearms. Although the mechanism of these rifles was far more complicated than for the match-lock rifle, this disadvantage was outweighed by greater accuracy and penetration. A milled wheel, driven by a powerful spring, spins round, striking a piece of flint or pyrites held by the cock. The resulting sparks cause the very fine priming powder to ignite, which in turn makes the main charge in the barrel explode. The great advantage compared with the match-lock is that the spark is created internally. This design was not ideal either, but at least you no longer needed to carry a smoldering fuse around with you through forests and fields.

Wheel-lock rifle, early 17th century, known as the Tschinke

Anyone new to the subject of powder-flasks will be surprised at how fascinating they are. Scarcely any other utensil has been produced in so many different shapes during the last three hundred years. The majority of these powder-flasks were the property of the nobility, though some were owned by the Emperor or the King. Many of them were pure status symbols, to be displayed at royal hunts; they were exchanged as gifts among the noble lords and ladies and were probably never used, which would explain their excellent state of preservation. For noblemen, weapons and their appurtenances were more than merely attributes appropriate to their noble estate, they were as valuable to them as jewels were to their wives. Elaborately fashioned by renowned master craftsmen, these documents of cultural history reveal their uniqueness only to those who study them carefully.

For centuries hunting was the privilege of the nobility, and it was exercised with a ruthlessness which brought much misery to the rural population. At the same time the hunt ensured a good living for a whole range of craftsmen. Not only bowmakers, winchmakers, swordsmiths, gunmakers, stockmakers, carvers, ironworkers, gold- and silver-smiths, engravers and etchers, but also bagmakers, girdlers, saddlers, strapmakers, hornmakers, trumpetmakers, and blacksmiths were employed in the manufacture of weapons and their accessories, as well as equipment for dogs, horses and riders.

With the invention of the wheel-lock at the beginning of the 16th century, hunting weapons became easier to handle for riders and hunters, and hunting bows and crossbows were used less and less. Pistols and hunting rifles soon became established, although many great hunters rejected them as inappropriate. Before he could actually fire his weapon the hunter had to have all kinds of additional utensils to hand: he needed a bullet pouch and plaster, containers for gunpowder and priming powder, ramrod and wheel-lock spanner (or key), as well as a pricker for cleaning out the touch hole. Other items in the hunter's equipment included game pipes to lure the game, hunting-horns for communication, not forgetting cloths, rags and nets for the battue.

Powder-flasks served to carry the gunpowder safely and, more importantly, kept it dry. The simplest containers were made from ox- or stag's-horn, hence the term "powder-horn". Powder-flasks of artistic merit were produced from 1535. They were used both for the coarse-grained black powder for loading the barrel of the gun, and for the finer powder for the priming of the charge.

This relatively modest 18th century hunting belt with powder-flask seems more suitable for actual use than do the more ornamental versions. The hunting bag with pearl embroidery and gold mounts, the heart-shaped powder-flask and the hunting horn with elaborate relief work (right) are from the 17th century.

◁ This splendid powder-flask with a lid in the shape of an Electoral Coronet and a surrounding boar-hunt motif on the body of the vessel was made in Paris between 1726 and 1730 by Remy de Cuizy for the Bavarian Elector.

There are very few still in existence compared with the great numbers of weapons that have survived.

The great museums in London, Paris, Vienna, Munich, Madrid, Brussels or Copenhagen are generously stocked with weapons, but most have no more than five or six dozen valuable powder-flasks. Old military powder-flasks are more plentiful, but these have only historical value as they were mass-produced and of poor quality. They were larger than those taken on the hunt, owing to the higher consumption of gunpowder.

Flasks for priming-powder contained the much finer powder that was poured into the priming-pan—whether of the match-lock, wheel-lock or flint-lock guns. The oldest containers were small, round and made of metal, generally of fire-gilded or silver-plated brass. Wooden flasks of trapezoid shape, musketeer style, covered in velvet and decorated with brass mountings, were popular, though some people preferred these flasks to be the size of the larger gunpowder type. Iron priming-powder containers in combination with wheel-lock spanners and tools were commonly used from 1550 onwards. They became super-fluous when in the course of the 17th century the wheel-lock was superseded by the flint-lock.

Antique dealers frequently offer for sale as priming-powder flasks small iron pear-shaped containers, inlaid with threads of silver or gold.

Many of these are beautifully carved out of boxwood. All are from the 17th century, and many of them are miniature masterpieces, with motifs drawn from life, but unfortunately they are not powder-flasks, but rather perfume-bottles, snuff-bottles or sand shakers.

Up until 1750, 90 percent of all powder containers were made of one of three materials: ox-horn, stag's-horn or wood. From 1550 to 1650, the wood of fruit-trees was the most popular; then from 1650 it was superseded by walnut, with its attractive grain. Either of these woods might be ebony stained.

Apart from these, every kind of material was used which could be carved and decorated or engraved: gilded bronze and beaten brass, elab-orately carved and turned ivory, pressed leather and incised mother-of-pearl. There are containers made of chamois horn, animal bones, tortoise shell, pumpkins, coconuts and shells. Not even objects as improbable as lobster claws have escaped the attention of ingenious craftsmen.

From 1750 to 1850, powder-flasks for hunting made of copper were industrially produced on a large scale, mostly having the same unimaginative motifs stamped on both sides. Some collectors are keen on these motifs, some having specialized in brass caps and different measuring devices. Well preserved flasks from this period have become very rare today, although they are now being specially made and are widely available again.

Old weapons are easy to date. They have long been collected and great numbers of them exist. Museums and private collectors have an extensive literature at their disposal, city authorities have the records of master craftsmen, royal armouries have inventories, and most weapons are identified, if not by a signature, at least by a master's mark or a monogram.

It is quite a different story when it comes to powder-flasks. Many thousands of them have been lost, partly because of their small size, but no doubt also because they seemed less attractive than the weapons themselves (which would have been useless without them).

One of the earliest powder-horns, dated 1531, is in the Victoria and Albert Museum, and is said to have belonged to Henry VIII. The Wallace Collection owns a powder-horn dated 1532, although the author of the catalogue, Sir James Mann, is of the opinion that the date was added later (Volume II, Arms, p. 596, No. A 1248). Datings from before 1550 are extremely rare and always somewhat questionable. After 1550, dating is more reliable, especially when the inscription is properly integrated into the decoration.

The first powder-horns for hunting were very much alike. They were made from two-point stag antlers and decorated with fire-gilded silver mountings. One particularly valuable specimen is a powder-horn from Augsburg, dated 1545, and the accompanying priming-powder flask is a genuine rarity.

It is very difficult, if not impossible, to date these objects precisely. There are few extant hunt paintings, tapestries or drawings depicting powder containers, although those few are very helpful. Just as in dress fashions, trends are discernible in powder containers, and this makes it easier to establish a chronology. Thus hemispherical priming-powder flasks inlaid with horn are associated with "buffer pistols". The few surviving flasks with silver mountings can be more precisely dated by means of the hallmarks. And there can be no doubt about flasks made of pressed leather in combination with metal wheel-lock spanners—they are certainly old.

The gunpowder that was used consisted of sulphur, saltpeter and charcoal. As one shot required considerable quantities of powder, the gunbarrels were often overloaded, causing numerous accidents.

The use of coarse, granulated powder in handguns was a significant factor in the handling of these weapons. At first two kinds of powder were required for firing: the coarser kind for the main charge, and the finer priming powder to ignite the main charge in the barrel. By about 1700, the gunpowder had been improved to the point where hunters could dispense with the priming powder altogether. Using special tools, a measured sample of powder was ignited and tested for quality.

By the middle of the 19th century the muzzle-loader had been rendered obsolete, and breech-loading weapons with cartridges began to take over, and thanks to their convenient handling properties and their increased safety these modern weapons soon became firmly established. The hunter's powder container thus became superfluous, and was soon consigned to history.

◁ This ivory powder-flask with the carved hunting motif so neatly fitted to the shape of the vessel, was produced in Augsburg in 1690. The medallion in the center shows Endymion leaving for the hunt.

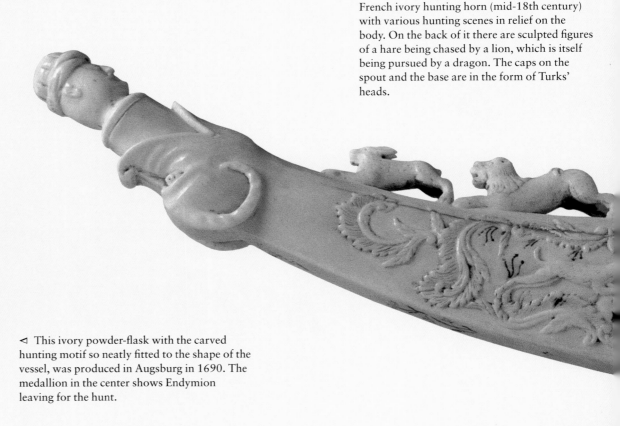

French ivory hunting horn (mid-18th century) with various hunting scenes in relief on the body. On the back of it there are sculpted figures of a hare being chased by a lion, which is itself being pursued by a dragon. The caps on the spout and the base are in the form of Turks' heads.

An unusual powder-flask with richly ornamental decoration from Persia (18th century). The body is of wood with geometrical inlaid work of engraved ivory. The circular cover is surmounted by a turned ivory cap.

This French powder-horn with trapezoid wooden body and lavishly worked metal mountings dates from 1581 (height c. 10 inches (26 cm)).

Powder-flask, wood with intarsia work, German, c. 1580, length c. 10½ inches (27 cm)

Louis XII powder-flask, wood with intarsia work, Augsburg, c. 1640, (signed I. Kilian), height c. 5 inches (12.5 cm)

Powder-flask, bronze, dated 1545, Augsburg, diameter about 2½ inches (6.5 cm)

Powder-flask, stag's horn, German, c. 1790, height 7½ inches (19cm); portrays disembowelling of a deer

Powder-flask, wood, covered with embossed leather, Italian, c. 1580, c. 10 inches (25.5 cm)

Powder-flask, stag's horn, German, c. 1800 (view of the base plate)

BRIEF CHRONOLOGY OF POWDER FLASKS

c. 1550–1850, whole of Europe
Stag's horn, usually cut from two-point antlers, but sometimes from three- or four-point antlers, the so-called "heart horn type"; front carved or engraved, back left plain, with metal trimmings; cap with spring lock; loops for carrying.

c. 1550–1800, whole of Europe
Oxhorn, plain; round, curved body, marbled, bleached, pressed flat, carved, engraved, partially transparent, wooden or horn base; spout with stopper, turned, horn, metal, with or without carrying-loops; from 1700 with powder lock and from 1750 with measuring device.

c. 1550–1620, Southern Germany
Metal, bronze, silver, steel, cast, chased, fire-gilded, a few with clock, sun-dial, compass, all very rare.

c. 1550–1700, Germany
Iron; priming-powder containers with wheel-lock spanner, combined with tools: screwdriver, hammer, ramrod, pricker for cleaning out touch hole, powder measure; partially engraved, some of bronze, fire-gilded, oxhorn with metal mounts; there were conical ones, and round ones, and some with hand-grip in the form of a bird or a heart.

c. 1550–1700, Germany, France, Italy
Wood, covered with velvet, metal mounts; spout with lock; carrying-loops; musketeer shape, trapezoid or cowhorn-shaped, pressed; inlaid with iron, silver or horn, some with belt-hook.

c. 1580–1600, Brunswick, Dresden, Nuremberg
Wood, inlaid with engraved ivory, some with medallions; iron spout with spring lock; two carrying-loops, particularly suitable for "buffer pistols".

c. 1580–1700, Italy
Wood, covered with leather (sometimes embossed), iron mounts, belt-hook; spout with spring lock. Metal, longitudinally ribbed, semi-oval conical form, flat back, with belt-hook; spout with spring lock; carrying-loops.

▷ Gilded silver powder flask from Germany; early 18th century. Depicts hounds attacking an ox, a stag, a wolf and a boar.

Powder-flask, wood with metal mounts, Nuremberg, c. 1600, height c. 8 inches (20 cm)

Powder-flask, ivory, Schwäbisch-Gmünd, c. 1670, "Maucher School", diameter 4 inches (10 cm)

Powder-flask, stag's horn with metal mounts, Schwäbisch Hall, c. 1580, height 10½ inches (26 cm)

Powder-flask, wood with silver mounts, Schwäbisch-Gmünd, c. 1705, diameter c. 5 inches (13 cm)

Powder-flask, stag's horn with carved boar-hunt motif, Bohemia, c. 1820, height c. 7 inches (18 cm)

Powder-flask, wood inlaid with metal threads and engraved ivory, Nuremberg, c. 1570, diameter c. 2½ inches (6.5 cm)

Powder-flask, beaten and engraved metal, French, c. 1570, height 8½ inches (21.5 cm)

Powder-flask, painted coconut mounted with silver, French, c. 1675, diameter 3½ inches (9.3 cm)

Powder-flask, wood with inlaid engraved ivory and metal mounts, Nuremberg, c. 1600, length 24 cm. (9½ inches)

Powder-flask, silver, and attached plate with decorative relief, Nuremberg, c. 1580, height 4½ inches (12 cm)

Powder-flask, bronze, South German, c. 1580, height 4½ inches (12 cm) (spout without closure)

Powder-flask, brass, French, c. 1580, height c. 6 inches (15 cm) (short spout without closure)

c. 1580–1650, Germany
Wood, ring-shaped and bulbous, turned body inlaid with engraved ivory in the shape of blossom, foliage, leaves, fruits; some with medallion, inlaid with silver, many are very richly inlaid with round-shaped ornaments, bright ornamental ivory rings, ivory points, mother-of-pearl, circular strips of ivory; spout of turned ivory or metal; two carrying-loops; smaller versions as priming-powder flasks, larger ones as powder-flasks.

c. 1580–1850, Sudetenland, Hungary
Stag's horn, highly polished all round, Y-shaped, with geometrical ornamentation; since 1950 many imitations have been in circulation.

c. 1600–1750, countries bordering North Sea
Oxhorn, pressed flat, pouring spout carved in shape of fish-head, some inset with eyes of two colors.

c. 1600–1750, Germany, France, Holland
Ivory, round or oval, ring-shaped and bulbous; turned, carved, some with iron mounts; arabesques, hunting motifs, animal motifs, animals entwined or entangled with each other; spout with spring lock; carrying-loops.

c. 1600–1820, Italy, France
Shells, mother-of-pearl, scallop, avalin shells; with brass or silver mounts.

c. 1650–1750, Belgium (Spa), France, Holland
Boxwood; finely carved priming-powder flasks, pear-shape, sometimes in the form of a heart with inlaid silver wire and mother-of-pearl.

c. 1650–1800, Southern Germany, Austria, Italy
Ibex horn, body left plain; with stopper, sometimes carved, and metal mounts; wheel-lock spanner; a few examples are made of chamois horn.

c. 1650–1706, Schwäbisch Gmünd, Augsburg, Nuremberg
Wood or ivory, ring-shaped and bulbous with metal mounts; carved; favorite subjects: animals entwined and entangled together, making optimum use of the body of the vessel, pack of dogs tracking down quarry; "Maucher School" is predominant (surrounding Johann Michael Maucher and his sons); spout with spring lock; carrying-loops.

c. 1650–1800, Scandinavia
Oxhorn, natural shape using round cross-section, closely carved, Christian motifs, mostly with text and name of owner, dated.

c. 1680–1850, Holland, England, France
Tortoiseshell, with metal mounting; spout; carrying-loops.

c. 1700–1750, Germany
Oxhorn, pressed flat, with erotic engravings, for the hunting bag; without carrying-loops.

c. 1720–1770, France, Germany
Animal bones, pumpkin, coconut, cowhorn; engraved with hunting scenes, a few with miniature paintings.

c. 1750–1820, France
"Galuchat" leather, wood, covered with ray skin.

c. 1750–1820, countries bordering the North Sea
Lobster claws, with pewter or brass mountings.

c. 1750–1850, France (Dieppe), Germany (Erbach), Poland
Ivory, boar's tooth; always very finely carved; never used for the hunt, produced purely for decorative purposes or as gifts; favorite subjects: departure for the hunt, St Hubert, boar-hunt, wolf-hunt.

c. 1750–1880, England, France, Germany
Copper, beaten; spout with brass closure device including spring lock or powder measure.

c. 1800–1840, France
Koroso, palm fruit from French Guyana; the hard shell was imported for the manufacture of buttons.

c. 1800–1840, England, Germany
Glass, engraved, for the hunting bag; with stopper or silver spring lock.

c. 1800–1850, England, France, Germany, Poland
Stag's horn, two-point antlers with finely carved, highly polished hunting scenes, remainder plain (often erroneously taken to be ivory inlay); pouring spout turned from ivory, with stopper or metal spout with measure.

c. 1890–1930, Germany, Italy
Animal bones, mostly from hip of mule and shoulder of ox; mass-produced for purely decorative purposes; easy to recognize, as they are mainly designed to stand up; the spout is always lathe-turned, without lock; no metal mountings apart from loops; engravings are stained black; motifs: Greek, mythological, or hunting scenes showing foot-soldiers without firearms, acanthus leaves above and below; some were popular with rifle clubs.

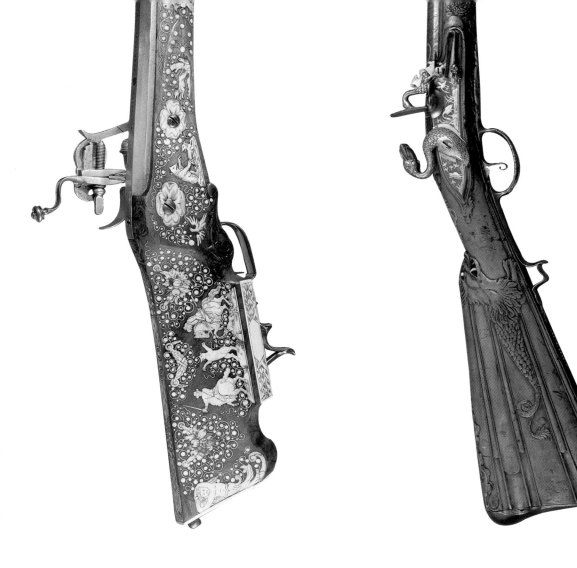

△ left: Wheel-lock rifle, Dresden, signed and dated on the barrel: Gottfried Hahn 1680
center: Flint-lock gun, Netherlands, around 1680.
right: Ladies' flint-lock gun, Germany, around 1750.

◁ Wheel-lock rifle, Franz Joseph Mahr, Prague, around 1760; detail of the engraved iron lock showing Diana, goddess of hunting, seated on a throne, with dog.

▷ Set of flint-lock guns by J. G. Kolb, Suhl, 1747. The details of the engraved iron decoration indicate that this was a lady's weapon.

Game birds could only be shot on the ground, because if the gun were raised the powder would be sure to spill out of the pan. As late as 1719, in his book "The Complete German Hunter", Hanns Friedrich Baron von Fleming, Minister of Forests and Game in Electoral Saxony, proclaimed that "the invention of this harmful gunpowder had been inspired by the Devil to bring about the downfall of all living creatures, whether or not endowed with reason. He who shoots with a rifle is no hunter but merely a marksman..." The true horse-riding hunters also rejected powder and shot, as they feared that the noise and the smell would frighten off the game.

The invention of the snaphaunce lock at the end of the 16th century caused a sensation, and led, after technical improvements, to the development of the classical flint-lock in the 17th century. The ignition speed was considerably increased, and a tumbler kept the cover on the pan containing the priming powder until the cock was released. It was now possible to shoot at birds in flight, at fleeing game, on horseback and even in wind and rain. Loading, however, was still complicated. The exact amount of powder had to be poured from the powder-flask into the barrel, a piece of felt was pushed down with the ramrod, then the ball was

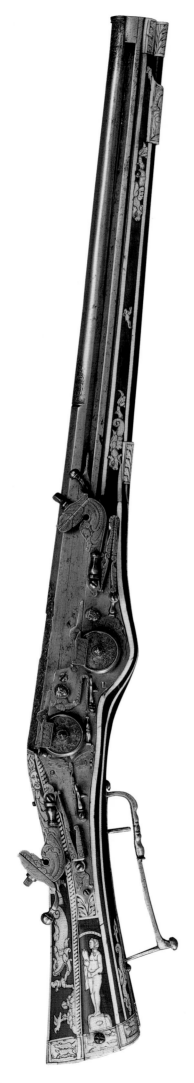

All-purpose set of tools for preparing a weapon for firing, German, 18th century.

◁ Wheel-lock rifle, early 17th century.

put in and pressed down. The priming powder was poured into the pan and the cock brought under tension. The detonation often produced so much smoke that it was hard to tell whether one had hit the target. Those who could afford it later used double-barreled guns, or increased their rate of fire by having a number of weapons with them, which a servant would prepare for firing.

The invention of percussion ignition at the beginning of the 19th century proved a decisive step. The key feature was a little thimble-shaped copper cap, known as the percussion cap, attached to the hollow nipple and filled with an explosive mixture of potassium chlorate and mercury fulminate. The cock was replaced by a hammer, which hit the percussion cap, thereby causing ignition. Many fine flint-locks were converted to percussion and were lost to posterity.

18th century airguns are a hunting curiosity. By means of a handpump, air was compressed to a pressure of 40 atmospheres in a small pressurized air container attached to the weapon. 20 shots could then be fired with no kick, noise or smoke.

The first breech-loader, built in the year 1835 by Lefaucheux, by no means meant the end of the muzzle-loader, the latter persisting right up to the beginning of the 20th century. In principle,

gunpowder weapons can be divided into two groups: the rifle, so-called because of its rifled barrel, for shooting bullets, and the shotgun, with its smooth barrel, for firing shot. Whereas until the age of the flint-lock, sportsmen had to make do with heavy, usually octagonal, bored steel barrels, the twilight of the age of black powder ushered in the lighter barrel of Damascus steel, invented in Liège. Three layers of iron and steel bands were wrapped around a mandril of toughened steel and welded together in the furnace. After browning, the surface was given beautiful patterns by variation in texture and coloring, such as the fine rose damask or the plainer 'strip' damask.

For over four centuries craftsmen created works of art of rare beauty, and it is hardly surprising that many of the most exquisite weapons were not used for hunting at all, but for display in cabinets.

However good the weapon, one still needed to be able to shoot. For those deficient in this area Heinrich Wilhelm Döbel had the following advice in his "Hunting Practices" (1746): "... first charge the barrel with powder, then catch a young Grass Snake and put it into the barrel, leave it in there for a few hours and then fire it at an oak tree. It will not be long before it is dead."

The hunter on horseback armed with a pistol had to make every effort to ride as close as possible to his quarry. Once he had reached it he drew his weapon and fired at point-blank range, aiming from above. The wheel-lock pistol pictured here was manufactured in Nuremberg in the late 16th century.

The most important accessories to old handheld firearms were powder-flasks and powder-horns. These rivalled the weapons themselves in their elaborate ornamentation, and the variety of materials used were even superior. This brass-gilded powder-flask dates from the late 16th century.

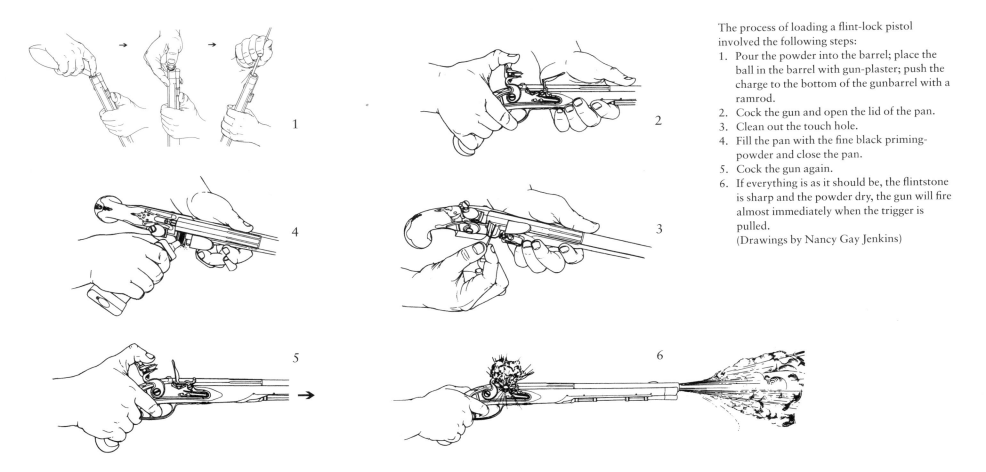

The process of loading a flint-lock pistol involved the following steps:

1. Pour the powder into the barrel; place the ball in the barrel with gun-plaster; push the charge to the bottom of the gunbarrel with a ramrod.
2. Cock the gun and open the lid of the pan.
3. Clean out the touch hole.
4. Fill the pan with the fine black priming-powder and close the pan.
5. Cock the gun again.
6. If everything is as it should be, the flintstone is sharp and the powder dry, the gun will fire almost immediately when the trigger is pulled.

(Drawings by Nancy Gay Jenkins)

A pair of wheel-lock pistols, early 16th century. The enlarged butts ensured that these weapons were well balanced.

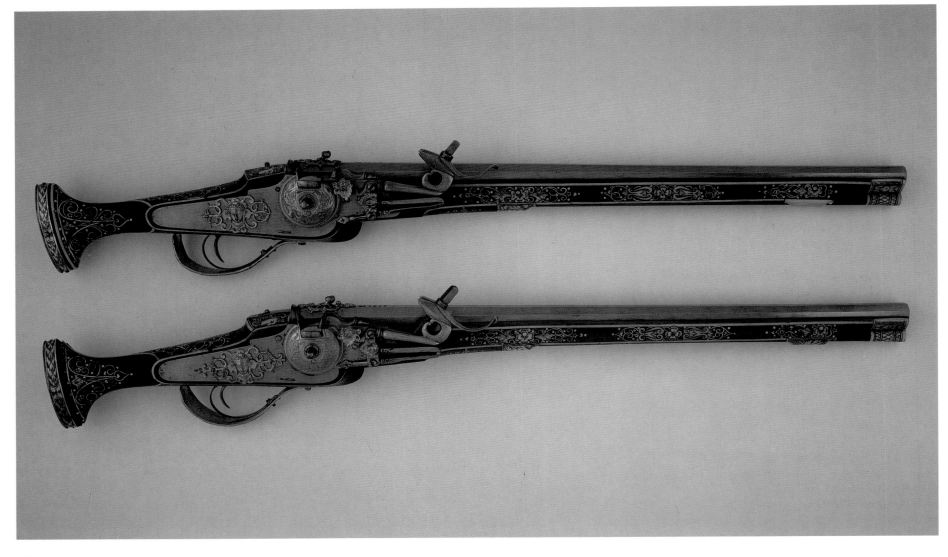

This valuable set of flint-lock firearms from 1741 by the gunmaker Johann Christoph Stockmar of Suhl have all the characteristics of this master craftsman: the finest wood, the discreet deer's tooth mounting, the filigree silverwork and the gilded backsight in the shape of a miniature stag on the barrel of the rifle. Aristocratic hunters liked to act as patrons of expensive sets of weapons such as this, which could consist of as many as 24 guns and pistols, all of which may well have been used during the course of a hunt.

Illustrations to pages 310/311:
A pair of wheel-lock guns belonging to Duke Johann Georg IV of Saxony, with work by Christian Herold, Dresden, 1669. The lavish ornamentation of the weapons called for the most varied craft skills, as can be seen from the detail of one of the two locks.

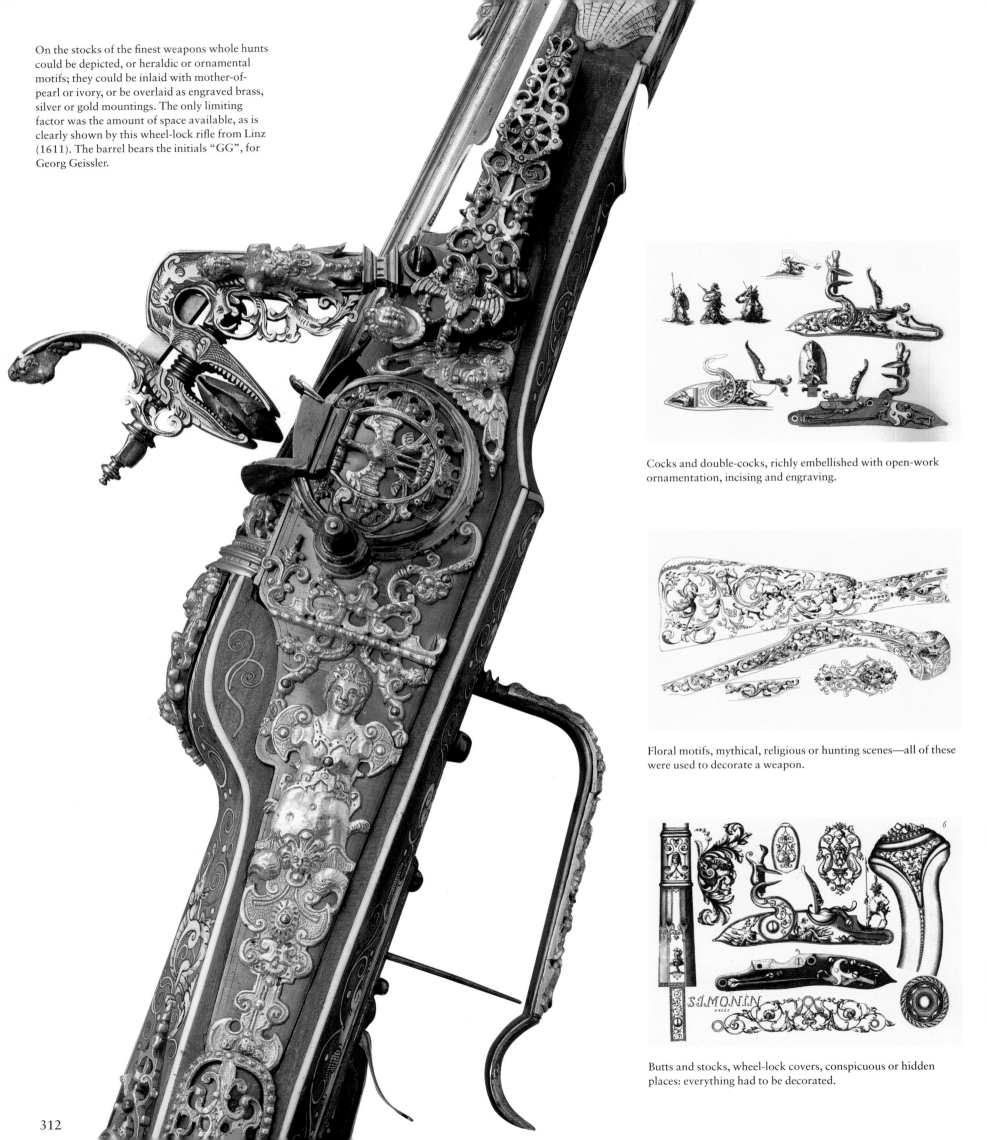

On the stocks of the finest weapons whole hunts could be depicted, or heraldic or ornamental motifs; they could be inlaid with mother-of-pearl or ivory, or be overlaid as engraved brass, silver or gold mountings. The only limiting factor was the amount of space available, as is clearly shown by this wheel-lock rifle from Linz (1611). The barrel bears the initials "GG", for Georg Geissler.

Cocks and double-cocks, richly embellished with open-work ornamentation, incising and engraving.

Floral motifs, mythical, religious or hunting scenes—all of these were used to decorate a weapon.

Butts and stocks, wheel-lock covers, conspicuous or hidden places: everything had to be decorated.

A splendid pair of lavishly worked stirrups, made by Daniel Kellerthaler in Dresden around 1615/1618. A royal parforce hunt had to be resplendent down to the last detail.

The filigree, detailed decoration of this wheel-lock rifle from the 17th century has some surprises in store when figures, fabulous beasts and items of weaponry suddenly emerge out of what at first sight looks like pure ornamentation.

TARGETS

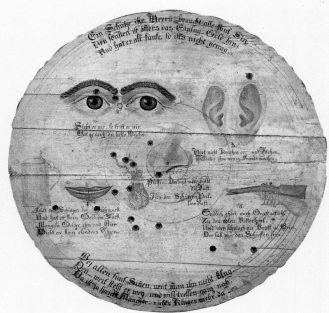

▷ Target in honor of Karl IV Philipp Theodor, Elector of the Palatinate and Bavaria, South German, 1749.

▷▷ "The Five Senses of the Marksman" (Sebastian Wohlmuth), South German, around 1830.

▷ "Resting after the Deer-Hunt", South German, 1840

▷▷ Commemorative target for the marriage of Crown Prince Maximilian of Bavaria and Princess Marie of Prussia (J. Kleininger, Schwabach), South German, 1842.

▷ Diana at Rest, South German, second half of 18th century.

▷▷ Decorative target, South German, around 1860.

◁ ◁ Commemorative target for the German schützenfest (rifle-club festival) in Frankfurt, South German, 1862.

◁ Commemorative target for the re-introduction of the goose shoot, Trostberg, October 21, 1868.

◁ ◁ Target in honor of the Sedan Shooting Festival, Munich, 1875.

◁ Target of the Trostberg rifle club in honor of the oldest marksman F. Sonnenleitner, Trostberg, 1899.

◁ ◁ "Three hares, three ears, and yet each has two", humorous target, South German, 19th century.

◁ Target in honour of the Wood Turners' Shooting Festival, Schliersee, 1908.

315

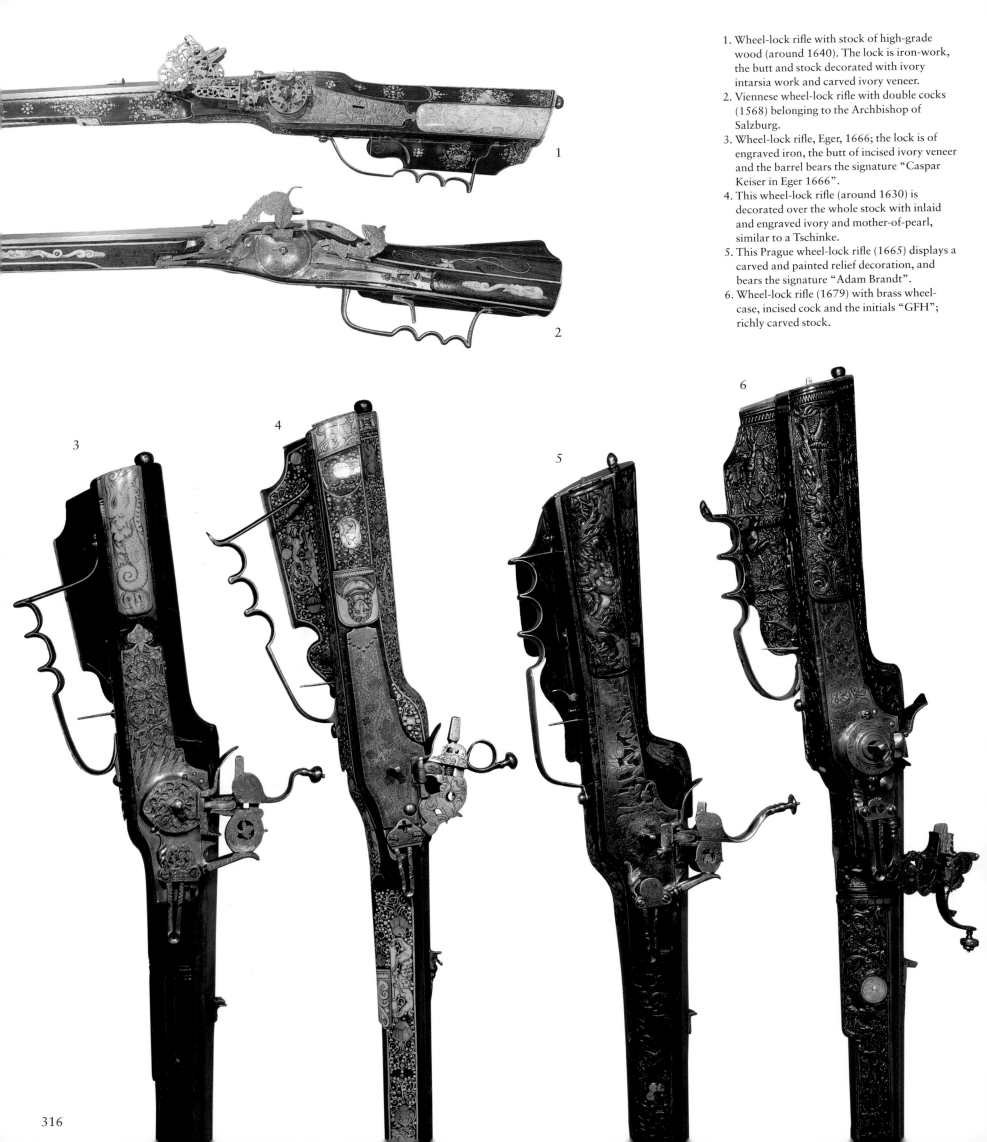

1. Wheel-lock rifle with stock of high-grade wood (around 1640). The lock is iron-work, the butt and stock decorated with ivory intarsia work and carved ivory veneer.
2. Viennese wheel-lock rifle with double cocks (1568) belonging to the Archbishop of Salzburg.
3. Wheel-lock rifle, Eger, 1666; the lock is of engraved iron, the butt of incised ivory veneer and the barrel bears the signature "Caspar Keiser in Eger 1666".
4. This wheel-lock rifle (around 1630) is decorated over the whole stock with inlaid and engraved ivory and mother-of-pearl, similar to a Tschinke.
5. This Prague wheel-lock rifle (1665) displays a carved and painted relief decoration, and bears the signature "Adam Brandt".
6. Wheel-lock rifle (1679) with brass wheel-case, incised cock and the initials "GFH"; richly carved stock.

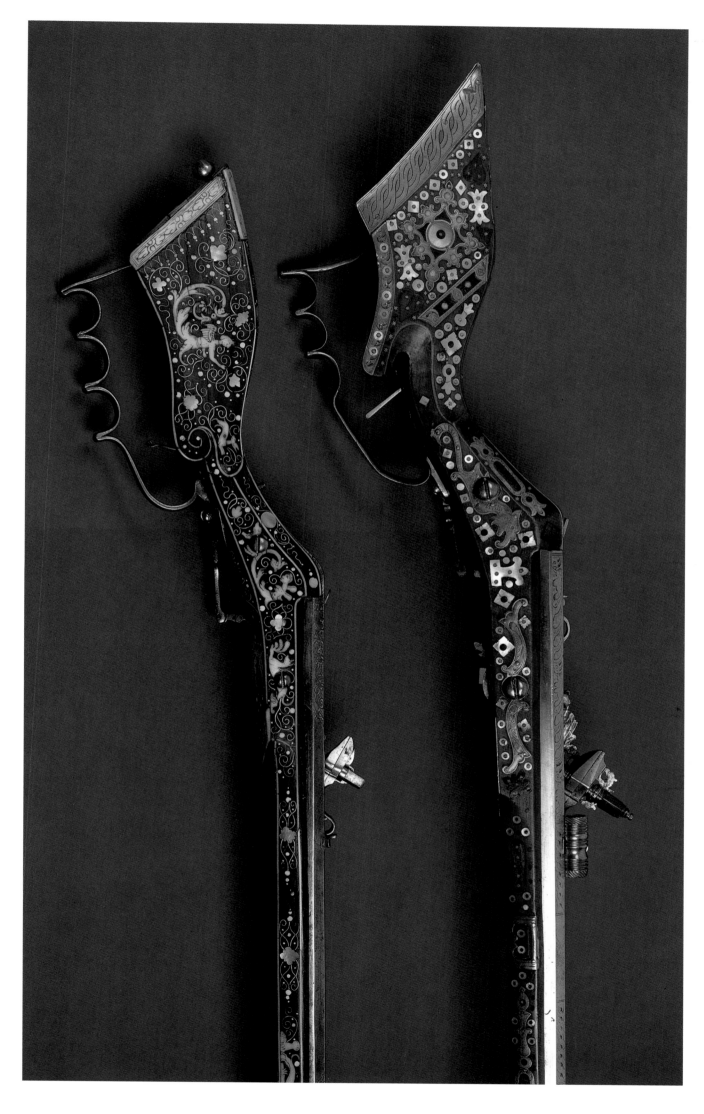

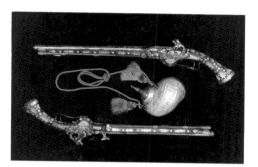

Pistol set from Tsarist Russia.

The left one of these two wheel-lock Tschinke rifles (around 1620) is a lady's gun. It is not only daintier, but the whole stock is covered with a particularly delicate filigree of engraved ivory inlays. The term "Tschinke" is said to be derived from the famous gunbarrels forged in Teschen, in Silesia.

The front of this ivory powder-flask with clock shows a relief of a lion hunt. (South German, early 17th century)

Richly embellished wheel-lock pistols with butts
in the shape of figures, made by Wolf Danner,
Nuremberg, around 1550.

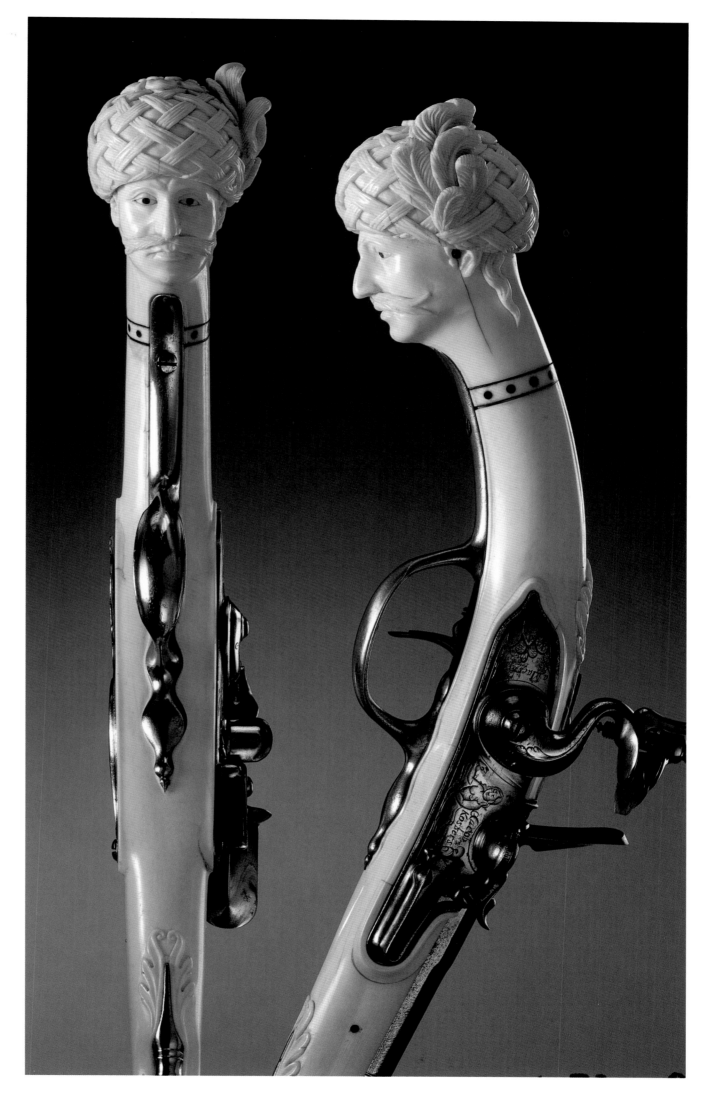

Flint-lock pistols belonging to Augustus the Strong. The elegant figured butt is the work of Jacob Kosters, Maastricht, 1660.

GAME AND HUNTING

KURT G. BLÜCHEL

GAME AND HUNTING

VOLUME 2

KÖNEMANN

© 1997 Könemann Verlagsgesellschaft mbH
Bonner Straße 126
D – 50968 Köln

Design: Peter Feierabend
Coordination: Birgit Beyer, Peter Feierabend
Editing: Martina Schlagenhaufer, Sylvia Hecken
Assistants: Karl Georg Cadenbach, Lydia Wegener
Translation from
the German: Christine Bainbridge, Clive Norris,
                         Martin Walters, Gordon Wells for Hart McLeod, Cambridge
Copy-editing: Martin Walters for Hart McLeod, Cambridge
Typesetting: Goodfellow & Egan, Cambridge
Production manager: Detlev Schaper
Picture research: Verlags-Service K. G. Hütten
Reproductions: Imago Publishing Limited, Thame

Printed and bound by: Neue Stalling, Oldenburg

Printed in Germany
ISBN 3-89508-471-9

Contents

HUNTING—FROM ANIMALS TO MAN

SIGRID SCHWENK

It is a legitimate question to ask if hunting, so intimately linked as it is to the natural world, has anything whatsoever to do with culture. Does claiming that there is a link between hunting and culture fabricate relationships which distort the essence of hunting? In the simplest terms, culture may be considered as everything which is alien to animals, and the uniquely human faculty of purposeful thought is one distinctive feature of "culture".
No animal has yet been shown to be sufficiently "intelligent" to give an idea a form permanent enough to outlive it, by means of a creative act.
Humans reached one of the high points in their development into cultural beings when they became capable of thinking about themselves and conceptualising an image of themselves, such as the creative act that produced the self-portrait by François Deportes, Louis XIV's hunt painter.
Placing hunting at the very start of the process of the birth of culture does nothing to distort this historical development.

If we view hunting as something which is specifically human, thus clearly differentiating it from the pursuit of animals by other animals, the currently widely accepted definition of hunting requires the simultaneous use of tools, such as weapons, traps or other catching devices. Animals do not use tools in this sense, because, by their very nature, tools presuppose the deliberate modification of an object that occurs in nature, a stone, a piece of bone or wood. This action must be purposefully directed into the future and must show signs of intention to accomplish something using the modified object.

One logical consequence of planned, intentional development is the striving for improvement, and a willingness to replace a conventional tool by another improved implement is therefore a further aspect of hunting. Only if these prerequisites are met can we properly talk of "using tools". Otherwise tools are simply makeshift contrivances of the sort used by many an animal.

Because of the small number of random finds dating from the time of prehistoric humans, we will probably never be able to reconstruct the beginnings of cultural activity with any certainty, and the long period during which our ancient ancestors remained gatherers and scavengers must be viewed as a pre-cultural phase in their development. From the viewpoint of the history of civilization, the developmental step that qualified these ancestors as human was only completed once they satisfied the criteria discussed above.

Even though, on the basis of prehistoric finds, we can now trace their development back millions of years earlier than was possible even half a century ago, this has not undermined the validity of the fact that the first humans were hunters, or that hunting is as old as the human species. Precisely when and over what period of time humans came to be cultural beings is a question that remains unanswered for the time being.

Two major achievements were crucial for the development of technology as an important aspect of our culture: the realization that a flint could be transformed into a tool by deliberately napping it, and that fire could be created, maintained and exploited. Both these steps can be reliably traced back to prehistoric times. The question of the extent to which less durable materials such as wood and bone were also used cannot be answered with such certainty. However, it is clear that the objective of technology from the outset was to improve the productiveness of hunting and also its domestic usefulness. The development of technology was geared toward perfecting hunting implements in order to improve the chance of success when hunting wild animals, thereby creating a reliable, lasting basis for supplying food and obtaining important raw materials, such as bone and animal hides.

Technical progress was therefore largely determined by the demands of the hunt. One need only consider the variety of flint tools, ranging from the hand-ax and arrowheads through to scrapers,

Supporters of hunting have always stressed its positive effects on character traits such as patience, persistence, courage and fast reactions.

knives, borers, chisels and spearheads, or the large number of bone tools, such as picks, shovels, awls, needles or harpoons, to glimpse a world which was shaped by hunting implements and hand tools for dealing with game. This culture was molded by hunters. Animal skins were just as indispensable for clothing, protection against cold, building shelter or for camp bedding as were animal stomachs and bladders for carrying liquids. Hand-held weapons probably predominated initially: hewn wooden lances which were later made more effective by attaching a flint head, striking weapons, cudgels and axes, and this arsenal was soon supplemented by thrown weapons such as spears and spear throwers. Bone or stone fish hooks are also of great antiquity. If it were not for all these creative achievements of the human brain it would be hard to conceive of culture.

Hunting activities were not merely the cradle of economics and technology—they initially determined every aspect of life. Here we can only give a few pointers, but they are crucial to understanding the full extent of the cultural importance of hunting.

The first consideration is the impact of hunting practices on the social system. The earliest hunting methods, identified by silent witnesses from a remote past, and making allowance for environmental conditions, all presuppose that hunting was a communal activity. Hunting carried out by individuals certainly cannot be ignored completely but can probably be regarded as an exceptional occurrence. The maintenance of the entire group depended on joint action during the hunt. Such group hunting could not have been successful without a clearly defined hierarchy and clearly allocated duties within the group. Success, without which there was little prospect of survival, would have been uncertain if subordinates did not take orders, and if tasks were not clearly allocated. This encouraged the establishment of a firm social order which must have had an impact on the status of an individual and on his importance in the interlocking system of households.

This also brings us to the beginnings of law. Obviously, there was no hunting law in the modern sense of the term, and it would undeniably be misleading to postulate an "unrestricted right to catch animals" at this time. Nevertheless, significant precursors to the general development of laws can be regarded as closely linked to the hunting-oriented existence of our ancient predecessors. These precursors relate primarily to problems of ownership and distribution. Game that was killed by joint effort was distributed in accordance with fixed rules. We know that this remains true, even in modern times, among all those tribes where hunting forms the basis of obtaining food. Accordingly, distribution favored the leaders of the group and those who had made

a decisive contribution toward hunting success rather than other individuals. Because it was probably seldom possible to determine who, in the final analysis, was responsible for the death of an animal, this decision may have been made much simpler by applying an owner's mark to hunting implements. This might explain certain markings on arrows and throwing spears that have survived: they would make it apparent who fired the fatal arrow or delivered the decisive blow.

Hunting in a group must have encouraged language, because it is virtually impossible to imagine social hunting without verbal communication between the participants. We know little about the beginnings of language but the necessity of the hunt must have provided an additional impetus toward its development.

Wherever we look there is always a hunting link. The path from early bone whistles, which were no doubt used during hunting, leads us to pipes made of bird bones and thus to the beginnings of music. Animal depictions in the form of carved drawings, cave and rock-paintings which we are used to looking at from an artistic point of view probably had a highly ritual significance. Their purpose was to ensure successful hunting or to ward off the vengeance of a slain animal's spirit. Necklaces and bracelets strung with bears' teeth are among the earliest items of adornment and items of hide or feathers which have been lost for ever no doubt served the same purpose.

These early humans, who differed from animals essentially in terms of what we now regard as culture, were hunters. Unlike animals, they were aware of the finite nature of their own lives and the inevitability of death—early records of objects included in burials prove this—and their remembrance of things past constituted an early form of historical awareness. This phase of human culture

In addition, hunting is said to promote physical toughness by teaching one to brave the inclemency of the weather.

which was molded by hunting only came to an end some 12,000 years ago.

With the emergence of cattle breeding, even more so than arable farming, economic life took a new direction in which hunting no longer had any appreciable importance. This transition from hunting to keeping domestic animals, and the associated reorientation of all areas of life, was as decisive a step in human development as the discovery of flint tools or fire in the history of civilization, a fact often not stressed sufficiently. We can assess precisely how drastic this change-over was for all those affected by such momentous change by examining bone material from the many trash piles that have been found and analyzed. These important material finds initially contain only the bones of wild animals, but at a certain point in time these bones are abruptly replaced by bones of domestic animals. The proportion of wild animal bones drops to roughly 1–2 percent by the end of the Neolithic Period (about 2200 B.C. in Europe), mirroring the sudden transformation of human culture.

This was a point in time which is extremely important in the history of hunting—namely the time when human hunting activity changed from being a vital necessity to a voluntary act performed for the enjoyment of the event in its own right. The oldest hunting author known to us, Xenophon, who wrote in the early fourth century B.C. states, in his book entitled "Kynegetikos": "I exhort youth not to neglect hunting since it will make them proficient for war and for everything

else that necessarily leads towards thinking, speaking and acting correctly." His words make it obvious that hunting has been elevated into a means of character training.

Over the next two thousand years, or more precisely up until the end of the 18th century, every author who examined hunting from a moral viewpoint gave their verdict on this question. Naturally, those who justified hunting outnumbered those who condemned it. To assert that hunting strengthened and toughened people, that it demanded discipline, discretion, courage and fast, well-considered reactions became one of the standard phrases in eulogies. Hunting was in the state's interest because it produced strong men suited for service in the field, able to cope with physical exertion and who were unaffected by the inclemency of the weather at a time when combat was still a hand-to-hand affair. Critics, on the other hand, claimed that hunting had a coarsening effect and, when practiced to excess, brought with it disadvantages for people. The main point to grasp here is that comments, whether in favor or against, always related to people and their organizational structures, such as the state, but never extended any further to include nature, the environment or animals.

The major turning point in the history of hunting is characterized by the emergence of three new factors representing a break with ancient times and which are of differing importance: firstly the confinement of hunting activities to a socially specific minority of the total population; secondly a widespread decline in the principle of inheritance; and thirdly the dependence of hunting ethics on the particular laws that prevailed at the time. The effect of these factors continues into present day times. This observation takes us up to that part of the period of the history of hunting that stretches from ancient times right up to the end of the 18th century. During the long period starting from highly advanced civilizations in the Middle East until the present, various social groups engaged in hunting to the exclusion of third parties: royal households with their retinues of attendants, the higher or lesser nobility, hunting enthusiasts prepared to pay for their pastime through to politically reliable cadres—just to mention a few examples. They all determined and continue to determine the cultural image of hunting by imposing their own cultural connotations.

Where ideological considerations displaced economic considerations, the hunting bag became insignificant and incidental. Despite this, hunting activities demanded ever increasing expenditure.

The lion hunts of Assyrian and Babylonian kings in Mesopotamia, the hare coursing of Celtic knights, hunting individual quarry animals by riding to huge packs of hounds, falconry and

The responsible hunter is first and foremost a person who looks after the game population in his hunting ground or shoot and can also make an important contribution toward preventing damage to woodland and agricultural land.

"holding" hunts requiring huge amounts of human and material resources—they all demanded vast financial investment which only a minority could afford. The development of hunting technology itself largely excluded the possibility of the "common man's" involvement in hunting.

On the other hand, major cultural accomplishments are not feasible without the deployment of correspondingly lavish resources. If it were not for such expenditure, we would not have the many products of art which record hunting events, or baroque hunting lodges which were built for the enjoyment of those who, as well as being passionately devoted to hunting, also wanted to see this affection expressed in the culture of their day, which was decisively molded by hunting. There are many examples of this in literature, poetry, art, music, opera, theater and, not least, in the handcrafted objects used for hunting, artistically decorated weapons, the work of silversmiths and the magnificent hunting uniforms produced by tailors at courts. Hunting finds its expression as a cultural phenomenon in the full diversity of artistic achievements that grew from hunting, and not just during the final phase of "holding" hunts. None of the objects cited above would ever have seen the light of day if hunting had been no more than a cheerless trade. The fact that advocates of hunting wanted it to be perceived as an art does, therefore, have a deeper significance.

We are now living in the middle of the next phase in the development of hunting culture, and are witnessing a change in human consciousness. The starting point for this change was the discovery of nature in all its beauty, as well as an exciting awareness of a new force which springs from nature regardless whether it is experienced with the emotional urgency of the Enlightenment, the carefree cheerfulness of a young generation that throws out all old traditions, or restrained introspectiveness. Everything in the past, even hunting, is projected into an environment that is determined by nature.

A second step is also taking place: the discovery of animals as living beings. Animals are no longer regarded as creatures with no souls which humans —the crown of creation—can use as they see fit; the theory of evolution has elevated animals to the status of close relatives (unfortunately, an opposite extreme will soon be reached due to excessive misguided sentimentality toward animals, an attitude which serves them equally ill). A comprehensive change of position is taking place. The latest phase of hunting history which is characterized by this change will not be completed in the near future and opinions still differ for the time being.

The progression from inanimate matter to life was a crucial event in the history of the earth which

The life or death importance of success and the inadequacy of their equipment led the first hunters to hunt in groups — this was fortunate because it endowed them with some of the social attitudes on which part of our modern ability to co-exist with each other is still based. In contrast, the modern hunter can allow himself the luxury of deerstalking on his own.

still has not yet been fully explained. The progression from animal to human is in some ways no less mysterious. Nobody has yet proved that any animal possesses even the rudiments of anything which is specifically human—a feeling for law and justice, conscience, duty, responsibility, compassion, altruism, solace, a sense of history, awareness of death and, above all, belief in God.

This is the situation in which the hunter finds himself when the question of hunting as a cultural phenomenon in modern times has to be answered. We view hunting as something which is specifically human. This means that we assume responsibility for it, a burden which only we humans have to bear. This is reflected, at least incipiently, in the hunting literature of the last hundred years, which has placed increasing importance on the conservation of game and habitats and on ethics. Ethical considerations relating to hunting would have had a place in both the previous phases of the development of hunting culture, not just among the hunting moralists of the 16th and 17th centuries.

Responsible hunting has many links to our cultural life, such as the fundamental duty to protect animals and species and to help prevent damage to woodlands and agricultural land, the all too rarely emphasized economic importance of hunting and its many spin-offs, the impact of hunting on literature and art and, not least, the significance of hunting in the development of law.

HUNTERS' TALES

Hunters' tales are an inextricable component of hunting. Wherever two hunters gather, sooner or later they are bound to discuss their first hunting experiences, and we can confidently assume that this was already happening long before the first accounts were set down in writing. Whereas this rich oral story-telling tradition is inevitably linked with romantic notions of good friends around the camp fire, written stories are intended more for the solitary edification of individuals. We can identify with the hunter who writes, who understands the tension just before the shot is fired and we appreciate the inclemency of the weather as we lounge in our comfortable armchairs and just sit back—an invitation surely not to be missed.

On the Polders
Friedrich Karl von Eggeling

Alert pink-footed geese

The beam of the Kloosterzande lighthouse swings around the estuary harbor: a short flash, then a long flash and another long flash. A heavy truck rumbles along the road from Antwerp, brakes and comes to a halt.

I am sitting in a deep gulley in the middle of the Polder, up to my knees in water and swathed in my waterproof woolen coat. A morning breeze is blowing in off the sea. Last year's dry dead grass is rustling and the willow bush whispers. The rye has been painted by the night frost and gleams like silver in the light of the setting crescent moon. As the first dawn light breaks I can hear the call of partridge somewhere far out on the marsh, the high-pitched call of the lapwings and the sound of mallard. Still plenty of time: geese are late risers!

I count my cartridges, peer through the binoculars to check that the wooden decoys set out on the crop have not blown over, and think about this and that to distract myself. I am trembling with tension, excitement, expectancy and cold.

Things stir in the village in front of the dyke, lights are switched on and I can hear voices and noises carried on the wind. Things are also stirring among the birds, I hear whirring wings, the calls of pintail, a snipe chattering and a hare

Graylag geese in flight

which looks huge silhouetted against the horizon hops by and startles me.

I'm ready for them!

Suddenly I am warm, almost boiling; somewhere in the distance behind a dyke I hear the quick, breathless laughter-like calls of the first white-fronted geese. Everything happens so fast that I only come to my senses once it is all over: a sudden loud whistling noise from the darker part of the sky, a goose call right in front of me and above me, a whirring of wing feathers as they land. I snatch up my gun, a right and left from a semi-prone position as the birds almost hang in the air, two dark bodies crash down, one in front of me, the other close to me in the gulley with a splash.

There is no time to reflect, that has to wait until later, drinking tea by the fire and having a smoke. The sky is full of geese, large and small, huge flights, hundreds and thousands and the air is thick with their calls. They fly high and low in V-shaped formations on their long journey inland. The geese that will settle here on the Polder are disorganized and fly low. They float back and forth, climbing and swooping, wheeling in wide circles, climb again, skim across the water and return. I have already picked up the two geese and

covered them with my coat. I move a short distance to the left almost as far as the willow bush which gives me cover but also restricts my field of view. Cover is more important, the be-all and end-all of wildfowling in the early dawn light. Better to miss a flight than be spotted by ten flights while they are still well out of range. Then they break off their descent, climb and are much too high and far away within seconds.

My bush is good, my gray jacket and green waders are well camouflaged and I get shots off again and again, leap out of the gulley, pick up the shot geese, place them beside me under the coat and crouch down again just above the water so that they cannot see my pale face as yet another flight approaches. I peek up from underneath the brim of my hat and only shoulder the gun once I can see whether the birds have dark stripes across their chests (this means they are old birds) or whether the chest is still white (then they are this year's birds), and when they are close enough to shoot, only then do I jump to my feet or flip over on my back and raise my gun. In a fraction of a second I have to pick out the target and nerves, hand and eye must be perfectly coordinated. Of course, I'm not always successful, I pull many a

shot, fail to give the geese enough lead, rush my shot, or miss with one or both barrels. It is a cure for arrogance and, anyway, wildfowling would not be the same if one never missed. It is sometimes nice to remember even complete misses, admittedly with a suppressed feeling of rage.

The action continues until it gets light, the morning flight subsides and I find time to collect my thoughts. I see the yellowhammer in the willow bush, hear the larks floating over the field —the first harbingers of spring, even in January.

I look at my watch and realize that scarcely an hour has passed. How eventful, how filled with tense excitement and exertion this hour was. It only finished a while ago but is already in the distant past. If it were not for the nine large grayish-white birds lying under my coat, the old ones with dark stripes across their chest and the young ones with creamish white chests, I could be convinced that it had all been just a dream.

Bagging a bird is often just a moment, a brief instant, but shooting is much more. It is the anticipation of pleasure, expectancy and the journey, the friends, fire in the hearth and a mug of hot tea clasped between fingers still stiff with cold. Shooting is times of remembrance and reflection.

Graylag geese fly elsewhere once a feeding place has been exhausted.

15

A WOOD SPRITE IN THE BOHEMIAN FOREST
Egon J. Lechner

The invitation to the hunting ground in Bohemia promised a rarity in hunting terms. Never before had I acted quite so capriciously, I immediately cancelled all my appointments and urged Kurt to join me on the trip. A pathological growth on an antler caused by "lack of the male sex hormone as a result of atrophy, injury or loss of the male genitalia", as defined in the hunting glossary, is rare nowadays and the misogynist roe buck thus afflicted shirks its reproductive duties.

It took less time than expected to drive the roughly 125 miles and complete the customs formalities. On the journey to our destination we hardly gave the enchanting summer countryside of the Bohemian Forest, the pretty villages or the impressive historical architectural monuments a second glance.

Brief interrogation of taciturn Pavel revealed that the sudden mowing of a huge alfalfa field a few days beforehand had disturbed the area in which the secretive animal was usually found. Because of the approaching rutting season, every aggressive roe buck in the area was fair game. At seven thirty precisely we were standing in front of Pavel's farm. We drove along narrow lanes often bordered by wild apple trees through gently rolling hilly countryside covered in maize and other field crops into this historically important landscape in the heart of central Europe which, as the nucleus of the Czech state, reflected an eventful history. Everything we saw was just the way we had imagined the Bohemian Forest.

We dropped Kurt off at a rather unpromising spot. He clambered up a rickety ladder with amazing confidence—unfortunately without his camera—and, certain of success, bade us goodbye with the words "Now for something exotic!". Although I glimpsed several fine roe bucks, over the next two hours as I stood at the edge of a clover field I had plenty of time to go through the alternative strategies of the roe buck with the deformed antlers which had presumably been expelled from this Eldorado long ago by his pugnacious relatives.

When darkness fell we picked up Kurt from the raised stand and could hardly believe our ears when he spoke to us. As he had jokingly predicted, the antler show-off had turned up within 65 yards of him in full daylight and appeared again a quarter of an hour later on the meadow which was sprinkled with hayseed and thistles.

Not believing him, I warned my gloating friend not to "make up stories" but his description left us in no doubt of his veracity: the antler abnormality had not yet grown into a "bishop's miter" or into a "beehive" growing over the eyes. "His six-point antlers are covered in thick velvet and really stand out, you'll be amazed!" enthused my friend Kurt.

It was tough luck that I had not seen him myself and I was restless with impatience. Tomorrow morning I would have better luck if I could only call the roe buck closer ...

The night was short, and just after midnight I was woken by a strong wind and flashing sheet lightning. A violent storm soon broke, rain spattered down and became continuous, which was invigorating, but not exactly what I would have wanted for deerstalking that morning.

We reached the sleeping village of Klenova in pitch darkness and steady rain. Soon afterwards I was on my way to Kurt's "surprise lookout". The lukewarm rain shower thankfully petered out as soon as the light was good enough for shooting. The first birds were stirring, wild pigeons were emerging from the freshly mown grain-fields and the cackling of thousands of Bohemian geese drifted across from the nearby village.

Apart from a spirited six-point stag, this dream morning failed to produce anything really exciting. I was relieved when this domineering resident stag, who would obviously not tolerate

This roe buck's bizarre antlers are misshapen but because of its exceptionally pronounced pearling it is a royal buck.

Healthy mixed forests are rare.

16

any rival in his vicinity, disappeared into the nearby bank of alder shortly afterwards.

Though the trail remained cold, the confirmed sighting of the secretive stag the evening before put me in a good mood and I suddenly found myself humming the old familiar tune "Long ago in the Bohemian forest...".

Just before dusk fell the six-point buck once again brightened up my evening watch from the raised stand. The time after the previous day's 'stage appearance' witnessed by Kurt passed without the curtain as much as twitching. Doubts welled up again. I knew him well, but what if Kurt had made it all up after all?

And suddenly there it stood in the middle of a dense tangle of thistles: in the fading evening light it looked like a bewitching red patch with the bizarre head briefly exposed almost as far as the bottom of the neck. The striking 6-point antlers, on which each beam was too thick to be grasped in the hand, extended a good hand's width beyond the ears, and were fascinatingly lumpy with their velvet covering. This was a great, perhaps unique, chance I thought. Should I shoot through the tangled thistles? I was overcome by scruples, what if the shot missed? But what a trophy!

Torn with doubt, I tentatively placed the butt against my cheek. Target practice! to fire or not to fire? In an instant I was freed from the horns of my dilemma. The shirker was becoming nervous at even the slightest sound, leaped and then disappeared into the darkness of the mixed forest. If only I could have called him closer... I was tormented by gnawing self-doubt until I finally fell asleep: shouldn't I have fired?

Long before the first cock crowed I was sitting in the cherry tree again. I tried to imagine what the buck was up to, played all kinds of absurd mind games and swore an oath on all that was holy in hunting. As everybody knows, hunters, like farmers and fishermen, are never totally free from superstition. Walter Niedl said that "Anyone who lives close to nature is affected by and keenly interested in anything that is unprovable, unexplainable and apparently supernatural".

As I feared, I returned to the car a defeated man and well aware that I had been visited by an extremely furtive wood sprite of a kind which a hunter is lucky to glimpse even once in a lifetime. I returned to the hunting area around midday. My every thought and wish were aimed at the stag with malformed antlers which, as I was soon to discover, some of the locals had already missed.

I returned to the raised stand in the evening lost in my own thoughts which had meanwhile become somewhat despondent. As I clambered up

The pygmy owl is the smallest European owl.

the rickety ladder I consoled myself that it would all be over in a couple of hours, and once in the stand I made myself at home and fell to morose brooding.

An oppressively sweltering heat hung over the clearing. There was not a breath of wind as late afternoon gradually gave way to evening twilight. Only the scolding of a blackbird nearby disturbed the heavy silence as the minutes ticked away.

What was that! a slight snap. As night fell I resigned myself to the fact that there was no prospect of any action, and then noticed something breaking cover directly underneath my feet: the buck on his evening patrol. It would have been impossible to get a closer look at him with the naked eye. Out of habit, I followed the resident buck with my binoculars as he paced through the meadow and noticed from the stand when he suddenly changed direction toward the clearing where the maize had been harvested.

A thought suddenly flashes through my mind as the stag pricks its ears and stares fixedly forward. Like an invisible radar beam, I followed the ruffian's gaze straight to the edge of the maize, some 85 yards away where, despite the failing light, I made out the shadowy but clearly silhouetted massive adornment of the extremely furtive buck

with the malformed antlers. Unbelievable!

As I carefully slide the butt of my semi-automatic rifle to my shoulder, I notice, to my horror, that the old warrior buck has already lifted his foreleg and is bellowing, preparing to attack. It's now or never! Before I can release the safety catch and take aim, the lily-livered "parukash", as Pavel insists on calling the buck with velvet antlers, is already trotting off hesitantly to the left. In the next second the swaggering buck will disappear in the maize, never to be seen again.

Swing the rifle, quick! My soft-nosed bullet strikes the sauntering buck from the rear at a semi-oblique angle. He is down, I rejoice within, and before the shot has echoed away in the distant woods I am already down from the stand and so sure of my shot that I carelessly forget to reload. Shortly afterwards I am kneeling in front of the wonderfully adorned giant and touch a deformed antler for the first time in my life. The 6-point antlers are almost as thick as a forearm, and overgrown with fleshy, waxy pearls of velvet as though cased in soft suede. They have a velvety feel and are much bigger than I imagined them.

The flashy misogynist did not heed the black-bird's warning. I am very happy, and it takes some time for my good fortune to sink in.

This doe is watching the photographer. She will bound off in an instant.

OBITUARY TO A HUNTING HAT
Johannes Daniel Gerstein

Yesterday I should have buried my hat—my seven-year-old Styrian loden hat. Weeks ago it fell out of a raised stand into a dense thicket of raspberries on a warm fall day and proved impossible to find in the dark. When I returned to the shoot two days later, it was lying on the deerstalking path and gazing up at me sadly with a large hole in the dark gray felt. Mice had probably reduced it to this sorry state in just two days. They had gnawed around the brim, but that in itself would not have been so bad. The hole in the felt at the front was large enough to put your fist through.

My lovely old hat! a trusty companion through seven summers and winters. You were more than a mere item of headgear during all those years. The cold water from the spring in the fox-wood tasted delicious from your crown. I used you to carry home chanterelles, ceps and cauliflower fungus on the way back from early morning stalking along the boar-bank. Once you inadvertently ended up under the rear wheel of my car and were crushed deep into the mud. You endured this indignity without grumbling. No hat maker had to clean or steam you—water and sunshine restored you to your previous state, and you returned to your former shape without any assistance.

How willingly and often you wore the small green branch with special pride when it was the first red deer or wild boar which we both shot in the Rhön. But you never liked feathers, you tolerated them being pinned on you but shed them at the first available opportunity. You never got lost—unlike other hats such as your predecessors, or town hats which possess neither brains nor soul. In the later years of your life you were as a crown that endows its wearer with prestige and dignity. Wherever I was invited as a newcomer I was cheerfully welcomed as a 'veteran' hunter after just one discreet glance at your honorable patina.

What do hatters nowadays know of the soul of a hat such as you? Only yesterday I showed you to a chap in this trade and asked him whether a piece of felt could be used to patch your gaping wound. He laughed scornfully, showed me the door and advised me to bury you, but this I cannot do. Maybe on sunny days I shall wear you again in the rutting season or when partridge shooting so that I can show you the hills, fields and woods all around which you always loved so much.

TWO RIVALS
Eduard Paulin

Anyone seeing Ulanchen—posh pedigree name Ulan de Wynen—for the first time probably wonders about the long-haired boar hound's diminutive 'chen' suffix, given the fact that he has grown to a height of 30 inches at the shoulders, and weighs in at no less than 88 lb (40 kg) on the groaning deer scales.

Who would have dreamt that the fat little winner of a private puppy selection contest, during which he flirted shamelessly with my wife, could have grown into such a giant, although his unmistakably dominant dog manners and big paws did strike me as a little suspicious.

Despite my tentatively expressed reservations in this respect, my preference for a cute, fine-limbed bitch was somehow overruled during the controversial selection debate and wife and dog, arm in arm so to speak, left for the new arrival's home and, for a long time, did not miss any suitable opportunity to reproach me for my heretical behavior. They immediately formed a steadfast alliance against which I was powerless from the outset— except when out hunting—despite repeated attempts at bribery.

The pup itself thrived splendidly and reached

the large but perfectly proportioned size mentioned earlier; this was hardly surprising because, as a true Bavarian, he was quite capable of polishing off a five-pound portion of his favorite meat loaf served up under various pretexts without pausing even once.

Ulanchen did not waste a single minute of his life in the kennel which I spent ages laboriously building. He remained largely untainted by any 'authoritarian training pressures' and, like certain badly brought-up children, always managed to play off master against mistress successfully, eventually developing into the charming rogue that he is today.

His stubbornness, caused by this unequivocal training defect which was attributable to humans, somehow blended strangely with a childlike disposition which is often encountered among 'big babies' and, just as he never took excessive advantage of any of our mistakes, it was impossible to hold a grudge against him for long for any of the many silly things he did. These facts, the bottomless trust which the boar hound placed in his humans, as well as his unfailing predisposition to daftness of every kind meant that, even when

This long-haired boar hound is gripped by the excitement of the chase.

22

he was four years old, little Ulanchen was still not grown-up Ulan, at least not in our eyes.

Given his highly individual character, it came as little surprise that all Ulanchen's obedience training results turned out somewhat mediocre, despite thoroughly good facilities; at obedience training this thoroughly unruly boar hound always felt it was his most urgent duty to show his fellow pupils 'where the action was'. We endured this with equanimity, we had no desire for a perfectly trained tail-wagging dog which would win obedience competitions anyway, and Ulanchen always performed the tasks required of him—albeit in his own fashion.

However, it would be a great injustice to accuse the boar hound of carrying over such behavior from his private life into his professional life, namely hunting. He might have been affectionate and naïve at home, but he hunted in a wild, unbridled manner and I was often surprised how much his temperament changed as soon as we approached the boundary of the hunting grounds. Having said this, among human hunters there are also many who, masquerading as inoffensive pen-pushers, go about their usually humdrum business during the week, but give full rein to their primitive passion for hunting on weekends, and I am sure that two such souls dwelt within the breast of Ulanchen.

Given his unrestrained temperament and without any effort on our part, he developed into an uncompromising foe of game animals and predatory animals. This fact was duly noted by the game population and was usually accepted with a grin by hunting companions, even when, on one occasion, he chased a cat into the sanctuary of a hayloft. After being unmistakably discouraged from this behavior, Ulanchen began to specialize in dealing with the fox population which had grown considerably and, despite his good nose and running ability, repeatedly managed to chase and despatch almost full-grown young foxes in cornfields on favorable terrain without any intervention on our part.

However, it should be mentioned that a fox which was already at bay once managed to escape the deer hound unnoticed when he was briefly distracted by our arrival. He then conscientiously tried to find his worthy opponent by looking at all the tops of the surrounding trees. No one drops out of a tree as a master, certainly not a fox.

Apart from such minor mistakes, basking in an otherwise uninterrupted string of successes, and despite the internalized hierarchy that only exists in our imagination anyway, Ulanchen soon became convinced that he was the uncrowned ruler of the hunting ground and brooked no competitors.

Reynard the fox peers warily from his earth.

This story could have been written in half the time had he not insisted on being the exclusive center of attention.

He felt obliged to behave in a clumsy, wooden, gentlemanly fashion to the Viszla bitch who had been at home when he first arrived, and who had lovingly mothered him when he was a puppy. He retrieved the grandmotherly Pekinese several times without causing injury but, basically, he never took to her.

This sunny state of affairs which was not troubled by even the smallest cloud was, however, one day overshadowed by a major thundery front which would later regularly send Ulanchen into a hitherto unknown state of frenzy. The change of weather in question was black and brown in color, consisted of a bundle of sinews, muscle and teeth, answered to the name of Basco and was our friend Max's terrier. Basco, a scarred dare-devil and battle-hardened terrier, shared Ulanchen's predilection for foxes in a most unwelcome manner and, although his talents in this department lay more in working underground, every now and again the interests of both dogs clashed to such an extent that they tore into each other. The advantage that the one had in terms of strength and fighting weight was balanced by the agility, pluck and experience of the other and, seeing the wounds inflicted during even brief bouts, we could not summon the nerve to follow the advice of old dog handlers and let these totally uncompromising adversaries fight it out between themselves.

We avoided hunting with the two arch enemies whenever possible, but if one of them even caught the merest sight of the other it produced such a racket that half the village turned out. It was therefore just a question of time before a scrap on a scale that would have done credit to any village fair in Lower Bavaria took place. The occasion for this was not as expected and will therefore be related here.

Theoretically we had planned to dig an earth in winter and both the dogs were to deploy their respective talents separately. Whilst Basco vented his anger underground, Ulanchen was assigned the task of tracking, rounding up and retrieving, roles which both of them could happily have accepted. The counting of entrances and exits from the obviously occupied earth, repeated several times that morning as always in such cases, produced an unexpected result. At around midday we reached the extensive earth in good spirits after an admittedly somewhat problematic walk with both the roughnecks on the lead. Because each dog felt it was incompatible with its honor to lag even one step behind the other my friend Max and I had not really needed to use our own legs to reach the scene of the crime. It was sufficient to

simply plant one's moon boots flat on the ground and allow oneself to be dragged across the thin covering of snow in true Husky style, occasionally throwing in a few short shuffling steps when confronted with any particularly treacherous tree roots.

This race, which came about through lack of sporting spirit, ended with jealous, malevolent sidelong glances and dreadful panting by both the quarreling thickheads and a standoff near the earth. The only person who derived any enjoyment from this sight was probably my wife whose cheers of encouragement made the whole affair funnier but no more pleasant. I breathed a sigh of relief when Basco's docked tail finally disappeared into one of the many tunnels, accompanied by the terrier's usual 'war cry'.

We were left above ground listening attentively and it was Ulanchen who pulled the oddest faces, and who soon noted the distinctive barking which unmistakably announced that Basco had struck lucky and was attacking the fox with his characteristic vehemence. Maybe the terrier begrudged his colleague lying in wait above ground even a partial success, or perhaps it was due to a particularly successful attack that the black and brown dog, rather than unearthing the fox so that it could be shot, seized it by the neck and, despite fierce resistance, attempted to drag it into the daylight. Of course, we were able to follow events underground by sound alone as the terrier put up a tremendous performance and reversed flat on its belly along the long winding tunnel. No colorful dawn sunrise was ever observed with more rapt attention than the earth-caked rear of the brave dog as it finally emerged after an hour or so of heavy toil. Even Ulanchen was so fascinated by the entire business that he stood there rooted to the spot, only his slightly bulging eyes betraying inward strain.

The carbine was already trained on the red plunderer to deliver the coup de grâce when fate took one of those unexpected turns which so often causes us to lapse into gloomy meditation. At the very instant when the brave fox terrier was about to go for the throat, another fox bolted from a secondary tunnel off to one side and was immediately hit by my wife's shot after miraculously eluding my two excessively hasty shots. It may well have been due simply to the fact that my Diana was standing in a better position, but she dropped the fox so cleanly with just a single shot that my annoyance at my own blunder was forgotten (almost) immediately.

As the shot fox lay there still twitching, I ordered Ulanchen to retrieve, something which I did not have to ask twice. He sprinted off toward the fallen animal like a high-velocity bullet and everything would have been fine if his route had

Illustration from Max Haider's 'Mr. Petermann's hunting book', a collection of not entirely serious hunting scenes.

not taken him of all places past the doggedly struggling terrier. After the event we postulated several explanations for the scene which ensued, although the true explanation will probably always remain the dogs' secret. Maybe Ulanchen found the fervently longed for opportunity offered him in the form of the expansive, unprotected neck of his detested rival irresistible, maybe he begrudged him the fox or, faced with his adversary plastered in red sand and smelling strongly of fox, was simply confused—an excuse which any counsel for the defense would have advised him to plead— whatever the case he bit into the considerable folds of skin on the scruff of the terrier's neck in a manner of which any Canadian lumberjack would have been proud.

Both the terrier and the fox onto which it was still hanging were shaken so violently that lumps of earth detached themselves from skin and fur and flew through the air. The only time I have ever seen a similar 'centrifugal' effect was when a hunting friend was performing a folk dance but, to the great discomfort of his hostess, had forgotten to clean clumps of dirt from the soles of his shoes before starting his performance.

There could be no other outcome: Basco, sick and tired of the unfair attack, released the fox, which made off toward its earth with an irritated expression and upcast eyes, so that he could devote his entire attention to his new foe. It goes without saying that the fox, stirred by the tremendous din around it, struggled to its feet and slunk off unnoticed.

We have never again exchanged such dumbfounded looks, and eventually managed to separate the dogs who, oddly enough, observed a kind of tense truce from that day on, but never became real friends. After a brief search we eventually found the fox which had been shot and left its badly-treated companion in peace, deciding not to hunt the old earth again, for the rest of the winter at least.

The fox emerges from his earth in the evening.

FLORIAN
Friedrich Karl von Eggeling

We got to know each other last year in the scorching hot month of July, the wild boar and I. More precisely, I got to know him and he did not notice me. It was the rutting season and the forest was burning near the lignite mines in the west. The entire heath stank of lignite and the air was thick with smoke pierced by vivid harsh yellow beams of sunlight which baked the parched earth.

In the morning I had attempted, without success, to decoy a roe buck and was walking along the path through the piece of moorland that cuts off the shoot from the neighbor's land. The stalking footpath runs along the spoil dug out of a drainage ditch and is so densely covered with birch trees that one can rarely see further than ten paces. Something gray moved in front of me at a point where the visibility was better. I saw two powerful haunches either side of a long tail, ending in thick bristles, which was constantly flicking to the left and right to drive off the tormenting midges. It was quite unmistakably a relatively large wild boar moving along the embankment in search of the cool and quiet of the moor, after probably spending the night in the neighbor's field of oats.

The wild boar walked slowly in front of me, keeping to the footpath, the birch trees swayed, sometimes I could see its powerful hind quarters and sometimes it disappeared. Suddenly the wild boar came to a halt, there was a splashing of water and, for an instant, I caught a glimpse of its head and gleaming tusks through a bush before it was swallowed up in the stand of young spruce, I heard the clucking alarm call of a blackbird, another splash in the stand of young trees and then everything was silent. I turned back along the same route I had taken.

Old wild boars do not have an established routine, they are here, there and often nowhere, and it was therefore highly unlikely that he would follow the same trail again soon. Even if he did it would certainly not be at this time of day, halfway through the morning. Or maybe he would. Perhaps this jungle of birch, aspen, spruce and brambles offered a sufficient degree of security to make him alter his accustomed habits.

Close to the neighbor's boundary there is an old ladder in a standard holdover of pine from where one used to be able to look into the stand of young spruce. Now it was disused but still a vantage point I could use to look at least a hundred yards down the overgrown stalking footpath and there would even be a narrow, unobstructed field of fire from the top of the ladder.

I went to the ladder every morning over the next few days and, to be honest, had seldom ever been so bored. I only saw the wild boar once in the first gray light of early dawn, when he predictably failed to walk along the footpath, crossing it in a single huge leap. Because there was an especially strong smell of fire and smoke that morning I said a fervent prayer to Saint Florian—the one that goes "Please spare our house and let those of others burn!", and this is how the wild boar got his name which was to stick with him through five or six hunts during which he honored me with occasional visits.

By August 10 the rutting season was already over but, out of habit, I woke up at the usual time before dawn, tried to get back to sleep unsuccessfully, made a coffee and drove to the shoot as the sun was rising.

Red deer sometimes hang around for a long time at this season and I did need a hind in its second year for the pot, so perhaps it was not quite so odd to sit on the 'giant'. This was a 40-foot high ladder with its back facing the marsh and its front facing the meadow and which lay beyond a monotonous, lifeless stand of young pines. For some reason red deer were fond of spending time among these pine trees and only later moved into the marsh area with its alders and spruce. I still had quite a good view into the stand of pines which was only just beginning to grow and close in.

I had hardly taken up my position in the raised stand when, completely on cue, a hind in its second year appeared in the narrow strip of mature timber in front of the stand of young trees, grazed a few dry stalks of grass as a dessert after the rich meadow grazing, stood there daydreaming for a while and started to move straight toward me along the narrow path at the edge of the stand of young trees. I had raised my rifle much earlier because the hind below me was slight in stature and weighed about 77 lb (35 kg). It jumped into the pine trees after I shot and collapsed. Almost before the crack and echo of the shot had died away there was a snapping noise behind me and a wild pig grunted in alarm, as I turned round and reloaded I caught a rear view of my wild boar as it shot off like a rocket. He then ran in a curve, reached the strip of old timber which was full of dry wood left from the last tree felling, shot through it and disappeared into the back of the plantation. I knew it was 'my' wild boar because I had seen its distinctive tail bristles and shining tusks. The population density of wild boars as powerful as this was not so high that I could have seen two animals which looked as alike as twins.

During the next encounter the chances were not bad, about fifty-fifty. The water bailiff had lowered

Mature wild boar often lead a solitary life, well away from others of their species.

Wild boar relaxing – circus tricks in the undergrowth

the level in the pond which is surrounded by thick oak trees where the goldeneye breed in holes and rotten parts of tree trunks. The acorns that drop into the water are a particularly tasty titbit for the wild pigs and must taste delicious when they are so swollen and tender. Whenever the pond is drained in late November or early December, herds of boar come from near and far and root through the bed of the lake. This happened last year and the tracks included a large wild pig. I stood at the edge of the pond for a long time undecided what to do.

I had four options, but the wild boar undoubtedly had many more. There was the trail back to the main stand of young trees which followed a wide sandy path: it was fairly unlikely that he had gone into the nursery, but the rut had started so it was not out of the question. He might also move along the river westward alongside the stand of young alder trees that had grown from seed dispersed by the wind, and here I would be

able to see him from the raised stand in the bottom meadow. The third possibility was for him to cross the local road into the endless marsh and ponds; I could lie in wait for him by the mail route. But when I really tried to get inside the head of a wild boar, I decided that his regular haunt on the marsh where I saw him the first few times exerted the strongest pull on him. There I would have a chance of waylaying him in the red oaks before the marsh if he only stayed there a while until it got light enough.

I was very proud of my intellectual accomplishment. "Even the most cunning wild boar cannot outsmart an old hunter like you" I thought to myself. It was just a matter of patience, but patience is really not my forte, even though I have held a game license for fifty years.

It happened on the first day: I had set out before dew and daylight, stalked into the red oaks, keeping the wind behind me, and took up position between the roots of a tree which was wide enough to

◁ Wild boar sow and piglet

With its sturdy build and powerful head, wild boar can penetrate almost any thicket.

conceal me completely. As it began to get light and the dampness of the earth gradually began to penetrate my trousers I heard rustling to my left and the old doe with her two fawns walked past. A small fallow buck then appeared hastily from the opposite direction as the sun rose, jays chattered, wild geese called in the distance, a solitary heron flapped over, it was daylight and the shoot was over.

I picked up my things, grabbed the climbing stick in my left hand, threw my rifle over my shoulder and marched off. Rather than returning directly to the car, I first went to the broad gravel path which preserved animal tracks so well; maybe the wild boar had crossed it.

Before you reach the old wood through which the gravel path leads, you have to walk a short distance through a young forest stand down a path overgrown with grass which precisely bisects the young forest stand of some two acres.

Occasionally, when walking through the woods as both a forester and hunter, one personality may sometimes get the upper hand and the other is ignored. Lying in wait for game, this is not important because one can think like a forester and observe like a huntsman, or vice versa. Stalking demands full attention, all the senses and every muscle. I have known this for ages, but I must be a foolish person because I have learnt nothing from my many mistakes and so it was in this case in this stand of young pines. They were obviously in desperate need of thinning and maybe lopping, 160 trees per acre, possibly 200, yes 200 would certainly be better than the prospect of a heavy infestation with pine beetle. How things had changed since my student days when, before our exam, the professor told us that we need only remember the name of this pest because it caused insignificant damage—and now it was suddenly eating entire forests, one consequence of trees being weakened by air pollution. I almost laughed out aloud.

But the urge to laugh passed quicker than it arrived: I was being watched by the wild boar

standing not ten paces in front of me. It was standing in the middle of the grassy path with its mane raised and not at all frightened, surprised at most. I should have seen him much earlier through the peeling stems of the pines, but no, I chose to gaze up to the tops of the trees from whence enlightenment concerning forestry matters comes, whether to take action, if so when, how extensively and at what cost. For Heaven's sake!

My instant of surprise lasted much longer than the wild boar's, assuming he was surprised at all. He was already well on his way with his fine tail raised high by the time I had shouldered my rifle. The shot, which I fired as he jinked slightly to one side just before the spruce trees, slammed into the vegetation behind him. The small trees at the edge closed around him, the sun shone high in the sky, still more geese were flighting to the fields, behind me a raven croaked in expectation of scraps from the gutted quarry which he as usual associated with the shot, and I stood there 'like a dying duck in a thunderstorm' as my father used to say whenever I pulled a particularly stupid face.

This pig was odd, behaved unnaturally, schizophrenically, and showed no respect for a serious hunter. I felt hard done by and offended.

Winter arrived on time in the month of January, the snow settled for once and fresh snow even settled on it, I had almost forgotten that such a thing existed.

I waited until around 10 o'clock in the evening, looked at the thermometer which read 12 degrees below freezing, wrapped myself in fur and my snow shirt and trudged off over the sheep bridge into the woods. The ducks were quacking in the thick layer of mist that hung above the water, the ponds had frozen over long ago. The snow crunched beneath my feet somewhat too loudly for me and I dragged my feet so that it crunched less noisily. I always think that no noise can be heard so far off as the loud crunching of snow. I halted near the old guidepost stone as I always do, firstly to acclimatize my eyes to the dim moonlight, forest and shadows, secondly to give my ears time to tune in so that they can pick up and distinguish quiet noises and, finally, stalking by moonlight is such a rare, unusual event that you first have to calm down your excitement so that mind and body blend to produce the necessary composure. It was then that I made my decision: I would stalk along the ridge to Schöpsaue into the wind and staying in the shadow of the ancient oaks, take a look at the plowed field, ending up by the weir. The latter was built over 250 years ago in order to create the millrace and embellish the park with a maze of canals.

Moonlight is enchanting and bewitching, memories linger, stories and faces come alive. I remembered standing there with my father and talking of how we intended to renew the wood which had been damaged in gales by planting oaks, beech and limes.

And now? Now I stood there in the same place with the same thoughts by the same wood which was now half a century older and more open, its

◁ A wild sow wallows to groom herself, not just for pleasure.

▷ There he was again, just when least expected. This promising sighting was all over in just a few seconds.

The distinctive plumage of the jay brings a dash of color to the forest and it also scares off the quarry of many a hunter with its warning call.

Even if the jay were to raise the alarm, this wild sow would probably not react – being photographed is far more interesting.

oaks more gnarled with an impenetrable undergrowth of fallen timber, bracken and elder.

A muffled snapping and stamping in the undergrowth brought me back to my senses but it was just the dark fallow stag walking across the sandy path towards the red oaks near the pond. I started stalking when he disappeared. I quickly covered the first stretch because the wallows underneath the alder trees were frozen solid and it was unlikely there would be any game among the mature pine trees because the hard hair-grass there was no good for browsing. Then I came to the first stand of oaks which protruded from the wood into the meadow on a high stretch of dunes. These used to be the only link to the old fortress which stood in the middle of the moor on dunes of the same height and could only be reached across a plank bridge over the swamp. There was no game among the oak trees, no rustling of leaves, no crunching of crisp snow beneath hard hooves.

I carried on along the edge of the young pine trees to the plowed field but it was cold, white, grazed bare and covered in snow, with just a few maize stalks sticking out of the white blanket and the moonlight casting harsh shadows through the branches of the surrounding oaks. There was no point waiting here, since every animal apart from the hare shunned this gleaming whiteness.

I continued stalking back along the ridge to the meadows and heard the water cascading and rushing across the mill weir. Ducks gabbled on the river and suddenly quacked in fright, a flying bird whirred past me down river. Maybe the otter was hunting? Last year I had seen him at dusk among the ducks. He swam toward me with a two-year-old carp in his mouth, brought the fish ashore almost at my feet near the roots of an oak tree and enthusiastically consumed the flank fillets scarcely a yard in front of the tips of my boots.

The weir was now in front of me to the left, and the loud roar of water pouring into the mill pool drowned out all other noise, even the scrunching of my footsteps in the snow and leaves. Before me was the large stand of oak trees with interspersed beech and alder, and the marsh which, in my grandfather's day, was used to hold carp in wintertime and also served as a soundboard for his academy-trained baritone voice which occasionally replaced the organ on Sundays if the organist played too slowly. This piece of woodland was now a real ancient forest, with dips and hollows and remains of fishponds containing trees more than three hundred years old, an undergrowth of elder and ferns, and hornbeam and spruce that had grown from wind-dispersed seeds. No ax had fallen there since the day this wood was established on meadow ground in its original state in 1732. A loud noise like a thick branch snapping or a dead tree falling and breaking

Mallard in the morning mist

emerged from this tangle of trees, saplings, branches, foliage and bracken. It came from the darkest part of the wood and I could see nothing, even using my binoculars. I had to get closer despite the difficulty of moving through the tangled branches. If only eyes could walk! I slowly approached closer and heard several cracking noises from the same spot.

There was a sudden movement in front of me, a blurred black silhouette, stout and long but much shorter than a red deer—a solitary wild boar? My wild boar?

I had already dropped down onto my left knee behind an oak with the rifle ready to aim and peering through my ×6 sights, but the sow was in dark shadow and I had no idea which was the front and which was the rear. The pig just stood there sniffing the air and listening, but there was a steady wind in my face. A sharp twig was sticking into my knee, the cold slowly but surely crept up my legs, but there were beads of sweat under the brim of my hat. Still the sow stood still as my hands started to tremble and my trigger finger became numb with this terrible waiting.

The pig shook itself, gave a contented growl from deep in its throat, moved one step forward, turned, disappeared in one of the old pond dips,

emerged on the other side out of shadow, and turned again so I could see it side on, but in the half shadow of the oaks. The telescopic sight scanned across it, withers, tail, unmistakable tail—my wild boar! The bead floated towards the front again, wandered around the pig—this damned excitement—then came to rest in the right spot well behind the foreleg. The shot was a deafening dazzling flash, then came a crashing and cracking of dry branches, a thump and perfect silence.

There were grooves in the snow at the spot where it stood when shot, dark splashes on the exit wound side and lots of blood on the tracks on both sides of the final dash imprinted in the snow.

He lay there under the shelter of a wide-crowned beech tree and I sat beside him on one of the flat roots of the old tree. The extreme tension of the last few minutes slowly subsided, thoughts and memories went round in my head, memories of all the things I had experienced with this wild boar and other sows which I had hit or missed in the moonlight. The last most important realization was that this was the first big sow on what was almost my own native soil again, and thanks for this night mingled with gratitude to my father and forefathers who had made this piece of land so lovely and so bountiful.

A FAMILY SECRET
Eduard Paulin

Initially I was somewhat perplexed and absent-mindedly fingered the bright card bearing the words "Invitation to a duck-shoot" and an appropriate hunting motif. Little by little this feeling heightened to amazement as I read the enclosed list of guests; the illustrious names of the twelve guns invited in addition to myself read almost like an extract from the European edition of Who's Who —if there is such a list.

Princes, counts or other aristocrats had evi-

Drake and duck mallard

dently decided to invite me to shoot in their ranks even though my blood only contains blue and white Bavarian components at best and, like that of any true Bavarian, is of largely dubious lineage.

Closer examination of the sender's name reminded me of a small favor which, by chance, I had been able to do for the host of the shoot and for which this invitation was evidently a token of appreciation. The invitation was confirmed by a brief phone call and it was not long before I set off one fine autumn day on my trip to the far-away Rhineland. There a prince, here a count—I had no intention of being upstaged and, in addition to an outfit that had been updated in line with the dictates of the very latest fashion, packed a semi-automatic shotgun, also referred to as an Italian muzzle-loader—with which I had familiarized myself sufficiently by shooting at clays. Since an unbelievably huge bag was in prospect, I imagined that I was kitted out ideally for any contingency, a belief which proved to be gravely mistaken.

As I arrived in the spacious forecourt of the magnificent Rhine castle I caught sight of a group of strangely shabby looking men who I first took to be the underprivileged servants but who turned out to be the noble shooting party itself. I received a thoroughly friendly welcome despite my comparatively foppish costume and there was never the slightest hint of any snobbishness on the part of Their Graces and Majesties during the entire weekend shoot.

Nevertheless, it was impossible not to notice the unwritten rules within this social group where members had had years to become perfectly attuned to each other's ways as is the case in any social group.

After a brief acclimatization period I had plenty of opportunity to subject individuals to closer scrutiny and I cannot recall ever having met such distinctively individual characters before or since. I am convinced that all of them, without exception, must have graduated in eccentricity a long time ago.

A dyed-in-the-wool English lord, who managed to embody every possible stereotypical feature including nonchalantly loose long limbs and reddish sideburns down to a shag pipe and even a deerstalker hat, stood out in particular. The hat which, with its two side flaps and checked pattern, would have undoubtedly made anyone else look quite hilarious, was worn by the peer from Olde England with the dignified matter-of-factness which is unique to those from the British Isles.

An aged, extremely kind-hearted gentleman of well-known princely blood caught my attention in particular and stood out from all the others thanks to his indefatigable liveliness; he was always

on the lookout for something and I soon secretly christened him, somewhat disrespectfully, 'Ahndl'. Both these gentlemen subsequently played a special role in my story.

The aforementioned 'Ahndl' was the first to make his mark, he was with heart and soul a shooter, spoke of little else but hunting and contributed to the fun had by everyone during a lively get-together on the evening of the first day with his extremely witty observations on the art of catching flies, an insect which, as far as he was concerned, had apparently assumed the importance of a substitute for game birds. 'Ahndl' had developed this discipline to a level of mastery, as was repeatedly proven by abundant specimens, and had developed stalking, decoying and extermination methods so fiendishly clever that they would have done credit even to a Borgia.

He achieved a respectable bag and I must admit that this reached a truly substantial size during the course of the evening. It was not just this specialist discipline but rather the extremely colorful stories which the other guests told of shooting red grouse, quail and black francolin—all game birds which I only knew from hearsay—which soon strengthened my conviction that I had obviously fallen in with an internationally experienced group of excellent game bird shots. My thoughts turned wistfully to the annual average of three or maybe five hares which succumbed to my scattered lead shot back home. There was nothing I could do about this, but it did rankle slightly that I was scarcely able to make any contribution to this swapping of experiences and good advice. This was soon to change, but in a slightly dubious fashion.

My situation was made problematic by a rule of etiquette which apparently dictated that only double-barreled guns of English or, if the worst came to the worst, French manufacture of twenty gauge or less were worthy of a true game bird shooter. Circumstances therefore obliged me to answer occasional questions regarding what type of weapon I used by attempting to suddenly reduce the volume of my body and mumbling some incoherent response. Thankfully the topic which was not really a topic in this company was soon forgotten as the gentlemen outdid each other in describing and demonstrating, with abundant gestures, the advantages and particular speed of their personal technique for reloading after emptying both barrels. This could easily have created the impression that reloading both barrels as quickly as possible was at least as important as the first moon landing had been in its day, a fact that, I must admit, had hitherto not occurred to me.

A gray heron searches for food.

This area of activity had produced good-natured competition between my new friends which had been going on for years, competitions were timed to within a tenth of a second with a stopwatch and so far no winner had emerged. Nobody expected a significant contribution on this world-shaking topic from me in particular and this was fine by me at the time, even though I would have loved to chip in.

My extremely tactful host must have noticed that I had dropped out of the gun and loading technique discussion groups because, after we rose from the table, he took me to one side where escape was impossible. He was initially somewhat indignant when I bashfully owned up to the large-bore gun but was fair enough, in view of the lack of information given, to accept his share of blame for the present situation. In response to my assurance that I was bound to miss everything with the gun he offered to lend me and which I might well break in my clumsiness, after brief reflection he put forward a breathtaking proposal which, after all the discussions that had taken place, left me nonplussed and which I could only interpret as an invitation to commit high treason.

The plan involved allocating me a stand obscured by brushwood and reeds at the end of the line of guns which I would take up officially carrying one of his dainty smaller-bore guns. He assured me that he would place my own gun inconspicuously under a straw bale before the shoot began. I was then to swap guns so that I could use the semi-automatic without losing face. He was no child of sorrow and the thought of this violation of the rules may even have amused him. Given the way things were I was also happy with the plan and looked forward to the next morning with feverish anticipation, heightened by the additional attraction of breaking the rules, a feeling which was intensified even more by the tremendous quacking which could be heard from the wild ducks on the water and which suggested there would be a huge number of birds.

The scene as I made my way towards the marked stands in the autumnal morning mist still remains unforgettable and among even this experienced shooting party there was that high level of expectancy which customarily precedes only the most vivid experiences, and is made somewhat unreal by the total silence of those involved. There was a good hundred yard gap between each stand, which ensured that a sufficient number of ducks would be able to fly down the line of guns unscathed since taking shots beyond reasonable

Damp habitats have become rare as rivers are straightened and riverbanks stabilized.

range was obviously out of the question in this party. At a hand signal from the host, just two men in a small boat would expend considerable energy zigzagging along this branch of the river, which was completely overgrown with reeds, without any effort to make additional noise so that the ducks would be put up in pairs or small groups, the main objective being to prevent a huge mass breakout.

This well-proven stratagem succeeded perfectly and during the entire drive the sky was full of the flashing wing feathers and whistling wing beats which are music to the wildfowler's ears. I was unable to see the guns alongside me but the air above the entire line of guns was perfectly visible from every stand so that each individual could observe his neighbors' shots, thus increasing the general level of excitement by a factor of twelve. I could not help but admire the unique sureness with which these fellows picked out their ducks among the birds which were flying as swift as arrows. I did my best, got my eye in as soon as possible and, because I was watching out and concentrating so much, almost overlooked a sideshow which it would have been a great pity to have missed.

His lordship at the neighboring stand had deigned to send his retriever, which was not terribly experienced in the water, into the river after

The garganey and its habitat; it spends the winter in tropical Africa.

a winged duck and, for the dog, this venture came within a hair's breadth of disaster. The entire line could see that the dog had become so hopelessly caught up in some clinging aquatic plant some distance from the bank that he was unable to untangle himself and was slowly sinking in the water and casting despondent looks at his master on the bank. Under the circumstances, his master's loud shouts of encouragement in the best Oxford English were of little help and my trousers were already round my ankles when the concerned dog owner, every inch a gentleman even in this trying situation, prepared to rescue the dog and stepped gingerly out into the very cold water toward his dog in the poised, deliberate manner of a crowned crane on the lookout for fish.

Other guns in his vicinity were struck by this spectacle, judging by the sudden lull in shooting, for the noble member of the House of Lords was wearing nothing but a hat and pipe and was so unbelievably scrawny that he looked more like a sack full of deer antlers. The tension dissipated very quickly because the mere sight of his master rushing to the rescue seemed to give the retriever new strength and there were friendly shouts of encouragement from all sides and allegedly witty comments of the sort that are invariably proffered so exceedingly generously to any creature in a perilous situation.

Mallard take off somewhat laboriously, but they fly well

Master and dog were within a few yards of each other when the Englishman suddenly disappeared under the surface of the water with a gurgling shriek. Having fallen victim to one of the apparently numerous trenches left by dredging in this part of the river, the crowned crane was suddenly transformed into a great crested grebe, and the nobleman's somewhat arrow-shaped body plunged down into the depths of the river at such a velocity that it took a good twenty seconds until he reappeared at the surface without even being parted from his hat, which he had very wisely fastened beforehand, or even his pipe. With even fiercer determination and completely unaffected by this trifling incident, his lordship continued his rescue operation to a successful conclusion, an accomplishment which predictably received appropriate, not to say slightly exaggerated, recognition during that evening's toasts.

The crowning achievement as far as I was concerned was the fact that, because I had given the matter no thought, nor imposed any restraint on myself, and thanks to the fire power of my large-bore gun, I had inadvertently become the focal point of interest. It was impossible for my fellow hunters to begin to imagine the real reason for my rapid rate of fire and the only alternative was to presume I employed a completely novel, revolutionary reloading technique and the gentlemen were itching to get to the bottom of it. They were far too refined to ask outright questions but my illustrious companions' numerous diplomatic investigative efforts were impossible to deflect and I became quite concerned for the wellbeing of my host, the only person who was in on my secret and who, in an attempt not to arouse any suspicions,

feigned occasional fits of choking to mask a bright red-faced struggle to suppress his mirth. Eventually, at a late hour, 'Ahndl' took me aside with inimitable dignity and I immediately suspected him of wanting to ferret out details of my supposed technical prowess for his own benefit alone. At last I was sitting pretty.

His highness launched his main offensive "Young man I have been shooting for well over sixty years now, always with my own gun, and pride myself on having achieved a certain level of mastery of the art. By dint of practice over many years I can now reload and be ready to fire again two and a half seconds after firing my second barrel. I timed your shots and know that you took no longer than a second to continue your salvo after firing your second shot. Please just tell me one thing for heaven's sake: how in the world do you manage it?"

"Your Highness" I replied, savoring the fact that I had the upper hand and not without a slight trace of guile, "With all respect I would ask you to spare me the obligation to answer this question because it involves an old family secret that can only be handed down from father to son."

His Highness accepted this explanation in a somewhat sulky fashion but without further pressure or demur. After all, where else could one hope to find understanding for old family traditions if not among people such as himself?

THE TRANQUILITY WHICH ONLY HUNTERS EXPERIENCE
Egon J. Lechner

Here Spain is still poor and its earth is still reddish brown, a serious land steeped in melancholy and a great sense of the past. The Sierra de Gredos and its snow-covered granite peaks with steep ravines, its deep wooded circular valleys and impenetrable maquis surrounding the barren goat-grazed land had never been an idyllic area. Far away from the thronging tourists, this is a region that appears behind the times and forgotten by time. As well as being the birthplace of the Roman Emperors Trajan and Hadrian and the great philosopher Seneca, other foreign races have left their imprint on this land: Visigoths, Phoenicians, Carthaginians and, above all, Arabs and their prophet Mohammed. They molded this land and its inhabitants just as much as its early hunting tradition.

What a privilege to be able to hunt the fascinating 'macho montés,' as the Spaniards call their highly sought after ibex, in this largely unknown, slightly hostile world of the Gredos. When hunting far away from one's home area the urge to stalk is accompanied by a real yearning for far-away places and adventure. The need to escape from time to time and forget about everything undoubtedly provides the strongest incentive for accepting an invitation to hunt in a foreign country—after all one can always shoot at home.

Red-bearded Chema, guide and organizer, allowed us hardly any sleep. In the dawn light we snaked up through the steep Sierra along narrow hairpins past stone pine and broad-leaved forests planted hardly ten years ago. Further up the mountains we encountered a few people gathering mushrooms and resin—there are few jobs here in the uplands of Central Spain. It is hard to reconcile draining heat, dry air, rain for days on end, floods and the onset of bitter frosts with the usual Spanish cliché of dreamy sunny beaches, blue seas and unending summer. As they say in Spain "Up there it's nine months winter and three months Hell". Nevertheless, the locals are loyal to this stretch of land—Mi tierra! My homeland!

The men's hats and women's clothes are black—oppressed and full of bitter experience, as gray as the distant landscape. Gloomy fortresses, monasteries and endless churches surrounded by centuries-old groves of twisted olive trees and ancient palm gardens dating from Roman times bear witness to a proud history. "Green, how I love your greenness!" exclaims García Lorca, the famous Spanish poet, speaking of the quiet longing for the plateaux of Castile, whose foothills we were conquering in first gear.

The sun was overhead sooner than we expected. Filled with the curiosity of the hunter, I cast my gaze over the brightly lit mountain slopes which faded from light orange to green and were covered in moss, lichen and broom and then became increasingly bare. My thoughts turned to the barren rocky regions where several thousand ibexes live scattered over a hundred square miles and have been protected for many years.

The upward slog began as soon as the forest path ended. The craggy, intimidatingly precipitous steep slopes of the Sierra soared before us, the wild home of *Capra hispanica victoriae*, one of the three subspecies of ibex that live in Spain.

Despite continuous rain during the previous week, the gorge into which we were climbing was bone dry. Many of these mountain streams often stay dry for forty years or more as the merciless sun scorches the earth. "You'll find no tears" people say and tell how the mortar to build their churches was more often mixed with wine than with water because the latter was usually more expensive than grape juice. Predictably, the water tap had been shut off in our accommodation and a bath full of cold water was available only for 75 pesetas.

Once beyond the bushy habitat we passed through an area of rubble and debris full of football-sized well-weathered or sharp-edged boulders where the going was slow, and walking was a tough grind. Later on, smooth, flat slabs of rock overgrown with moss and as big as a room were dangerously slippery and demanded full concentration—one false step meant the end of more than just the hunt.

We allowed ourselves our first rest stop at the edge of a layered block of rock which looked like an outsized sandwich. As we unpacked the Serrano ham, a decent chunk of dry sheep's cheese and fresh white bread, I gazed across the landscape which stretched as far as the eye could see: this was the land of everchanging colors, with its strangely contradictory blend of cheerfulness and tranquility, the melancholic world with which we are familiar from the landscape paintings and portraits of El Greco, Murillo, Goya and Pablo Picasso's early works.

Once we had finished the two-liter skin of wine which we chilled in old snow, we resumed our walk and, after further climbing, reached the precipitous gorge of a mountain stream that babbled down into the valley. My experienced companions suspected that the ibex would soon move in our direction back up from the bottom of the valley, which we could hardly see, up onto the more breezy higher ground.

"Select the darkest one" Chema reminded me before taking his Spanish siesta which was sacrosanct regardless of circumstances. Despite the drowsy midday stillness I managed to stay awake.

Very few hunters indeed will have the good fortune to get as close to a Spanish ibex as this photographer.

The azure-winged magpie is a native of Spain and Portugal.

The barren landscape of Extremadura is home to the Spanish ibex...

Alongside me blackish-gray lizards darted here and there over slabs of rock that had been warmed by the sun, and fair-sized grasshoppers with luminous orange markings on their bellies scurried among half-withered clumps of grass. Two eagles circled overhead, well aware what we new arrivals were up to, as was the pale-yellow Egyptian vulture with its bent neck and low-slung, forward-thrust head as it scrabbled through the scree and which Chema referred to as a condor, either in error or in an attempt to talk up business. With one trailing wing and swaying unsurely like an old trouper with a wooden leg, it seemed to be waiting for better times. Its larger relative, the griffon vulture, has tripled its numbers over the last ten years and is now seen even over the capital city Madrid.

Despite the babbling and murmuring from the narrow gorge, we suddenly heard the noise of falling rocks from below us: at last, the ibex! I scanned the ravine below through my handy 10 x 40 binoculars, having placed my rifle within easy reach on my rolled-up parka. Chema surfaced again without even being woken—that's hunting instinct for you.

Then the ibex emerged from the depths of the canyon, at least two dozen of them. The herd was completely unsuspecting as it moved up across the slope well over 400 yards away. Half-way up they came to a narrow point where there was an overhanging ledge. It was interesting to watch the disciplined fashion in which these muscular, powerful animals queued up almost demurely despite the general crush and how, one after the other, they climbed over the rock platform that overhung the torrent, before jumping onto the scree opposite in one huge leap.

The ibex continued walking up the slope in single file without standing quietly and testing the wind. Two dominant males who stood out clearly because of their color and size and were well screened in the midst of their harem were in the midfield. Now they were no more than 200 yards away, fine, I knew that my 7 mm Remington Magnum could easily handle this range and the last act could begin.

The herd was quiet, but suddenly turned away from us and continued climbing, why? Had they caught our scent? No, the 'machos' were still up wind and completely unwary. Swing, aim. The words went through my head almost like a charm. The hair trigger snapped and the shot fired. The ibex were running in all directions, but despite the chaotic confusion I could see quite clearly that my shot had flipped the horned animal round on the spot and he was slowly sliding into the dense broom at the edge of the gorge. What should I do?

...this exceedingly agile climber has found an ideal spot.

I froze for an instant when Chema barked "Missed!" Impossible! I had heard the bullet strike! The rifle shot was drowned by the loud crash of the rolling scree. Irritated by Chema's general state of panic—behind me he kept shouting "Shoot! For heaven's sake shoot!" I moved the sight, almost compulsively, underneath the dark stripe on the back of the largest male who was rushing to the nearby mountain crest in huge bounds. The images were like time-lapse photography, no time to think, reflexes were in control. The bead overtook the body of the fleeing ibex as though of its own accord and before the buck disappeared behind the safety of the crest he stood still, tested the wind and, for an instant, was silhouetted against the light as my trigger finger squeezed. With the crack of the shot the buck collapsed onto the scree in front of us on his last journey.

The hunt was over! The noise of the rock rolling down into the valley slowly faded away. As usual, during the first minute after my shot, the now empty scene was one of strange tranquility, the tranquility which only hunters experience. Time to reflect and take deep breaths.

This last act of the drama at Cir Vunal was worthy of the title of Hemingway's famous book *Death in the Afternoon*, if the reader will allow this comparison, and brought the curtain down on the rocky arena and, despite my success and joy in having bagged the 'macho' over on the slope, left me with a brief feeling of unease. The Spanish know that "a good matador weeps when he has killed the bull". I felt more like swearing and hoped that I really had missed the first buck, help us St Hubert.

We moved off cross-country after a short breather. Crossing the gorge was child's play and uncertainty made us walk even faster. Conscience always urges us on faster. Arrived at the scene we discovered what we had inwardly long feared: the ibex which I had supposedly missed lay dead hardly twenty yards from the second animal on the previously hidden shaded side of the crest. Like twins, both bucks had equally impressive horns. This had been a serious, unforgivable mistake.

Chema laughingly congratulated me "Muy preciosa" and seemed well pleased. It took some time before I could share his enthusiasm about the successful completion of the hunt and the two trophies. To this day I cannot make up my mind whether my over-zealous guide shouted "Missed!" through well-meaning eagerness, lack of self-control or shear business acumen. In reality it is irrelevant but it still upsets me even now.

ALMOST NOTHING HAS CHANGED
Johannes Daniel Gerstein

I am not one to tell impressive stories, the kind that make headlines. I would like to tell about a peaceful side valley in Upper Bavaria which is less than an hour's drive from Munich.

I first went there thirty years ago and remember it as though it was yesterday. I drove down the narrow dirt road into the middle of the valley as far as the isolated farm which had once been a mill and lumbermill. I closed the car door, pulled on my rubber boots and, with the aid of a map, walked round the 250 acres which, a short time later, was to become 'my' shoot.

I walked for over a mile along 'my' future stretch of river suitable for fishing where red speckled river trout and silver scaled chub lurked in the deep water in the shadow of the willow trees. I saw a few roe deer and the tracks of foxes, badgers and marten, and there were signs of hares and ducks. A kestrel sat on the telegraph pole, buzzards wheeled over the spruce trees and I heard the call of the cuckoo.

As soon as I came to an arrangement concerning shooting and fishing rights with the farmer who owned this paradise, I felt as though I had won the lottery. This was a valley that the world had forgotten. Only two signs bearing the words 'Nature Preserve' at the beginning and end of this small area revealed that the competent official department had noticed the beauty of the landscape and intended to protect it.

The small boggy peat meadow was only some 2.5 acres. In the spring it was blue with spring gentians, interspersed with the delicate red of mealy primrose. An enthusiastic knowledgable friend on his first visit to my shoot counted twelve different species of orchid.

Everything remained the same until my farmer drained and planted saplings in the small meadow in the mid sixties, an initiative which I could understand because rare flowers do not produce any profits. Now there are sterile, stunted spruce trees in the old meadow. The lazy adder and the alert grass snake disappeared like the flowers but, after all, it was just a couple of acres.

The other marshy meadow was a little larger, maybe seven acres, and stretched to the right and left of the stream. It was also full of orchids, along with butterworts, cottongrasses, yarrow and cuckooflower—a favorite spot for butterflies and grasshoppers. I have never seen so many grasshoppers flying and leaping in a meadow and my trout grew into stout heavyweights with the abundant food.

The cattle were less fond of this meadow and so it was understandable when it was also drained and deacidified, thus improving the quality of the

grass after applying copious amounts of fertilizer. This did make life difficult for the varied fauna, but it was only seven acres.

The road was unpaved and riddled with potholes and puddles which provided the swallows with sufficient material to build their nests, but the potholes were less beneficial for tractor axles. Who cares if cows prefer to walk to pasture along dirt roads rather than asphalt roads? In any case the parish council tarred the road in the early 70s. It was given subsidies by government and it would have been irresponsible to have wasted the money, and when a road is surfaced it also makes economic sense to straighten it.

Admittedly, road straightening required work here and there, especially where the old road passed through reed-beds and hay-meadows, both of which disappeared at the same time because no one felt they were of any use anyway. It was a matter of five, or at most seven acres.

One useful side effect was to give the village youths a race track from one village to another and because the valley was so isolated, a practice circuit for learner drivers. This was only at the expense of the odd flattened hedgehog and maybe a roe deer but there were still plenty of hedgehogs in Upper Bavaria. There are still a few hares and deer there. Many people think that it is the deer who are guilty when nature ails.

As the sixth year passed I realized why small red posts had been staked out across the meadows. The large electric power station had discovered that 'my' valley was an ideal route for the new high-voltage transmission line. Now there are just four, admittedly huge, pylons on my shoot.

The damage caused to nature is not so serious: several thousand square feet of scattered meadow met their fate. After all, the protection of nature and the countryside does not override everything —we need more energy and we all benefit from it in some way.

Consolidation of arable land came to the valley two years later. It allowed farmers to cultivate the larger meadows and hay-meadows more efficiently. It was relatively time consuming for large farm machinery to avoid small stands of trees, hedges, ponds and stagnant water, so it probably made sense to eliminate such troublesome obstacles.

It was fascinating to observe how quickly modern machinery could fill in the half-mile long old mill-stream and how quickly forty or fifty-year-old alder and willow trees could be rooted up. The entire stream was filled in and leveled in less than a week, as though it had never existed.

The new stream-bed, equipped with culverts made of corrugated iron and sterile banks made of

The female hare suckles her young in a sitting position.

Even when browsing nothing escapes the roe buck.

44

Martens are strictly nocturnal and are seldom glimpsed during the day.

Mixed forest – the Laubacher forest is shown here – imposes high demands on forestry and hunting...

...and offers both hunters and walkers moments of contemplative tranquility.

The woodpigeon is a common woodland bird, and the only pigeon of any importance in shooting terms.

fieldstone, held the water of the old stream with ease. The mallard, which used to hatch their young there, soon realized that the times were changing and flew away after wheeling around for two days in the sky above the landscape which had changed so suddenly and so drastically.

We used electricity to stun most of the fish so that we could move them to the bottom stream. We rescued some of the crayfish at night, but some of them had already wandered off.

I have no idea what became of the frogs and large grass snakes near the pool of stagnant water. It was only some 450 yards long, but also had to be filled in. Reeds, marsh marigolds, water crow-foot, reed mace, bogbean and many other plants and animals that accompanied it also disappeared, to be replaced by tempting juicy grass which encouraged the cows to add to the butter-mountain.

This all happened in the 60s and 70s. In the mid 80s people started to give the matter a little thought: a small association for the protection of orchids reintroduced new flowers into the spruce plantation for my farmer and a few orchid species returned within two years.

My farmer decided to participate in the meadow rehabilitation scheme and now mows some meadows only after the roe deer rut. This led to more frequent sightings of swallowtail butterflies and camberwell beauties, among others, and the number of fawns killed by mowing with heavy machinery decreased. Thank heavens, since the new neighbors built their raised stands right on the boundary and have started shooting any deer that crosses on to their land, so the new generation of deer is needed more than ever. It is becoming

harder for any buck to reach the kind of age that was still possible in the days of the old neighbor.

The number of horse riders, mushroom gatherers, cyclists and walkers has tripled over the last 25 years but most of them take their litter away with them when they eat their sandwiches at the edge of the wood. If you talk to them calmly they sometimes even keep their dogs on the lead and stick to the footpaths. So far they have not sawn down any of my raised blinds.

This year I saw a red-backed shrike for the first time in three years and the wild mallard are nesting on the stream again which is slowly becoming more overgrown. We joined forces to excavate, construct and plant two new small ponds with some success and now the crayfish are returning and even breeding.

The wild roe deer population is up to forty or fifty percent of its old level—too many according to forestry officials but too few according to us hunters. I now have six-point bucks again and occasionally they survive. One can conserve game even in just a couple of hundred acres if the will is there.

Once again I can shoot 'my' 250 acres and enjoy nature the way I used to do. Maybe one day I shall live to see roe deer promoted from forest pest to a necessary part of the countryside. Already some farmers are complaining that they no longer see any roe deer and they also see that consolidation of arable land had disadvantages as well as advantages.

Many things may change before I eventually have to give up my shoot. Nature can regenerate herself if we only give her a chance and time to do so. People in general, and not just we hunters, must grasp the fact that we are all responsible for nature.

AMONG THE GEESE
Gert G. von Harling

The weather is like a game of chance: it is always good for a surprise. It can only rarely be forecast accurately and what is good for one person can bring another person to the verge of ruin. Breweries and ice cream factories depend on the weather just as much as the quality of wine or the harvest of the already hard-pressed farmer. What is true of brewers, ice cream manufacturers and winegrowers is just as true of huntsmen, especially wildfowlers who shoot geese. Fog, wind, rain and low cloud are all ideal conditions for shooting geese.

As Hubert, Bodo and I approached Bodo's former family estate in Brandenburg along a wide linden avenue under a clear, cloudless evening sky the weather was far from ideal for wildfowling. Bodo stopped the car abruptly by the side of the road. Through our binoculars we could clearly make out a densely packed flock of geese feeding on the crops a good 550 yards away, and we watched the field covered in graylag geese for five minutes or more.

These birds are cunning and seldom roost on growing crops, memories of bad experiences having probably been handed down from one generation of geese to another. Just before darkness falls they normally flight to water and return to their feeding grounds the next morning. If, as on that day, the weather is clear, they fly high, but if it is cloudy or misty they fly low and are relatively easy to hit.

As if in response to a secret signal, almost all the geese took off suddenly and flew high over us in the direction of the Oderbruch. We watched them for a long time as they became smaller and smaller and finally disappeared as tiny dots on the horizon in the clear evening sky. Other flights came toward us and darkness fell quickly. The sky was loud with the almost uninterrupted shrill honking of graylag geese as they flew over. They remained visible as shadowy figures for a few seconds and then they were lost in the darkness, becoming half-glimpsed shadows floating overhead as their cries eventually faded in the distance. Even though the weather was far from promising, we decided to intercept the dawn flight here.

At around five o'clock the next morning we were outside again and lying in a dip some twenty yards square and overgrown with nettles, bordering the field where we had had the good fortune to see the geese the evening before. The moon was still up and we could smell the wild chamomile. Before the first birdsong announced the approaching dawn, I spotted the shadowy shapes of several roe deer in the meadow to our right.

Since the time of Galileo we have known that the earth revolves around the sun, not vice versa, but the expressions 'sunset' and 'sunrise' sound much more romantic and beautiful than saying

White-fronted geese in their wintering grounds in Holland.

Wild geese flying in formation.

48

49

The barnacle goose is found in coastal areas.

The Canada goose originated in North America.

A flock of barnacle geese takes off.

'The earth completed another revolution'.

A quail called intermittently and a skylark sang in brief snatches. Although it was early August, the weather that day was quite autumnal after the prolonged period of rain.

It gradually became lighter, almost imperceptibly at first. A few midges found the unprotected areas of my wrist between sleeve and glove. At last we heard the first goose calls in the distance and my heart instantly started beating faster as their cries became increasingly clear and loud. They were getting closer and closer. The air was filled with shrill cries to the left and right, behind us and in front of us, we could hear nothing else, but it was still too dark to see the geese clearly.

I kept searching the sky as it became lighter and then they were suddenly over our heads. Six large V-formations were descending and slowing down, still well out of range, and eventually landed on the crop. They settled cautiously two or three hundred yards away from us and then one stretched raised neck after the other disappeared and, apart from a few sentries, the geese began to feed unconcernedly.

With our collars raised and the wide brims of our hats pulled down over our faces we lay flat on the ground waiting for other flights. We needed to be virtually invisible to even the sharpest goose eye, for geese are extremely smart and exceedingly suspicious. The term of abuse 'silly goose' is misleading, stupid and obviously has its origin in typical human arrogance.

A large insect buzzed past lazily, the sun appeared on the horizon and the dawn sky was filled with more and more geese. They initially circled over us at a considerable height, cautiously descended and eventually dropped down in the opposite end of the field, to the accompaniment of lively cackling. Other groups arrived as the light got brighter, now less cautious and flying in lower. The sky was now light and we could have taken shots, but they still seemed out of range to me. Then there were geese everywhere for minutes on end and the air was thick with hundreds of voices cackling and gabbling in every register. There were so many geese, hundreds, possibly thousands, too many to count.

Huge formations stood out sharply against the sky which was now bright with just a few thick red-tinted, blue-gray clouds. They were still way out of range and we had obviously not chosen a good spot. Each new flight was preceded by shrill cries.

Each formation received a noisy greeting as it

The graylag goose often rests with its eyes open.

A short exposure time captures a graylag goose as it takes wing – 'walking on water'.

landed and the piercing cries blared like fanfares as flock after flock arrived and spun down to land without even bothering to circle. Geese were still in the air and still well out of shotgun range.

We watched this natural scene for a good half hour, lying flat on the ground and keeping our heads well down.

Callas, the labrador bitch, became impatient now and again, looked into the sky and stood up from time to time but lay down again in response to softly hissed commands.

Then it became quieter for a time, the large gray-brown birds fed on the sprouting green shoots at a safe distance—from the goose's point of view. Several sentries were continuously on duty and we dared not raise our heads. We could only see the vast flock of birds indistinctly though the dense nettles.

The invasion of the geese may have been an astonishing spectacle, but their departure after one or two hours was the highlight of that memorable morning: individual geese suddenly lifted into the air with metallic honking cries, followed by larger groups, and flew directly toward us in snaking ribbons. Small gaggles of four or five, strings of up to ten or twenty and entire flocks of a hundred or more birds approached us. The countless calls blended into a loud, overwhelming din which

completely enveloped us, a fascinating cacophony similar to the sensation experienced by young people listening to techno music I would think.

The first group was scarcely twenty yards above us. Four shots rang out in quick succession as we leapt up and three Michaelmas geese thumped to earth.

We immediately crouched down again and blended into the thick nettles. Several dozen geese were suddenly overhead again and flapping their powerful wings in an attempt to gain height as soon as they saw us stand up from our sparse cover, but it was too late. Another four shots rang out, one goose veered to the right, one tumbled over forwards and two dropped to earth like stones. The rest of the flock climbed steeply into the air with piercing alarm calls and before we had time to reload the countless birds were long gone and well out of range.

The noise of our shots had caused utter confusion among the flock of geese as it was about to take off. The honking and screeching, heavy wing beats, soaring, gliding and flapping of the birds was heartstopping. This powerful symphony of natural sounds almost made me tremble and gave me goose pimples.

THE RUTTING SEASON IN BEAR COUNTRY
Dietrich Stahl

The enchantment of the Carpathian Mountains as described by the classic hunting writers of that area has retained its magic throughout all the twists and turns of history and fate and never fails to cast its spell over us.

The last ten days of September are the best time for deer hunting in the Carpathians; any earlier you usually have little luck, and any later you will have even less.

The rut in the forests back home had got off to a slow start and it was therefore easy to take one's leave and set off. Nowadays it takes about two hours to fly from Munich to Bucharest. Once in the air it is even easier to see how tidily and orderly my native soil is, planned down to the smallest plot of land and only later do the huge wooded mountains and expansive fertile plains appear below: Romania—a potentially rich country ...

I receive a cordial welcome at the airport as I am reunited with my old friend. The visa and firearm import formalities are quickly dealt with, then there is the drive through Bucharest, the oppressed city, which contrasts starkly with its remembered former elegance and unique atmosphere in earlier times.

It was a pitch-black night as we set off and as dawn broke we were already crossing the Carpathians toward Kronstadt (Brasov). Our journey took us through countless Transylvanian towns and villages with their well-fortified churches and lines of gables typical of German farmsteads. The vast majority of the "Saxons" who once lived in Transylvania have already left. The testimony of a culture that was visibly dying after eight centuries punctuated our journey and put me into an increasingly pensive mood. If you are looking for carefree shooting, you should drive through the plains and lowlands as quickly as possible.

We drove through the oldest area of German settlement near Bistritz (Bistrita) without pausing, knowing that we would be able to tour the town at a later date. The distinctive buildings with their characteristic archways and colonnades near the old grain market are fortunately largely intact.

We drove toward the western foothills of the Caliman Mountains along a hazardous road before reaching open pastureland where the idyllic sight of herds of peacefully grazing sheep and cattle can sometimes be deceptive. The dogs which watch over the livestock are often extremely aggressive and the only way to escape them is to jump into your car or, if need be, to fire warning shots. By law the farmers and herdsmen are obliged to fit thick wooden sticks on their dogs' collars to make it harder for the dogs to hunt game.

Our sturdy little car which had been built in 1980 was significantly overloaded and climbed hills at a sedate pace but eventually we found ourselves standing in front of the spectacular Dealul Negru (black mountain) hunting lodge which the once all-powerful Conducator had had built on a narrow slope and which afforded a scenic view of the foothills of the Caliman Mountains. This was the residence of Joan Andres, forest ranger and chief hunter. The oversized rooms of the former head of state had been disused for several years. The more unassuming guest will find appropriate accommodation in the kitchen wing where the wives of the professional hunters look after the guests.

In hunting terms, the Bistritz region has a special reputation as first-class bear country. Above all, bears are enticed from near and far by the fruit in countless orchards in the fall. Every year considerable concentrations of bear build up in this area. This produces excellent opportunities for drives and high bags. The success of these drives is often ensured, during the preparations for such shoots, by encouraging the bears to stay in the area in which they are found by putting out sweet plums, apples and a special cornmeal mixture rather than by using the carcass of an old horse or cow as is often described.

Our first trip into the hunting area was simply to watch bear rather than shoot one. We came across our first light-brown medium-sized bear before we reached the ladder of the raised stand we were heading toward in the valley floor not far from the hunting lodge. It fled with astonishing agility as soon as it caught our scent.

Evening brought a variety of further sightings: a female red deer too old to breed, a fawn, a two-year-old stag, a second bear, jet-black this time, and a young wild boar which was possibly two years old but was already of considerable size. Finally, on the way home and in the fading light at one of the lures and feeding places, we came across two large older bears, perceptible only as mysterious shadowy figures underneath high beech trees in the dim twilight. We decided that a discrete retreat was our best option.

Over the following days we were repeatedly able to observe how surprisingly tame the legendary king of the Carpathian forests can become when fed. One is enriched by experiencing many an impressive sight, but also loses many an illusion, especially when one is told how the "boldest hunter in the Carpathians", as the head of state modestly styled himself, shot many fine bears at a range of only 30 meters at the feeding trough and not uncommonly under the light of a spotlamp. The spotlamp still hangs above the gun

A red deer stands majestically in the morning mist.

slit of the solidly built impregnable tower of the raised stand.

Romania boasts roughly 7.6 million acres of suitable bear habitat. A total population of approximately 5,000 bears would be reasonable for such an area, but Dr Almasan estimates that there are at least 8,000. This means that 500 bears would need to be culled every year but, at present only 60 to 100 are shot. Such an excess population of large wild animals protected by game laws is not without problems for people living in the same areas. Bears repeatedly attack flocks of sheep and herds of cattle, destroy beehives and apiaries and cause considerable damage to orchards. Many an attempt by countryfolk to take emergency measures has come to a tragic end. Not long ago one person grabbed his scythe and paid for it with his life.

We rounded off the first evening with a liter of red wine as our nightcap and planned the next morning. The chief hunter thought we should walk a long distance, there were apparently deer an hour or two away. Our destination would be the Tailor area of the shooting ground, named after a poacher who had once been caught there and who had previously pursued the honorable trade of tailor. Chief hunter Andres knew that

there was an old deer there, and that one couldn't wish for a better animal: a slight hint of brow antlers topped by two beams with a marked bend in each and two completely unequal surroyals each with four tines. His description of the animal haunted my dreams for the next two nights.

Twenty years before, we had walked up into the mountains in Bukovina with small, wiry pack ponies, but now we drove in pitch darkness to the first morning shoot in the four-wheeled drive vehicle which has now become customary almost everywhere in Romanian forest enterprises. Thoroughly shaken about and wide awake, we climbed out of the vehicle which had taken a fair battering and began to walk up the bed of a stream as the stars gradually grew paler. In addition to chief hunter Andres, I was accompanied by a second professional hunter, Doruj Bresfelean.

For foresters and hunters in the Carpathians, streams are still important routes for gaining access to their timber and deer. In the fall they are fortunately usually quite dry, but the coarse scree and slippery stones make them dangerous. The constant murmur of the stream drowned out all the other forest noises in the early morning. As we rested briefly on a fallen tree trunk we heard the initially faint roaring of a deer. The ascent became

increasingly difficult, at least for a relatively untrained northern European plains dweller. Both the professional hunters were well ahead of me like young wolves.

There was a sudden starting noise, a snapping of dead wood and a blurred fleeing shape close to the edge of the mature timber stand. In the still gray dawn light it was impossible to identify the strongest stag in the rutting place or unwarrantable stags. A little later in full daylight, a relatively young bellowing stag of fifteen points walked along a mountain ridge in front of us—what a wonderful sight.

Then there was an older eight-point stag with long beams which ended in thick spires standing above us on a slope—it bellowed down at us without pausing for breath. We really should have shot it but it did not seem right to bag an eight-point stag on the first morning. Sparing him was pure recklessness because there was little likelihood of finding a particular deer again in these woods. Nevertheless, the old abnormal stag was in my thoughts and this quick, easy kill was far less appealing. The eight-point stag eventually trotted over the crest, never to be seen again.

Later that morning we followed the promising voice of a roaring stag until we lost it in the in-creasingly dense forest stand. The higher we climbed the more natural the forest became, usually there was still the original mixture of beech, fir and spruce, but the shapes of individual trees were increasingly massive and bizarre.

The management activities of the forester in terms of timber production, attenuation and maintenance were apparent at lower altitudes, at higher levels one is in the real virgin forest of the Carpathians which has been described so many times and which is far more impressive in reality when experienced first hand than in all the written accounts put together.

This first morning's stalk ended there underneath sturdy trees with a long rest and a substantial hunter's breakfast. Hunter Doruj's bulging rucksack yielded plenty of tasty local delicacies which we spread out on the forest floor, not forgetting a small bottle of plum brandy.

Appropriately fortified, we set off on the descent which afforded fascinating fresh panoramic views across the mountains, valleys and endless forest. On the way down we looked at the supposed place where the 'dream stag' rutted. We only saw a hind in its second year roaming around but the tracks promised many more animals.

In the afternoon we left the deer in peace because dusk falls early in the deepest valleys.

A small group in the rutting season. The red deer typically ruts in a highly visible location such as a hillock or clearing.

Illustration pages 58/59:
An edifying sight for any hunter: a royal red deer stag in its territory. The well-developed antlers are an indication that the animal is in good condition as well as a much sought after trophy.

58

We stalked up the valley of another stream in the Tailor area. After just a few hundred yards a huge old stag appeared on the slope to the right, a stag of twelve or fifteen points. Both the professional hunters estimated that the antlers weighed roughly ten kg (22 lb), but it could easily have been eleven. We had a choice and watched the magnificent deer in wonder and enjoyment until it disappeared at a lazy trot.

Our nightcap of local red wine finished unusually early that night because we aimed to get down to serious business the next morning. Once again we groped our way up the bed of the stream in complete darkness as far as the familiar tree trunk, waited silently and listened. It was as silent as the grave until daybreak and we heard no roaring above the murmuring of the stream.

As soon as there was enough light we moved off cautiously toward the rutting spot. We finally saw a red deer: he was bellowing impressively from high up on one side, in a section of the valley and walking parallel to the slope so that we could glimpse him only briefly between fir and beech trees. Chief hunter Andres was convinced it was the one we were looking for but I wanted to see and identify him myself.

He remained invisible for a long time but made himself loudly heard in the meantime. Then suddenly he was standing on the crest between tree trunks, roared several times gruffly down into the valley and eventually lay down and continued bellowing fitfully. It was an image that will always remain with me.

I could only see the head and neck but it was enough to allow definite identification of the antlers, everything matched: the suggestion of brow antlers, the bend in both beams and tines only on the completely unequal surroyals.

I had enough time to select a good firing position and to arrange pieces of wood, my rucksack and parka to make a serviceable rest for a steep uphill shot from the prone position. I fired when movement above stopped and the right-hand shoulder was exposed. The deer crashed down the slope, raised its head obviously seriously wounded and took the second bullet from the front and fell noisily several yards down the slope after a brief renewed attempt to flee.

The second shot was probably unnecessary but better safe than sorry, especially in these wooded mountains. Without this last fatal dash the deer may well have simply collapsed in front of us without falling and breaking off a small tine from its four-point surroyals, but all the same it was a dream stag.

It only had one eyetooth and subsequent examination of its teeth revealed that my trusty old break-barrel rifle had preempted death from old age caused by wolves and winter. I lingered long beside

the dead ancient stag of the Carpathian forest, the fulfillment of my dreams, hopes and desires over several decades. Eventually chief hunter Andres lifted the head and antlers of the deer onto his shoulders in the fashion of Carpathian hunters and carried it down the bed of the stream in front of me, reminding me of images from the old times.

A timber tractor later picked up the deer and took it to the hunting lodge where it was gutted extremely carefully to make sure that the venison, which was destined for export, would be clean and, apart from the powerful scent of the rut, of high quality on delivery.

There was certainly no shortage of brandy, red wine and riesling that day, and this real high was to be followed by other absolutely wonderful days in the rut. Chief hunter Andres and his assistant Doruj had no other stalking guest to take care of for the time being and went out with me whenever I wanted, that is to say every evening and every morning. This was the perfect fulfillment of my journey, to experience the rutting season in the Carpathians, and the wide open unrestricted stalking and walking filled me with fresh enthusiasm every day. The hunting there is totally different to the way we hunt back home in our tiny hunting grounds where we are mostly confined to shooting from a raised stand.

There were bright early fall days when we walked through rustling grass covered with hoarfrost early in the morning; days when the morning stalk often ended somewhere high up in a position which afforded hazy, distant views across the fringe mountains; days when we enjoyed a rest and the contents of the rucksack in the warm morning sun, to the sound of bellowing stags below us in the Tailor area; days when our evening stalking seemed to lead directly into the fiery red setting sun, days which held fresh heightened experiences and sublime, unforgettable sights.

I finished up with a day in the Colibita hunting area which is famous for its deer and other game, up in the harsh spruce zone of the Caliman Mountains. This brought several more hours of stalking and long walks, abundant sightings of capercaillie and, eventually, red deer. The rutting season was noticeably coming to an end, heavy rain clouds descended towards evening and the next morning not a single stag was roaring.

As we said our farewells, Joan Andres gave me a liter of homemade brandy and an eyetooth from an old stag to match the one in the upper jaw of my stag. It is hard to imagine a more beautiful token of mutual understanding between hunters.

Anyone who harbors dreams and plans of a hunting trip should give thought to putting them into action while there is still time, otherwise they risk finding that they have missed out somehow at the end of their life.

A BLACKCOCK IN THE TYROL
Eduard Paulin

"In the winter of 1805 the Bavarian battalions escorting Napoleon poured along every mountain road into the holy province of Tyrol where they wreaked terrible devastation until they were finally completely crushed and captured between Innsbruck and Bozen by the Tyrolean leader Andreas Hofer and the poacher Josef Speckbacher." These memorable lines from Carl Oskar Renner's novel *The Müller-Peters of Sachrang* came into my thoughts as I crossed the border between Bavaria and the Tyrol near Plansee on Ascension Day, 180 years after this notorious invasion by my fellow countrymen. I had no idea what awaited me and certainly no idea that within the next twenty-four hours I would atone for a fair number of the 'sins of the father'. One fact was clear: the 'Bavarian battalions' were there again, maybe not wearing blue and white uniforms with horses and carriages, but dressed appropriately in golf caps and shorts for the midsummerlike May temperatures. A stout manly 'warrior race' in fashionable polo shirts covering usually generous beer bellies. They came in buses and cars and most of them were obviously tipsy by midday but I appreciated their laughing faces—it was Father's Day.

But I had other thoughts in my mind, my luggage contained my long-barreled Hornet with its ×6 telescopic sight, and the object of my trip was the displaying blackcock, that prancing love-smitten clown of the alpine mountains. There are certainly more awe-inspiring sights in the hunting line than this black, white and red suitor lost in his ecstatic love song, but I have never seen anything finer anywhere.

So far I had only been familiar with the classic method of hunting blackcock from hunting writers, whose magic descriptions enchant me. For a long time I had deliberated whether it was at all justifiable to hunt a game species whose numbers were constantly dwindling due to excessive exploitation of its habitat by humans given the fact that, for opponents of hunting, this is grist to their mill. Preventing damage to the habitat is still the decisive factor for the survival of grouse and for any game species. Excessive exploitation for tourism and forestry measures are the main culprits for shrinking capercaillie and black grouse populations as scientific investigations have proved well enough.

If, despite all the unobjective animosity and adversities, we decide not to lay down the shotgun because hunting really means something to us, we should seek out the enjoyment of shooting and preserve it. It is more than a matter of the undisturbed hunting enjoyment of one or two generations of shooters, it is a question of hunting per se.

The dilemmas which we nowadays have to face are mostly far from new: the hunting author Ludwig Benedikt von Cramer-Klett, an amazingly intelligent observer of both people and nature, makes the laconic statement, in his book entitled *Dream of Green Earth*, that the desire to annihilate game and social hatred of hunting always occurs when there is unrest in domestic affairs. There is nothing I can add to this.

The reader may accuse me of digression, let's get back to the point: my almost 10,000 acre hunting area contains just three blackcocks, and the magnanimous lady owner of the shoot has earmarked one of them for me. Obviously, the hens of this polygamous game species are not hunted because they are significantly more vital for the survival of the species, I point this out only for non-shooters. A single black 'knight' can 'service' up to a dozen hens perfectly adequately, a fact which incited lusty old Ludwig Ganghofer to write these partly envious, partly contemplative lines of poetry of which I have no wish to deprive the reader:

In truth I have often thought to myself
If only I were a blackcock!
But when there are shots and when it swings
then I did think again:
No, I'd rather be
a hunter than the blackcock!

On arrival I met Martin, the hunter, the youngest of three professional hunters employed in the hunting area, a Tyrolean through and through with a considerable bugle. I can certainly compete with him in terms of size of nose but I carry the extra weight of a fair-sized chamois buck round my waist, not to mention an extra twenty years—differences that were eventually to make themselves felt.

He greeted me with a grin and asked "Are you the Boarfrack?" in his guttural Tyrolean accent and nodded with a laugh in response to my immediate counter-question as to whether he was the 'Kraxentrager' who had been assigned to me. Given the historical background I mentioned earlier, it is understandable that for a long time there was no love lost between Bavarians and Tyroleans. This may explain these two derogatory names which survive even today although, obviously, only in a humorous form. The term 'Boarfrack' is probably best translated simply as 'Bavarian pig' whereas the expression 'Kraxentrager' is essentially a more subtle allusion to the widespread habit, which was unavoidable in the Tyrol in earlier times, of carrying any type of burden on one's back, the so-called 'Kraxen'.

The blackcock is specially fond of displaying in open areas: here he makes use of his spread tail feathers which are highly visible from far away.

I enjoyed our walk in the mountains together even though Martin made it clear that the display grounds were free of snow because the weather was much too warm and the mating behavior of the blackcocks would therefore be unpredictable. "Let's give it a try anyway" he said, a proposal which I could only endorse.

It was already three o'clock in the afternoon and by evening we had to reach the hunting lodge at an altitude of some 5,500 feet, just below the tree line. The rest of the ascent would begin at around two o'clock in the morning before dawn broke. This meant that we had to reach the blind in the dwarf pines at the edge of the selected display ground no later than four o'clock.

Because there was no snow cover, the climb would be an average stroll in the opinion of the 'Kraxentrager'. I was taken in but wanted to set the pace and set off up the narrow winding path at a brisk pace. I was carrying my gun and rucksack but had forgotten my climbing stick and was using a completely stupid patent ski pole instead, made of sections which telescoped together and predictably collapsed to Bonsai dimensions whenever I put my full body weight on it.

On this first leg we had to climb to an altitude of about 3,300 feet. This may not sound much, but in real terms represents a three-hour climb. Rotting leaves made the path slippery, and after about twenty minutes I stopped being unhappy about the lack of knee-deep snow. In the final analysis I knew what I was in for, it wasn't the first time I had hunted in the mountains and I would not have wanted it any other way. I motivated myself by remembering that, ultimately, the value of the bag depends on the effort expended.

After an hour of strenuous uphill walking it gradually dawned on me that a spreading waistline and a smoker's lungs are not ideal equipment for mountain hunting and that my previous mountain walks must have been of a significantly more innocuous nature. My shirt and trousers were sticking to my back and buttocks and I was taking breathers at ever shorter intervals under the pretext of a pressing need to observe nature. The 'Kraxentrager' grinned but said nothing and, like a true professional, let me believe that he understood my tendency to admire the scenery.

Completely exhausted, I finally glimpsed the hunting lodge, perched picturesquely on the steep slope and shimmering through the trees and made a final sprint worthy of any racehorse.

I could already hear the inviting babbling of the trough of the spring-fed fountain from far off and plunged my head and shoulders into it without even bothering to take off my hat. I swallowed great gulps of the refreshing water as greedily and as eagerly as an old dog after a six-mile walk across a potato field.

The rock partridge is roughly the same size as a partridge and is a protected bird in Germany.

The ptarmigan is an essential part of alpine fauna – this rare bird is also protected in Germany.

Marmots in spring

Passably invigorated but with my pulse still racing, Martin suggested that I got the practice target shooting out of the way because dusk was already falling and there was no time for a rest. I was aware that I would hardly be performing under rifle-range conditions but was nevertheless surprised by the target. It was a small unopened can of sausage, about two inches in diameter and very appropriately labeled "Smoked Tyrolean hunting sausage". The 'Kraxentrager' rejected my objection proposing a more sensible use of our supper on the grounds that there was no alternative and even claimed that the small hole would be no problem and might save using the tin opener.

Strongly suspecting that he was banking on a miss, I lay in a cramped-up prone position aiming at a point a hundred paces down the slope and hit the edge of the small can. The can of sausage took off vertically like a jack-in-the-box and disappeared downhill in a series of rapid cartwheeling bounces. Martin, surrounded by an avalanche of stones, hurtled downhill and caught up with it, thus saving our supper.

At two o'clock in the morning Martin roused me from my bed onto which I had slumped, after our dented meal. It was pitch dark and seeing the long-pointed crampons, helmet lamp and sturdy

ice axe with which the 'Kraxentrager' was equipped, for the first time I began to have serious misgivings about what I had taken on.

He eased my worries by claiming that such gear was really superfluous for our short walk across the snow-free stony ground but that it would make life a bit easier anyway. I scrambled along behind him in the dim beam of the fairly pathetic lamp as we crossed the tree line. The terrain was becoming increasingly rugged and I was very glad of the darkness which prevented me from seeing how steep the drops were in certain places. The sound of rocks rolling downhill faded in the distance and left me in no doubt that both of us could well be taken home in a bag if we went down the mountain other than in the prescribed manner.

We eventually reached the blind, as dawn was already breaking and I could clearly see a steeply sloping alpine meadow beneath us which was roughly two hundred yards long—the lekking ground was ahead of us. I had made a rough-and-ready attempt to dry my clothes in the hunting lodge but they were already sticking to my skin again and this, together with the ice-cold morning wind, made me begin to freeze; it was certainly not hunting fever making me shiver. Because of the alleged 'short walk' I had thoughtlessly ignored

A blackcock in flight, a rare sight in much of Europe – blackcock are only common in Scandinavia, where they are also hunted.

Once a blackcock selects a location for its lek display, it is very reluctant to abandon it. In hunting terminology, such a bird is a 'resident cock' or an 'old rowdy' – names which are quite appropriate, as this series of photos shows.

A capercaillie reaches the climax of its mating display.

The hazel grouse is fond of buds and berries and is well camouflaged in the branches of a tree.

The ptarmigan also cuts a fine figure in flight.

the advice to take a change of clothes, but the spirits of the mountains showed me consideration because events then followed in rapid succession.

All of a sudden we heard a whirring noise in the air and a dark bundle of feathers shot low over our heads as we ducked. A single blackcock arched down onto the display ground scarcely thirty paces from the blind, stretched its neck and looked around somewhat warily. Our necks also stretched jerkily to three times their normal length, not unlike the damned ski pole, but we dared not risk making any other movement. The blackcock then began the performance for which I had dragged myself there. There were alternating sequences of gurgling and bubbling noises and one flapping, fluttering leap after another. It reminded me vividly of our Bavarian folk dancing which some people claim was actually inspired by the blackcock's wild mating dance and I was totally engrossed in the sight of this tiny suitor who was equally absorbed in his love song.

Martin's elbow jabbed me in the ribs, he was understandably worried that the blackcock would not stay long because of the unsuitable weather situation. I rested the Hornet on the supporting branch of a dwarf pine in front of me cautiously, but the blackcock saw or sensed that it was in

mortal danger. He immediately interrupted his mating dance, stopped, looked in our direction and crouched down in order to gain height by taking off vertically. At this moment of last opportunity the cross hairs were on the wing joint and I squeezed the trigger.

The blackcock jerked as the rifle cracked and I knew that only a bird which is fatally hit behaves like this. I still held my breath because the blackcock, although already dead, was close to the precipitous track and was gobbling. The gaping chasm of the steep gorge lurked at the end of the display ground. The 'Kraxentrager' jumped up like a madman, overtook the tumbling blackcock in similar fashion to his race with the can of sausages the day before, grabbed it and held the bird up in front of me a hundred and fifty paces away with a shout of triumph.

I stood in the blind completely numb with cold and, because of my inadequate yodelling talents, relieved my tenseness with a litany of curses of joy spoken in a low voice. Martin placed the blackcock on the rucksack, decorated it with a small green branch and carried it down into the valley in front of me. I cannot remember ever having felt more pride when wishing someone Good hunting!

PRECIOUS MEMORIES
Gert G. von Harling

The hour of winter's death nears and soon spring will be reborn. A solitary lark already floats over the rye fields, which are turning greener every day. The pied wagtails must have arrived overnight because in the morning two of these songbirds are happily scampering along the roof ridge of the manor house with their long bobbing tails as I go downstairs to let the dogs out.

I had been expecting the pied wagtails for weeks, they normally fly back from the south with the woodcock to the northern regions where they spend the summer.

I had already prepared a plan. As for many years, this spring I am once again drawn to the wood that borders onto the extensive moorland to a spot where my father and grandfather used to stand in wait for the birds with the long beak. But this time, unlike on previous occasions, I shall not take my shotgun, but I do want to capture the mood which has always taken me ever since my youth at this time of year, a mood which no one can take away from me. I want it to remain more than a memory, now that ill-informed politicians have made a traditional form of shooting controversial despite scientific evidence.

My grandfather was a passionate huntsman and in the village they still tell how, when he was too old to tackle the long arduous walking of the shoot because of his rheumatism, he used to be pushed in a wheelbarrow to shoot woodcock. It must have been a strange sight to behold the estate forester's son pulling the misappropriated barrow with a thick length of rope and the father pushing it from the rear.

In the summer when I occasionally used to lie in wait for roe buck, I often used to see and hear woodcock flying grunting and squeaking through the clearings. Even in the fall, when the leaves and grass were already on the turn, I used to listen to them and watch their mating flights. Once our landlord found a woodcock nest with two eggs and two freshly hatched chicks. By the time he found me and we went to the supposed nest a few hours later there was no sign of it apart from a few pieces of eggshell. Did the woodcock move her chicks because she had been disturbed?

It was late afternoon when I left the house with the weimaraner on the lead and noticed that the redstart had returned from its wintering grounds and was curtsying friskily on a paddock fence post. Although it was still quite cool I was in no doubt: the woodcock would be flying.

A few years ago when it was still possible to shoot the long-bill in spring I once shot one in a very heavy snowstorm. Our gamekeeper had obvious misgivings about my sanity when I went out with

my shotgun in such weather. In the late evening on the way back home there was a slight frost and, as well as the woodcock, I caught a cold into the bargain. As I presented my bag to my unhappy-looking tutor, my teeth were already chattering.

This story came back to me as I stood at the old stand far too early in the afternoon. A slight wind had got up and blew the sound of the spruce trees toward me, not particularly favorable weather for a flight of woodcock early in the year.

The ground was still frozen, even where the sun's rays had begun to penetrate. I ambled past the brown poultry pens which always look abandoned at this time of year and two calling buzzards circled overhead. Several lapwings and a flock of starlings announced the imminent change of season just before I reached the wood.

I disappeared into the bare alder trees and nearby dark spruce trees, and dead leaves rustled beneath my feet as I walked to the spot where I had been allowed to shoot woodcock with a shotgun for the first time over thirty years ago.

I was so excited then that I shot a plump out-of-season mallard with my first cartridge, a wicked act which fortunately became less culpable long ago through time. I was far from displeased with this clean shot and, smugly confident that I would also hit any woodcock, carried my bag home and was duly reprimanded. This did not prevent the entire family consuming the illegally obtained roasted bird with considerable enjoyment.

But I was despondent, after my first successful shot at a game bird my next ten cartridges fired at woodcock achieved nothing apart from possible damage to the tops of the tall alder and spruce trees. The birds seemed to have no desire to award their highly sought after painter's feathers as a modest trophy to a crazy young shooter who was bursting with enthusiasm, and he in turn could not understand this.

My self-confidence was in tatters and my score remained zero.

At one point a woodcock landed just a few paces in front of my stand to probe the damp pasture. It stopped and looked around for some time, walked hastily to and fro, stuck its beak in the ground, turned and pulled a large worm out of the damp soil. While it was eagerly attending to the worm, the evening quietness was shattered by a tremendous bang. My tutor would have undoubtedly forbidden me to shoot for the rest of my life if he had ever discovered that I had 'assassinated' my first woodcock while it was sitting. So much water has flown under the bridge since then but I can now confess my crime with remorse.

Afterwards I did hit birds and took many a bird with a long beak home but, honestly, I normally shot only a single bird on any one evening.

My nephew once accompanied me to lie in wait

for game. He sat quietly behind me on a tree stump as we both savored the delightful evening atmosphere. A woodcock suddenly flew towards us and I dropped it straight into his lap. The amount of pain which a small bird can cause when it strikes certain parts of the human body is amazing. On this occasion Schiller's claim that 'all goodness comes from above' applied only to me. My 'badly winged' nephew never came woodcock shooting with me again.

I was actually quite pleased about this because even one person often makes too much noise when out shooting.

I reached my stand just as the sun seemed to slowly touch the horizon, and as I had often done in past years, I made myself comfortable by resting on an old slanting tree and gave way to my thoughts. My dog made a bed for itself by turning round restlessly in circles several times. His initial attentiveness was followed by loud yawning and he soon fell asleep. I listened to the piping, warbling and singing of the various bird species. The concert given by the feathered songsters seems to be loudest when dusk approaches. Several blackbirds trilled their evening song and I could also hear the melodic voice of a song thrush. A robin was shyly clicking somewhere and a wren called excitedly in front of me in the raised root ball of a spruce tree that had been uprooted by the last storm.

I heard sudden wing beats and a woodpigeon settled not far away. His mating call drifted across to me after a brief pause. It would probably have been easy to lure him closer by cupping my hands and imitating his call but I was not in the mood even though he had no cover. He called again and his cooing seemed more insistent than before. I then heard a response from the nearby spruce wood.

It was becoming cool and the scent of rotting leaves, pine resin and fresh earth became stronger. The bird song faded almost imperceptibly. I could only hear the scolding call of two song thrushes, and it seemed that their heated argument would never end. Mice rustled beside me in the dry fallen leaves and I heard the far off hoot of a tawny owl but the light was fading and everything around me suddenly fell silent as though in response to a secret command.

The dog woke, got up, yawned, stretched thoroughly and looked at me questioningly. How was he to know what I was feeling, he was young and had never been with me when I had shot a woodcock.

There were three roe deer to my right, scarcely discernable against the brown background, only their gleaming white rumps betraying their presence. They were unwary and carried on walking without noticing us.

The shadows had become much longer as I sat there. Another roe deer gave the alarm in the far-

The tawny owl is more often heard than seen. Its characteristic call is an essential part of the evening mood in any wood.

Illustration pages 68/69:
The twilight flight of a woodcock

off distance—was that a wild boar over there? A song thrush scolded again briefly, and then silence. The tops of the alder trees stretched skywards and took on a light purple hue. I felt chilly. In the old days there would have been a few single shots somewhere in the neighborhood at this time of day, but for years now there has been silence.

A shadow flew over me, I started, only a tawny owl on the lookout for prey. He instantly swerved and flew back toward me as I pressed my lips together to imitate the squeaking of a mouse but he soon saw through the ruse and glided away silently until the darkness of the trees enveloped him completely.

Something that looked like a swallow was flying in a zigzag line along the edge of the wood: a bat hunting for insects overhead in the evening sky. When I was a boy we often used to have fun with

bats by throwing our hats into air. Now and again these animals which fly as fast as lightning were fooled and swooped down onto what they thought was their quarry.

And then there was nothing but silence and the excitement of waiting expectantly and listening for sounds. I was beginning to have my first doubts, and then I heard the far off unmistakable 'quork, quork, quork, pisik, pisik' noise. They were suddenly flying directly overhead, bird after bird.

I have no doubt that I could have shot two or three of these birds, but in our neck of the woods large bags of woodcock are off limits because of their numbers and circumstances. They are one of many species of game that we should now watch rather than shoot.

The woodcock uses its long bill to search for tasty titbits; worms, insects and larvae are on its menu.

HUNTING DOGS

KARL WALCH

Legend has it that when a rift developed between man and animals, the dog
was the only animal to spring over to man's side. However the bond had not
always been so clear-cut. Initially man and wolf had been hostile toward
each other, and even now the "big bad wolf" still pursues innocent Little
Red Riding Hood. Ice Age hunters allegedly developed friendly contacts
and bred wolf cubs, and only another 20,000 years have past since man
discovered dogs, yet he has already conquered the moon. Dogs have
meanwhile been bred to become man's best friend, and like everything
which is dear to us, we have also turned him into an objet d'art.
For example, the Saint-Germain Pointer in a hunting still-life by
François Desportes evokes the words of the Persian prophet Zoroaster:
"The world exists through the intelligence of the dog!".

73

The wolf was domesticated very early on, but it is not known whether it was used simultaneously as a hunting hound. Pictures like these Bronze Age cave drawings from Hultane in West Sweden are considerably later. Here a group of dogs is harassing a wild boar which is then killed by the hunter.

◁ The dog as guardian is based on the Egyptian idea of Anubis, the God of Death.

An unknown artist depicts the dramatic moment when the wild boar is held at bay by the hounds.

74

Good Hounds are Almost More Important than Good Weapons

This quote from Count Czernins' "Hunting Manual" (1935) is a rather clear definition of the relationship of the hunter to his hound. Flavius Arrianus (around 95–175) saw it quite differently: "A hound with a really good pedigree is a mighty possession which will not be bestowed on the hunter unless the Gods favour him".

Harmony between hunter and hound originated at a time when Stone Age hunters and collectors hunted game with spears and spear-slings, and there is a striking connection between the dog as hunting companion and the greater effectiveness of the spear used with the sling. It is really tempting to connect the appearance of the dog as hunting companion with the necessity to track down fleeing, injured game over greater distances. The so-called "peat" dog (*Canis familiaris palustris*) of the Mesolithic (8000–5500 B.C.), which has been found relatively often in excavations, was both hunting dog and guard dog. Presumably it would also have been used as food in hard times. Out on the hunt he proved invaluable for tracking down and pouncing on game which tried to defend itself, and it is mainly in this connection that the hunter made abundant use of the intelligence of his four-legged companion. The individual capabilities of dogs resulted from their natural disposition. Man's influence will have been limited to pure utilitarian breeding and the

exploitation of hereditary instincts. The main capabilities of individual dogs was therefore different.

In around 3,000 years of a generously measured "transitional phase" during the Neolithic Age (4000 through 2200 B.C.) and the Bronze Age (2200–750 B.C.), different dog breeds gradually emerged, and these can basically be divided into four groups. Alsatians, Huskies, Spitze, Terriers and Pinschers belong in the first group; Sheepdogs, mountain dogs, hunting dogs (hounds) and Poodles in the second. Greyhounds comprise the third group, and Pugs and Bulldogs the fourth. The dogs of this period were already on average bigger and heavier than the "peat" dog.

Let us interrupt the history of hunting dogs at this point and pick up the threads approximately 2,000 years later.

In the Middle Ages, and in some cases far earlier, attempts were made to breed "tracker" dogs and "assault" dogs separately, by specific mating of particularly successful types. In addition the agile Staghound emerged, as did the hawk- or bird-dog which was particularly suitable for falconry.

Riding to hounds and stag hunting became increasingly important. These two types of hunting were especially popular in England and France, where they concentrated on the breeding and handling of hounds which required a passion for

English Greyhounds are considered the swiftest and most reliable of dogs.

The leading tracker-dog at work – an illustration from Hans Friedrich von Fleming's "The Complete German Hunter" (1719/1724).

Hunting was also successfully portrayed in porcelain figures in the 18th century, riding to hounds and dog handlers being particularly popular.

Even though this dramatic scene of a bear hunt as portrayed by the Antwerp painter Frans Snyders (1579–1657) may appear somewhat fanciful, we are left in no doubt of the keenness of the hounds attacking the wild game.

The warlike appearance of these barbed dog-collars was supposed to protect the valuable hounds from bites from cornered game.

This detail from the Devonshire Hunting Tapestries (Arras or Tournai around 1445) shows that hounds used for bear hunting also wore protective hunting garb.

François Desportes (1661–1743), painter of hunts at the court of Louis XIV, here creates a still-life of two hounds and a hare in an evening landscape.

In portrait painting dogs fulfil different roles; they reveal the identity of the hunter, give information on the character of the person portrayed and are a symbol of faithfulness.

The fox-hunt is brought to a successful conclusion.

Im Winter hat der Bär die größeste Gefahr,
Derweil zu solcher Zeit sein Peltz sehr frei von Haar.
Es stellt Ihm der Polac mit allen Listen nach,   **Der**
Doch dient die Englisch Dock am besten zu der Sach. **Winter.**

Une Saison fort mauvaise l'Hiver,
à l'egard de l'ours et de sa peau,
Le Polonois avec les Dogues,
Tâche à l'attraper, où elle est à trouver.

L'Hiver.

This Meissen porcelain figure from 1744 is of "hunter Wenzel" and his dog.

Johann Elias Ridinger (1698–1767) advises using English dogs for hunting bear in winter, as practiced by the Poles. This page is an extract from a four-seasons series.

hunting, stamina, keenness and a flexible neck.

In his handbook (1737), Georg Friedrich Probst relates a conversation between Nimrod and Hubertus. Hubertus answers Nimrod's question as to which is the best dog as follows: "English (...) have good stamina, do not underestimate the exertion, are also more likely to stand the stinging lash of the whip than others. By contrast, French dogs look far more beautiful, but are highly-strung and do not have as much stamina as an English one (...)."

A bird dog or field dog, which was kept singly, was expected to have a controlled hunting instinct, but retained a strong bond to the falconer. His task was to find the game, mostly birds, and flush it, that is, drive it out of its hiding place, so that it could be attacked by the hunting bird which had been carried to the spot. A special kind of Bloodhound emerged during this period in the form of the leader of the pack which was used for detecting and picking up the scent of the game or following the deer trail.

With the decline in feudal supremacy in the mid-19th century, hunting methods changed, and this also had an impact on the handling of hunting dogs. In place of spectacular riding to hounds and "regulated hunts", which had required big packs of hounds, the individual hunt now emerged. This took the form predominantly of falconry with the bird dog, and later with the Pointer which was

Der Hasen werden viel, zur Frühlings-Zeit gefangen,
Bevorab wan sie sich, ins Grünen Feld vergangen,
Doch wan mit höchster Wuth, die Hunde an ihn setzen,
So hat der Schirmer Sorg, daß sie ihn nicht zersetzen.

Der Frühling.
Le Printems.

Le Printems la Saison fort propre,
Pour la chasse des lievres,
Mais pour defendre les chiens,
De les dechirer, chien est gardien.

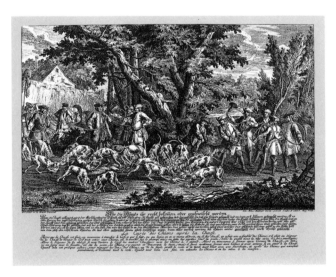

The spring extract from the four-seasons series depicts the small game hunt for hares.

Adriaen Beeldemaeker (around 1618–1709) portrayed dogs specialized in different tasks in his "Returning home from the hunt" (above right).

Ridinger shows how after the hunt the dogs were "made familiar" with parts of the stag (below right).

bred from the former. The Pointer or Setter was trained not to flush or drive out wildfowl, but had to stand or lie rigid with its nose pointing in the direction of the spot, until hunting apprentices had placed a net in position, so that the startled wildfowl could be trapped. In falconry, the dog had to stand rigid next to the game it had found until the hunting bird had been brought to a favorable hunting position by the falconer.

Two factors led to a significant re-evaluation of the pointer; the invention and general spread of firearms and a rise in the hunting of gray partridge, quail and pheasant as arable land was extended. The characteristics of the Pointer were further improved by cross-breeding them continually with hounds (Foxhound, Greyhound and Bloodhound). Although the "new age" in hunting terms, marked by a decline in small game in nearly all parts of Europe, permits an almost limitless exchange of all breeds in existence, traditional and proven methods of training, handling and breeding nevertheless still differ from country to country, and even from region to region. Whereas versatility is expected of most dogs in Germany, specialist dogs are kept and trained as such in large parts of Europe. The owner of an English Pointer may jokingly refer to the utilitarian German dog as a "Poodle," but in turn, there is much criticism of English special breeds by many German huntsmen.

The hunt breakfast and pack, "whips" and visiting servants rest together; both the latter, according to Ridinger, enjoying "a cold roast, bread and a bottle of wine".

A copperplate engraving by Ridinger depicts how the "lead-dog" picks up the scent of the noble stag (top right).

Hunter and dog in spruce forest—the stereotype of the hunter since the 19th century.

Handing over the retrieved wild fowl.

Captions to page 81:
Still-life composition (1714) by François Desportes of hunting game and equipment (top).

Philipp Ferdinand de Hamilton (around 1664–1750) portrays a very keen hunting dog on a black grouse hunt (below).

HUNTING HOUNDS

HOUNDS

All hound breeds can be traced back to a distinctive early type of running dog which can be encountered in vivid detail in drawings by the Romans and the Celts, and also in ivory carvings from the Orient; it had long, lop-ears and a slender body. The original large varieties were replaced by smaller and slower breeds, as a result of the need to adapt to the individual hunting operation, and ultimately to the reduced size of hunting areas.

Parallel to the change in hunting conditions, the maintaining and breeding of the once widespread hounds declined considerably in European countries. Especially hit are densely populated industrial nations and those regions where the link between hunting right and landownership, and the preference for certain hunting practices (e.g. ambush and deer-stalking) leave little room for the long-term use of hunting hounds.

Many of the regional breeds of hound, for example the Holstein, the Hanover Heath, the Ammerland and the Cronenberg Hounds, fell victim to these changes and became extinct. Their lineage, however, lives on in a whole series of breeds which still exist today. The last surviving examples of Holstein Hounds, which disappeared around 1880, laid the foundations for hounds in Denmark, Sweden and Norway. The Hanover Heath Hound lives on in the Hanover Bloodhound, with which it was cross-bred to improve its hunting instinct.

The most important local breed in Northern Germany was the Westphalian Hound, officially recognized as the German Hound in 1990. Its main area of distribution is still the Sauerland, even today.

Earlier local breeds were classed as Holzbracke (Wood Hound), which are large and Steinbracke (Rock Hound), which are small. In and around Olpe (North-Rhine Westphalia) between the wars a smaller Holzbracke stock was bred—the so-called Olper Hound—which was approximately 18 inches (40–50 cm) in height. Its somewhat reduced hunting stamina (by contrast with the old Wood Hounds) and its pleasing appearance contributed to the fact that the German Hound basically corresponds to the triple-colored Olper medium-sized breed.

Apart from the long-legged German Hound, there is still its smaller cousin, the Westphalian Basset (Dachsbracke = Badger Hound), which was also introduced into Sweden around the turn of the century and became very widespread there under the name of Drever (Swedish Dachsbracke). Today the Drever is occasionally used to slightly extend the small breeding stock of the few Westphalian Bassets kept in Germany and to protect them from the dangers of in-breeding.

The Alpine "Erzgebirgler" Dachsbracke is not related to the Westphalian Basset, despite the similarity of its name. It apparently emerged via selection from the Segurian Hound. Its homeland is a wide area of the Alps and the Ore Mountains (between Germany and the Czech Republic). In the opinion of leading dog breeders and experts, the Dachshund (Teckel) developed from this race. It therefore represents the link between long-legged hound and Dachshund. In the JGHV (German Utilitarian Hunting Dog Association) it is officially recognized as a breed of Bloodhound, although in terms of provenance it belongs to the true hounds. It is bred as a brindle, that is, black with rust-red markings and dark deer-red.

Today hunting with hounds is widespread in Austria, where the Austrian Hound (Brandlbracke), Tyrolean Hound and Styrian Wirehaired Hound are still very much in evidence. In the 1960s, to improve the bark and alertness of the Austrian Hound, which is the dog preferred by mountain hunters, it was specifically crossed with the Slovak Hound (Slovensky Kobov), to which it is related.

PACKHOUNDS

Parallel to the emergence of short-legged dog breeds on the continent, England devoted its time to the breeding of Packhounds. Even though fewer pedigrees were bred there than for example in France—the latter including the original breed, the "Chien de Saint Hubert" (the Saint-Hubert Hound = Bloodhound)—a standard was reached in England which has lasted into modern times, and could not be even remotely matched by any other country.

The most common breeds today include Foxhound, Harrier and Beagle. They are used in packs in their country of origin for hunting fox

"Many dogs are the death of the hare." However, even big and swift hunting dogs cannot usually catch a healthy fleeing hare. But if the hare is ill and is accidentally found and chased by two dogs at the same moment (as in the photo), he will be caught and brought to the hunter.

(Foxhound) and hare (Harrier and Beagle). Whereas it is usual to ride to (behind) hounds on fox-hunts, even in England hares are mostly hunted on foot, and thus hare-hunting, especially with Beagles, was common even in less wealthy circles. This contributed to the extensive spread of the Beagle. The Beagle is also used in small numbers in Germany as a keen "flusher" and for sending off on safe hunts for dead prey as a tracker dog.

TRACKER HOUNDS

As direct descendants of original hounds, the Hanover Hound and the Bavarian Mountain Hound are used exclusively to track injured cloven-hoofed game. As specialists in this field, they produced quite outstanding work.

The ancient legacy of the leaders of the pack, those formerly calmest and most sensitive-nosed dogs of the pack, lives on especially in the Hanover Hound. Although the leader of the pack was still used in the Middle Ages exclusively for "launching" and detecting and picking up the scent of healthy deer (it was even feared it could lose its abilities, if it was involved in tracking work), nevertheless, at least since the widespread introduction of firearms, it has been used on the trail of wounded deer. Even today the Hanover Hound is mostly trained according to the so-called gamekeeper circle method on the healthy, cold (at least two hours old) scent of a single piece of deer being pulled along under observation, instead of with an artificial scent, because it is important that the hound becomes acquainted with the individual scent of each animal.

The Bavarian Mountain Hound developed from a cross between the Hanover Hound and the Tyrolean and Austrian Hounds. The Bavarian Hound is slighter in build than the Hanover Hound, and is a tracking specialist in mountainous terrain. Nevertheless there are a great many of these dogs in Northern Germany today, and even there they have demonstrated their high potential for work on the trail of injured game.

DOGS USED TO FLUSH GAME ("BEATER HOUNDS")

A good hunting hound often follows the scent of hunted game for hours until the latter is exhausted and can be trapped and brought down by the waiting hunter. By contrast, the task of the "beater" dog in hunting operations is firstly to seek out and locate the exhausted game. Once the "beater" hound has located the game, it then flushes or drives it out from cover, by reacting noisily to the warm scent or trail it has detected. The game, which always knows where the noisy

Ideally hunter and dog make a perfectly co-ordinated team.

hound is, does not flee panic-stricken, as it would if confronted by a silent hound, but instinctively changes the direction of its flight and can be brought down by the hunters who are ready and waiting there.

The group of dogs which flush game also includes dog breeds which generally briefly ransack any shelter or cover in the search for woodcock, pheasant, rabbit and hare, with the hunter and his shotgun standing by. These are referred to as gun dogs. Classical gun dogs are Clumber Spaniels, Cocker Spaniels, Field Spaniels, Irish Water Spaniels, English Springer Spaniels, Sussex Spaniels and Welsh Springer Spaniels.

The absolute classical dog which flushes game, and versatile companion of the forest hunter, is the German Quail Hound. The "Quail" is bred in two color types; the brown short-distance hunting dog and the white, in which the legacy of long-distance hunting hound is still very prevalent. Since color separation during breeding is not always strictly maintained, today it is no longer possible to distinguish the characteristics of the two color types.

POINTERS AND SETTERS

The names for this useful group of hunting dog indicate the typical "pointing" or "setting" (crouching) stance the Pointer or Setter adopts when it detects the scent of the game. It is a visible signal for the hunter that the dog has found game, and always something of an experience, when the solid dog, in the midst of its lively and all-encompassing search, darts around at lightning speed as if pos-

sessed, and then stops short as if transfixed, until the approaching hunter drives out the huddled, marked game and kills it.

Since the spread of firearms and the increase in the hunt for small game, everyday hunting has become unthinkable without the Pointer or Setter, though these breeds were originally used mainly for falconry. Even today, the Pointer or Setter is the most common hunting dog found throughout Europe, although the stock of small game has sharply declined in many places. Within Europe, however, Pointers or Setters are used rather differently in different regions. Whereas in England, Pointers or Setters are still regarded as field work specialists, in Germany they have been bred for a long time for their versatility. Known breeding characteristics are also attuned to different specific uses.

Whereas a German Pointer or Setter must demonstrate its ability in field, wood and water, and work before and after the shoot, an English-bred Pointer or Setter is selectively bred for the field work before the shoot. The English Pointer must be regarded as the epitome of the classical field dog, with its big movements, its sensitive nose and fine pointing stance to the game. Psychologically and physically totally attuned to field work, it is capable of extraordinary achievements. Nevertheless, if trained in the classical manner, even the retrieving of game shot under the "nose" of the Pointer is handled by Retrievers which have been specially trained for this task.

The three long-haired Setters also qualify as English "Pointer" Dogs. They are the mahogany-colored Irish (Red) Setter, the black and tan

He roams inquisitively through the meadow,
Nothing escapes his sensitive nose.
He detects even the minutest scent
in the long grass.
How skilled, how cleverly and sensibly
he keeps a watch on everything.
It is divine watching him work.
(Christian Karl Josias von Bunsen 1791–1860)

Correct retrieval of a mallard

Hunting party at rest

▷ German Hunting Terrier

◁ The hunting instinct can occasionally be difficult to contain in the enthusiasm for action.

Two magnificent Alpine "Erzgebirgler" Dachsbracke

Leather hound-collar with brass mountings and initials
(German, 18th century)

Dog muzzle made from bands of perforated filigree brass
(German, 16th century)

Iron hound-collar with brass mountings and the initials ASPA (German, 17th century)

Iron dog-collar with brass mountings, coat-of-arms and the initials EGVK (German, 18th century)

Leather dog-collar with the initials HVM (German, 18th century)

Leather dog-collar with the initials PZ and the coat-of-arms of Zweibrücken

Leather dog-collar with the owner's remarks as follows: "J'appartiens A.S.A.S. Monger le prince Max de deux ponts colnel propre du Regt d'Alsace" (dated 1771).

Hunting in water requires keen, dedicated hunting dogs who enjoy being in water. It is always a pleasure to watch such dogs at work—how he dives into the water with one leap, reaches his target with supple movements and proudly returns with the game.

brindle Gordon Setter, and the predominantly white (with several different large black or brown patches) English Setter. As the name suggests, they crouch ("set") rather than stand when taking up the pointing stance. The pointing stance is overall slightly different according to the breed, but also differs from dog to dog.

Among the numerous French Pointer and Setter breeds, which can be divided into three different fur varieties—the French Shorthaired Pointers, the Longhaired Spaniels and the Wirehaired Barbets (Water Poodles) and Griffons—the smallest member, the Brittany Spaniel, enjoys big international acclaim. This obedient, albeit highly keen, small Pointer is very highly rated, especially for falconry.

Finally, German Pointers have an outstanding reputation world-wide as versatile working dogs both before and after the shoot. This can ultimately be attributed to the fact that even utilitarian hunting dogs have been handled with typical thoroughness here, which is still the case today. Examination and breeding systems are strictly regulated. All one year's examination results are recorded annually in the so-called DGStB (German Working Dog Pedigree Book) breed for breed, and dog for dog, and published. In addition, the use of "serviceable dogs"—a term entrenched in law in Germany only—is specifically binding for numerous different types of hunting.

These hunting dogs are bred in shorthaired, wirehaired and longhaired varieties.

The German Shorthaired variety enchants lovers of this breed with its outstanding field manners. Whether it is in the heat of Spain, or in the wide expanses of the North American Prairie, or in the Scottish Highlands or in neighbouring France, the German Shorthaired Pointer can hold its own anywhere and everywhere. In this connection the breed not only excels in field work, but also in numerous cases on a long lead, and as a reliable retriever of wounded game.

This large dog, whose body measures between 22 and 26 inches (58 and 66 cm), is bred as a brown or black brindle. A hunting dog breed of very special interest is the Weimaraner, which is bred both in longhaired and shorthaired varieties. The leader dog legacy together with the legacy of the old German Pointer lives on in it. The Weimaraner is a calm, working dog which searches in a somewhat hesitant manner, and is especially suitable for the work after the shoot.

Among Roughhaired German Pointers the German Wirehaired is the oldest breed. His ancestors doubtless include the old Water Poodle —the French Barbet—to whom it owes its amazing keenness for water and also its rough, wiry coat. The German Wirehaired Pointer is today found predominantly in the area of East Frisia. The small litters, however, mean that it has become a rare sight even there.

In 1881, upon the initiative of Baron of Zedlitz and Neukirch, better known under the pseudonym of Hegewald, the Poodle Pointer emerged by crossing Poodle and Pointer. The aim of this cross-breeding was to combine the water enjoyment, keenness, intelligence and leading qualities of the Poodle with the outstanding scent detection, style of searching and "pointing" aptitude of the Pointer. Over 110 years later the objective of this cross-breeding appears to have been largely successful. The Poodle Pointer is today presented as a highly productive fully working dog

Carrying the dog along in search of hoofed game.

Nothing escapes that sensitive nose.

94

A well-coordinated team.

German Wirehaired Pointer barking over the kill.

which works well in the field and in water.

At the end of the last century, a Dutchman named Korthals who lived in Germany produced Belgian, French and Dutch Wirehaired Pointers from crossbreeds, and the now entirely separate breed of Griffon from the Barbet. The rough and coarse fur with long top coat, the prominent beard and bushy eyebrows are the typical hallmarks of this dog. The Griffon's strengths lie in field work, and particularly in water.

Although it is not the oldest German Pointer, the German Wirehaired Pointer nevertheless corresponds to the widespread visual notion of the original German working dog. It is the extremely successful result of cross-breeding between

German Wirehaired Pointer, German Shorthaired Pointer, Griffon and Poodle Pointer over a decade and is today the most popular Pointer in Germany. It is difficult to pinpoint any particular ability, some definite sign that it really does represent the breeding objectives of the breed founders, but it is a versatile working dog. It is bred with a coarse, wirehaired coat in brown, brown brindle or black brindle.

Examples of longhaired German Pointers are the German Longhaired Pointer, Large and Small Münsterländer, and the Longhaired Weimaraner. The German Longhaired Pointer is even today still associated with prestigious old German companion dogs. Old working dog virtues, for

example calm, scent detection and alertness have been displayed by this dog over many decades through breeding. Its special talents lie in work in wood and water, where it is conspicuous by its toughness on itself, and its energetic and zealous way of working. Guided in a consistent manner on a long lead, it demonstrates fascinating work on the scent of red deer. It nearly always hunts noisily and shows its genetically firmly entrenched alertness even on wild boar when standing its ground against game which defends itself. It is bred as a pure brown dog and as a brown and white dog with different proportions of brown and white (dark-brown brindle, light brindle, whiteish-brown brindle, "trout"-colored brindle).

The Large Münsterländer also belongs to the group of German Longhaired Pointers. It was originally nothing more than a black and white version of the German Longhaired Pointer (Deutsch-Langhaar). In 1919, when the "Deutsch-Langhaar Association" excluded the black color, friends of this color variety formed the "Association for the pure breeding of the Longhaired Black & White Münsterländer Pointer" that same year, and undertook to breed and spread it. In the recent past there have been several matings with German Longhaired male dogs, in order to improve the breed, particularly in terms of keenness for game. Thus the offspring of black and white parent animals today continually revert to brown and white. We must wait and see whether or not both breeding associations—Deutsch Langhaar (German Longhaired) and Large Münsterländer—merge again one day, thereby putting an end to the quarrels of the past.

The Small Münsterländer Pointer is the third longhaired German Pointer. It is not a smaller version of the Large Münsterländer, as people like to maintain, but an entirely separate breed. Being the smallest German Pointer it enjoys great popularity amongst the hunting fraternity. Its friendly nature and uncomplicated attitude, however, have also contributed to the fact that no other German Pointer is bred in such enormous numbers (except for the hunting breeding associations) as is, regrettably, the case with the Small Münsterländer, which are bred for their beauty, rather than as hunters.

GROUND DOGS

The preservation of small game would be unthinkable without hunting down foxes and badgers. Apart from hunting with traps, or hiding places near lures, a particularly successful form of hunting is "burrow hunting" (digging out). The Terriers and Dachshunds bred for this purpose drive the fox out of the burrow with sharp attacks, so that it can be killed by the hunter. Or, they hold a badger, which they have found in a burrow, at bay

Whether in search of game in the deep snow of a forest in winter or hunting small game in autumn, you need good hunting dogs.

Receipts, to heale sundrie diseases and infirmities in houndes and dogges. Chap. 79

▷ "Turbevile's Booke of Hunting" illustrates how to administer medicine to dogs, 1576.

Caption to page 97:
A Münsterländer proudly retrieves a rabbit.

The Longhaired Dachshund is suitable for flushing and burrowing work. Unfortunately it is often the victim of breeding for beauty's sake.

The Cocker Spaniel is more suitable as a gun dog than for flushing game. It searches in close contact with its handler who has his gun at the ready.

The English Beagle is used in England for hunting hares.

The Austrian Hound is the ideal companion for the mountain hunter.

Longhaired Weimaraners are rarely seen.

The Labrador is a classical retriever.

The Hanover Hound belongs to the oldest breeds of hunting dogs and is the descendant of the leader dog.

The Finnish Hound is closely related to the German Hound.

Magyar Vizsla (Shorthaired Hungarian Pointer).

The Greyhound was also a popular and swift hunting dog, which hunted game over long distances. This kind of hunting is prohibited today.

Nordic Elk Hounds have upright (pricked) ears.

The Labrador is a favorite hunting companion—especially in England.

English Pointers, living up to their name.

in the farthest tunnel until the hunter digging there kills the badger in the excavated hole. Both Terriers and Dachshunds are used for ground hunting and also as tracker dogs on safe hunts for dead game. In addition, these short-legged dogs are used extremely successfully for noisy tracking and flushing of game. A hunt where wild boar are flushed is practically unthinkable without the use of German Hunting Terriers, and that is a reflection of the quality of performance of the black and red dogs, which are bred as smooth-haired and wirehaired varieties.

The Fox Terrier, which is predominantly white with black or tan markings, has the same coat. In his homeland of England it was and is still used for riding to hounds on fox-hunts, mainly if the Fox evades the pack of pursuing Fox Hounds by retreating into a burrow. When it has been taken out of the saddle-bag, it is the Fox Terrier's task to persuade the fox to emerge again, so that the hounds can continue to chase him until he can be killed. Only very small numbers of Fox Terriers are bred as actual hunting dogs nowadays.

Among terrier breeds native to the British Isles, the Jack Russell Terrier enjoys great international popularity as a "burrow" and "flusher" dog. The Jack Russell is an English cross between the Old Terrier, the White Bulldog and the Beagle, which was attributed to the Reverend John (Jack) Russell around 1820. After he died in 1883, the new breed which emerged was named after him.

RETRIEVER

To support Setters and Pointers, which were used in England purely for "pointing", Retrievers were bred on the island specifically for retrieving. Retrievers are a cross between the Newfoundland St. John's Labrador and Water Spaniels, Poodles, Setters and even Newfoundland dogs. Retrievers occur as several different breeds, which are sometimes longhaired, sometimes shorthaired, and also curly-haired. Unfortunately Retrievers hunt mostly silently and only very seldom have a keen instinct for predatory game. They therefore have a very limited use in terms of hunting. Their good nature and calmness, combined with their marked play instinct has meant they have become popular family dogs over and above their hunting use.

NORDIC DOGS

In terms of their historical development, Nordic dogs are not derived from hounds, but have their own roots in earlier Nordic dogs, and in particular in the Danish "Torvmose" Dog.

Nordic dogs are on all accounts good "flusher" dogs, even though they mostly hunt in silence. They are usually specialized in certain species of game. Thus the Karelian Bear Dog or the Karelian Bear Laika have emerged, whose legendary ability is the all day search for sable. Then there is the "Jämthund" (Large Swedish Elkhound) and the Gray Norwegian Elkhound, which on long leads follow the trail of the elk until their handlers take over, or, roaming freely, search for elk and independently flush it from cover, then hold it at bay and bark until the hunter arrives. Furthermore Finnish Spitz Dogs and "Norrbottenspets", the Swedish equivalent, are used for tracking down game birds. Nordic dogs are used for hunting almost exclusively in their area of origin.

EUROPEAN GAME—MAMMALS

BRUNO HESPELER

Two types of game have traditionally been hunted in Europe— mammals and birds. The mammals range from seals to reindeer. Mammalian fur serves important functions: protection from the weather and from predators, and in social behavior as a method of signaling.

The mammalian game of Europe are represented by ten large families and still include a wide range of species, despite the encroachments of urbanization and industrialization. The populations vary from species to species and from region to region, some being threatened by loss of habitat, whilst others, such as roe deer and red fox, are still found in large numbers. Hunting and field sports—no longer the privilege of royalty—have therefore taken on an increasingly ecological dimension.

WHICH SPECIES MAY BE HUNTED?
Susanne K. M. Linn-Kustermann

Only a small selection of wild mammals may legally be hunted, and the laws relating to hunting vary from country to country, and also sometimes from region to region within a country. In general these are medium-sized or large species which can or could be used in some way, usually because they provide (or provided) edible meat or a warm pelt. They include some species which are now rare or threatened and which have therefore been removed from the category of game animal or placed under strict restrictions, or in some cases totally protected. Examples of rare mammals enjoying full protection over most if not all of their range are brown bear, lynx and spanish ibex. The sportsman or hunter must always check on the legal situation before going into the field in pursuit of a particular quarry.

In most countries hunting is restricted to particular seasons. Thus, in Britain for example, the open season for stags or bucks of red and fallow deer is 1 August through April (although in Scotland it is 1 July until 20 October for red deer stags). For hinds or does, the corresponding dates are roughly late October until mid-February. In England, Scotland and Wales, ducks and geese may generally only be shot between September and the end of January, whilst the season for Pheasant and Woodcock is October through January, and for red grouse between 12 August (the famous "glorious 12th") and 10 December.

Most game mammals belong to the following groups: hoofed mammals (zoologically, these are all even-toed ungulates—order Artiodactyla), such as wild boar, deer, chamois, wild goats and wild sheep; rodents, which include beaver and marmot; lagomorphs, the rabbits and hares; and carnivores, for example fox, wolf, wild-cat and brown bear.

Some species, for example the hoofed game and lagomorphs, yield edible flesh and are widely taken for food. Carnivores are notable predators of other wild species. Huntsmen have always had rather an ambivalent attitude to such species. On the one hand they yield useful pelts and are also admired for their nimbleness and cunning. On the other hand some predators have been persecuted because of the effects, real or imagined, they may have had on the populations of other game species or farm animals. Bear, wolf and lynx have all been persecuted in this way, to the extent that they are now threatened or extinct over much of Europe.

Some animals are hunted because they may become pest species, often being referred to

colloquially as "vermin". Species in this category include grey squirrel (in parts of Britain), brown rat, carrion crow, magpie, jay, woodpigeon, and occasionally feral cat.

Sika deer grazing

The raccoon—an immigrant from North America—is now firmly established in the European fauna.

106

Much of Europe north of the Pyrenees, Alps and Carpathians belongs to the temperate zone and enjoys a climate which typically varies between warm, frost-free summers and more or less cold winters. In winter, most plants have a period of dormancy and for the herbivorous mammals at least there is then little food available.

Some species get through the winter by resting for long periods, others by hibernating, migrating or lowering their metabolism and reducing their activity. Some sleep for much of the time during the coldest weather, without drastically lowering their body temperature or heart rate. Such species, for example badger, brown bear, raccoon dog and raccoon, need to break their rest from time to time to forage for food, even in winter.

True hibernation is mainly seen in certain rodents and bats, and also in hedgehogs. Such species select a deep hole or other safe place in late autumn and then fall into a deep sleep-like state. In true hibernation, the body temperature can fall as low as 39°F(4°C), and energy consumption is reduced to some 10–15 percent of normal, thus eking out the fat reserves right through until spring.

The onset of hibernation is governed by the light-dark regime (photoperiod). Some hibernating animals wake occasionally to pass urine or feces, and a few also to feed. On final awakening in spring, normal body temperature is restored in just a few hours. True hibernators include alpine marmot, hedgehog, hamsters, dormice and bats.

Another strategy for winter survival is to migrate to warmer regions to avoid the barren period. Migration involves the regular seasonal switch between summer and winter quarters, rather than daily travel between resting and feeding sites, movements to rutting or display grounds, or dispersal of young animals into new territory.

Some hoofed mammals, such as caribou/reindeer and Siberian roe deer, travel hundreds or even thousands of miles, often in enormous herds. Red deer also undertake seasonal migration in parts of their range. In the Alps for example, almost the entire red deer population descends to the river valleys in winter to feed. Much of this vital winter territory has been lost to housing or affected by developments such as power stations, or access cut off by motorways. Red deer are therefore forced to spend all year at higher altitudes, and are often fed during the winter. In the Swiss National Park, where such supplementary feeding has been discontinued, the annual migration to lower ground has reinstated itself. The trails followed are apparently passed on from generation to generation. Migration from winter

to summer quarters takes place at the end of May or beginning of June, that is before calving takes place. The deer usually move quickly, often completing the journey in a single night, apparently responding to fresh growth in the vegetation. Return to the winter quarters is usually in October, but may be earlier if food is particularly scarce. Roe deer also make such seasonal migrations, but usually in smaller numbers and especially when there is no supplementary winter feeding.

Some species move only short distances to more suitable sites in winter. Thus chamois and ibex seek out sites exposed to the sun or wind, where the snow tends not to lie or where it melts more quickly, such as south-facing slopes.

Wild boar are specialists in the art of survival, thriving under diverse conditions. These omnivores are active even in the cold of winter.

Fallow buck. Unless given supplementary food these herbivores must migrate to warmer regions for the winter.

DEER FAMILY (*Cervidae*)

The members of this family of even-toed ungulates are found throughout the world, as are the bovids (horned ungulates). Only four of the seven main European species are native: elk (moose), roe deer, red deer and reindeer (caribou); fallow, sika and white-tailed deer being introduced. Fallow deer came originally from Turkey and possibly other parts of southern Europe, although bone finds have shown that between the Ice Ages they were found as far as north as the Baltic Sea. Nevertheless, all present northern European populations can be traced back to introduced stock. Sika are from east Asia and have been introduced to many places in Europe, notably the British Isles and north-west Germany. The American white-tailed deer has been introduced to southern Finland. Other introduced deer are the axis deer of India, with small scattered populations, for example in Italy, Poland, and Ukraine, and the dog-sized Chinese muntjac, now common in much of England. In all except the reindeer, only the males have antlers.

RED DEER (*Cervus elaphus*)

Often known as "king of the woods," red deer have been prized by huntsmen of the nobility since the Middle Ages, and poaching this species was often punishable by death. Now widespread throughout the whole of Europe albeit missing in some regions – except for Finland, and much of Greece and Portugal.

Adult stags stand at between 45 and 60 inches (115 and 150 cm) at the shoulder and weigh, varying over the geographical range, between 175 pounds (80 kg, in Corsica, Sardinia, Scotland) and 550 pounds (250 kg, in Bulgaria and Romania), and occasionally as much as 770 pounds (350 kg). The female (hind) weighs about half to two-thirds as much.

The rut starts as early as the beginning of September in the south and south-east, rather later further north where the climax is usually early October. The single fawn (occasionally twins) is born after a gestation of 33–34 weeks. The fawns lie up for most of the day in the first two weeks, are suckled right into the winter and stay with their mothers until the next fawning season.

Stags first grow antlers—usually a simple spike —in their second summer (rarely earlier). The

Distribution of red deer.

Red deer – *Cervus elaphus*.

length of this depends mainly on the social rank of the mother in the herd, and has no influence on future antler development. These first simple antlers are shed the next spring (older stags shed in early March or earlier). In the third year the antlers are usually six or eight-pointed (tined), and often rather blunt. Fully developed antlers do not normally develop until the stag is ten years old. The size and shape of the antlers depends partly on the age of the stag, but also on its state of nourishment and health, and on its social standing. Antler development appears also to depend on genetics and on food quality. Well developed antlers may have as many as 12–14 tines, sometimes even more.

Red deer live in herds. The older animals move out from the herd shortly before calving, and at this time the calves from the previous season leave their mothers, either wandering alone or in small groups. In early summer the pregnant females temporarily abandon the herd when the young are born. Although the newborn calves are quite capable of standing and walking, they spend the

first few days hidden under the scrub or tall grasses waiting for their mother to come back and feed them. Family groups tend to consist either of hind, young female and calf, or of hind, young buck and calf. The hinds live together with calves in small herds, in which one adult female is usually dominant. Adult stags form separate herds in summer, which break up at the start of the rut.

Unlike roe deer, red deer do not have fixed territories, and stags fight not over land, but only over hinds during the rut. After the rut, the stags accompany the hinds for a short time, before forming stag herds again after shedding their antlers. In woodland and forest habitats red deer are mainly crepuscular or nocturnal, but on the open Scottish moorland where they often form large herds they are mainly active by day.

It is mostly rutting stags that are hunted, in woodland often from raised blinds, and in Scotland by stalking. In some parts of Europe hinds and young stags are hunted by beating through the woods and undergrowth.

Red deer stags in velvet.

Red deer hind with calf.

Red deer stag

Red deer in drawings by J.E. Ridingers,
18th century

FALLOW DEER (*Cervus dama*)

Fallow deer were spread to many parts of southern Europe, first by the Phoenicians and later by the Romans, mainly from their stronghold in Turkey and some other pockets in the Mediterranean region. The Romans brought them to England by 150 A.D., and by the 16th century they had become established in Germany. There have been many deliberate introductions to parks and forests over much of central and western Europe.

An adult buck measures 30–43 inches (80–110 cm) at the shoulder, and may weigh between 175 and 285 pounds (80 and 130 kg), depending on the region. The wild type is reddish brown above, flecked with white spots, with a white rump patch with dark borders. In winter the coat is gray-brown with less distinct spotting. Artificial selection has led to the existence of a number of color forms, including albino and melanistic varieties.

Fawns begin to develop antlers at 5–6 months and these are fully grown by February. These usually develop the first branch by the first half of August, although some yearlings may have a second branch. Older bucks mostly shed their antlers in April, whilst the younger bucks shed in May and so come into velvet earlier. The second set (head) of antlers is somewhat broader-stemmed, and by the third set they become markedly flattened and shovel-like.

The fallow deer rut starts as the red deer rut peters out, and finishes about the beginning of November. Unlike red deer, fallow bucks use traditional rutting grounds and remain true to these for decades. Often several bucks will stand close together, separated by small, invisible territories. If a buck strays into an adjacent patch this can lead to fierce disputes. The rutting bucks advertise their presence through distinctive belching and groaning sounds and thus attract the does.

Gestation is about 33 weeks and usually a single fawn is born. Unlike red and roe deer, the fawn follows the doe immediately to the protection of dense undergrowth, before they both join up with others.

Unlike red deer, which have become largely crepuscular or nocturnal at least in central Europe, fallow deer are mainly diurnal and generally prefer open country or parkland, often fleeing into open fields even when hunted, and waiting there for the "all-clear" signal.

After the rut the bucks gather into all-male herds and wander some distance from the rutting grounds. Some bucks however, usually the younger ones, separate from the herd and live alone. At about the beginning of September the bucks separate before gathering at the rutting grounds. Here they scrape out hollows in which they bathe and wallow. During the rut the bucks seldom eat and lose up to 20 percent of their body weight.

Fallow deer have a characteristic, goat-like way of running, in which all four feet leave the ground almost simultaneously.

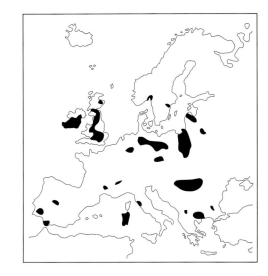

Distribution of fallow deer

Fallow deer – woodcut

Fallow deer – from Conrad Gesner's "Thierbuch," 16th-17th century

Fallow deer

113

Cervus dama: Fallow deer bucks. By the third season most bucks have flattened, shovel-like antlers. First-year bucks have simple spiked antlers; branching begins in the second year, with the number of points increasing steadily each year.

Fallow deer bucks...

... shedding velvet

Cervus dama

Rutting bucks

Fallow doe with fawn

SIKA DEER (*Cervus nippon*)

Introduced from Japan and China to many sites in western, central and eastern Europe. Scattered populations in England, Scotland and Ireland, as well as in Austria, the Czech Republic, Denmark, Germany, and Poland.

Between fallow and red deer in size, rather like a small version of red deer, but variable in size and proportions. Summer coat color red-brown, speckled yellow-white at all ages and browner than a fallow, and gray below; gray-brown in winter, unspotted or with indistinct spots. Adult stags have an obvious mane in season.

The rut is very long, from mid-September until early December. The usually single fawn is born between early May and mid-July.

Sika are rather more nocturnal than fallow deer, but are also active by day, and they tend to stay in one area rather than move about. Rutting behavior resembles that of red deer, although the rutting herds are smaller. The hinds live together with young animals in herds, the stags in small groups or solitary. The antlers usually have at most three or four tines. The first simple antlers start to appear in March of the second year, but the deer are not in velvet until August or as late as October. Older stags shed their antlers between mid-April and the end of May, and are in velvet between mid-July and early September.

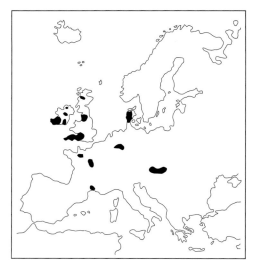

Distribution of Sika deer

Sika stag

Sika hind

Sika deer—*Cervus nippon* ▷

118

WHITE-TAILED DEER
(*Odocoileus virginianus*)

This deer is native to North and Central America, south to Brazil, but has been introduced to southern Finland. In size it is between red and sika. In summer it is pale or reddish brown, without spots; grayer in winter. The large ears and tail are particular features, as is the spreading white rump-patch. The antlers lack a front fork, and the upper tines point forwards and upwards. The first year antlers are mostly simple spikes. Antlers are shed from the end of November to late January, and regrown between June and August.

Rutting takes place between October and December. After a gestation of about 30 weeks, two, occasionally three, fawns are born.

Like roe deer, white-tailed deer are highly territorial, living in family groups or larger winter herds.

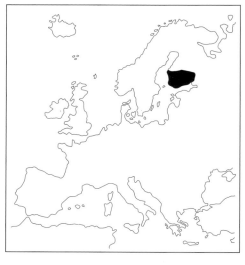

Distribution of white-tailed deer

White-tailed deer – *Odocoileus virginianus*

120

REINDEER/CARIBOU *(Rangifer tarandus)*

Caribou, or reindeer as they are known in Europe, live in the northern forests and tundra of Eurasia and North America. Both sexes have curved and branching antlers, and one of the forward-pointing branches is often flattened. The fur is very thick and dense.

Reindeer make annual migrations between summer and winter quarters. They leave the forests in spring for the treeless tundra, covering distances of over 600 miles (up to 1,000 km). As highly selective feeders, they take only very nutritious food such as fresh shoots, buds, flowers and leaves. Using their deeply cloven hooves they dig through deep snow to reach the vegetation below. Reindeer is the only deer species to have been domesticated. They are still herded in many parts of their range by the Lapps, and they provide meat, leather and milk.

Herds are usually active by day and led by an adult female. Caribou may weigh as much as 330 pounds (150 kg), grow to 6.5 feet (2 m) long and live for 15 years. The fine, spreading antlers are a highly prized hunting trophy.

Reindeer

ELK/MOOSE *(Alces alces)*

Moose (known as elk in Europe) are found over a wide area of North America and once ranged widely in the northern forests of Europe and Asia. Nowadays the European strongholds are Norway, Sweden, Finland, the Baltic states and Poland, although they occasionally wander south to Germany, the Czech Republic and Austria.

The largest living deer, about the size of a horse. The male (bull) usually has flattened, shovel-shaped antlers with up to 40 points, spreading almost horizontally and weighing up to 44 pounds (20 kg); the female (cow) lacks antlers. The bull also has a characteristic bearded throat lobe.

The rut is from the end of August until November and the calves (often twins, rarely triplets) are born after a gestation of some 33 weeks.

Moose are mainly crepuscular. Unlike most other large deer, the females stay with their own families, sometimes accompanied by young of previous years. Each male remains with a single female at a time, often leaving the first after mating to go in search of another.

The traditional method of hunting is with elkhounds which track individual animals. The huntsmen either follow the hounds or wait nearby.

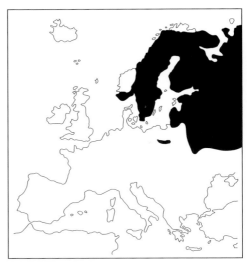

Prehistoric drawing of an elk
Norway

Alces alces: female with calf

Bull elk

Two bull elks rutting

Elk—*Alces alces* ▷

Much has been written about the origins and function of antlers. Today there is broad agreement amongst scientists that they arose out of the rivalry amongst the males of the species to propagate their own kind. Whereas female ruminants expend a great deal of energy nourishing the growing foetuses and producing milk, the contribution of the male animals to the procreation of offspring is limited to the insemination of the females. They can therefore afford to channel a high level of energy into building up powerful antlers or horns to use as weapons and to help them to attract and defend fertile females. The fact that these weapons may be used against pursuers seems to be a side-effect rather than a significant factor in their origin.

In the course of evolutionary history many different kinds of horns (in the broadest sense of the word) have evolved. Two basic zoological types can be distinguished: the horned animals of the family Bovidae, and the antler-bearing animals of the family Cervidae. Horns and antlers differ firstly in their material: horns consist of horn, antlers of bone; secondly they differ in their durability: horns last a lifetime, whereas antlers are renewed annually. Their growth proceeds differently too: horns become progressively larger, whereas antlers grow to a different size each year. Furthermore, in the case of horned animals the females bear these "weapons" too; amongst antler-bearing creatures this is true only of reindeer.

Antler growth is cyclic. In winter, after the fighting for supremacy is over, the antlers become not only superfluous but also burdensome. They are therefore shed, and new ones begin to form under a protective skin, the velvet. Amongst all European Cervidae the antler cycle—from the shedding of the old to the rubbing of the velvet from the new antlers (known as fraying)—is linked to seasonal changes in vegetation, that is to say, to the available food. The external (photoperiodic) trigger for the antler cycle is the proportion of daylight to darkness. At a certain point on this curve, which differs for each species of deer, hormone changes are triggered which control the shedding and the regrowth of the antlers.

Amongst the hormones which influence the antler cycle, testosterone plays the major role in almost all species of deer. It is only in the case of the reindeer, the only species of deer in which the female also bears antlers, that the antler cycle is controlled by different hormones. For the new antlers to grow, the testosterone level must steadily rise, which is why the animals are at their most sensitive and temperamental when their antlers are fully formed, and this in turn has an effect on their social relationships. As a rule, the groups of bachelor males break up soon after they have finished fraying their antlers, as by then stags and bucks have become too quarrelsome.

A rapid fall in the testosterone level leads to the

The famous 66-pointer, killed by the Elector of Brandenburg Frederick III (later King Frederick I of Prussia) on September 18, 1696 near Berlin, was the subject of numerous paintings, engravings and silver figures. The trophy is on show in the Hall of Freaks in Moritzburg hunting lodge near Dresden.

The Hall of Trophies in the former Munich Stadtpalais of Maximilian Count of Arco-Zinneberg (1811–1885). The collection, currently housed in the German Museum of Hunting and Fishing, Munich, includes more than 2,000 roe deer antlers and chamois horns, as well as numerous red deer antlers.

casting of the antlers. This hormonal change brings about a natural fracture at the pedicle, an excrescence of the frontal bone, on which antler branches begin to grow. The fracture soon heals over and becomes covered by the velvet, under which the development of the new antlers now begins. Out of the soft tissue of the frontal bone, which contains a copious supply of blood, the hard, bony structure of the antlers develops through calcification from the base upwards. Until it becomes mineralized and hardened the bone remains covered by a protective layer of velvet. Between the velvet and the bone tissue run numerous blood vessels, the course of which remains visible on the fully-grown antlers in the form of more or less deep grooves. During this period, the antlers are very sensitive, and stags and bucks in this condition behave cautiously, so as not to injure their antlers. Injuries at this stage can result in misshapen antlers and serious loss of blood.

Only when the ossification of the antlers is completed, with the formation of the tines, does the bone tissue calcify and harden, becoming insensitive to pain. The superfluous velvet, which dies and is rubbed off on the trunks of trees, is highly nutritious, and is then eaten by the deer. The bony substance of the antlers is at first snowy white, its final coloring being determined by the pigments found in tree sap and from the traces of blood in the velvet. Whether the antlers acquire a darker or lighter color is thus dependent on the type of tree on which the stags fray their antlers.

In contrast to the horn-bearing animals, whose horns carry annual growth-rings, it is not possible to tell a deer's age from its antlers. The idea that the stag grows one more point with each year of life is a popular myth with no foundation in fact. Nevertheless, antler growth follows a certain progression, depending on the age of the animal. For all antler-bearing animals the antler makes its first appearance at the pedicle. This first antler growth, in the form of a little knob or tiny spike, does not follow the same cycle as the antlers of the adult deer, as, of course, the calves are too young to be involved in the mating process.

The development of the antlers follows different patterns according to the species. Various factors can influence antler development, these factors include diet, the social environment or social structure of the herd, and the extent to which the deer can find opportunities for undisturbed quiet and rest. The genetic make-up also plays a part in the different levels of growth of the antlers. The following indications of age-related development are therefore only guidelines, from which individual animals may deviate markedly.

For its "first head" the young red deer nearly always produces just two spikes. For its "second head" it generally forms its first proper antlers

with a greater or lesser number of points, according to its constitution and the environmental conditions. At the age of seven it is fully grown, and from this point on until the age of twelve to fourteen it grows the strongest antlers. The antlers attain the peak of their development when the deer reaches full maturity. At that stage the branches are at their longest and strongest, and have numerous points, which may be quite long. This occurs at about the tenth or twelfth "head". Thereafter the antlers gradually get smaller, as the stag grows old.

In the roebuck a distinction is made between the yearling's antlers and the first "proper" antlers, which even in the fawn grow as small, inconspicuous buttons. The yearling, on the other hand, may form shorter or longer spikes, or may have either forked branches or six points. The peak of antler development in the roebuck varies greatly between individuals and regions. It is fair to say, however, that bucks grow the strongest crowns between the fifth and seventh years of life.

Fallow deer form spikes in the "first head", and in the second and third "heads" develop rudimentary palms. Fully developed palms do not appear before the "fourth head." The peak of antler development for this species of deer occurs around the ninth and tenth "heads". By this time the palms of a healthy animal are broad, and the branches thick and heavy.

The first antlers of sika deer are almost always simply spikes. From the "second head" on, however, it may have as many as six or eight points. In contrast to red deer, in sika even a fully mature pair of antlers, which is normally only attained at the age of about nine or ten years, seldom consists of more than eight points.

Antlers of a "royal" 24-pointer. Each branch bears (from bottom to top) the brow tine, the bay tine, the tray tine and the crown. The points on the crown are known as top points.

Roebuck in velvet

ROE DEER
(Capreolus capreolus)

Roe deer have expanded their range considerably in recent decades and are now found throughout Europe except for north Scandinavia, Iceland, Ireland and the Mediterranean islands. They are also found in northern Asia across to China. Roe deer can tolerate a wide range of climates, from the dry heat of the Balkan karst to cold sites high in the Alps where they can be found at altitudes of up to 3,000 meters, even in the depths of winter. They have also adapted well to living in cultivated areas, often close to human settlements, benefiting from intensive forestry and being relatively insen-

sitive to air pollution. Roe vary in weight and size, influenced both by the habitat and by their population density. Bucks are generally somewhat larger and heavier than does, and measurements vary from about 24–28 inches (60–70 cm) shoulder height and 44–77 pounds (20–35 kg) weight. They live for up to about 20 years.

The summer coat is red-brown, except for the grayish face. In winter the coat turns to gray-brown. The tail is almost absent, and there is a prominent white rump patch. Partial and full albinos occur, and also melanistic individuals in some regions, notably in the lowlands of north-west Germany. The antlers are fairly small, and 6-pointed when fully developed.

Roe buck with first antlers

Roe buck with uneven antlers in velvet

Roe buck with 6-pointed antlers

Roe deer family ▷

126

The once commonly held belief that one can judge the age of roe deer by the points of their antlers has been shown to be false. Even yearlings can grow well-developed 6-tined antlers if they are well nourished and favorably placed in the social hierarchy. For a roe buck neither the strength nor degree of branching of its antlers appears to be important, and these seem to affect neither survival nor social rank. Nor are they useful as weapons against prey, for which purpose simple spikes would in any case be more effective than branched antlers.

Antler growth takes place from December to March, with calcification complete by mid-March, and the drying skin (velvet) being shed in April or May. They are shed each year between October and the end of December.

The rut runs from mid-July until early August, finishing somewhat later at higher altitudes, some does staying in heat until mid-August. The bucks seek out does in heat and remain paired up with them for two or three days. Sometimes yearling bucks will pair if all the full-grown bucks are fully occupied.

After mating, the fertilized egg or eggs remain in a state of suspended development until early the next year, resulting in a gestation of over 40 weeks. Interestingly, the roe deer is the only ungulate species in which this phenomenon has been recorded. The fawns are born in May or early June, with twins being the norm (exceptionally triplets), although weaker or older does may have just one.

For the first few days the mother leaves the fawns in a safe site, returning often several times a day to feed them. Imprinting on to the doe does not occur until the age of about three weeks. At two days old the fawns deliberately eat soil to help their digestion and by a week old they start eating plants. With ovulation in the autumn season, the does' milk drops off, and the fawns must by then rely mainly on plant food. Sometimes the fawns suckle well into the autumn, but this probably has more of a social function than providing much nourishment.

Roe deer are most at home in a varied habitat with quite a lot of cover. At two or at the oldest three years the bucks start defending their own territories which they often keep all their lives. They mark the territorial boundaries by scratching with their front feet, using scent secreted from glands between the hooves. There are also scent glands on the forehead which come into play when the bucks rub their antlers against young trees. After the rut, territoriality declines again. They tend to inhabit different but overlapping

Roe deer—doe with fawns

ranges in summer and winter. Does also occupy their own, rather less distinct territories when giving birth and rearing young.

Yearling roe leave their home territories to look for a place some distance away where they spend the summer (a behavior which reduces the danger of incest), and may occasionally travel as far as 30 miles (50 km). Roe are not particularly gregarious, although the young deer do sometimes stick together in early summer. After the rut, one typically finds family groups, consisting of a doe and fawn, together with a young doe or yearling buck. Larger groups gather together at feeding sites, but these are made up of several family groups which have come together by chance and which disperse again soon afterwards.

Roe are essentially deer of scrub or woodland margins, and when danger threatens they tend to respond by sticking to cover and hiding, rather than by running away as would red deer. They seldom move more than about 300 meters, then they wait silently until the disturbance subsides, before retracing their steps.

Roe are hunted by different methods in different regions. Thus in Scandinavia and parts of France, in Italy and in Switzerland they are shot, a selection pressure which has produced some-

what stronger animals. Elsewhere, in Germany for example, roe are only hunted in the mating season.

These differences developed as long ago as the end of the last century. Roe bucks are generally hunted in summer, enjoying a close season from mid-October, and this applies in much of central and eastern Europe (except Switzerland). Does and young deer are mainly shot from September 1 through to mid-winter. In Germany and Austria some 1 million and 260,000 are taken each year respectively.

Roe buck

Distribution of bison

CATTLE FAMILY *(Bovidae)*

These are horned, even-toed ungulates with a digestive system allowing them to cope with a relatively unspecialized diet. Unlike antlers, horns are permanent rather than shed each season and are carried by both sexes, although in mouflon some females have only very small stumps. There are six species in Europe: bison, musk-ox, two species of ibex, mouflon and chamois. There are also some populations of wild goats, mainly in Turkey and on some Greek islands, and feral populations of once domestic goats scattered in the British Isles (notably in Wales).

BISON *(Bison bonasus)*

Originally found throughout Europe, but brought to the verge of extinction by the early Middle Ages. The last wild bison dates from 1919. Fortunately it has now been reintroduced using captive-bred stock, notably to the Bialowieza Forest in Poland. Today there are some 700 animals in Poland and Belarus, and efforts at re-introduction have also taken place elsewhere, for example in Romania, Bulgaria and Hungary. Both sexes have short, curved horns and a characteristic body shape with the head carried rather low so that the shoulders are the highest part of the body. The bison is closely related to the American buffalo (*Bison bison*)

Bison veterum...

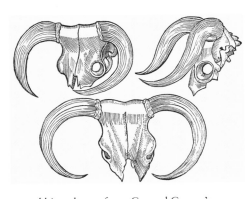

... and bison horns from Conrad Gesner's "Thierbuch"

◁ Bison ▷

MUSK OX *(Ovibos moschatus)*

During the Ice Age, musk oxen lived as far south as central Europe, but nowadays their European range is restricted to parts of Norway and Sweden. They are also found scattered in Arctic North America, Greenland, Spitzbergen, and Arctic Russia. The body length is from about 90 to 98 inches (230 to 250 cm), with a shoulder height of about 60 inches (150 cm). The horns droop to either side of the head and curve upwards, growing from broad bases which almost meet across the forehead. The fur is mainly dark brown and unusually long. The mating season is from July through September, and a single calf is born after a gestation of eight and a half months.

Musk oxen are related to sheep and cattle and are predominantly herd animals. They also provide thick, soft wool which is much valued by the Inuit, who call it qiviut.

The species takes its name from the strong musky odour emitted by the bulls during the breeding season. Musk used in the perfume industry, however, originally came mainly from the Chinese musk deer.

◁ Musk ox—*Ovibos moschatus* ▷

ALPINE IBEX
(Capra ibex)

This species became extinct by the 18th century, except for a small population in the Gran Paradiso area of Italy, from which derive all the present colonies in France, Switzerland, Italy, Germany, Austria and Slovenia.

Adult bucks reach 35 inches (90 cm) at the shoulder and can weigh up to 275 pounds (125 kg), with impressive curved, ridged horns up to over three feet (a meter) long. The females are only about half as heavy, with smaller horns, to about 16 inches (40 cm) maximum length. The mating season is in winter (December–January) with usually a single kid born after a gestation of about 24 weeks (variable). The young animals can follow their mothers over the rocky terrain at just a few days old and by about a month they start to form small clubs within the herd. Adult bucks tend to spend most of the year separate from the rest of the herd. Ibex inhabit high mountains, rocks and alpine grassland above the tree-line, and are diurnal.

In certain areas the alpine ibex populations can now support hunting again, with the main quarry being the oldest animals, mainly bucks. Very old bucks and females are generally the easiest to kill.

Capra ibex

Distribution of alpine and Spanish ibex

◁ Alpine ibex—*Capra ibex* ▷

◁ Rutting alpine ibex ▷

136

Spanish Ibex *(Capra pyrenaica)*

This close relative is restricted to isolated colonies in the Iberian peninsula, notably in the Pyrenees, Sierra Nevada and central Spanish mountain ranges. It is somewhat smaller and lighter than the alpine ibex, but the main difference lies in the shape of its horns, which are twisted in a slight spiral and lack the transverse ridges. The buck's horns can be over 3 feet (up to a meter) long, but those of the female only about 8 inches (20 cm).

The body colour varies from gray-brown to brown, with a black stripe along the back; the underside is white. The main diet in the harsh environment is grasses, mosses, lichens and buds. One or two kids are born after a gestation of about 23 weeks. They are suckled for about six months and reach sexual maturity themselves at about 18 months.

Like the alpine ibex, the Spanish ibex was hunted almost to extinction for its horns, which are hunting trophies, but this endangered species is now recovering, albeit slowly.

Spanish ibex—a tough mountaineer which has only just avoided extinction   Alpine ibex ▷

The origin of these strange objects has a simple and rational explanation. Many mammals clean their fur by regular licking, which results in fur entering the digestive tract. Some fur also enters with the food. This hair remains largely undigested and gradually accumulates in the stomach where it turns into compact balls of felt-like hair fragments. These balls, which range from pea- to egg-sized, gradually absorb both organic substances and inorganic salts and eventually gain a smooth, hard, chalky patina. They can be found inside the stomach or intestines of ibex, wild goats and chamois.

The name for these stones comes from the Persian "bazahar" which means "remedy," and the wild goat is also known in some areas as the bezoar goat, although the term later came to be used for the stones from other species too, notably ibex, chamois, horse, ox and wild boar.

These stony balls were traditionally thought to have marvellous medicinal and magical properties, and to be effective against a wide range of complaints, including sterility and poisoning. Whether worn as amulets, ground up and taken as medicine, or used as a tincture, they became a cure-all for almost any bodily or spiritual illness.

This belief is closely bound up with their origin. The entrails of animals (and of people) have long been regarded as the site of divine revelation, and early soothsayers sought explanations for events by studying their appearance and composition. Entrails were studied as signs of a higher power, and this was important for early hunting communities who needed to rely on the support of a higher authority as they competed with wild animals for survival in an often hostile natural environment. So it is easy to see how the discovery of such unusual objects as these bezoar stones was regarded as a sign of supernatural significance.

Early medicine regarded most illnesses, be they of the body or of the soul, as a form of poisoning, the result of an imbalance of the life-fluids: blood, bile and phlegm. Bezoar stone was used as a cure for all kinds of such poisoning, from stomach aches, sickness, and even plague, epilepsy and spiritual problems. The famous Tyrolean chamois stones were held to render walls transparent and to protect their owner from cuts, stings or shot! Thus a certain Dr Velschius, in the early 19th century, commented that "even chamois did not help". Some people bestowed a quite different value on bezoar stones, irrespective of their supposed medical or magical effects: they were surrounded by gold and embellished with precious jewels. But we have no record of whether this improved their powers.

Bezoar stone with emeralds, around 1570

Bezoar stones encased in gold, around 1610

◁ Alpine ibex bucks

Gold-decorated bezoar stone ▷
mounted on a plinth, around 1650

MOUFLON (*Ovis musimon*)

The precise origin of the mouflon is unclear, but it probably came under domestication from the Near East, first to Corsica and Sardinia. Subsequent introductions have spread mouflon (sometimes crossed with other breeds of sheep) to other mountainous regions in Europe, except for Britain, Ireland, Norway and Finland.

Rams reach about 32 inches (80 cm) at the shoulder and weigh up to 120 pounds (55 kg), although the ewes are somewhat smaller. The ram is reddish brown with a white saddle marking, the latter less obvious in summer and sometimes lacking altogether. In winter the coat is darker. Ewes are generally paler. Rams have tightly curled horns; ewes either lack horns altogether or have shorter horns.

The breeding season is from October through December, and at this time the rams seek out the flocks of ewes and get involved in frequent bouts of butting. The usually single lamb (occasionally twins) which follows its mother within a few hours, is born after a gestation of 22 weeks.

Mouflon are originally sheep of dry, stony mountain areas, but they have been introduced to mixed woodland and parks. They avoid open fields and dislike crossing barriers such as roads, railway lines and even small rivers. Ewes and rams live mainly in separate flocks, although young rams will also accompany flocks of ewes and lambs.

The hunting season for mouflon rams runs from August through January, while ewes and lambs may be hunted from September.

Mouflon—*Ovis musimon*

CHAMOIS (*Rupicapra rupicapra*)

Chamois are found throughout the Alps, and in many other high mountains of central, eastern and southern Europe, such as the Pyrenees, Abruzzi, Tatras and Carpathians, also in the Balkans and in Turkey; introduced to a number of other mountain ranges in Europe, including the Vosges and Black Forest.

Chamois vary across the range in weight and size, mainly according to population density. Bucks reach to about 34 inches (85 cm) shoulder height and weigh up to 110 pounds (50 kg).

They have a relatively low reproductive rate compared with other wild ungulates, only reaching maturity at two or three years, with even healthy adults sometimes remaining barren. The rut begins early in November, reaching a peak at the end of the month. After a variable gestation of 25–27 weeks, they produce a single young (rarely twins). Juvenile mortality is quite high.

Their tameness, where not hunted, combined with their sociable behavior, make chamois beloved of hillwalker and mountaineer alike. The young follow their mothers soon after birth and, like ibex, form "youth clubs" within the flock. The flocks are made up of coalescing family units and therefore vary in size and composition as families come and go. The young bucks often peel off to form separate smaller flocks in summer, whilst the older bucks are either solitary or go about in twos or threes.

Chamois tend to avoid unsuitable weather at all times of the year, moving to cool, shady sites in hot weather, returning to sunnier slopes in the evening and in winter. They live mainly on the higher slopes in summer, moving down into the montane forest with the snows of winter, especially in areas disturbed by winter sports. They are also highly sensitive to impending danger such as avalanches or rock falls.

In the early 20th century, chamois were hunted on their land by the nobility using beaters, and the area then protected for one to three years to build up the stocks again. The decline in this ecologically sound hunting strategy results not just from changing views of hunting and the reduction in range of the quarry, but also on the lack of suitably skilled and willing helpers. Nowadays hunting is mainly by stalking, from the beginning of August until the middle or end of December. The hunter tries to take the weaker bucks, young or ewes early, whereas older bucks are shot mainly during the rut. Bucks with well developed winter coats and beards are particularly sought after.

Distribution of chamois

Chamois—female with young

Rupicapra rupicapra

144

Chamois in snow

Chamois fleeing danger

Female chamois with young at play

145

PIG FAMILY (Suidae)

Pigs are even-toed ungulates, but, unlike deer and bovines, they are not ruminants. They are true omnivores, digesting their food with the aid of a voluminous single-chambered stomach, resting the while for long periods. Much of their food is gleaned from the soil, as evidenced by their shovel-like snouts.

WILD BOAR (Sus scrofa)

Wild boar have a superb sense of smell, so much so that they have even been used by police instead of dogs to sniff out explosives and drugs.

They are found in most of Europe, north to the Baltic and North Seas, but are extinct in the British Isles, although re-introduction is being considered. They also live in central and south Asia, in North Africa, and as introductions in parts of North and South America and Australia.

Males (boars) can weigh up to 550 pounds (250 kg) in Europe and be as tall as 39 inches (1 m) at the shoulder. The summer coat is bristly and dark with a silver tinge, turning to a darker brown or black in winter, when a thick underfur also develops. The piglets are reddish-brown or ocher, with yellowish longitudinal stripes for the first four or five months.

Distribution of wild boar

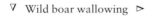

▽ Wild boar wallowing ▷

Sucking piglets

Few native wild animals react as quickly as wild boar to changes in food availability. A rich food supply guarantees rapid growth and maturation, and under good conditions both sexes can reach maturity within a year. Sows come into heat between October and May, with the height of the breeding season in November and December. In many herds, the timing of breeding is set by the dominant sow. When she comes into season, the others become receptive as well (an example of breeding synchronization). An average litter of five piglets are born, after a gestation of 15 to 16 weeks, and strong and especially older sows can produce as many as eleven, although young sows seldom have more than four piglets. The piglets are looked after in a soft nest sited in a sheltered spot.

Wild boar live in groups consisting of females and young of different ages, usually led by the oldest sow, with a definite hierarchy, established by strength and age. Animals from outside are not usually tolerated. Sows generally only leave these groups to tend their new-born piglets, until the latter are about two weeks old.

Fully grown boars by contrast tend to live a solitary life outside the breeding season, wandering randomly about their territory, although younger boars do associate for a short period in summer. These are usually superfluous animals, expelled from the female groups before the new piglets were born.

Hunting methods for wild boar vary quite widely in different parts of Europe. According to recent ecological and hunting theory it is best to protect them from general stalking, at least in summer and in woodland habitats, restricting this instead to local hunting using beaters. This results in mainly young or superfluous animals up to 88 or 132 pounds (40 or 60 kg) weight being taken. Individual adult boars or sows are hunted mainly by stalking.

In areas where they are hunted throughout the year, wild boar are hardly ever seen by day, but nevertheless they often cause damage to crops, especially grain and potatoes. They also damage hay meadows by churning the ground as they search for worms, grubs and small rodents. Where not hunted they can be surprisingly tame, even feeding on household waste in some suburban areas.

Litter of young

BEAR FAMILY (Ursidae)

Bears walk on the soles of their feet, and are omnivorous, although plant material features more than animals in their diet. The exception is the polar bear which is almost entirely carnivorous. Stone Age paintings and bone fragments found in caves indicate that our early ancestors hunted bears. In many cultures bears have been the subject of myths and cults, and they were often regarded as "King of the Animals" because of their size and strength.

BROWN BEAR (Ursus arctos)

Brown bears once lived across the whole of Europe, except Iceland. They are now mainly in north and east Scandinavia, Russia and south-east Europe, with scattered populations in the Pyrenees and in central Italy. They are absent from the British Isles, Denmark, the Benelux countries and Germany. There are some 30 subspecies of brown bear, including the larger Grizzly and Kodiak Bears in North America.

A fully grown male brown bear can be 45 inches (115 cm) at the shoulder and weigh up to 770 pounds (350 kg), although most remain smaller. The mating season is in May and June, with a gestation of six to seven months, including delayed development.

Remarkably, the tiny cubs (usually twins), weighing only about 400 g, are born in mid-winter, when the mother is in her den with access to neither food nor water. She then has to use her body reserves to provide milk for the young, seldom leaving the den until mid-May. In southern Europe the cubs remain with the mother for about a year, further north two or three years. Apart from people, brown bears have few natural enemies and they can live for between 35 and 60 years, although the mortality amongst young animals is very high.

Brown bears have very large territories, within which they are usually solitary. From September they enter a period of hibernation, although the length of the dormant period depends on the local weather.

Bears usually pose no danger to people, normally fleeing long before they are spotted. Nevertheless, if one gets too close (nearer than about 15 m), or encounters bears which have become accustomed to foraging close to houses, there can be problems. Then it is vital to remain calm, backing off slowly before making a dignified retreat.

The commonest hunting method is by shooting, at baited feeding sites, and in south-east Europe bears are often hunted by use of beaters. One rather unpleasant method involves tracking them down in their winter dens.

Distribution of brown bear

Brown bear cubs

Brown bears are adept climbers

Brown bear

The loner: *Ursus arctos* ▷

Raccoon (*Procyon lotor*)

The raccoon belongs to the family Procyonidae, which contains the pandas and their relatives. It is native to North and Central America, with the exception of the far north. Raccoons have been deliberately introduced into many parts of central Europe and have also escaped from fur farms. The main areas are in Germany (mainly north of the Main River) and Belarus, but they have now spread as far as north-west France, Austria, the Czech Republic and Poland.

Raccoons are rather badger-like in overall appearance, and grow to about 14 inches (35 cm) at the shoulder and 15 pounds (7 kg) in weight.

Breeding begins at the end of January, after hibernation, and at this time the males wander long distances in search of a mate. Gestation is about nine weeks, after which between two and five (rarely seven) young are born.

Raccoons are mainly crepuscular or nocturnal, and, as omnivores, they profit from human waste and rubbish. They are also not particularly fussy when it comes to habitat requirements, but generally avoid open mountain country, preferring a varied landscape. They use hollow trees, fox or badger burrows and occasionally piles of brush-wood in which to breed or overwinter. They are sociable animals and can achieve high population densities.

Raccoons use their front paws like hands to find and manipulate food. They also turn over small stones in shallow water in their search, leading to the erroneous belief that they habitually wash their food before eating it. Their natural enemies are lynx, eagle owl and wolf, and dogs also take young animals.

They have long, thick fur which gives them a rather squat appearance, and a short, pointed snout with a black and white face mask. The latter is reminiscent of the raccoon dog.

Raccoons often forage around human habitations, being found for example near barns, stables and camp sites, but they do not normally travel more than about three miles (5 km) from their dens, unless spreading out to colonize fresh territory. We can only guess at the European population, but a figure of 100,000 has been quoted for western Germany alone.

Raccoons are usually caught by accident. They are very nosy and therefore easily trapped. In America a popular method uses coonhounds, which chase the raccoons into trees, where they are pinpointed by torchlight before being shot.

Raccoon—*Procyon lotor*

Raccoon

Procyon lotor at den

DOG FAMILY *(Canidae)*

Dogs are carnivores, but they also take a certain amount of plant food as well (mainly berries and other fruits), at least occasionally. All have well developed social systems, especially at high population densities. So highly developed is their social hierarchy, that it is often only the dominant adult female which comes into heat and breeds. The other pack members concentrate on hunting and helping to rear the cubs. After copulating, dogs remain joined for a variable amount of time. The young, which are blind for the first week or two, are born in a den which is either dug specially, or taken over from another species, such as a badger.

WOLF *(Canis lupus)*

The wolf, responsible for eating both Little Red Riding Hood and her grandmother in Grimm's fairytale, has always been regarded by Europeans from their earliest childhood onwards as the embodiment of power, nastiness, cunning and grave danger. However, we have long known that wolves avoid people and are even afraid of them, and this highly intelligent, predominantly crepuscular or nocturnal animal is actually very shy.

Although once found across the whole of Europe, only remnants of the former population remain, mainly in eastern Europe, scattered in Scandinavia, and in the mountains of south-east Europe, with pockets in Spain, Portugal, Sardinia and Italy. Wolves are also found in North America and in Asia.

The breeding season is from December through March. Gestation is 9–10 weeks, after which five to eight pups are born. Pack size and hunting technique are strongly influenced by the available prey, with only large packs being capable of overpowering big animals such as moose. Small packs and solitary wolves will even take prey as small as mice and amphibians, especially in times of need.

Wolves may be found in a wide range of habitats, including forest, swampy country, steppe, desert, tundra and mountains. As pursuit hunters they particularly like open country, where their hunting territories can be up to 115 square miles (300 sq km).

Wolves are mainly taken when driving for wild boar, although they are sometimes hunted using bait as a lure at night.

Canis lupus

Wolf cub

Distribution of wolf ▷

Wolf ▷

RACCOON DOG
(*Nyctereutes procyonoides*)

Raccoon dogs come originally from the borders of Russia and China, in the Amur and Usuri catchment area, but they were introduced into many other parts of Russia in the first half of this century for their fur. They had reached Finland by 1935, Poland by 1955 and south Germany (records from Munich and Augsburg) by 1964. They are now found throughout central and eastern Europe, and also in parts of Sweden.

Raccoon dogs weigh up to about 22 pounds (10 kg). They are rather squat and badger-like, with short legs and a black facial mask, reminiscent of a raccoon.

The breeding season is somewhat later than that of the fox, being February through April, and between five and eight young are born after a gestation of nine weeks.

Mainly crepuscular or nocturnal, and carnivorous, although they will sometimes take up to 80 percent vegetable food. Shows winter dormancy, depending on the severity of the weather.

Raccoon dogs ▷

Nyctereutes procyonoides

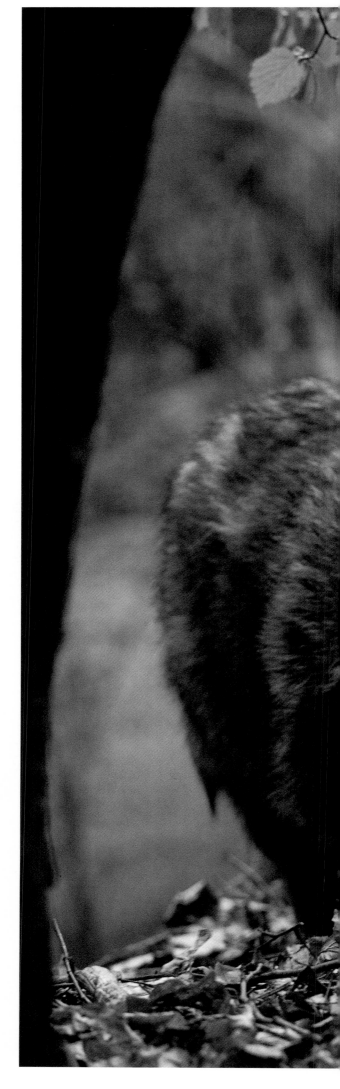

156

ARCTIC FOX (Alopex lagopus)

The arctic fox lives in the Arctic and subarctic parts of both the Old and New Worlds. It is somewhat smaller than the red fox, with relatively longer legs and short ears and nose. Most Arctic foxes are gray-brown in summer, turning pure white in the winter; rare "blue foxes" brown or ash-gray throughout the year, with bluish tinge in the winter.

The breeding season is a bit later than that of the red fox, being in March and April, but otherwise the life history is similar. Arctic foxes are diurnal, living in small groups.

Mainly hunted by trapping, but also pursued on skis or snowshoes.

Arctic fox with cub

Arctic fox in winter coat

158

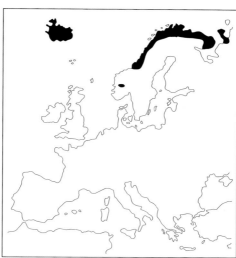

Distribution of arctic fox

Arctic fox in summer coat

159

RED FOX *(Vulpes vulpes)*

Do foxes take geese or not? The zoologist Erik Ziemen locked up a goose with a large group of foxes. The result was that the goose attacked the foxes so much that none dared approach. After five weeks Ziemen removed the goose, which had scarcely an unruffled feather!

The red fox is found throughout the whole of Europe except Iceland, and also in much of Asia, North Africa, and North America.

Dog foxes grow to a maximum of about 20 pounds (9 kg) in weight and to 16 inches (40 cm) at the shoulder. They are very elegant in build, with a long, bushy tail. They are mature by the first winter and the mating season is in January and February, when more than one dog often tracks a single, wandering vixen. Three to five cubs are born after eight weeks gestation.

As darkness falls, foxes move about in search of their food; fox territories can cover up to 500 hectares. Nowadays there are well-established suburban fox populations in many areas and foxes can increasingly be seen close to houses.

Contrary to popular belief, foxes spend most of their time away from their homes, although the den is a key center of communication. In recent decades foxes have been identified as the main vector of rabies in continental Europe. The rabies virus is transmitted in the saliva of an infected animal, usually when it bites. Mice often carry the virus, and may infect foxes by biting them on the lips when they are attacked. A rabid fox usually bites very aggressively and thus readily transmits the disease further. Rabies outbreaks tend to erupt in cycles every few years, petering out when the fox population declines resulting in reduced frequency of contact between individual animals. Millions of foxes were shot or gassed in an attempt to halt the spread of rabies, but such attempts have had no significant effect on the disease. More recently foxes have been fed an oral vaccine (via bait) and this is having some success in Switzerland, Germany and parts of France.

Young foxes begin hunting expeditions at three to four months. Cubs are rather sensitive to cold, wet and infection, and many die before reaching maturity. Foxes are hunted in many different ways, including tracking, driving or beating, luring to bait or call, pursuit by hounds, or trapping. In some areas they are killed using poisoned bait, which also often results in other species being killed accidentally. In Britain there is a long tradition of hunting to hounds, using packs of foxhounds followed by huntsmen on horseback. Despite all this pressure, fox numbers remain high, nor would the huntsman wish otherwise. The anti-rabies vaccinations have resulted in large increases in fox populations in parts of central Europe.

Distribution of red fox

Red fox cubs

Red foxes at play

Red foxes in winter coat

Red fox in summer coat

DANCING WITH THE FOX
Erik Ziemen

Stories of Saint Francis and dreams of close unison with nature strike a chord in all of us. Who hasn't imagined swinging, Tarzan-style, on lianes through the forest with friendly chimpanzees, or joined Mowgli and his wolf-pack in the jungle? Why are we so fascinated as children by the likes of Lassie and Flipper? Similar feelings explain the joy and happiness at hearing about the experiences of Günther Schumann and his foxes.

Such longing for harmony between man and animal often starts in childhood with a pet guinea pig, cat, or even a horse. Even large families often have a dog as an extra member of the household, and for the old, and often lonely, a pet is sometimes their only true friend. Such cosy, jolly and faithful companions can certainly be of special importance to a child, a family or the elderly.

Even more fascinating are relationships between man and free-living wild animals in their natural habitat. I shall never forget traveling on horseback with two friends across the east African savanna, when a huge herd of wildebeest approached, surrounded us and traveled with us for the whole day. They always kept slightly aloof, but remained inquisitive and playful. It was just like a dream.

Nowadays, in place of animals one tends to find tourists, all anxious to get close to an ever-retreating natural world. Wild mammals do not as a rule seem to have an innate fear of people as do many birds which react even to a model of a bird of prey. Nevertheless mammals do learn to avoid people if they are persecuted, and such behavior transfers rapidly to the young. On Ellesmere Island in northern Canada my friend Dave Mech

Red fox

Günther Schumann and his foxes

"Fox"—natural history photograph ▷ of the year 1991

162

Vixen with cub

A problem with transport

Vixen with litter

has shown that even wolves can be very trusting, providing they have had no negative experiences of people. This is amazing, considering that wolves, which have been hunted for thousands of years, are normally amongst the most wary of all wild mammals.

The most commonly hunted mammal in most of Europe is the red fox, which, with the virtual extinction of wolf, bear and lynx, ranks at 11 to 22 pounds (5 to 10 kg) with the badger as our largest predator. Badgers eat mainly earthworms and insects, while foxes take small mammals, and also the occasional slow hare or clutch of pheasant's eggs, a competitive habit which makes them unpopular with some huntsmen and gamekeepers.

Foxes are rigorously hunted, partly in efforts to control rabies, and there is no close season. Research into red fox populations in Saarland for example has shown that in May and June most foxes killed were suckling vixens. The vixens are particularly vulnerable because they have to hunt by day in order to get enough food to feed their cubs. The huntsman, however, more often through ignorance rather than malice, often forgets about the cubs in the fox's den, or the fawns in the case of a roe deer hind, which are then doomed to a slow death by starvation. Such events are to be deplored.

Despite these pressures, red foxes are found throughout the whole of Europe, in almost all available habitats—from the high mountains, to the coast, deep forest, cultivated prairie, and even close to people, sometimes within large cities. Indeed some of the densest fox populations of all are in built-up areas, such as around Bristol in England, and the Ruhr area of Germany.

The explanation for such remarkable adaptability lies with the fox's ability to distinguish the potential threats posed by different types of people. I once watched a fox wandering along a forest edge, near Saarbrücken. It seemed completely oblivious of people walking along a nearby track, who were also unaware of the fox, even though it was very close and had jumped several times whilst hunting, eventually successfully, for small rodents. Just minutes later, however, this same fox came across the scent of a person in the wood and immediately leaped for the cover of thick undergrowth.

Another fox, a vixen, raised her cubs not five meters from a university bus stop, with thousands of people passing nearby every day and just a hedge between them. The cubs played, just as if they were in a peaceful woodland den, as the vixen lay in the sun, taking very little notice of all the bustle close by.

Foxes also gradually became more trusting of myself and my colleagues. At first we had to use special infra-red nightsight equipment, but we were soon able to observe them using regular torchlight. Each fox had a radio collar and we used a directional aerial and receiver to track them, either on foot or from a car. Using such high-tech biology we could follow foxes throughout their nightly excursions and determine exactly which thickets or burrows they used to rest up during the day.

Despite this, one false move, such as getting out of the vehicle too quickly, or any sudden unexpected meeting, and the foxes would disappear in a trice. However much we wanted to get close to them, to track their wanderings, see them hunting and watch their encounters with other foxes, and with their young, in the end, despite all our efforts, we were treated as a threat, and, as in all other similar scientific investigations, this wish was unfulfilled. The foxes remained private and reserved, deeply suspicious of even the most harmless people.

Our observations led us to conclude that this helps to explain the red fox's success. Foxes live close to us, but not with us, at once dependent but at the same time independent, influenced by us in all their activities, yet remaining at heart a free spirit. Typical fox, we decided!

But it seemed to us that even a fox must have its price. Günther Schumann, a passionate animal photographer from the mountainous areas of Hesse, showed us how to get close to wild foxes, not by hiding and secretly using sophisticated technology, but quite openly and simply. Günther Schumann, a man with life-long knowledge of the woods, did not impose himself on the foxes, but instead they virtually invited them to visit him!

This resulted in wonderful observations and superb photographs! Foxes had never before been observed so intimately in the wild. I found it particularly interesting how the male fox gradually accepts his family, which then slowly disperses again toward the end of the summer. The young male whelps then move away, leaving at least one daughter with the vixen. Perhaps she will then help her mother raise the next litter, before having offspring of her own the following season. Who knows? I hope Günther Schumann will soon be able to tell us a lot more.

How did such an unusual relationship between man and animal come about? Was it a lucky chance? Did Günther Schumann suspect from the start that woodland foxes retained a stable social structure? Certainly here they can escape much more easily from persecution and hunting, and their supply of hiding places is almost inexhaustible.

Outside in the open fields foxes have long been killed, partly to protect hares and pheasants, by many methods, including trapping and shooting. This has resulted in a complete change in their social behavior. The foxes have no fixed ter-

Günther Schumann

ritories, nor stable pair-bonds. Each wandering vixen finds her mate almost at random, moving on to another after breeding. Such vixens also tend to raise larger litters than their woodland cousins, the young tend to wander further afield and the foxes are generally more aggressive, with a higher mortality. Vacant territories are however quickly filled.

The more foxes are hunted, the more they increase and spread. This means that increased hunting pressures on foxes in these open habitats hardly ever results in a decrease in their numbers. Worse still, the disruption of territorial and social systems in the wake of intense hunting pressure increases the rate of infection, notably of rabies.

Modern hunting methods thus tend to increase not diminish the risk of epidemics.

It was not always this way. Huntsmen and foresters once earned extra money from the sale of animal skins, notably red fox, martens and polecat, many taken from deep woodland. Nowadays the woods and forests have become something of a haven, and now act as a reservoir for foxes, which replace those lost from neighboring open country.

The older woodland foxes behave in the ways so wonderfully demonstrated by Günther Schumann's beautiful photographs. In this context we and Günther Schumann must be grateful to those huntsmen and foresters who gave up hunting in Reinhardswald.

Sucking cubs

165

WEASEL FAMILY (*Mustelidae*)

The members of this family are mostly slim, narrow-bodied and short-limbed, although the badger can hardly be described as slender. They also have sharp, curved, retractile claws on front and hind limbs. Again, the badger is an exception, with long, non-retractile claws which it uses to help dig in the soil. They have anal scent glands whose secretions have a variety of functions. Although they are carnivores, most species do take some plant food, especially berries and other fruits. Mating behavior usually involves the male holding the female by biting the fur of her neck. The young are born helpless. Weasels and relatives use their sensitive whiskers to help them hunt by night (badger, martens) or in murky water (otter). Territorial boundaries are marked out using urine and droppings, usually on a raised site. They also use their feet to mark branches, stones or soil with anal secretions.

PINE MARTEN (*Martes martes*)

Pine martens are found in most of Europe, except Iceland and much of Spain. They also occur in Turkey, the Caucasus, and in western Siberia. They prefer large, closed woodland and forest, and tend to avoid human habitations.

Males can be up to 4.4 pounds (2 kg) weight and 30 inches (75 cm) length. They are chestnut or dark brown, with a characteristic yellow chin and breast patch, and furred soles to their feet. The mating season is mainly July and August and this is followed by a period of delayed development, with the 2–4 young being born around April. These open their eyes at 34–38 days.

Pine martens climb exceptionally well, and can even catch squirrels, but they also hunt on the ground. They use holes in trees, and sometimes squirrel dreys or old birds' nests as daytime resting places.

Historically, pine martens were trapped, mainly for their soft, silky fur, but nowadays they are only taken by accident.

BEECH MARTEN (*Martes foina*)

Sometimes known as the stone marten, the beech marten is found mainly in central and southern Europe. It is absent from most of Northern Europe, the British Isles, Corsica, Sardinia and the Balearic Islands. Somewhat slimmer and shorter-legged than the pine marten, with a white, usually divided bib. The soles of its feet are not furred.

Its reproductive biology is similar to that of the pine marten, but beech martens usually nest on the ground, amongst rocks or in a building. They are even found in some cities. Presumably they take advantage of the food available in suburban areas, where their territories are smaller than those of their country cousins. They can be very useful in villages and towns because they catch a lot of mice and rats. However they do occasionally cause damage in hen coops or pigeon lofts. They have a bloodthirsty reputation, but most accounts of massacres of poultry can probably be explained by panic behavior, or confusion caused by the inability of the prey to escape, or the marten being unable to drag the prey through the narrow gap by which it entered. In some parts of central Europe beech martens cause a lot of damage by biting through cables in parked cars.

Few of these highly nocturnal animals are shot, but they are relatively easy to catch in traps, a practice which seems to have little effect on the populations.

Distribution of pine marten

Pine marten—*Martes martes*

Distribution of beech marten ▷

Beech marten ▷

Martes foina ▷

166

WESTERN POLECAT *(Mustela putorius)*

The distribution is similar to that of the pine marten, comprising the whole of Europe, east to the Ural Mountains, but excluding Ireland, Iceland, northern Scandinavia and the Mediterranean islands. In Britain it is found mainly in Wales, from where it is now spreading slowly into western England.

Males can be up to 3.3 pounds (1.5 kg) and to 18 inches (46 cm) in length, noticeably smaller than the martens. The mating season is from March through July; the gestation six weeks, with 3–7 young per litter.

Polecats like similar habitats to foxes, and they tend to overwinter in agricultural areas. When attacked, they release a foul-smelling secretion from the anal gland. They make winter food stores, often gathering up torpid amphibians.

Distribution of polecat

Beech marten

169

THE RARE MARBLED POLECAT
Günther Schumann

In east and south-east Europe there are two more species of polecat, the steppe polecat (*Mustela eversmanni*) and the rarer marbled polecat (*Vormela peregusna*). Both are found mainly in open, treeless steppe grasslands, normally far from towns and villages.

The marbled polecat is somewhat smaller than the western polecat. It is well-named as its brown back and body fur is mottled yellow, giving a marbled effect. The face is dark, with a white snout and chin and a striking white band above the eyes. The relatively large ears are surrounded by long, white hairs. The face pattern in particular gives it a truly exotic appearance.

The beautiful fur was once valued highly by local people and their pelts were given as presents by the nobility to honored visitors or to high-ranking citizens.

The European range of the marbled polecat is mainly in Bulgaria, eastern Romania, northern Greece and Turkey, with isolated pockets in Yugoslavia. From here the range stretches east into the Russian steppes.

It is nowhere common, and usually rather rare, which explains why this polecat is one of Europe's least known and studied mammals.

Although marbled polecats are normally crepuscular or nocturnal, I have seen them in broad daylight in the Dobrogea region of Romania, north west of the salt Lake Techirghiol.

The habitat is a hilly, steppe-like grassland with a loose growth of cypress spurge and scattered thistles. Other mammals here include sousliks (an eastern squirrel-relative), hamsters and the occasional red fox.

After many excursions into the steppe I suddenly found myself standing 80 to 100 feet (25 to 30 m) from a marbled polecat, which then quickly disappeared into a burrow. As I approached the spot, its head appeared above ground. I noticed an opening about 2.5 inches (6 cm) across, but could not tell whether this belonged to the polecat or to a potential prey animal.

I settled down some five meters away on the ground in order to try and photograph it. After a long wait it nervously poked its head out again, but immediately vanished. I then settled down behind a large clump of thistles. Eventually, it reemerged and started preening itself, before spotting me again and retreating into the burrow.

Next, I lay flat out on the ground in an attempt to try and get a rare photograph. This time it was a full four hours before my quarry peered out again. It noticed me, and apparently sensed that I posed no danger. At that moment I took the photograph you see here!

Romanian marbled polecat

EUROPEAN MINK (*Mustela lutreola*) and AMERICAN MINK (*Mustela vison*)

European mink have been replaced in many areas by the similar American mink, introduced from North America, mainly via fur farms, where it is reared for its valuable pelt. Both species are restricted to wet habitats.

About the size of a polecat, the European mink is blackish-brown, whereas the American mink is more variable, although the original native species is dark brown, but lacks the white chin spot and lips of the European mink. They are both trapped in some parts of Eastern Europe and Scandinavia, but are only usually shot by mistake.

American mink – *Mustela vison*

Distribution of European mink

STOAT (*Mustela erminea*) and WEASEL (*Mustela nivalis*)

Both are found throughout Europe except for Iceland, although the stoat is absent from the Mediterranean region as well, with the exception of northern Spain and Croatia. They occur from sea-level up to alpine habitats, and weasels also occur in agricultural land.

Stoats can weigh as much as 450g, but weasels are much lighter, especially north of the Alps, and in the south of the range stoats are rather smaller than they are further north. Stoats turn white in winter, as do weasels at high altitudes. The stoat always has a black tip to its tail, and this is the best distinguishing feature at all seasons.

Stoats have a gestation of some 56 days, but this may seem as long as 9–10 months including delayed implantation.

Both species can run swiftly, and climb and swim well, and they live in tunnels or holes in trees. Both are carnivores and in defense the stoat produces a foul smelling secretion from its anal gland.

Before cats were domesticated, stoats were encouraged as mouse catchers. They catch a range of prey, from hamsters and squirrels to birds, amphibians and fish.

Stoats are trapped in eastern Europe for their white winter pelts (ermine), but they otherwise do not feature much in the European hunting scene.

Stoat – *Mustela erminea*

Distribution of stoat

Weasel – *Mustela nivalis*

Distribution of weasel

171

BADGER *(Meles meles)*

Badgers are found throughout Europe, except N Scandinavia, Iceland, Corsica, Sardinia, Sicily and Cyprus; also in temperate parts of southern Asia. They occur in many habitats, from deciduous and mixed woodland, hedgerows, gardens and parks, but avoid purely agricultural areas.

They reach to the weight of a roe deer, and grow to 100 cm long. Their short legs make them look very squat and plump. The black and white face markings are very distinctive.

The mating season varies from January to October, with or without a variable length of delayed implantation period (the development of the embryo takes 60 days).

Badgers are social animals, living in groups in large burrows (setts). They use regular pathways and also dig latrines not far from the sett. They do not hunt as such, but tend to behave more as gatherers, being omnivorous. Their food includes soil animals, many kinds of insects, frogs, earthworms, small mammals and carrion (even young roe deer); also roots, buds, fruits and berries.

Badgers were hunted in various ways, including digging out (a cruel and illegal practice), shooting in the fields at night, chasing with hounds, and trapping.

WOLVERINE *(Gulo gulo)*

Also known as the glutton, this species is found in the taiga and tundra of Europe, Asia and N America. In Europe mainly in Norway, Sweden and Finland, sometimes to the Baltic shores.

Resembles a small brown bear but with a bushy tail, broad paws and powerful claws.

Wolverines can kill prey as large as reindeer or elk, although with such large prey it is usually the weaker or sick individuals which are taken. They also eat a lot of carrion and sometimes rob other animals of their prey (and may even steal from hunters' cabins).

The mating season is in March or April, gestation (including delayed implantation) about nine months, after which 2–3 (sometimes more) blind young are born. These are independent at 6–9 months and may live for 18 years.

Active by day and night, solitary; climbs, jumps and swims well, but lives mainly on the ground. Its broad foot pads enable it to move quickly even over loose snow and thus gain advantage over its prey.

Hunting is illegal in most areas, but if allowed is undertaken by experienced hunters on skis.

Badger   Wolverine

Otter (*Lutra lutra*)

Once found throughout Europe except for Iceland and the larger Mediterranean islands. A vulnerable species which has become extinct or much reduced in numbers over much of its range.

Males can weigh up to 15 kg and reach 140 cm length. Excellent swimmers and divers, with webbed feet. The thick coat has an oily secretion covering it which makes it waterproof, retaining a layer of air when submerged; it simultaneously prevents waterlogging and keeps the body warm. Both ears and nostrils close when diving.

Mating season February–April, sometimes throughout the year; gestation 62 days, sometimes extended through delayed implantation to nine months; 2–3 blind young with grayish hair; these open their eyes at five weeks, can swim at 10 weeks and first leave their family in the following spring.

Otters prefer smaller watercourses, without too strong a current, including ditches, and they sometimes cover long distances over land (even alpine passes). Mostly nocturnal, hunting fish, also locally muskrat, water birds, frogs, crustaceans. Smaller prey are eaten in the water, larger items on land. Breeds in a burrow in the bank or a hollow tree in riverside vegetation, with the entrance usually below water.

Hunted historically for their pelt, but now protected almost everywhere.

Otter

Lutra lutra

Otter – mother with cubs

173

CAT FAMILY (Felidae)

"The food their bodies need they catch for themselves, being neither beggars at another's table, nor carrion eaters. They require warm blood to drink, direct from the spring of life." So wrote Hans-Wilhelm Smolik in his famous book *The Animal World*. The family is found almost worldwide, with some 40–50 species. Only two occur in Europe: lynx and wild cat.

All cats have rounded faces, with eyes facing forwards, and very sharp teeth with which to kill their prey. They are graceful movers, and their toes (five on the front paws, four on the hind paws) have retractable claws. Their hearing is excellent, and their sensitive whiskers allow them to orientate in darkness. Their sense of smell is moderately good (short nose). The European species are solitary, and have territories which they defend well, at least against same-sex members of their own species. The young are born furred, but blind and helpless at first. Although cats were domesticated as long ago as 3,000 B.C., they retain, unlike dogs, the air of wild, rather secretive and self-contained creatures.

LYNX (*Lynx lynx*)

Formerly found throughout Europe, but today restricted to Scandinavia, eastern Europe and the Carpathians, with isolated pockets in the Pyrenees and south-east Europe; also in central Asia and North America.

Male is up to about 30 kg, and 70 cm at the shoulder. The mating season is February and March; gestation about 10 weeks; litters of 2–4 kittens which open their eyes at 16 days, are suckled for five months and stay with their mother for about a year.

Lynx hunt by stalking their prey, then pouncing and overpowering them, but they rarely run further than about 20m.

Their territories can be very large (20–150 square kilometers) depending on prey density, and adjacent territories may overlap to some extent. By hunting in different parts of the territory, they keep prey disturbance to a minimum.

Lynx have been successfully reintroduced in a number of regions in recent decades. They pose no danger to people and they also have little effect on wild populations of game animals. Where they are taken, they are shot, and are even tracked on skis in parts of Scandinavia.

Note: Lynx are protected over most of their range and may not be hunted.

Distribution of lynx

Lynx – *Lynx lynx*

Wild cat ▷

174

WILD CAT (*Felis silvestris*)

You know it must be a wild cat if you cannot see it. So goes the old huntsman's joke! Which means that if you do come across a wild cat, in a forest for example, the chances are that it is a domestic cat which has gone native, rather than the genuine article.

This species originally occurred throughout Europe, except for Scandinavia, Iceland and Ireland, but today numbers have dwindled, although there are signs of increases in recent years (notably in Germany and Scotland).

The kittens (usually 2–4) are born in May after a gestation of some nine weeks in a den which is usually in a hollow tree, although sometimes in an abandoned fox or badger burrow. The breeding chamber is often lined with grass, fur or bird feathers. The young start to leave the nest at 4–5 weeks old and rehearse their adult behavior through play. At two months old they start to accompany their mother on hunting forays.

Wild cats prefer sites which are warm in winter, such as sunny rock-slopes, and avoid cold mountain sites. They also avoid dense coniferous forest, perhaps because of the relative shortage of mice there. Hard winters reduce the populations considerably, and under these conditions they sometimes seek refuge in buildings.

Note: The wild cat is a protected species over most of its range and may not be hunted.

Lynx

175

TELLTALE SIGNS IN FIELD AND FOREST
Susanne K.M. Linn-Kustermann

TRACKS

If the ground is soft enough, many game animals leave imprints from which it is possible to tell the species, sex (in the case of hoofed game and larger game birds) and, to a limited extent, age. The depth of the individual footprint in a track, the stride and the cross trace are significant. The stride of a full-grown red deer is roughly 60 to 80 cm, while that of an older animal is only 50 to 55 cm. The cross trace is the lateral deviation of the footprints from an imaginary center line. The heavier a red deer, the broader its cross trace.

The gait of the animal can be determined by examining the sequence of footprints. When moving at a leisurely pace or at a fast trot, the prints left by the left and right hind feet more or less coincide with the prints left by the corresponding fore feet. When running, the hind feet are pushed forward between the fore feet, the hooves are spread, and the dewclaws (just above the hooves) also leave marks. Only wild boar leave dewclaw marks in their tracks at slow speed, and in all other species of hoofed game a track with dewclaw marks indicates that the animal is running fast, perhaps fleeing.

The soft pads of predators often leave prints that are less distinct than those left by sharp-edged hooves. Some species (mustelids and canids) leave claw marks in their tracks, those of the badger being particularly distinctive. In contrast, all cats, including lynx, retract their claws when walking and leave no claw marks.

In the days of riding to hounds, skilled trackers studied the marks left by game very closely, and from these they could tell much about the deer being hunted. A number of features of tracks left by red deer are claimed to have provided evidence not only concerning the sex and age of the deer but also its weight and even its antlers—a claim which modern hunters who are expert trackers find hard to believe. It is clear that the marks interpreted by trackers skilled in deer stalking formed part of the formal knowledge of professional 'huntsmen' who were members of a guild. For this reason alone it is important that they do not pass into oblivion.

Heinrich Wilhelm Döbel included only 72 features of tracks in his *Newly published hunting practices* (1746). This was a great deal fewer than the features mentioned in earlier literature. Later on, even fewer features were accepted. These included the depth of the footprint, the cross trace and the stride, toe turn-out (deer walking with fronts of its hooves turned outwards, a tendency which increases the older or heavier the animal).

The following are some of the characteristic marks: leading or lagging (imprint of hind feet in front of or behind that of fore feet); imprint of hind feet beside those of fore feet; imprint of hind foot does not coincide precisely with that of fore foot; marks in a place where an animal has lain up (individual imprint left by hind foot which is folded underneath the animal's body when it lies down, leaving an imprint as it stands up).

TRAILS AND RUNS

Many game species use regular tracks between their resting-place and feeding grounds, and this produces visible evidence of wear and tear on vegetation. In the case of larger species like deer, these are referred to as trails, in the case of smaller game species, such as fox and hare, they are called runs. Trails and runs are very important in hunting. Game animals tend to use familiar paths rather than fleeing headlong cross country, and this particular behavior is exploited during drives by moving as quietly as possible through areas in which larger game animals are usually found and placing the guns selectively on trails rather than attempting to cover the entire area. In trapping, knowledge of game trails is also crucial in order to place the traps correctly, although spring traps which are set on the actual trail and sprung when the animal treads on them are largely prohibited nowadays in Europe.

Trails which are only occasionally used by a game species when moving longer distances play an important role, in biological terms, in the repopulation of lost habitats, as a route for genetic linkage between populations. Individual animals migrate along centuries-old long-distance trails into areas in which they may have become extinct long ago. Biologists make efforts to use ancient knowledge of such long-distance trails in the context of projects to reintroduce certain animals.

SIGNS OF FEEDING AND DAMAGE CAUSED BY GAME

Apart from signs left by movement, the best traces of the presence of animals are those left by feeding. Where such feeding affects vegetation used by people, we regard this as damage, such as the notorious damage caused by barking of trees. This can lead to rot and reduce the value of trees as timber. Bark damage is caused primarily by red deer, sika deer, sometimes by mouflon and elk and, more rarely, by fallow deer. Roe deer, however, never eat bark. Bark damage has caused and continues to cause serious problems in forestry in some regions. In places where the forest is a reserve rather than an economically productive crop, attempts are made to prevent bark damage by culling the game population. The reasons why red deer in particular are now beginning to eat bark on a wide scale have not been thoroughly investigated, but it is known that stress brought on by incompetent or excessive hunting and large-scale disturbance can cause increased bark damage and that unbalanced, irregular feeding in winter may also encourage the habit. In populations with a natural social structure and where winter feeding is moderate, there is not so much bark damage, the latter being associated more with small, unsuitably confined deer populations.

Sheep and goats can also cause bark damage, as can hares in orchards, whilst rabbits can eat the bark of pine trees and also damage stands of broad-leafed trees. Small rodents sometimes damage the bark of saplings by gnawing it. Finally, beavers can also cause considerable damage to trees.

Apart from bark damage, forest plants are also damaged by browsing, especially of fresh shoots, and this kind of damage can be caused by hoofed game and smaller game alike. The grazed surface that is left yields clues concerning the culprit who caused the damage; ruminants have no incisors in their upper jaw and rip off the young shoots, whereas hares and rabbits leave a clean-cut bite.

Various hoofed game species, especially wild boar, can cause significant damage to crops. Wild boar dig up woodland and meadow soil by grubbing for protein-rich food in the ground. Wild boar, deer, hares and flocks of migrating geese are also fond of valuable agricultural plants such as oats, wheat, corn and other field crops, as well as fresh grass and grain (especially geese). Even badgers are sometimes responsible for causing damage by grubbing in the soil for small invertebrates or feeding on oats and corn.

REMAINS OF PREY
Small prey animals such as mice, rabbits and hares caught by predators are rarely found because they are either eaten immediately or dragged away. The situation is different in the case of larger prey, and the pattern of bites or removal of parts of the prey often reveals the identity of the predator, be this fox, lynx or dog. A predatory cat such as the lynx does not normally eat the innards, whereas foxes and dogs eat the soft parts of their prey first.

DROPPINGS AND DUNG
Heaps of dung left by game animals may also be characteristic, and each species has its own characteristic form of dung or droppings. When examining dung, the location, its smell, the food remnants it may contain and other special characteristics reveal the presence of a specific animal species. Many species regularly use the same latrine (e.g. badger, wild boar, rabbit) whereas other species (particularly predatory animals) mark their territory with dung and therefore leave small heaps in particularly obvious locations. Finally, the diet of each species is reflected in the indigestible remnants that are passed out. Fruit pips betray the beech marten's sweet tooth, crayfish shells are a tell-tale sign of the gourmet otter, and the hedgehog, which eats insects, leaves evidence in the form of beetle wing cases.

FRAYING SPOTS
All deer species fray their antlers, which regrow every year, that is to say they rub off the protective velvet by scraping and rubbing their antlers against small trees and branches. The size of the trees used, and the height and nature of the damage caused helps to identify the deer species. Among members of the same species, antler fraying sites also provide visible sign and scent signals used to mark territory boundaries.

SCRAPES
Deer make scrapes, depressions in the ground, with their front hooves and their antlers. These places give off a strong scent, revealing rutting sites shortly before the season starts.

RESTING PLACES
When a game animal lies down to rest, this may leave signs, according to the weather, soil consistency and vegetation; hunters often refer to such sites as 'beds'. The snow may be slightly melted, green vegetation crushed, or a slight depression visible in soft soil. Hair and dung are also occasionally found in the vicinity. Hares leave noticeable body-sized depressions in the ground in open fields; these are called 'forms'.

MUD WALLOWS AND DUST BATHS
A few species of hoofed game have a regular grooming routine which involves mud baths in so-called wallows. A wallow is a wet depression in the ground filled with mud of varying consistency. Red deer, wild boar and sika deer need to wallow throughout the year, even in winter, fallow deer less often (primarily before the rut), whilst roe deer never wallow. Nearby trees are used as rubbing posts after their mud bath and such trees can be recognized by a thick crust of dried mud. Depending on the season, wallowing is used to cool down, for killing parasites or for scenting purposes, or perhaps may also be indulged in simply for pleasure.

Hare Family (Leporidae)

Hares have long ears, well supplied with blood vessels, which act as temperature regulators. Their eyes are on the sides of their heads, giving all-round vision, but without the definition offered by binocular vision. The rootless incisor teeth grow throughout life and behind each one is a peg-tooth. The gut has a large sac attached (the cecum) in which cellulose is partially digested with the aid of bacteria. Soft dark cecal pellets, rich in vitamins, are passed out and eaten, to be digested a second time around. Cheek glands secrete a chemical used in transferring information and in marking territories.

Brown hares 'boxing'

Brown Hare (*Lepus europaeus*)

The Romans regarded the hare as the favorite of the goddess Venus, and thus as a symbol of her legendary fertility, and hares traditionally give us eggs at Easter. This story may have arisen because eggs were often found, almost magically, close to where hares had been lying in the open fields. In reality these were probably lapwing clutches.

The brown hare is found throughout Europe except for Iceland and N. Scandinavia; it is also absent from most of Spain and Portugal, Ireland and most of Scotland. Also found eastwards to Turkey and to central and eastern Asia. In west and central Europe, it has declined markedly in some places due to the mechanization of agriculture and the increase in traffic.

Unlike rabbits, their ears are always tipped black.

The mating season is mainly from January until fall, and there are group displays, often involving several animals. This 'mad March hare' behavior is usually unreceptive females chasing away males. Sometimes more than one male will follow a female, and fights may then ensue.

Up to four litters a year, each with 2–5 well-developed young which can run after just a few hours. The females are fertile again from the 38th day of pregnancy.

Hares have suffered from field enlargement and rapid harvesting techniques, with stress and food shortages taking their toll, both at harvest and in winter. They tend to do better in areas with smaller fields, when their territories are also smaller.

Largely crepuscular and nocturnal, but may be seen at almost any time. Hares lie up in a shallow scrape (often called couch or form) in the open, both to save energy and to avoid predators, and if disturbed they bolt out, as if from a catapult.

Hunted by using beaters in some lowland areas, from raised platforms in woodland, and occasionally using dogs.

Brown hares displaying ▷

Distribution of rabbit

RABBIT *(Oryctolagus cuniculus)*

Rabbits were originally restricted to the Iberian Peninsula and NW Africa. Since Roman times their range has been extended, and they have been introduced to many other regions either to provide food or for hunting, and are now found in most of the milder parts of Europe (but not in north-east and south-east Europe) especially where the soil is suitable for burrowing.

Smaller than both hares, with shorter, more rounded ears. They are preyed upon by a wide range of predators and have a correspondingly high rate of reproduction, with up to five broods a year, and up to 12 young per litter!

Rabbits live in colonies made up of several large families in burrow systems (warrens) where the naked, blind young are born. The dominant male mates with several females, although there are well-defined small territories within the colony. They prefer warm, dry areas with sandy soils and low plant growth, such as the edges of woods, heaths, pastures, parks and gardens, mainly in lowland sites.

Traditionally hunted using ferrets which chase the rabbits out of their burrows towards the hunters. Also shot using beaters, and occasionally hunted using a trained goshawk.

MOUNTAIN HARE *(Lepus timidus)*

Also known as Irish or tundra hare, this species is found in Ireland, Scotland, Scandinavia, north-east Europe, northern Asia, North America and Greenland, with an isolated population in the Alps. Smaller than the brown hare (to 3.5 kg); gray-brown in summer, pale below, and pure white in winter, except for the black ear tips.

Breeding season is later and shorter than the brown hare's, and there are usually just two litters a year, each with 2–5 young.

Behavior is similar to that of the brown hare, and it seeks shelter and refuge in snowy hollows or burrows. There is some evidence of a gradual retreat into the cooler regions, with climatic warming.

The Alpine subspecies, *Lepus timidus varronis*, occurs in sparse populations around the tree-line, only descending to lower levels in the winter. They like open woodland where food is more plentiful.

In Ireland and Scotland, mountain hares are hunted using beaters and also with pointers, in Scandinavia and, when permitted, in the Alps, with hounds.

Rabbit – *Oryctolagus cuniculus*

Mountain hare (Alps)

Distribution of mountain hare ▷

Mountain hares – *Lepus timidus* ▷

SQUIRREL FAMILY (Sciuridae)

Squirrels are rodents. The family also contains the flying squirrel of the northern taiga, the Alpine marmot, Siberian chipmunk and two species of souslik (genus *Citellus*). All have rootless and steadily-growing gnawing teeth for dealing with woody plant food, and they build nests in which to rest, hibernate or breed. They have four front toes and five, usually long hind toes, for climbing or digging.

RED SQUIRREL *(Sciurus vulgaris)*

Found in the whole of Europe except Iceland and the islands of the Mediterranean, but replaced by gray squirrel over much of Britain. There are two color forms, one foxy red, the other dark gray (sometimes almost black). The red form is commoner in lowland, the dark in mountainous regions. The bushy tail is characteristic.

Almost entirely tree-living, but may feed on the ground. Builds a twig nest (drey) lined with grass and moss and used both to rear the young and also as a resting place during the winter. Squirrels do not hibernate in the strict sense, but show a form of dormancy. In cold weather they are much less active and sleep, often for days at a time. They store food in hollow trees or buried in the ground. Shot in some areas both for its fur and meat.

North American gray squirrels *(Sciurus carolinensis)* were introduced to England around 1890, and this species is now predominant in most of England and Wales.

EUROPEAN BEAVER *(Castor fiber)*

Formerly found in most of Europe and central Asia; today restricted to a few areas (mainly the Rhone, the Elbe, south Norway and eastern Europe); reintroduced to a number of sites.

Body length of some 75–100 cm, and weight of 18–30: the largest European rodent. The breeding season is January–February, gestation 15 weeks, after which 1–5 fully-furred sighted young are born, capable of swimming and diving within a few days of birth.

Crepuscular and nocturnal, living in family groups. Beavers are excellent swimmers, and can dive for up to about 15 minutes. They nest in burrows in the riverbank or sometimes build elaborate lodges using branches, twigs and mud, with entrances always beneath the water. They can fell trees of up to 80 cm diameter, and regulate water levels by building dams. The flat tail functions as a rudder, and, when danger threatens, they also use their tails to make a loud warning splash.

In parts of Finland and eastern Europe the related Canadian beaver *(Castor canadensis)* has been introduced.

EUROPEAN SOUSLIK *(Citellus citellus)*

Sousliks live in Europe, Asia and North America. They grow to some 20 cm, and most live in large, underground colonies. They inhabit warm, dry steppe country. A second species, the spotted souslik *(Citellus suslicus)* lives further north and east, roughly from southern Poland to the River Volga.

Distribution of red squirrel

Distribution of European beaver

Distribution of Alpine marmot

ALPINE MARMOT (*Marmota marmota*)

This shy rodent lives in the central and western Alps and the High Tatra, and has been introduced to the Pyrenees, Carpathians, Black Forest and eastern Alps. Always found above about 1,500 m.

Grows to some 7 kg, and has a compact, plump body. Loses up to a third of its weight during hibernation.

Mating season Apr–May; gestation 34–35 days; usually 2–3 (up to 7) naked, blind young. The females may pause for up to four years between pregnancies.

Marmots are diurnal, and live in family groups. Sentries are posted near the burrows to warn of danger by shrill whistles.

In late summer they bite off long grass stems and lay them in the sun to dry. When the hay is ready it is collected, either in cheek pouches or in the mouth, and taken underground. The marmots also make underground stores of food for when fresh grass is scarce. The whole family goes underground, often before the first snow falls. They seal the entrances carefully using soil and hay and hibernate close together. They do however wake every 2-4 weeks mainly to excrete.

◁ ◁ Red squirrel

◁ European beaver

TRUE SEALS (Phocidae)

Excellent swimmers and divers which spend most of their lives in the water, they have closable nostrils and ears, and their five-digited hands and feet are modified as paddles. These diurnal carnivores eat mainly fish and crustaceans. They mate in the water, but give birth on land to a single pup, which soon makes its way to the water, the mother following. The young are suckled for around six weeks.

Although reproductive rate is slow, seals can live for up to 40 years. Their thick fat layer gives them good insulation even in icy water and also lets them go without food for long periods. The weight ranges from 50 kg (ringed seal) to 290 kg (gray seal).

Unlike the walrus, they do not have tusks, and their webbed feet distinguish them from most other carnivores, evolution having perfected them for their amphibious existence.

COMMON SEAL *(Phoca vitulina)*

Also called harbor seal or spotted seal, this species is found in coastal waters of north temperate latitudes; in Europe from Portugal to northern Scandinavia and Iceland.

The body is torpedo-shaped, with short limbs, and individuals may weigh up to 250 kg. The coat is mainly yellow-gray and consists of shiny, bristly hairs. Although ungainly on land, they can swim at up to 35 kph and young seals can swim almost from birth. Pups call loudly when separated from their mother.

Their habitat is sandy coasts, mudflats, and sometimes freshwater near the coast. Affected by disturbance from tourism, and by marine pollution, eg oil spills. Individuals may live for 20 years.

Distribution of common seal

Common seal – *Phoca vitulina*

GRAY SEAL *(Halichoerus grypus)*

Atlantic coasts of central and northern Europe; North Sea and Baltic, east coast of Canada.

Bulls reach 250 kg, and up to three meters long. The coat is gray to dark gray with irregular black spots. The head shape, with elongated rather heavy muzzle, is characteristic.

RINGED SEAL *(Phoca hispida)*

Baltic, some inland lakes in Finland and north-west Russia, Arctic sea coasts of North America and Eurasia, in coastal waters, fjords, ice-fields and on pack-ice.

Resembles common seal but smaller and slimmer; coat colour ocher to gray-brown with rather irregular darker patches, each with a pale border (hence the name); yellowish white below.

Gray seal

THE HUNTER AS ECOLOGIST
Heribert Kalchreuter

Hunters have always been concerned with the preservation of game. Hunting goes hand in hand with conservation, and is only possible if the populations of game animals are healthy. Huntsmen will only be successful if they ensure that they maintain or increase numbers of game.

In modern society hunting is ever more restricted and controlled, the main problem being the spreading human population. People compete directly with wild animals for territory, altering natural ecosystems and making demands on nature and the environment.

Wild animals react in different ways to human-induced changes to their habitats, with specialized species at most risk—the losers in agricultural and suburban landscapes. These are often the smaller game species.

Other species thrive in altered landscapes, and even reach higher densities. These are the winners, and include several hoofed game species. Man removed the main predators to protect cattle and sheep and so some of their natural prey species have thrived. Red and roe deer have also adapted well to conifer monoculture, and wild boar

Roe deer

186

Roe deer fawn

supplement their natural diet with potatoes and maize.

The red fox is a splendid example of a flexible species, and has profited better than most from living close to man. It has a very varied diet, and also benefits from increased rodent densities in agricultural landscapes.

There are many such generalist and opportunists amongst birds too, for example many members of the crow family, which feed on some of the products of human society. Goshawks also have a broad spectrum of prey and have adapted well in some areas.

Both the losers and winners can prove problematic in different ways, through their rarity or because of their very success.

Wild boar, woodpigeon, red fox, crows and goshawk can all profit from man's activities and sometimes become a nuisance. Roe and red deer can also cause damage, above all where the living forest has been transformed into an economically managed monoculture.

It is small wonder that wild species damage crop trees, often by grazing shoots and damaging bark, if all that is available to them is a dark monoculture of spruce, with an impoverished ground flora.

Wild species can also produce ecological damage, as for example where foresters have attempted to return monocultures to more natural forest communities. Some of the introduced species are eaten in preference, thereby inhibiting the development of more natural woodland.

Other winners influence the species diversity. Examples are opportunistic predators which may reach unusually high densities through increased food availability, thus causing a problem for their natural prey, whose populations may already have been weakened by human activity.

Such ecological consequences are often the subject of controversial and ideological discussion. Goshawks, for instance, have reached high densities in some areas, with the benefit of full protection and a ready supply of semi-domestic birds, such as pigeons. But they do not concentrate on these, taking natural prey species such as the declining blackcock, in its ever-diminishing moorland habitat. There are indeed cases where goshawks have been responsible for driving this characteristic moorland bird to local extinction.

Similarly, several members of the crow family have profited from cultivation, and like to steal the clutches of many other species.

The red fox provides another example of man-induced ecological change. Its present high density may well account for decreases in prey species such as brown hare and gray partridge.

It is worse still, because red foxes themselves suffer from their own success. Nature eventually controlled numbers through the deadly rabies virus. Where this struck, hare populations quickly recovered, but rabies is a danger to domestic animals and to people. Although the infection and death rate remained low, veterinary authorities to immunized the fox population by distribution of vaccine in bait from airplanes. This initiative was successful, at least initially, and led to even greater fox populations, with all the negative effects on prey animals, including game species.

Nature then avenged herself for these unnatural

Winter hunting scene

contrary, foxes and crows quickly learn to concentrate on these refuges and develop 'search-images' for them, systematically hunting along field margins and hedgerows for egg clutches and leverets. Thus these havens can become traps for the very species for which they were created. The only answer is a drastic reduction in predator numbers, where these are at high density—precisely the solution denied by today's conservationists. The stress is on 'today's', as only a few decades ago even conservationists were pleading for a reduction in goshawk numbers to help blackcock and curlew numbers, booty was paid for killing crows and intensive fox hunting was the norm.

Quite different claims and ideas come from foresters, and from biologists and ecologists, when it comes to species which feed on forest plants rather than other animals, namely those such as red and roe deer, which also now have few natural enemies. Food supply and habitat structure determine their populations. Again, parasitic illnesses play a role, particularly with roe deer.

Regular hunting is necessary if vegetation damage is to be avoided. Foresters' claims go much further. To them each nibbled young fir or beech represents damage, even though only a proportion will be recruited into the future forest. Research has also shown that nibbled trees actually regenerate quite well and grow back quickly rather than dying off.

It is a similar story with red deer and the barking of tree trunks. Nevertheless hoofed game are generally regarded as detrimental to forests.

Thus the once noble stag, subject of so many crests and inn-signs, has sunk to the level of pest to be eradicated. There are few objections, even from a conservation-conscious public, when red deer are removed from yet another area, even though this means the local extinction of our largest remaining wild game species.

Huntsmen and hunter-foresters should try and prevent this, and attempt to maintain species-rich ecosystems. Indeed they achieve this, often unwittingly, and by quite a different method: through the quest for hunting trophies, in this case the antlers of red deer stags and roe bucks.

Certainly there have been almost incomprehensible excesses in the collection of antlers, but the modern, civilized, hunter understands the importance of his role in the natural world. Joy of hunting can thus support the whole ecosystem—now as it did two hundred years ago.

methods. Mites flourished and afflicted the foxes with another painful and deadly disease—mange. Hairless foxes—an unattractive prospect. Worm parasites also increased. These do not harm the host, but can produce illness and even death in humans if they are infected by the tiny eggs, and vets now warn people not to eat wild berries unless they have been cooked. It must be feared that efforts at vaccination against mange could again have negative side-effects on the environment.

These examples show how complex some of the issues connected with hunting have become in cultivated areas. Hunters should strive to balance out the negative effects of ecosystems which have been altered by human activities, by supporting game and their habitats. But huntsmen are only a minority of the public, so how can they achieve this?

Various guidelines should help to encourage game species:

Gray partridge can be supported by not treating field margins with weed killers.

Leaving stubble, rather than ploughing it in, leaves food and shelter for brown hare and partridge.

Overproduction is also having some good consequences, with land being set aside. Such land can be left to benefit game species.

The aims of the hunting community and conservationists are thus often identical, although problems, often of an ideological nature, do arise in practice. With the high levels of some predators, provision of islands of suitable habitat is not by itself sufficient to raise the levels for instance of brown hare and gray partridge. On the

Rooks

EUROPEAN GAME – BIRDS

FRIEDRICH KARL VON EGGELING

Seemingly weightless, birds enjoy freedom of movement like no other life form—reason enough to marvel, and even to wish to follow them into the air. Huntsmen have managed this after a fashion by using firearms: now they can confront birds in their own element. Previously they were hunted mainly by trapping or flushing. Hunting with traps and nets tended to be carried out by the common folk, whereas flushing using beaters was a sport for the privileged. In our century, bird populations have been decimated by a combination of factors, including destruction of forests, pollution of waterways and the air, and the use of chemicals in agriculture. Protection of species is therefore also one of the main aims of the modern bird hunter.

GAME BIRD BIOLOGY
Susanne K.M. Linn-Kustermann

Without their oil gland...

...ducks and geese would find swimming difficult.

The pheasant has beautiful shiny plumage.

Apart from feathers, the distinctive features of birds are their bones, which are more or less hollow, and their skull with its toothless bill. In contrast to mammalian game, their high nutritional requirements and fast digestion are distinctive characteristics. The most important sense in the case of birds is sight, their sense of smell being rudimentary.

FEATHERS AND SKIN
All birds share one feature: they have feathers; but not all birds can fly. The feathers form a covering that is used to regulate the heat of the bird's body. The large wing and tail feathers make flight possible. Feathers also give a bird its color, which is either designed primarily for camouflage or plays a role in its social behavior.

A distinction is made between contour feathers, flight feathers, down feathers and filoplumes, which all have a different structure.

The contour feathers cover all the body and help with streamlining. The larger flight feathers are longer and stiffer; they are found in the wings and tail.

A typical feather has a central shaft or rachis, a hollow cylinder, which is attached to the skin. On the shaft of the feather there are lateral processes called barbs which form the feather vane. These lateral branches bear second-order barbules which interlock like a zip fastener and give the vane a solid, compact surface. This helps produce the smooth contours which are important for streamlining and the ability to fly.

Down feathers have a similar structural plan but are fluffy, with reduced rachis and barbules. The initial juvenile plumage consists of down. In an adult bird, down feathers are distributed over its entire body underneath the contour feathers as an insulating layer.

The filoplumes consist of a thin hair-like shaft with a tuft-like tip. They are located next to the contour feathers and are sensitive to pressure and vibration, probably helping to maintain plumage in good shape and condition.

The feathers of owls have other distinctive features. All owls have very soft plumage which allows them to fly almost silently. The wing feathers, which produce a distinct noise during flight in other species, are serrated on their outer edge in the case of owls, and this prevents any loud noise during flight.

In some species of game birds the color of the plumage is plain and adapted to the bird's main environment, whereas in other species it is brightly colored. In some species both male and

female birds have the same plumage, in others the male is colorful and the female has a somewhat dowdy plumage. Strikingly colored plumages have evolved primarily in species where males compete for access to females and this helps the males when they are courting the females.

All young birds are initially covered in down. Chicks that keep to the nest are usually naked when they hatch and are brooded by their parents. Chicks that quickly leave the nest are covered in down when they hatch. The first plumage with contour feathers is usually similar to the least conspicuous parent. Many species have a typical juvenile plumage for the first year of life or even longer: examples are goshawk, peregrine and black-headed gull.

Feathers wear out and do not usually regrow. They are therefore shed and replaced at regular intervals—during the molt. The renewal of all feathers, which takes place every year as a rule, is called a full molt. Molting of the flight feathers takes place in a sequence characteristic of each bird species. In some species this sequence has evolved so ingeniously that the bird is always capable of flying, whereas in other species all the flight feathers are shed at the same time and such birds cannot fly for weeks or even months (e.g. some geese, ducks and swans). Most European bird species molt in mid summer. The beginning of the molt is genetically determined and controlled by hormones, but its progress may be altered by climate and feeding conditions.

Birds have no sebaceous glands in their skin, but most bird species have a preen gland which secretes a waxy preening oil. There is usually a feather wick at the outlet of the preen gland where the oil can be picked up on the bill and distributed over the feathers. The preening oil protects the bird's plumage against drying out and also helps keep it waterproof.

DIET AND DIGESTION
Birds have extraordinarily varied diets and have managed to colonize an exceptionally diverse range of ecological habitats on land, water and in the air. Because they are adapted to such a diversity of diets, it is possible to find a huge variety of bird species within a radius of just a few miles.

Food is ingested through the beak and esophagus, and in most birds the esophagus has an extension, the crop, in which the food is softened or stored. The glandular stomach (or proventriculus) is separate from the esophagus, and proteins are digested in it. Particularly hard food is mechanically crushed in the gizzard. In birds which eat grain, this process is aided by small digestive stones which the bird deliberately swallows. Indigestible food remnants are eliminated through the cloaca. Most birds, including all our game bird species, have no bladder, urine being eliminated together with droppings. Large indigestible food fragments such as hair, bones and feathers are regurgitated through the beak as pellets.

NUTRITIONAL REQUIREMENTS

As a rule, birds need large amounts of energy, especially when they perform strenuous activities such as running and flying or at times when other high demands are made on their metabolism, such as when laying eggs or molting. The size of the bird plays an important role in its metabolism. The smaller the bird, the higher its basic calorific turnover, the higher its relative nutritional requirements and the more often it must feed. This is particularly significant in the case of birds of prey. Whereas an eagle only needs to feed once every three days, sparrowhawks and kestrels need to make a kill every day in order to survive. An eagle needs to eat roughly a tenth of its body weight in food a day, the goshawk needs a sixth and the kestrel needs about a quarter.

Birds have developed various strategies to ensure they can continue to meet their considerable nutritional requirements: many species store food temporarily in their crop. Grain can be stored for up to 20 hours in a gallinaceous bird's crop, and the crop and stomach of a bird of prey can be so full that it has an adverse effect on its mobility. Another option is to lay down fat reserves; migrating birds in particular use large fat reserves in order to travel long distances, and these reserves are almost always fully depleted by the time they reach their destination. When a bird such as a goose is in good 'condition' before flying to its nesting grounds, this fact is externally visible to an observer.

In other species an expert can feel the breastbone to determine whether the bird is plump and in good condition or out of shape. Birds must have fat reserves for the breeding season as well as when migrating. Many species, including gallinaceous and duck species, only feed once or twice a day when incubating eggs; eider ducks fast completely when sitting on eggs and lose roughly half their body weight by the time they finish brooding.

A third way of ensuring a supply of food is to store it. Crows and relatives conceal food, jays being famous for their stores of acorns and beechnuts which they can find even when they are hidden under a solid blanket of snow.

BIRD SIGNS

The surest sign of the presence of a species of game bird in a hunting area is the feathers lost during the molt. Feathers from the remains of quarry of a bird of prey, plucked feathers which indicate that the quills were pulled out rather than bitten, are no less conclusive. Where and how they are scattered, in conjunction with any traces of droppings, often makes it possible to identify the species of bird of prey: goshawks and sparrowhawks prefer to pluck their prey at a slightly raised vantage point in a copse, and repeatedly return there. Because they are extremely wary, they change location while feeding, and the remains of their prey are therefore scattered. They pluck the hair from small mammals in clumps in the same way as they pluck game birds. The peregrine, on the other hand, plucks its prey in the open. Because it has no cover and must remain alert, it keeps turning round and therefore leaves a circle of feathers. It usually only feeds on the breast meat of its victim, the head, wings and feet remaining untouched.

The size, shape, contents and location of a pellet (the regurgitated bundle of indigestible matter) provide clues as to the species of bird which produced it. As a rule, a bird casts a pellet twice a day, usually at a place where it roosts, shortly before it moves off to search for food. The acid gastric juices of birds of prey, for example, can even digest bones, and their pellets contain mainly the remains of fur and feathers, as well as beaks and claws, or wing cases of relatively large beetles. Owl pellets contain tiny bones, mostly of rodents.

Just as mammals can be identified by their dung, game birds can be identified by their droppings, which have a typical consistency depending on the bird's diet. In the case of the capercaillie, its solid, well-formed tubular droppings contain pine needles and relatively hard seeds. Birds which eat green plants, such as geese and swans, leave quite soft, cylindrical, mostly green droppings. As the proportion of soft, low-fiber food such as grass shoots increases, droppings become more liquid, and duck droppings, for instance, may consist of small cylinders or quite watery splashes, depending on the composition of the diet. Carnivorous birds, because of their strong gastric juices, have more liquid droppings that are expelled farther away from the body.

Capercaillies produce droppings early in the morning from the tree in which they start their mating displays, and this dark, viscous substance is easily visible, especially in the snow.

Many birds, including songbirds and gallinaceous birds, look after their plumage by taking dust baths. Small to medium-sized indentations in the sand, depending on the particular species, reveal the presence of such birds to the observant hunter.

As ground-dwellers, game birds (here a red-legged partridge)...

are well camouflaged. So are ptarmigan, as well as...

this female capercaillie.

Game birds, found in various genera and families worldwide, are all ground-living running birds. They are found in most northerly moss tundra, rocky mountain tops and sandy deserts, as well as bogs, swamps and icy wastes of the Arctic. Although they vary in outward appearance, all are strong birds with short wings and powerful feet, and most have a short neck and bill and especially well-developed rump or tail feathers.

PARTRIDGES AND RELATIVES:

GRAY PARTRIDGE (*Perdix perdix*)

Originally a bird of the open steppe, the gray partridge spread over most of Europe following the forest clearances of the early Middle Ages. Now found from northern Spain and Italy (except Sicily) through central and northern Europe to south Sweden and Finland, and through the Balkans to Ukraine, Russia, along the north of the Caspian and Aral Seas to the Yenisey River, thence along the southern edge of the taiga west again to Archangelsk.

For centuries it was the most important gamebird in Europe, not just because it was common, but also for its good flavor, whether eaten roasted, warm or cold. Even Goethe used to take two gray partridge with him as a cold snack on his excursions around Weimar. There is also the well-known story about the Bishop of Dijon, imprisoned by Henry IV of France, with the instruction he be fed only on partridges which were originally the favorite food of the clergy. 'Toujours perdrix' is still an expression used for food offered too frequently and in excess.

Before the invention of the shotgun in the late 17th century, partridges were caught using nets. A dog was used to point up the game and hold them until a net could be held over to trap them.

Even today, except in England and parts of France, gray partridges are hunted using pointers or setters, which detect the game until it is flushed by the huntsmen.

In England where such sports are traditionally made more of a challenge, the partridges are flushed by beaters toward the guns, concealed behind a hedge or row of trees. The birds rise suddenly and fly rapidly overhead, calling for lightning reactions and marksmanship.

Unfortunately gray partridge have suffered a marked, sometimes drastic, reduction in numbers over most of their range, and so hunting them has had to be prevented in some areas. In Germany for example some 585,000 were taken in 1936/7, but this had fallen to about 17,000 in 1994/5, and

the density, once up to 10–15 pairs per 250 acres (100 ha) of farmland, is down to 0.5–2 pairs per 250 acres.

The reasons for this decline are many, but the main cause is the impoverishment of the habitat, with insufficient cover for breeding, and not enough food in winter. Up to 20 percent of hens fall prey to predators and up to 60 percent of clutches are lost to agricultural machinery or predators such as crows. In addition, hard winters kill many undernourished birds, resulting in ever-diminishing numbers.

As steppe birds, gray partridge like a mixed landscape with cover from tall grass, hedges and bushes, with undisturbed ditches and margins. When the coveys split up in March, the birds pair with individuals from unrelated groups. If there is no vocal contact with a neighboring group, pairing may not take place at all. They are mostly non-migratory, except in Russia where they may migrate from north to south over long distances, sometimes as far as central Europe.

A clutch of 8–20 eggs is laid in a grass nest from around the beginning of May and brooded for 25 days, under the guard of the cock bird. The young leave the nest about mid-June and feed first on small animals such as beetles, spiders, grubs and flies. They only feed if the prey moves—which means when the temperature is above 50° F (10° C)—and so a cold spell in June can wipe out an entire generation of chicks, since the hen only lays a second clutch if the first is lost in the nest, and not after the chicks have fledged.

The young are led by cock and hen and are able to escape predators by flying at 10 days old. The young are fully grown at some three months, when only their yellowish legs distinguish them. By mid-November the young birds can be identified only by inspecting their outer flight feathers—pointed in young birds, rounded in older birds. Cock and hen can be told apart by the fact that the cock has brighter colors and a larger belly patch. Fully grown birds weigh between 12 and 16 oz (350 and 470 g).

Many hunting organizations across Europe strive to improve conditions for the gray partridge, notably by protecting their habitat. The most important measures are retention of hedges and green strips, leaving streamsides and field margins unmowed, and planting fields with plants to provide both grain and cover. Many other initiatives, including the EU set-aside program, later mowing, and reductions in use of fertilizers and sprays, should also reduce losses of clutches and chicks.

Hunting for gray partridge has become the exception in Europe—the main aim now being protection.

Distribution of gray partridge

Gray partridge maintain contact by calling to each other in the morning and evening.

Distribution of quail

Quail are well camouflaged both as adult and as eggs.

QUAIL *(Coturnix coturnix)*

Smallest European member of this family, starling-sized, found scattered through most of Europe (but nowhere common), except for much of Scandinavia and northern Britain. Populations fluctuate according to their survival in the African wintering grounds. Also killed in large numbers on migration through Tunisia, Malta and Italy.

The expression 'fat as a quail' comes from the thick layer of fat under the skin of a quail in the fall, which means they can be cooked without adding additional fat.

They arrive around the beginning of May, and each male mates with several females, each of which lays a clutch of 10–12 eggs and broods them for about 17 days. The young can flutter after just 10 days. Both sexes have a stripy pattern above and the male has clearer face and chin markings. The male's call is a highly characteristic 'pick-wer-wick', often heard at night. Quail populations vary and they have become rare in many areas, although in others populations seem to be increasing again.

Note: Quail are protected throughout the year in most of Europe.

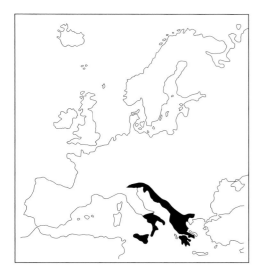

Distribution of rock partridge

Distribution of chukar

Distribution of red-legged partridge

The rock partridge (*Alectoris graeca*) is found in the western Balkans and in southern Italy and Sicily. Its gray plumage gives it good camouflage amongst the rocks.

The red-legged partridge is found in western and southern Europe.

ROCK PARTRIDGE (*Alectoris graeca*)

Found from high in the Alps to Italy and the west Balkans, but populations mostly sparse. Hunting is restricted in Italy and Balkans and in Germany and Austria this species has total year-round protection. Similar to red-legged, but slightly larger.

CHUKAR (*Alectoris chukar*)

Found mainly in Turkey and the Crimea, and from there south and east to India and Pakistan. Very similar to rock partridge but has cream colored, not white, chin patch. Often kept in captivity.

RED-LEGGED PARTRIDGE (*Alectoris rufa*)

Replaces the gray partridge in southern and western Europe. Slightly larger than gray, and has red bill and legs, and contrasty head markings. Introduced to England, where it now outnumbers the gray in many areas.

Mainly hunted by beating, as tends to run away from dogs. Flocks tend to split up when disturbed, an advantage for beating, but a disadvantage when hunting with dogs.

197

PHEASANT (*Phasianus colchicus*)

This species has a distribution stretching from the southern Black Sea through south Asia to Korea and Japan, and occurs in many races, from some of which the familiar hunted form arose, partly by crossing and partly through mutation.

Said to have been brought from Colchis in the Caucasus by Jason and the Argonauts, to Greece, pheasants were a staple part of the diet in Italy by the 2nd century B.C. The Romans then introduced it to France and many other parts of Europe, as proved by its depiction in many Roman mosaics.

Pheasant was also favored by the Merovingian Kings and by the Carolingians, as mentioned by Einhard in his "Life of Charlemagne." It seems that the birds were then kept in enclosures rather than as wild game.

In the 13th century, pheasants were kept in the estates of the nobility across Europe, in special enclosed gardens, as indeed were rabbits. From the time of the Crusades, pheasants were revered, along with peacocks. Knightly vows were taken over this bird which was brought roasted to the table, often partly feathered, and passed round for this purpose. In 1455 Philip of Burgundy founded the 'Order of the Pheasant' in which the initiates spoke the following words: "I believe in God, my Savior, above all others, and the blessed Virgin, and after our Lady and the Pheasant...", followed by the declarations, the central part of the oath.

With the Thirty Years' War pheasants lost this meaning, becoming more and more a game bird, especially after the invention of firearms.

By 1760, pheasant shooting was still such a rare event that Johann Conrad Seekatz depicted it in three oil paintings, although these birds were probably not hunted by his lord, Ludwig VIII of Hesse-Darmstadt, who preferred to shoot them from the trees by torchlight with his shotgun.

Pheasants were not maintained in the wild until around 1780, first in England, followed by France, and by about 1800 in Germany as well.

The original race, the rather heavy, slow-flying Colchicus pheasant, was not ideal for sport. Eventually, the opening up of trade with India, China and Japan, and expeditions to Iran and the steppes of Kazakhstan in Victorian times saw the introduction of lighter, faster-flying races, which were then crossed with the slower forms.

Hybrids between the steppe pheasant from Asia, *Phasianus colchicus mongolicus*, and the Chinese subspecies *P. c. torguatus*, produced the European hunting pheasant familiar today. Somewhat later the latter was crossed with the Japanese subspecies *P. c. versicolor*, the shiny green hill pheasant from Hokkaido, and a melanic mutation, *P. c. tenebrosus*.

Today's pheasants are therefore of mixed origin, showing varied characteristics, depending on their line of descent.

This mish-mash of hybrids was fatal: the new breeds certainly flew better, but this was about their only advantage. The hybrids seemed to lose their brooding behavior, and also to be more vulnerable to predators, and recently attempts have been made, with limited success, to select for the original race.

Nevertheless, pheasants are by far the most abundant of all game birds in most parts of Europe, especially in Britain, Netherlands and Italy, and in parts of France and Denmark. In all other European countries, especially those in which they are not bred for release, pheasant numbers have declined. In addition to the consequences of domestication, the reasons for this are, as with gray partridge, a reduction in the quality of habitat, including the use of insecticides and also changes in opinion about killing released animals.

Pheasants are polygamous, with one cock having a harem of several females. These are the dominant cocks, distinguished by their well-developed wattles during the breeding season in March and April. The hens make a rather scruffy nest into which they lay up to more than twenty eggs, between April and May, sometimes into June. These are brooded for about 24 days from the date when the last egg was laid.

Pheasant populations do not suffer as much as gray partridge from cold weather in June, because of the variation in brood and fledging period. Pheasants are fully grown at around three months and by this age the cock birds start to develop their colorful plumage. At this age the cock birds, unlike gray partridge, form single-sex groups and begin to disperse, especially if there is insufficient food available or provided. In winter they form larger flocks of both sexes which stay together until the displays begin early spring.

Pheasants are birds of the woodland and woodland margins, and their preference for meadows, wet places and woods perhaps reminds them of their mixed origins in steppe, rice-field or jungle. Compared with gray partridge, they are more generalist feeders, and require more cover. Ideal pheasant country are wet woods, reedbeds and open woodland with a rich undergrowth and a good canopy offering protection from storms and good sites for roosting.

They need protection, especially since they are such easy prey to predators, and also supplementary feeding from harvest-time right through until spring. In many places pheasants are reared and

Distribution of pheasant

Pheasants mark their territories with wing flaps and loud calls...

and may even come to blows with a rival.

released in huge numbers to provide sport in the autumn shoots. In Germany, where only birds which have been free-living for at least six weeks may be shot, this practice has declined.

The pheasant season begins around October 1, and shooting is usually with the aid of beaters. This is perhaps best developed in England where the aim is to provide fine sport for the hunters, but also to give the birds a good chance of escape. Wherever possible the marksmen are concealed, either in a deep ditch or behind a thick screen or hedge, and the birds either sent over high, or so suddenly that they only become visible when they are at close range. Pheasant are also sometimes hunted using pointers or setters or beater-hounds, usually at the start of the hunting season when the birds are still to be found in open fields and in copses. Pheasant were traditionally hung to tenderize the meat, but these days this is not necessary—a short spell in the deep freeze serving the same function.

A pheasant cock calls with a loud and clear 'kirrk-kok', then shakes his wings.

Pheasant hens start to lay in early May, in the nest, which is sited on the ground. There may be up to 22 eggs, which hatch after about three weeks.

Cock and hen pheasant live in harmony, as suggested in this photograph, but are not monogamous.

200

Pheasants start to display in March or April. This cock resembles a conductor in full coat and tails.

Cock pheasants are often seen by day and stand out in their colorful plumage.

GROUSE

CAPERCAILLIE *(Tetrao urogallus)*

Found in Scandinavia, Scotland, central and south-east Europe, capercaillie have declined over the last 50 years due to destruction of natural forests, and through disturbance, especially at lowland sites. On higher ground, above about 6,500 feet (2,000 m), where there is generally less disturbance, the populations seem to be more stable, as are those in Scandinavia and Russia. The Scottish population, re-introduced in the last century, is currently small and declining.

The cock bird is almost as large as a turkey, weighs up to 14 lb (6.5 kg), and is unmistakable, whilst the hen weighs a mere 5 lb (2.5 kg). The preferred habitat is well-structured, peaceful coniferous and mixed forest, with small clearings, and bushes with a good supply of buds and berries. Courtship takes place from the end of March to May, with birds displaying either from the branches or from the ground, the latter especially towards the end of the displaying period. Displays from trees are apparently rare in eastern and northern Europe. The 'song' is really strange, beginning with explosive gurgles and ending with

very quiet, scarcely audible grinding sounds. This display begins in the dark, before most other birds are singing and ends soon after sunrise. Rivals are repelled by loud, guttural calls.

Females select their mate, usually the oldest male at the display ground. They lay around eight eggs in a simple scrape and brood the clutch for 26–28 days. The young leave the nest early—as with all game birds—and take mostly animal food for the first few weeks, notably ant 'eggs'. The young birds start to disperse in late autumn and the cocks have by then already developed adult plumage.

In many countries, including Britain and Germany, capercaillie, although once hunted, are now protected throughout the year. Restricted hunting is permitted, during the display period, in certain alpine countries, although prohibited in some Austrian provinces; in Scandinavia there is some hunting in the autumn using dogs to drive the birds into the trees where they are shot; and in Russia both methods are used.

Distribution of capercaillie

The hen capercaillie looks rather like a hen black grouse (gray hen), but is larger. In summer they are found mainly on the forest floor.

A displaying capercaillie does not hear or see very well – luckily for the photographer, who can then get quite close. The cock ruffles out his feathers, dances back and forth and begins his remarkable display song.

BLACK GROUSE *(Tetrao tetrix)*

Found in similar habits to capercaillie, but also on heather moor and bog (including lowland bog), and on dwarf-shrub heath near the tree-line. Now extinct in many lowland sites. Populations have declined markedly across Europe, even in upland sites, due to cultivation of bogs and disturbance.

The hen (grayhen) is considerably smaller than the cock (blackcock), and adult cocks have shiny blue-black plumage and lyre-shaped tail feathers, fluffed out during courtship to reveal white under tail coverts. Both sexes show a white wing-bar in flight. The cocks meet at lekking grounds in the breeding season to display to females, with outspread tails and making cooing and gurgling sounds. These displays may result in genuine fights.

Although cocks and hens live together in mixed groups, the hens alone brood the eggs.

The traditional hunt at the lekking grounds in April and May, in which the huntsmen gathered in the gray light of dawn, is now illegal almost everywhere—with the exception of the Baltic states and Russia and certain Austrian provinces. In Scandinavia they are still sometimes hunted in the fall using pointers or other bird dogs.

Still sometimes hunted using beaters in Scotland, but traditional 'roughshooting' no longer takes place.

RACKELHAHN
(Tetrao tetrix x *T. urogallus)*

This is a rare infertile hybrid between a black grouse cock and capercaillie hen, and more rarely the reciprocal cross. Of limited importance to hunting.

Black grouse (*Tetrao tetrix*) have become rare with the loss of so much of their habitat – bogs and lowland mires...

... whereas the hybrid rackelhahn (*Tetrao tetrix* x *T. urogallus*) has never been common.

When capercaillie (lower photographs) and black grouse (cock shown above) cross, they produce the rackelhahn, which are infertile amongst themselves, but can reproduce again with either parent species.

▷ Black cock displaying. The hens come to the lekking grounds to choose a mate.

▷ The rackelhahn is like a small version of the capercaillie.

PTARMIGAN *(Lagopus mutus)*

Widespread across the Arctic and Subarctic to north Greenland, Spitzbergen and Franz-Joseph-Land, with Ice-Age relict populations in Scotland, the Alps, Pyrenees, Japan and Newfoundland. In the Alps they are found to nearly 12,000 feet (3,600 m) and breed at up to almost 8,000 feet (2,400 m).

Plumage is brown in summer and pure white in winter, with a grayish intermediate phase in the fall. In winter the blackish-brown tail feathers, which may be hidden at rest, are obvious in flight.

Hunting is illegal in most European countries, except for parts of Scandinavia where the populations are increasing. The smaller populations of Scotland, Switzerland and South Tyrol are more or less stable.

Ptarmigan (*Lagopus mutus*) is unmistakable in flight, with its pure white body and wings...

...but in spring is rather less spectacular in its speckled summer plumage.

RED GROUSE
(Lagopus lagopus scoticus)

This is a distinctive race of the willow grouse, and is sometimes regarded as a separate species. Unlike the willow grouse, the red grouse is a prime game species. The British regard grouse shooting as one of the finest of all field sports, and it is very challenging to shoot at these fast-flying birds. Grouse moor fetches a high price, and taking part in such a shoot is regarded as quite an honor. Red grouse are found on the upland heather moors of Britain and Ireland, with the main concentrations on high ground in Scotland and northern England.

Grouse shooting usually involves the marksmen waiting concealed in a semicircular dugout (the butts) and aiming at the birds, which are driven toward them by beaters. More rarely red grouse are hunted using English setters (laveracks) to point up the birds, and spaniels or labradors as retrievers. For late season shoots assistants known as ghillies prevent the grouse from flying too soon by trailing kites in the shape of birds of prey. Shooting parties are of three or four guns each, and a good bag can consist of as many as 600 grouse.

To maintain high grouse yields, a plentiful supply of fresh heather growth is traditionally ensured by regular burning. Predators are also hunted (where legal), and the grouse fed in winter, often with antibiotics against parasitic worms.

However, red grouse populations have recently declined as a result of loss of heather quality through overgrazing by sheep, and, more controversially, through an increase in predatory birds, now protected.

WILLOW GROUSE (Lagopus lagopus)

About the size of hen pheasant, willow grouse are found in northern Europe and northern Asia. Very like ptarmigan, but summer plumage is browner. Hunted using pointers or other hounds.

HAZEL GROUSE (Bonasa bonasia)

In the east of their range these birds inhabit lowland and taiga, but in the west and north they tend to be found in the mountains to about 5,000 feet (1,500 m). They prefer sunny, mixed forest with broad-leaved and coniferous trees. Now rather local in central Europe, with huntable populations only in the French Jura, South Tyrol and Slovenia. Rare in Germany, with pockets in certain areas including the Black Forest. Often hunted in the fall, by being lured to a whistle imitating the distinctive sharp call. In Scandinavia hunted using tracker hounds, and also trapped in Russia.

Willow grouse (*Lagopus lagopus*) in its preferred boggy habitat.

Hazel grouse (*Bonasa bonasia*) prefer wooded country.

Red grouse are found only in Britain and Ireland. These are birds of upland heather moor and nest on sunny slopes, often under the shelter of a large clump of heather, willow or birch.

Distribution of hazel grouse

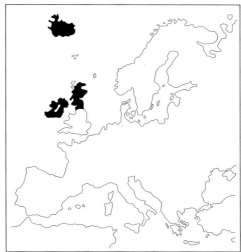

Distribution of red grouse

Distribution of willow grouse

Like many ground nesting birds, the willow grouse chick is in grave danger as soon as it leaves the nest.

PIGEONS AND DOVES

This family is widespread in all except the polar regions, in some 60 genera with around 400 species, and all members have the typical pigeon body shape.

Doves are a symbol of peace, ever since Noah released three of them, one of which returned with the famous olive branch. Since the Thirty Years' War the motif of doves with olive branch has been a common symbol used on coins, and Picasso's dove was used as the emblem of the 1949 Paris communist World Peace Conference.

WOODPIGEON (*Columba palumbus*)

Very common throughout Europe, and in most areas the most commonly shot species. In the British Isles the population stands at about 3,520,000 pairs. In Germany some 800,000 to 900,000 are taken each year—more than ducks, pheasant and gray partridge combined. This increase has several reasons: woodpigeons are opportunists which have adapted well to human society, especially in gardens and parks, even in cities, where they are safe from natural predators. They have also adapted well to the large fields of modern agriculture, finding safety in large flocks. They supplement their diet by feeding on many kinds of crops, including intermediate sowings, and the recent slight climatic warming has also helped provide them with nourishment through the winter.

Sometimes huntsmen find themselves in the almost grotesque situation of having to telephone around despairingly to gather up all the dead pigeons, especially in the open country of the Netherlands or southern England. Roast pigeon is however quite a delicacy, especially stuffed with parsley in a roasting brick, and has a characteristic powerful taste, and an aroma not unlike roast partridge.

Woodpigeons start to display in March or April and have a very characteristic drawn out owl-like cooing song with long phrases—'hoo-hóo-hu-hoo-hoo, hoo-hóo-hóo-hu-hoo-hoo...', ending rather abruptly. The female also has a nest-call, a deep 'rrru-kúuuh', which indicates that she has recently laid her eggs or begun brooding them. The clutch is usually two, pure white eggs, laid in a rather loosely built twig nest and brooded for 15-17 days. The newly-hatched young are fed for their first week entirely on 'crop-milk', by both parents. This substance is a milky, fat-rich glandular secretion of the crop wall. Two to three clutches may be laid each season, into July, and losses are high, with about a third of eggs being lost to the wind due to the feeble nest design; the first clutch is often chilled too much, and goshawks, cats, and members of the crow family all take nestlings and young birds. Nevertheless a pair raises on average two young each year, resulting in a doubling of the population by the autumn. Winter losses are small, since their flocking behavior gives them good protection from predators. It is therefore possible, even recommended, to take some 40 percent of the fall population, to avoid overpopulation, which

Woodpigeons (*Columba palumbus*) find safety in large flocks. In towns and cities however this in not necessary, and they have learned to survive in suburbia as well. But for breeding they seek out a quieter spot.

212

could cause consequent damage, and even diseases such as pigeon-pox (diphtheria) in the pigeons themselves.

In the first year it is easy to distinguish young birds from adults, as the former only develop the characteristic white neck marking after the second molt. This is important in the kitchen too, as young birds take only about half as long to cook, with the oldest birds needing a long steaming.

Woodpigeons are hunted in many different ways. One classic method is by luring. Woodpigeons return the call and react quickly, which requires speedy reactions by the huntsman. Imitating the call often results in the bird approaching so quickly that it is hard to get to the gun in time to get a good aim through the twigs and branches. Bird calls and lures made of wood or plastic are now available and these may improve success. In summer and early fall the usual methods involve waiting amongst crops or near a watering site.

By late fall most woodpigeons have gathered into large flocks, which move about in search of food, be this acorns or beech-mast in woodland or sprouts in the fields. Stalking in bare autumn woodland is rarely successful, and virtually impossible in the open fields. One needs to find a roosting site, which in still weather is usually a copse, and in windy weather perhaps in the middle of a wood. In relatively open landscapes, such as in England, the Netherlands and north Germany, the pigeons may be driven backwards and forwards between such sites, and this can result in large bags. In England, the numbers taken daily can be as high as 400 birds per huntsman, shot in the fields by day and at the roost in the evening.

Hunting using beaters is less successful since the birds tend to disperse rather randomly when disturbed. There is an exception, requiring careful preparation, and this involves encircling the flock in the field, and preventing early escapes by flying kites shaped like birds of prey. This can unfortunately be something of a double-edged sword, as pigeons which have been feeding all day on sprouts taste so bitter as to be almost inedible. Woodpigeon is destined to remain the number one European game bird for some time to come.

Woodpigeons are not very fussy about where they nest.

◁ The still blind young woodpigeon (squab) is fed on 'crop-milk'.

213

Distribution of stock dove

Distribution of turtle dove

Distribution of collared dove

The hole-nesting stock dove has declined in many areas.

214

STOCK DOVE
(Columba oenas)

This is the only hole-nester amongst European pigeons and doves, often using old black woodpecker nests in continental Europe.

Found over most of Europe, except the far north. In the British Isles about 270,000 pairs, with populations now recovering after earlier decline. Summer visitor in central, northern and eastern Europe, resident in the south and west. Migratory birds overwinter in Africa and also in southern Spain, returning to the summer quarters in early May. Their disyllabic calls 'oou-o, oou-o, oou-o...' can be heard in woodland and in copses through the summer.

Easily confused with feral pigeons from a distance, but the latter usually have a white rump. Smaller than woodpigeon and has shiny metallic coloring on the neck and breast, and double, broken wing bars. Protected in most areas.

TURTLE DOVE
(Streptopelia turtur)

Found throughout much of Europe, except the far north and north-west. Summer visitor and passage migrant, wintering in Africa, mainly south of the Sahara. There are three migratory routes: through the Balkans and Turkey to east Africa; through Italy to Tunisia; and through Spain to Morocco and Mauritania.

Our smallest dove, with rather delicate build, and graduated tail with white margin when spread. Plumage rusty-brown, with speckled wings and black and white markings at the sides of the neck. Prefers hedgerows and open broadleaved woods. Generally avoids populated areas. The song is a soft, purring 'turrr-turrr, turrr-turrr...'.

The loose, often see-through nest is built in a tree or bush. Turtle doves return from Africa in the spring.

Protected throughout the year in central and northern Europe, but shot in large numbers in southern and south-east Europe.

COLLARED DOVE
(Streptopelia decaocto)

The collared dove invasion began in the 1940s, from the Near East, since when it has spread throughout most of Europe, except the far north-east and much of Spain, mainly close to human habitations.

A pale, slim, long-tailed dove with a dark half collar at the back of its neck, and a pinkish breast.

The courtship song is a monotonous trisyllabic 'coo-cóoo, coo', accented on the second syllable, and it also makes a nasal flight-call. Resident and partial migrant, with good numbers in winter as well.

Mainly found in towns and villages, especially where there is an abundance of food, as in parks, zoos, at silos, grain stores, farmyards; often seen at bird tables. Nests in trees, bushes or even on buildings. Collared doves have several broods each year, and feed mainly on grain and seeds.

Hunted in the same seasons as woodpigeon.

The stock dove (*Columba oenas*) is somewhat smaller and darker than the woodpigeon.

The turtle dove (*Streptopelia turtur*) is a bird of woodland and scrub ...

... whereas collared doves (*Streptopelia decaocto*) have even colonized cities.

215

Distribution of mute swan

Distribution of whooper swan

Whooper swans can be seen at many lakes and rivers in Scandinavia.

The swan has landed. This majestic bird has inspired many a poet and artist, although its meat is not suitable for eating.

SWANS, DUCKS AND GEESE

These birds are divided into two families, with many genera and some 200 species, worldwide, and are mostly restricted to wetlands.

At the end of the 15th century the goose was the symbol of St. Martin (St. Martin's Day is November 11), but it seems graylag geese had been domesticated by the early Stone Age in northern and central Europe, and in the Near East by the 4th century B.C.

SWANS:

MUTE SWAN
(Cygnus olor)

This is the most widespread of Europe's three species of swan, and is a common breeding bird, mainly in central and western Europe. Whooper swans breed in Iceland and Scandinavia, and Bewick's swans breed mainly in Siberia, although both can be seen in certain places, notably Britain and Ireland, in the winter, and are protected at all times.

The mute swan has a reddish bill with a black base, and an obvious knob on the bill, more developed in the male, especially in spring. The other species have a black bill with a yellow patch. Mute swans are normally silent but their wings make a throbbing whine in flight, whereas whooper swans make loud, trumpeting flight-calls.

Mute swans are partial migrants, wintering on open water, and breeding on river banks or lake margins and reedbeds where they construct large nests. They hold their necks in a characteristic V-shape when swimming.

The threat display of a male defending its nest is impressive: he swims toward the intruder with neck held back and wings raised over his back.

Mute swans have increased markedly in recent years, partly through feral park birds, and a reduction would benefit other water creatures, although their damage to the underwater flora has probably been overstated.

They are shot in the fall, either at their grazing sites which they may use for weeks at a time, or en route between their feeding and drinking places.

Only the young swans (gray plumage) are particularly good to eat.

Note: In Britain, swans are Crown property and may not be taken.

GEESE:

GRAYLAG GOOSE *(Anser anser)*

There is no more impressive sight than flocks of wild geese passing overhead, with their constant loud and strange calls. How wonderful it would be to fly off with them into the unknown, just as Nils Holgersson did in the marvellous fairy tales by Selma Lagerlöf!

It is mainly the gray geese which affect us in this way with their behavior and calls as they migrate to and from their breeding grounds in the far north.

Graylag geese have increased in the last few decades and also expanded their range westward. Today there are some 4,000 breeding pairs in Germany, 1,000 in the Netherlands, 2,000 pairs in Britain and over 10,000 pairs in Scandinavia and the Baltic states.

Such increases, of many wild geese, may in part be due to climatic changes over the last 20 years and the slightly earlier onset of spring in the breeding grounds, and consequent better survival of the young birds.

The wintering grounds of northern European geese is mainly the British Isles and Brittany, the central European birds in northern Germany, Netherlands and France, and the eastern European geese on the Danube, Black Sea, Volga delta and Arab emirates.

Graylag geese like to breed at still waters with well-developed reedbeds, and on undisturbed boggy and marshy ground. The clutch is of 4–12 eggs, brooded by the female for 28–29 days. At first the young goslings feed mainly on larvae, grubs and flies. After some 55 days they can fly and leave the breeding grounds with their newly molted parents to join other flocks of geese on large lakes. From there they may fly up to 20 miles in search of food—mainly on grassland or arable fields. They often feed on rape or, more unfortunately, on winter wheat, which they may damage.

Hunting is usually by waiting under cover at a suitable spot, rarely by moving through reeds or from a punt. It is important to establish which fields are used regularly by the geese during the day. Once this has been discovered, then well camouflaged dug-outs can be constructed, in which the hunters wait from before dawn for the arrival of the flocks.

Distribution of graylag goose

Graylag geese rear their young in their territories, until the time arrives for the autumn migration. Then the geese fly off in wedge-formation.

218

WHITE-FRONTED GOOSE
(Anser albifrons)

This species has increased enormously in recent decades, with almost a four-fold increase in some areas. It breeds in the Arctic tundra. The Russian race winters around the North Sea and Channel coasts of England, France, Holland and Germany, and in the Near East, whilst the Greenland race winters mainly in Ireland and western Scotland. The adults have black horizontal barring on the belly, and a white forehead.

BARNACLE GOOSE
(Branta leucopsis)

These geese nest mainly on cliffs above river valleys or fjords in Greenland, Spitzbergen and northern Russia. They are regular winter visitors to Scotland, Ireland, and to the southern North Sea (mainly the Netherlands). The latter come from Russia, whilst those from Spitzbergen winter in north-west England and south-west Scotland (Solway Firth), and those from Greenland mainly in Ireland and west Scotland. From a distance looks black above and white below, the white face contrasting with the black neck.

BEAN GOOSE
(Anser fabalis)

This goose breeds on the tundra of north-east Europe. It is browner than graylag and has variable dark marks on the bill.

It winters mainly in central Europe, with small numbers in south-west Scotland (Solway) and East Anglia.

The similar but slightly smaller pink-footed Goose (Anser brachyrhynchus) breeds in Greenland, Spitzbergen and Iceland and winters in large flocks to traditional sites in northern Britain (notably Scotland and Lancashire), and to south-east Ireland. Also to eastern England, usually only after hard weather, and to the southern coast of the North Sea.

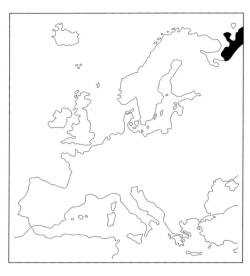

Distribution (breeding) of white-fronted goose

Barnacle geese (*Branta leucopsis*) likes to feed on saltmarsh and coastal sandbanks.

Distribution (winter) of barnacle goose

Distribution (breeding) of bean goose

The bean goose (*Anser fabalis*) winters mainly in central Europe and breeds in the tundra of north-east Europe and Russia.

The white-fronted goose (*Anser albifrons*), winters mainly in the British Isles.

Canada geese (*Branta canadensis*) on a lake

Distribution (winter) of Brent goose

Brent Goose
(*Branta bernicla*)

Small, dark, rather duck-like goose with black bill and legs. Two races visit Europe in winter: a pale-bellied and a (commoner) dark-bellied form. Irish birds are mainly of pale-bellied race, whilst those visiting southern England and continental Europe are mostly dark-bellied. Any damage caused by grazing is evened out by the fertilizing effects of their droppings.

Canada Goose
(*Branta canadensis*)

Largest European goose, and an introduction from North America, where it breeds on marshy lakes and river banks, right up into the tundra region. In Europe mainly breeds in the British Isles, and locally in Scandinavia, but also elsewhere, notably in the lakes of upper Bavaria. Resident and partial migrant to Germany and Holland. The Swedish population winters on the German North Sea coast.

Note: Hunting restrictions on geese vary from country to country, with some species protected throughout the year.

Distribution (breeding) of Canada goose

Brent geese (*Branta bernicla*) are very sociable.

DUCKS

MALLARD
(Anas platyrhynchos)

There is an old wildfowling saying that goes "The duck is an odd bird. Too much for breakfast, but not enough for lunch!" A fully grown mallard weighs about 2 lb (about 900 g), although yearlings are some 7 oz (200g) lighter.

Mallard is Europe's commonest duck, with around 3.4 million being taken each year—some 550,000 in Germany, almost 700,000 in Denmark and even more in the Netherlands.

Mallard have benefited from eutrophication of water, which has increased the year-round supply of plant food. Remaining long in their breeding grounds is also a disadvantage, especially for suburban populations, which have increasingly interbred with semi-domesticated ducks, resulting in many odd-shaped or colored hybrids, some with the thick head of domestic ducks rather than the flatter head of the wild type.

Mallard are found throughout Europe, including Iceland, being absent only from the far northeast, around the Barents Sea.

Mallard are partial migrants, moving a short distance south, migrating to warmer regions in the winter, or with only a proportion of the population moving. Thus, for example, German mallard migrate south to Italy, France or Spain, whilst Russian mallard move to the comparatively milder conditions in Germany and the Netherlands. From February they return to their summer quarters, the process taking several weeks. After their arrival they start chasing each other, each duck followed by one or more drakes. Breeding begins in March, or April, and the eggs are normally laid quite close to the water, although the nest may exceptionally be as much as a mile away from the water. The clutch of 6–10 eggs is brooded for up to 28 days by the female alone, with the drake keeping a watch until they leave the nest. The newly-hatched ducklings eat almost entirely insects at first, and whole broods can be lost in cold weather. They can fly at about seven weeks old.

The drakes molt out of their breeding plumage from the middle of June, and are almost flightless for a while. The ducks molt after the young have flown, and flocks in August are usually entirely made up of young birds, as their mothers are then flightless. During the eclipse plumage, drakes resemble ducks, except for the bill color: olive in the drake, brown in the duck.

The age can be told from the state of the feathers. In older birds the feathers of the wing coverts are square-ended, in younger birds oval. In young birds less than six months old, the tail feathers are worn (before the winter molt), whereas in the adult they are fresher.

The autumn molt begins at the end of September, or in early October, and by the end of October the drakes regain their full breeding plumage. After this time the birds are easier to pluck.

Mallard are hunted at different times of the year, and by many different techniques: from cover, and by tracking or beating. In all cases a good dog is necessary, not just a good retriever, but also one which will not mind working through thick reeds or in the water. Winged birds will often dive, and this can test even the best hunting dog.

Mallard sometimes cause damage, for example to grain crops in late summer. In the Netherlands the hunting season begins at the end of July, but is generally harmonized over much of Europe, with a close season at least in the spring migration.

Distribution of mallard

Mallard duck preening

▷ The streamlined body of this mallard drake is typical of waterfowl – the nest is usually near the water, in reeds.

GOLDENEYE *(Bucephala clangula)*

A sea duck, but breeds on lakes and fast-flowing rivers in the coniferous forest zone, using holes in trees. Outside breeding season mainly coastal; also on lakes, reservoirs and larger rivers, especially at the coast. Mainly Scandinavia and north-east Europe. In British Isles a rare breeding bird (protected), but increasing (about 100 pairs, mainly in Scotland). Winter visitor to British Isles, and central and south-east Europe.

RED-CRESTED POCHARD *(Netta rufina)*

Breeds in only a few places in Europe, mainly in southern Spain and Camargue (France), but also in the Netherlands, Denmark, and south central Europe (Lake Constance and southern Bavaria), and in the Danube delta. Sometimes escapes from collections. Generally rare, and protected throughout the year. Large, mallard-sized, thick-headed diving duck, sitting rather high in the water. Breeding male has chestnut head (crown paler) and bright red bill.

TEAL *(Anas crecca)*

Our smallest duck, with rapid, almost wader-like flight. Breeding male has chestnut and green head and yellow triangle (bordered black) at side of tail. Female has yellow-brown spots and dark gray bill. Both sexes show white wing-bar and green speculum in flight. Breeds on lakes with thick bank vegetation. Widespread in northern and eastern Europe, rarer further south. Accounts for some 5 percent of duck taken.

GARGANEY *(Anas querquedula)*

Resembles teal, but slightly larger yet slimmer. Breeding male has broad white eyestripe reaching to back of head. Female like teal but with rather striped face pattern. Male in eclipse like female, but with blue-gray front of wing. Flight not as rapid as teal. Breeds on shallow water or marshland with rich vegetation. Outside breeding season on lakes, flooded meadows and marshes. Summer visitor to much of Europe (but absent from much of northern and southern Europe), and nowhere common. Winters in Africa. In the British Isles a rare breeding bird and protected (about 50 pairs). Male call 'klerrb'.

SHELDUCK (*Tadorna tadorna*)

Large goose-sized duck, looking black and white in distance. Broad chestnut band around body at chest region. Male has knob at base of bill. Mainly protected and of little importance for hunting. The breeding range is around the coasts of north-west Europe, and patchily in the Mediterranean. Common breeding bird of North Sea and Baltic. Mainly on muddy and sandy coasts, and coastal lakes, where it nests in holes and rabbit burrows. Resident and partial migrant (Scandinavian populations summer visitors).

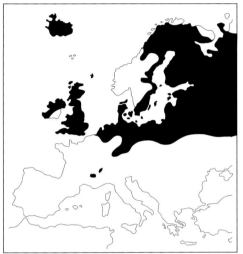

TUFTED DUCK (*Aythya fuligula*)

This species has, like pochard, expanded its range westward in the last two decades, and now breeds through Germany, the Netherlands and Britain, as well as in north-eastern Europe. In Scandinavia the numbers have increased somewhat. With pochard makes up some 20 percent of the catch.

SCAUP (*Aythya marila*)

Somewhat larger than tufted, without plume. Head larger and more rounded, bill wider. Male has green-black head, pale gray speckled back and white flanks.

Breeds in Iceland, Scandinavia and Finland, and occasionally in Britain in very small numbers. Summer visitor to breeding grounds; winter visitor mainly to coasts of north-west Europe. Feeds mainly by diving for molluscs, crustaceans and insect larvae. Often seen in flocks at sea.

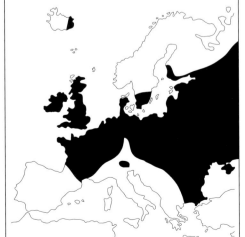

SHOVELER (*Anas clypeata*)

Squatter than mallard, with more pointed wings and long, broad bill. Male has dark head, white breast and chestnut belly and flanks. Female rather like mallard, but has pale blue forewing. One of the few duck species not to have increased or spread in recent years. Protected through the year in many countries. Scattered, mainly in central and eastern Europe. Breeds on shallow lakes, bordered by rushes, sedges or reeds, and in marshy areas with open water. Sieves crustaceans and other small prey from the water with specially adapted bill.

POCHARD
(Aythya ferina)

Widespread breeding bird, with similar (rather patchy) distribution to tufted duck, but absent from northern Scandinavia. Male has contrasting silver-gray back and flanks, black chest and tail, and chestnut-brown head. Female brown, with blackish bill and pale head markings. More associated with fresh water than is tufted duck, and less liable to taste oily.

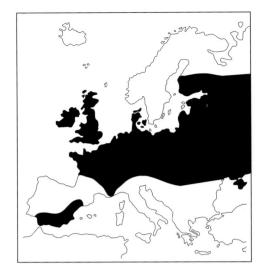

LONG-TAILED DUCK *(Clangula hyemalis)*
COMMON SCOTER *(Melanitta nigra)*
VELVET SCOTER *(Melanitta fusca)*

All three of these ducks breed in the far north and only appear at the coast during the winter, although velvet scoter are sometimes seen inland. Of little importance to the wildfowler. The photograph shows a male long-tailed duck in summer plumage.

EIDER
(Somateria mollissima)

Large sea-duck, heavier than mallard, but more compact and shorter-necked. Breeding male mainly black and white. Female brownish with darker stripes. Breeds on coasts and nearby islands; outside breeding season in shallow bays and estuaries. Breeds around the coasts of Greenland, Iceland, Scandinavia, the North Sea (scattered) and northern British Isles.

PINTAIL *(Anas acuta)*

Slimmer than mallard. Male has chestnut head, gray body and long, pointed tail feathers. Female similar to mallard, but has more pointed tail and smaller, gray bill. Breeds mainly on shallow lakes in northern coniferous forest or tundra of north or north-east Europe. Outside breeding season mainly on the coast, or on flooded washland, often in large flocks.

FERRUGINOUS DUCK *(Aythya nyroca)*

Small, dark, chestnut-colored duck, with white wing-bar. Uniform plumage is distinctive, with only the under tail coverts white. Breeds mainly in eastern Europe, Balkans and Turkey. A rare winter visitor to most of Europe and a protected species.

WIGEON *(Anas penelope)*

Medium-sized dabbling duck, weighing up to 1¾ lb (800 g). Breeding male has chestnut head with golden crown stripe; female similar to female mallard, but slimmer, with rusty-brown plumage and more pointed tail. Often forms large flocks in winter. Male has whistling call, given especially in flight. Breeds on lakes bogs and river deltas in northern Europe (mainly Iceland and Scandinavia). Regular winter visitor to North Sea, south Baltic, and other coasts.

GADWALL *(Anas strepera)*

Mallard-like but slightly smaller and slimmer, weighing up to 800g. Male relatively drab, with obvious black 'stern.' Like other dabbling ducks, can rise directly from the water. In flight both sexes show white belly and white speculum. Breeds on freshwater lakes with rich vegetation, and on slow rivers. Patchy distribution over much of Europe, but absent from most of Scandinavia. Call is a deep quacking.

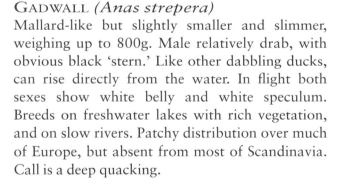

SAWBILLS *(Mergus spp.)*

The three European sawbills are protected throughout the year in most countries, and are therefore of little importance today for hunting.

SMEW *(Mergus albellus)*

Smew, the smallest of the sawbill ducks, nest in hollow trees in northern and eastern Scandinavia. Male in breeding plumage is pure white, with black lines on body, black eye-patch and back. Female gray, with red-brown cap, and white cheeks. Winters south to coasts of North Sea, Baltic and Channel.

RED-BREASTED MERGANSER *(Mergus serrator)*

Mallard-sized sawbill, breeding mainly in Iceland, Scandinavia and British Isles. Resident and partial migrant in Britain, summer visitor to breeding areas in northern Europe. Winters south to most coasts. Both sexes have a ragged double crest. Breeding male has dark green head, white collar and reddish breast; in eclipse has pale red-brown head with white chin and gray body. Female has indistinct boundary between head and neck coloration.

GOOSANDER *(Mergus merganser)*

Largest European sawbill, with long, hook-tipped red bill. Male mostly white, with salmon pink flush underneath, greenish-black head and black back; no crest. Eclipse plumage gray with brown head and neck. Female mainly gray, with brown head and upper neck and white chin and neck. Breeds on lakes and rivers in forested areas.

The red-breasted merganser (*Mergus serrator*) also breeds in Europe.

Smew (*Mergus albellus*) nest in holes in trees close to water.

▷ Goosander (*Mergus merganser*); the commonest in Europe as a whole

WADERS AND GULLS

The scientific order containing waders and gulls is divided into three suborders: auks; gulls and relatives; and waders and relatives. Despite their different appearances, these groups are quite closely related.

SANDPIPERS AND ALLIES:

WOODCOCK (*Scolopax rusticola*)

The woodcock is rather a strange bird, about which many stories have been told and handed down over the centuries—be these about their unusual movements, the question of whether they carry their young about in their feet, whether there is more than one species or subspecies, and lastly whether it is true that only a small number of cocks display, the rest taking no part. One last mystery remains. How do they make their odd ventriloquial grunting calls? Anatomical investigations have so far failed to elucidate the mechanism.

Until a few decades ago, somewhat heavier than usual woodcocks, early arrivals, so-called 'owl-heads', were considered to represent a distinctive form, compared with the lighter birds arriving later in the season. Since then it has been established that there is just a single species, and the weight differences are due to nourishment—the early arrivals having fed well in their winter quarters in nearby France or Spain, whilst the others have used up body reserves on the long migration from Senegal, Morocco, Tanzania and Mozambique.

Woodcock are true migrants, and only a few overwinter in central Europe, though even these move south in hard weather. There are three routes: through the Balkans and Turkey to East Africa; through Italy and Malta to Tunisia (unfortunately shot in large numbers on the way); and through southern France or Spain to Morocco, south to the equator. The return routes are not necessarily as strict.

Scandinavian birds winter mainly in the British Isles, and most of the British birds are resident. They have had the opportunity, possibly through this separation from European birds, to develop their own particular characteristics, which may explain why they are often found in more open habitats such as marshland or bogs, as well as in woodland, whereas on the continent they are almost entirely birds of woodland. The population density also seems to be higher in England and Scotland, and many birds cross the channel to settle in the Netherlands and northern France.

In mild, especially rainy weather, with southerly or westerly winds, the dominant cocks, representing some 20–50 percent of the cocks, begin to 'rode', in cruising flights along woodland rides, clearings and over plantations. This roding flight is accompanied by calls—a loud, very high-pitched sharp 'psi-vitt, psi-vitt', alternating with deep grunting 'orrk-orrk-ork', repeated two or three times. The hen birds remain on the ground

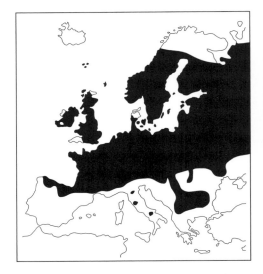

Distribution of woodcock

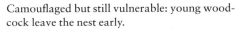
Camouflaged but still vulnerable: young woodcock leave the nest early.

and answer the cock birds with a soft 'psi-vitt'. They sometimes make a henlike clucking noise when flying off to feeding grounds. The hen birds are pretty sedentary in spring, so two or three birds calling close by are always males displaying and competing.

Woodcock hens lay four eggs in a simple nest amongst the undergrowth in moist or damp (but not wet) woodland, and these are brooded for 22 days. In bad weather many clutches and young birds are lost. In grave danger, the hen moves her chicks between her legs to a safer spot. If the first clutch is lost, they will lay a second in June, preceded by a similar courtship.

Woodcock have a palearctic distribution: that is west to the Azores, Madeira and the Canaries, through Spain, and along the Atlantic coast to about 70° N in Norway, then following about 65° N to the Sea of Okhotsk. The southern border goes through southern France and northern Italy, through the Balkans, Ukraine and along the southern edge of the taiga, over the Himalaya, to India and Japan, to Sakhalin Island.

In most European countries the hunting season for woodcock is from fall through February (in Germany for example from October 16 until January 15), and in some parts of south-east Europe they are also hunted during the courtship season.

Woodcock catches are very high in their winter quarters, with almost 1 million birds being taken in France, between 22,000 and 25,000 in Germany, usually during hare or pheasant shoots. Around equal numbers of both sexes are taken, whereas in shoots during courtship over 90 percent would be cock birds.

Populations fluctuate in Europe, with recent declines in Britain and Germany. Sharp declines in southern Germany may be a result of heavy losses to shooting on migration through the central Mediterranean route. In northern Germany numbers have remained more stable, possibly connected with the more westerly migration route.

Recent changes in forestry practice, notably planting of mixed stands, have favoured woodcock, whereas the lowering of water tables through drainage has been to their disadvantage.

Roast autumn woodcock, with its incomparably aromatic flavor, is a delicacy.

Woodcock feed mainly on worms, larvae and insects which they find by probing the soil with their long bill.

Distribution of snipe

SNIPE (*Gallinago gallinago*)

This cousin of the woodcock is protected in much of Europe (or hunting is very restricted).

Smaller than the woodcock, weighing only about 3 oz (100 g), with dark stripes on head (horizontal on woodcock). Very long bill, short neck and short legs.

Male makes high, undulating flights over breeding ground, plunging downwards and producing a humming or bleating sound (so-called drumming), by vibrating the stiff outer tail feathers. Therefore known as 'Himmelsziege' (sky-goat) in parts of northern Germany.

Repeated nasal 'etch' when flushed. Song is a repeated, 'ticka-ticka-ticka', often from a song-post.

Breeds in fens, bogs, damp meadows and other wetland areas with low vegetation. Also seen at lake margins, mudbanks, small ponds and ditches. Threatened by drainage of habitats, and declining over much of its range.

Hunted using dogs to flush birds from fens and wet meadows. The zig-zig flight is a challenge to the marksman. Tastes similar to woodcock.

Day-old chick

Camouflaged clutch

Snipe (*Gallinago gallinago*) live in fens, bogs and wet meadows, and are only about half the size of woodcock.

Distribution of curlew

CURLEW
(Numenius arquata)

Like snipe, curlew have declined in much of Europe, due mainly to land drainage, and are therefore protected. Some signs of an increase in British Isles, and expansion of range in Scandinavia.

Largest European wader, with long, gently decurved bill; about twice the size of snipe. Open bogs and upland moors, overgrown lake margins, damp meadows. Also breeds on damp and wet meadows. Common on mudflats and estuaries outside the breeding season, and on open fields.

Young curlew

Adult curlew ...

... and clutch

Distribution of black-tailed godwit

BLACK-TAILED GODWIT *(Limosa limosa)*
BAR-TAILED GODWIT *(Limosa lapponica)*

Both these species are fully protected, and are mainly seen wintering around the coasts.

Black-tailed godwits breed mainly in water meadows (rare breeder in England). Adult in breeding plumage has rust-brown neck and breast, and in winter both sexes are uniform gray. In flight it shows a white wing-bar and white base to black tail.

Bar-tailed godwits breed on damp tundra and mires in northern Europe and north Asia, but can be seen in large numbers on mudflats around the North Sea. Resembles black-tailed, but breeding male mainly rust-red, speckled brown and black on the back; female and winter male buff colored. In flight the legs extend slightly beyond the tail, and there is no obvious wing-bar. The tail has narrow bars.

Black-tailed godwit searching for food in a damp meadow. This species and curlew are both waders.

233

Distribution of coot

Coot (*Fulica atra*)

The only game species amongst the seven European rails. Moorhen (*Gallinula chloropus*), and Water Rail (Rallus aquaticus) were formerly hunted, but are now generally protected.

Coot are found throughout Europe, except the far north, and they live in nutrient-rich lakes, reservoirs, ponds, and slow-flowing rivers with well-developed fringing vegetation. Also found on small gravel pits and on lakes in urban parks. In winter coot often gather in large flocks on ice-free lakes, and often become tame where regularly fed, for example at jetties or in parks. Partial migrant, moving south from October to warmer regions in central Europe. Usually returns in early spring, a few weeks before mallard. Occupies similar habitat to Mallard, with which it may come into competition.

Coot weigh around 1–2 lb (700–1000 g). The sexes are similar, though the male has a slightly larger frontal shield.

The nest is built from early April, from plant material, usually over or close to the water. The young are fed by both parents. If the hen lays a second clutch, the cock takes over feeding the first brood of chicks.

Coot have a high reproductive rate, and their predators include marsh harrier, rats and, more rarely, white-tailed eagle and goshawk.

Coot are usually hunted like duck, but normally on the water, since they rarely fly, except in emergency, and then in a rapid hurried manner, like blackcock. Sometimes they are rounded up by boat into a bay, and eventually forced to fly back over the boats to regain the open water.

Coot are often regarded as inedible, but this is quite untrue. They just have to be skinned as soon as possible, the rump cut away, and then left to soak in buttermilk for a day or two. After this, the meat, either roast or as pâté, tastes excellent.

The white bill and shield of the coot are distinctive.

The smaller moorhen has a red and yellow bill.

Distribution of great black-backed gull

GULLS:

Gulls comprise a family of gray or white seabirds, which nest in large colonies, usually on the ground near water. They swim well but do not dive. They are mainly carnivorous, but will take a wide range of food, notably from rubbish and dumps.

GREAT BLACK-BACKED GULL
(*Larus marinus*)

Our largest gull, with black back and wings; otherwise white, with flesh-coloured legs. Found at rocky and stony coasts, particularly on small islands. Outside the breeding season at coasts and often at rubbish tips. Breeds in Iceland, Scandinavia, Finland, south to the British Isles and northwest France.

Great black-backed gull

BLACK-HEADED GULL
(*Larus ridibundus*)

Of all the members of the gull family, this species is the one which most often nests inland. Commonest of the smaller gulls, and commonest gull inland. Chocolate brown face mask (not extending down back of neck), with crescent-shaped white mark around eye. Wing-tips black, bill and legs dark red. In winter the head is white, with dark ear-patch.

Breeds in colonies (often large) at reedy lakes, and on small islands and coastal marshes. Very common at coasts and on inland waters and fields during the winter, even in built-up areas. Throughout Europe, especially in north and east. Colonies sometimes affected by disease (botulism) and by changes in water level.

Distribution of black-headed gull

The calls of the pigeon-sized black-headed gull can be heard on most coasts.

HERRING GULL (*Larus argentatus*)

Commonest large gull. White with pale gray back and wings, and black wing-tips. Bill powerful, yellow with red spot; eyes yellow; feet flesh pink. Breeds in coastal meadows, dunes, on shingle banks and small islands and rock ledges; in some areas even on buildings. Outside breeding season usually at coast, but also at inland water and rubbish tips. Mainly coastal areas of north-west Europe.

LESSER BLACK-BACKED GULL
(*Larus fuscus*)

Size and shape of herring gull, but with dark slate-gray back, and proportionately slightly longer wings. Legs yellow. Breeds both further north (to Arctic) and further south (to coasts of Spain and Portugal) than herring gull.

Distribution of lesser black-backed gull

Lesser black-backed gulls are mainly coastal, but come inland in the winter.

235

GREAT CRESTED GREBE
(Podiceps cristata)

Grebes can be divided into those which have lobed feet and live mainly in fresh water, and those with webbed feet which live mainly at sea, although they also breed in fresh water.

The great crested grebe, which has lobed feet, is the only European species which is still hunted, at least in some regions. About 20 inches (50 cm) long, with a straight, powerful, reddish bill, red eyes, white cheeks and grayish feet. The striking head and neck feathers form a ruff in breeding season. In winter has dark cap, white cheeks and front of neck and a clear white stripe above eye. Juveniles have striped head and neck. Swims deep in the water.

Common over much of Europe, except Scotland and much of Scandinavia, Portugal and Greece. In winter often in flocks on large lakes and rivers, and coastal seas. Inhabits large lakes with reedy margins, and reservoirs, and feeds on fish, insects, tadpoles and frogs.

The nest is usually floating and anchored with reeds. The stripy chicks often ride on their parents' backs. The courtship display is quite impressive: the birds face each other, necks outstretched, shake their heads alternately, and exchange nest material. In flight, the white wing patches are distinctive.

In general, populations have increased in most parts of Europe, and the range expanded northwards. However, there have been local declines, perhaps due to pollution and disturbance.

Earlier hunted from boats—like coot—but now fully protected all year-round.

Distribution of great crested grebe

Three chicks have already hatched from this clutch, but the fourth is proving more of a problem. The nest is constructed of water plants and twigs and floats on the surface. The sexes are very similar in the breeding season.

CRANES AND RELATIVES

These are mainly large, long-legged marsh birds lacking a true crop. They are found throughout the world and the families include the cranes and bustards.

BUSTARDS:

GREAT BUSTARD *(Otis tarda)*

Very large and heavy bird of the open steppes. Today found in open cultivated fields and pastures, and has been driven to extinction in many areas. In Europe now only breeds in Spain, eastern Germany (about 200 birds just south of Berlin), Poland, Czechoslovakia and Hungary, with remnant populations in eastern Austria. Good populations persist in the Ukraine and Turkey (inner Anatolia). Its decline follows intensification of agriculture, use of pesticides and division of territory by road building. Now fully protected.

A shy bird of open steppe country, and one which cannot tolerate disturbance.

Cock birds can weigh as much as 35 lb (16 kg), with the much smaller hens reaching 11 lb (5 kg). In courtship, the cock bird inflates his neck pouch to the size of a football, raises its rear with the tail lying along the back and twists its wings to reveal the white feathers beneath. A courting male in a green field resembles nothing so much as a giant snow-white ball of feathers.

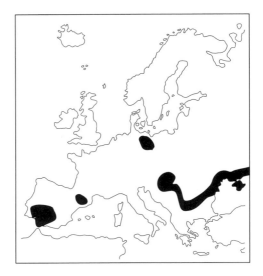

Distribution of great bustard

LITTLE BUSTARD *(Tetrax tetrax)*

Much smaller than the previous species, growing to some 18 inches (43 cm). Locally common, mainly in south-west Europe. Not hunted. Now extinct in central Europe, where it occurred until the beginning of the 20th century.

Threat display of great bustard. This species, which can reach some 3 feet long, is well named.

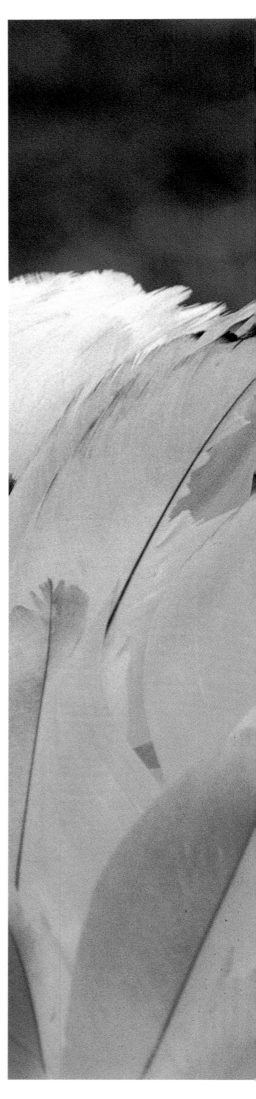

Little bustard (*Tetrax tetrax*) – like its larger relative, a very shy bird

Great bustards usually lay two (rarely three) eggs.

This ground-dwelling bird has a characteristically thick neck, with thin feathers.

◁ A great bustard cock displays by fluffing out his feathers and strutting proudly about.

HERONS AND RELATIVES:

Herons and egrets are long-legged, long-necked marshland birds. They are mostly medium-sized or large and they fly with their necks tucked in.

GRAY HERON
(Ardea cinerea)

Formerly the game bird of royalty, and hunted using falcons, as evidenced by the multitude of 'heron-lodges' adjacent to the great stately houses.

Increased both in range and in numbers in recent years, in central, northern and western Europe, with a decline in southern Europe. A wide distribution from the British Isles across the central part of Europe, taking in west Norway, south Sweden, France, north Italy, and across the southern taiga to east Asia. More scattered, or winter visitor only, in southern Europe (eg Coto Doñana).

Breeds in colonies in tall deciduous and coniferous trees, occasionally in reedbeds, where the birds build very large, twiggy nests. The 4–5 eggs are brooded for 30 days, and the young fly at around 9 weeks, dispersing to ponds and damp fields.

Herons are shot in some places, usually at fish hatcheries and the like, but local laws vary widely. The fish stocks are often better protected by nets or wires to prevent the birds from landing or standing in shallow water.

All other European herons and egrets, such as purple heron, night heron, great white egret, bittern and little bittern, are protected species.

Heron breast, often mentioned as a delicacy in literature, is of very doubtful worth, being very tough and still seeming like shoe-leather, even after the best of marinades.

Distribution of gray heron

Gray herons (*Ardea cinerea*) show admirable concentration when hunting.

▷ The night heron (*Nycticorax nycticorax*) is smaller and stockier than the gray heron ...

▷ ... which is very impressive in flight, with its wingspan of over 5 feet.

CORMORANTS AND RELATIVES:

The cormorants and their relatives (including pelicans and boobies), are mostly marine and often produce guano deposits at their breeding sites. They have webbing between all four toes, and feed mainly on fish.

CORMORANT *(Phalacrocorax carbo)*

The cormorant and its close relative the shag *(Phalacrocorax aristotelis)* are quite common around the coasts of Europe. Both are protected species, although cormorants are occasionally allowed to be shot where they compete with fisheries.

Cormorants breed in colonies in tall trees or on rocky coasts, usually near the sea, but also inland at or near large lakes, often close to gray herons. Their range includes the British Isles, Holland, northern Germany and Poland. Regular on larger lakes in winter.

Young birds, which mature at about three or four years, often stray inland to rivers and lakes, where they occasionally cause fish losses.

Cormorants are used by traditional Chinese fishermen, who train them to return with fish to their boats. The birds are prevented from swallowing the catch by a ring around the neck.

Damage to fisheries is sometimes considerable and licenses are occasionally granted to hunt cormorants, usually at their fishing grounds.

Distribution of cormorant

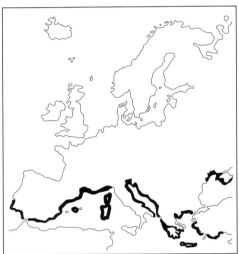

Distribution of shag

Like their relatives, shags are sociable and usually nest in colonies, on rocky coasts. They reach about 30 inches, have shiny blue-green eyes, a yellow patch at the base of the bill, and, in the breeding season, a tufted crest.

▷ Part of a cormorant colony. A cormorant's plumage is not very waterproof, so the birds spread their wings to dry after diving for fish.

BIRDS OF PREY

Birds of prey vary enormously in size but all have powerful, hooked bills with which they tear up the flesh of their prey. Their feet (talons) usually have sharp, curved claws. They are important in playing a cleaning-up role in nature, taking carrion and sick or weak animals. They pair in early spring, and the female lays (depending on the species) 1–2, or 4–6 eggs, usually sequentially. Males tend to keep watch during incubation and bring food to the nest. The young hatch at 4–6 weeks.

EAGLES:

GOLDEN EAGLE
(Aquila chrysaetos)

This magnificent bird, symbol in so many crests and coats of arms, has become extinct over much of its former range, but is now recovering in many regions. There are now some 400 pairs in the Alps, spreading west and north. The same is true for Scotland and Scandinavia, where the golden eagles now often successfully rear two young, which used to be the exception.

Golden eagles are about 3 feet long, and have a wingspan of some 6 feet. They lay just two eggs which are brooded for 44 days. The chicks are blind for the first two weeks, and fly at around 12 weeks.

SPOTTED EAGLE
(Aquila clanga)

This is a woodland eagle found in north-eastern Europe and Asia. It hunts hamsters, moles, sousliks, rabbits, hares, and also reptiles and amphibians.

LESSER SPOTTED EAGLE
(Aquila pomarina)

Another eastern European species found mainly in wooded country. Breeds as far west as north Germany and Poland. Smaller than spotted eagle – almost buzzard-sized. Migrates to east Africa. Feeds on voles and other small mammals, frogs, young birds, large insects, carrion. Builds a large nest high in a tree, and uses the same nest year after year.

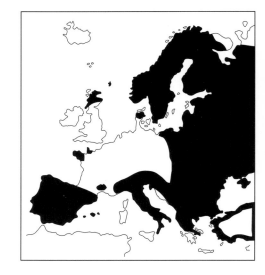

Distribution of golden eagle

Eagle (here a golden eagle, *Aquila chrysaetos*) has long been admired by people. It symbolizes power and watchfulness, and has legendary eyesight.

With its wingspan of over six feet...

the golden eagle...

is one of the most impressive birds of prey...

...of European mountains.

WHITE-TAILED EAGLE (*Haliaetus albicilla*)

White-tailed eagles weigh some 11 lb (5 kg) and have a wingspan of up to 7 feet. They breed near large lakes and rivers surrounded by forest, at the coast and in the tundra. Mostly extinct in central Europe, with relict populations in north-east Germany and Poland. Good populations also on the coast of Norway and also found in east Sweden, south Finland, Russia and east Balkans. Subject to re-introduction in the west of Scotland. Regular on certain large lakes (eg in the foothills of the Alps) outside the breeding season. Has bare, not feathered feet, unlike golden eagle. A very large, sturdy bird of prey with powerful yellow bill and short, white tail (adult). The large nest, built of sticks and twigs, is used for several seasons.

IMPERIAL EAGLE (*Aquila heliaca*)

This eagle breeds in Spain, south-east Europe and Asia (1), but is not common anywhere.

OSPREY (*Pandion haliaetus*)

Length about 20–22 inches; wingspan about 5 feet. Distinguished by very pale underparts and long, narrow, angled wings. Dark above, with pale crown. Dives almost vertically with wings half closed, thrusting talons forward shortly before hitting the surface, and often submerging completely for a short time. Specialist fish hunter.

Stable but small population in Scotland (2), frequent in Scandinavia, and also breeding in northern Germany, Poland and Russia. Regular on migration in spring and fall, on lakes and rivers.

Nests in trees, but will also use poles where provided in suitably open sites.

BOOTED EAGLE (*Hieraaetus pennatus*)
BONELLI'S EAGLE (*Hieraaetus fasciatus*)

Two small eagles which are rather similar in habit and appearance. Mainly found in southern Europe. Booted is a bird of wooded hills; Bonelli's (3) also occurs in more mountainous country, and is rarer.

SHORT-TOED EAGLE (*Circaetus gallicus*)

This reptile specialist is still relatively common in some Mediterranean countries, and also breeds (more rarely) in eastern Europe (4). Slightly larger than buzzard, and found in open, hilly landscapes with heath or maquis, woodland and cultivated land. The twig-nest is sited in the crown of a tree. The young are brooded and guarded by both parents.

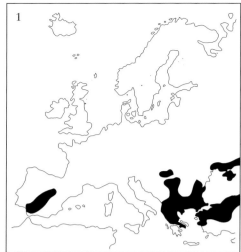

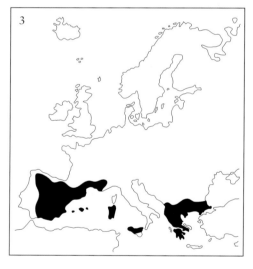

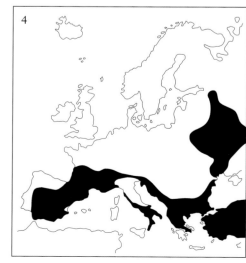

248

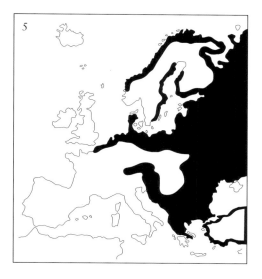

Distribution of white-tailed eagle

◁ Imperial eagle (*Aquila heliaca*; the photo shows the eastern race) feeds mainly on carrion, despite its majestic name.

◁ Female osprey (*Pandion haliaetus*), photographed in Florida, USA. In Europe it breeds mainly in the north and east.

◁ Booted eagle (*Hieraaetus pennatus*), like its relative Bonelli's eagle (*Hieraaetus fasciatus*), is found mainly in southern Europe.

◁ The short-toed eagle (*Circaetus gallicus*) feeds mainly on reptiles.

The white-tailed eagle (*Haliaetus albicilla*) is Europe's largest eagle. It eats mainly fish, birds, smaller mammals and carrion.

VULTURES:

GRIFFON VULTURE
(Gyps fulvus)

Commonest of the large vultures. Huge, with long, broad wings and short, rather square tail. Buff coloured, with dark brown flight feathers and whitish, fluffy collar into which it can withdraw its small head. Specialist carrion feeder, found in the mountains and rocky sites in southwest and south-east Europe (notably Spain and Greece).

EGYPTIAN VULTURE
(Neophron percnopterus)

Our smallest vulture and also the palest, in adult plumage. In flight shows small head, long, narrow wings and wedge-shaped tail. Adult creamy white, with black flight feathers. Juvenile dark brown, getting gradually whiter over four years. Note also the naked face and narrow head. Visits rubbish tips, often with black kites. Nests on rocks or in trees.

BLACK VULTURE
(Aegypius monachus)

This, Europe's largest vulture, has a wingspan of up to 9 feet. It looks like a darker version of the griffon vulture, with a larger head and longer, more wedge-shaped tail. Plumage is dark brown, but looks black from a distance. There are just a few hundred pairs in Europe (Spain, Mallorca and Greece). Black vultures eat mainly carrion.

LAMMERGEIER
(Gypaetus barbatus)

Also known as bearded vulture, this species feeds on carrion (especially deer, sheep and goats). It breaks open bones for the marrow (and sometimes tortoises) by dropping them onto rocks from a height.

In flight it resembles a huge falcon, with rather pointed wings and long tail. It reaches some 45 inches in length and has a wingspan of 8 feet.

Breeds in the mountains of southern Europe—mainly Pyrenees, Corsica, Greece and Turkey.

 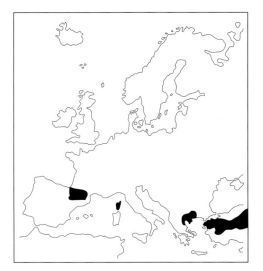

Vultures (here a griffon vulture) are not great beauties, and do not share the noble looks of the related eagles, which are true hunters.

KITES

RED KITE
(Milvus milvus)

A bird of hilly, wooded country. Widespread but scattered in central, southern and eastern Europe (as far as eastern Poland), with outliers in south Scandinavia and in Wales. About 25 inches long, with long wings and long, deeply forked tail. Breeds in hilly, wooded landscapes, with open areas such as small bogs, wetlands and clearings, but also in dry, flat areas with small pockets of woodland. Feeds on small mammals, birds, fish and frogs as well as carrion and at rubbish tips.

BLACK KITE
(Milvus migrans)

Black kites eat a variety of food, from fish, to young birds, smaller mammals, and carrion.

Normally breeds near to water, typically building its nest halfway up a tree, at the base of a branch. Prefers river valley forests and woodland margins. Often hunts over water, but also over land. Outside the breeding season mainly on rivers and lakes. Widespread but patchy in central southern and eastern Europe.

Plumage darker than that of red kite, and the tail is shallowly notched, rather than forked.

▷ Distribution of red kite

▷ Distribution of black kite

▷ Black kite in flight

Both red and black kites are carrion eaters and therefore play an important ecological role.

HARRIERS:

MARSH HARRIER *(Circus aeruginosus)*

Largest and most widespread harrier, found in much of Europe, but rare in Scandinavia, and local and rare in Britain.

Breeds in dense and extensive reedbeds on lowland lakes and rivers, with fresh or brackish water. Hunts over reeds, water meadows and nearby fields and open country. Lays 4–5 greenish-white eggs. Feeds on small mammals, birds including small ducks, also fish, amphibians, insects, and the eggs and young of water birds. The male has pale gray tail and upper wings, with dark plumage and black wing tips. The female is dark brown, with cream-colored head and shoulders.

MONTAGU'S HARRIER *(Circus pygargus)*

Very rare, graceful species, breeds in low vegetation near water, but also in damp heath, especially on fens, also in open fields and crops. Hunts mainly over wetlands with low cover, and in fields. It feeds on small mammals, insects, lizards, small birds, birds' eggs and nestlings.

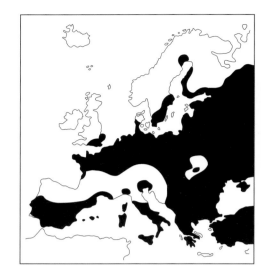

Distribution of marsh harrier

◁ Marsh harriers live in wet heath and marshland, where they feed mainly on birds and small mammals.

Young marsh harriers begging for food – as ground nesting birds, harriers are under threat both from natural enemies and from land use.

This Montagu's harrier (*Circus pygargus*) has caught a lizard. This harrier is generally rare, despite its relatively wide range in Europe.

▷ Hen harrier (*Circus cyaneus*) calling from the nest

Distribution of hen harrier

HEN HARRIER
(*Circus cyaneus*)

One of our most attractive birds of prey. The male is easily told by his ash-gray plumage, contrasting black-tipped wings and white rump. The female is dark brown above, pale yellow-brown beneath, with striped wings and tail, and a clear white rump.

Rather patchily distributed over much of Europe, from north Spain northwards, with strongholds in the north and east. In the British Isles mainly in the north and west. In central Europe much reduced by habitat loss and use of pesticides.

Breeds in open landscapes—bogs, heather moor, dunes, marshes and damp meadows, and occasionally in young plantations. In winter regular in open wet areas and cultivated land. Flight very acrobatic; sails and glides with V-shaped wings, often low over open country. May exchange prey in the air during courtship.

Feeds on small mammals to the size of rats, birds, especially small species, and young waders and ducks.

BUZZARD *(Buteo buteo)*

Europe's commonest and best known buzzard, found throughout, except for Iceland, north Scandinavia, most of Ireland and eastern England. Breeds in varied, wooded regions with fields, bogs, hedges and woods. Hunts over open country and nests mostly at the woodland edge. Weighs about 2 lb (1 kg), and has a wingspan of about 4 feet. Very variable in plumage, from almost white to uniform dark brown, but usually brownish with paler breastband. Eye dark brown to dull yellow. Rather compact in flight with wings held somewhat stiffly, and wingtips noticeably upturned when soaring. The call is a mewing 'heeyair,' at all times of year, but especially in spring. Population dependent upon prey availability, especially small rodents, young rabbits; also worms, reptiles, insects, and more rarely birds. Partial migrant, with those moving south being replaced by birds from further north. Often sits patiently on a post, waiting for small mammal prey, and in winter frequently looks for roadside casualties. Despite its size, often driven off by groups of crows or jackdaws.

Distribution of buzzard

The buzzard (*Buteo buteo*) is one of Europe's most widespread birds of prey. Here a buzzard mantles its prey (below). Buzzards take some carrion as well as catching their own live prey.

HONEY BUZZARD *(Pernis apivorus)*

Similar distribution to buzzard, but less dense. In Britain a rare bird with some 20 pairs. Summer visitor wintering to tropical Africa.

Slimmer than buzzard with longer wings and tail. Plumage variable—upperside usually dark brown, underside pale with large brown spots, or uniform brown. Head dove gray, with bright yellow eye, tail has three dark bands.

Feeds mainly on the larvae and pupae of wasps and bees, more rarely of bumblebees. Also adult insects, frogs, lizards and young birds. Rarely small mammals.

Honey buzzards are summer visitors to Europe...

ROUGH-LEGGED BUZZARD *(Buteo lagopus)*

Breeds in the mountains of northern Europe, mostly above tree-line, and in the tundra. In winter found on moorland and heaths, river flood-plains and open cultivated areas.

Legs feathered down to the toes (hence the name). Tail white, with wide dark band at tip; hovers much more frequently than buzzard. Variable plumage paler than buzzard's, but always with dark belly. Usually nests on the ground. Feeds on voles and lemmings, other small mammals and birds, also carrion.

and the rough-legged buzzard also migrates south from its northern breeding area (shown on map).

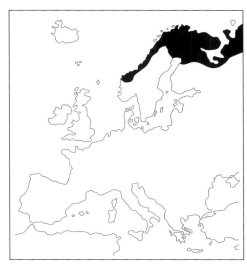

257

Goshawks mainly use their talons to catch their prey.

HAWKS:

GOSHAWK *(Accipiter gentilis)*

After the buzzard, one of the best known birds of prey in Europe, and disliked by many, including pigeon fanciers and poultry farmers, as well as many huntsmen. However, its population is not as dense as the buzzard's over most of the region.

Found throughout, except for Iceland, Ireland, and many parts of Britain. Formerly reduced by shooting and poisoning by pesticides, but numbers now recovering.

The length is from 19–24 inches (48–61 cm), and wingspan 40–47 inches (100–120 cm); male smaller than female. The eyes are bright orange or yellow. Underside whitish with horizontal streaks; in juveniles yellowish to rust-coloured with vertical dark brown markings.

Very varied diet, including birds to size of hens, and mammals to young hares; also birds of crow family, doves, partridges, rabbits, squirrels. The female is able to take larger prey than the smaller male.

The nest is built at up to about 60 feet in a tree, and the 3–4 greenish-white eggs laid in April or May hatch after 35–37 days. The female molts during this period and is fed almost exclusively by the male. The young are driven from the territory when fledged and generally move away, the original pair remaining.

SPARROWHAWK *(Accipiter nisus)*

Found throughout Europe, except for Iceland. Lays 4–6 eggs, brooded for 31–33 days. Resembles Goshawk, but smaller, and with similar size difference between the sexes. Underparts narrowly banded, rust-brown in male. Upperparts of female browny-gray, male blue-gray. Juveniles dark brown above, heavily streaked below (mainly horizontal). Builds twiggy nest in a tree, often a conifer.

Mainly in coniferous and mixed woodland, interspersed with open areas, hedges and copses. In winter also hunts in villages and towns.

Specialist aerial hunter, using surprise, and skillful in its use of cover. Takes mainly birds, up to size of collared dove (male to thrush size); more rarely small mammals. Uses a plucking post to deal with its prey.

Distribution of goshawk

Distribution of sparrowhawk

The sparrowhawk is like a small version of the goshawk. It hunts equally well in the air or on the ground.

▷ The female goshawk looks after her brood well – here sheltering them from a storm with her wings.

FALCONS:

PEREGRINE
(Falco peregrinus)

King of birds and also the bird of kings—such is the status of the peregrine and its even larger northern cousin the gyrfalcon (*Falco rusticolus*). The peregrine has, for centuries, and even, in the Orient, for more than a thousand years, been the ultimate hunting falcon, used to catch game up to the size of bustard and even as big as gazelle. It is strongly protected in the wild, with the result that it is now successfully bred in captivity, and the majority of (legally obtained) peregrines now have this origin. Peregrines are found in most hilly and mountainous areas, and at the coast, and also in the Russian forests. They usually need steep rocks or cliffs for nesting. Dramatically reduced through pesticide poisoning in the 1960s and 1970s, and through persecution and egg-stealing, but now recovering in most regions. Now conservationists, falconers and hunters are cooperating to protect the wild population.

Takes prey mainly in flight, from finch-sized birds to mallard, even occasionally heron, but only rarely hunts mammal prey. Like other falcons it takes over and adapts an existing nest, such as that of a crow, although peregrines often make minimal nests on rock ledges. Newly fledged young leave their territory, moving out of the area and returning the following season, often to a site nearby. The older birds tend to move off later, nearly always returning to their old territory the next season.

HOBBY
(Falco subbuteo)

Looks almost like a large swift in flight, and can match the latter in speed. Measure about 12–14 inches (30–36 cm). Found in wooded country in most of Europe, except the north of Britain and north Scandinavia.

Breeds in light woodland, at forest edges and in isolated trees, using an old crow's nest or similar.

Feeds on insects such as dragonflies and beetles; also small birds such as swallows, larks, sparrows, finches, and even swifts.

Distribution of peregrine

Peregrine

Distribution of hobby

Distribution of kestrel

KESTREL *(Falco tinnunculus)*

This widespread and familiar falcon is our commonest small bird of prey, often seen by main roads, and even in towns and cities where it often nests on tall buildings such as a church tower. On open country it nests in a hole in a tree or old crow's nest or similar. Often hovers.

A small falcon with long tail, long, pointed wings and brown upperparts. Male has weakly speckled red-brown back, gray head, and gray tail with broad terminal band. Female uniformly red-brown, with barred upperparts. The call, frequently heard, especially in the breeding season, is a high-pitched 'kikikiki...'

The male feeds the female as she broods her clutch of 5–6 eggs. The young fledge after four weeks. Kestrels eat mainly mice and voles, also reptiles, insects, and small birds.

Distribution of Lesser Kestrel

LESSER KESTREL *(Falco naumanni)*

Small falcon. Adult male back bright chestnut, diagnostically without spots *(see* Kestrel); head grey; tail grey with black terminal band. Underparts pinkish-buff, with dark brown streaks. Female and immature brown above, paler buffish below, heavily barred and streaked. In flight, from below appears much paler than Kestrel; hovers only occasionally. Gregarious; feeds, flies and roosts in small flocks. Voice: very vocal; chattering 'chee' and 'chet' calls, plaintive whistles. Habitat: open farmland, rocky hillsides and towns with old buildings. Widespread; sometimes common.

ELEONORA'S FALCON *(Falco eleonorae)*

Like a large hobby in build, but has longer tail. Occurs in light and dark phases, but slaty gray colors predominate in both. Breeds in colonies on Mediterranean islands. Mainly takes birds; sometimes insects. Summer visitor, migrating mainly to Madagascar in the winter.

Distribution of Elenora's Falcon

262

Young kestrels

This kestrel shows its characteristic plumage

PERCHING BIRDS

This order is the largest by far, with over 5,400 species, accounting for some 60 percent of all bird species. Most have more or less well-developed songs, although on that criterion alone one might wonder about the inclusion of those selected here.

CROWS AND RELATIVES:

RAVEN
(CORVUS CORAX)

This, our largest crow, is the legendary wise bird of the Norse god Odin. There have been some local increases in recent years, notably in parts of Germany and in Ireland, but numbers fluctuate, and ravens are now mostly found in rather remote, mountain areas. In lowland areas where they have increased, such as some maize-growing regions, they can be a problem, with large flocks roaming about and causing losses to ground-nesters such as gray partridge and lapwing, in addition to damage to the crops. For this reason they can be shot in some areas, by special license.

Ravens breed early, with clutches by February, nesting in isolated woods or amongst rocky crags.

ALPINE CHOUGH
(PYRRHOCORAX GRACULUS)

This agile crow-relative is found high in the Alps, Pyrenees and other mountain ranges of southern Europe. It is jet black, with red legs and yellow bill.

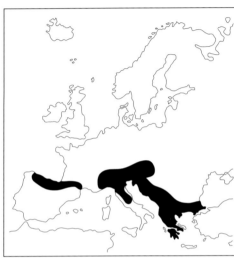

Distribution of raven (above) and alpine chough (below)

Ravens in icy landscape in Lapland (right) and alpine choughs on a sparsely vegetated mountain (below)

CARRION CROW (*Corvus corone corone*) AND HOODED CROW (*Corvus corone cornix*)

This species occurs as two subspecies—the all-black carrion crow, and the gray and black hooded crow. The latter looks very different, with gray body and black face, wings and tail. Carrion crows are found mainly in west and central Europe, from Britain to Spain, and east to Germany. Elsewhere (including Ireland and north-west Scotland) it is replaced by the hooded crow. Some hybrids result where the ranges meet.

The laws governing when and where crows may be shot are much disputed, and complex. They certainly cause damage to crops and to the young of ground-nesting species and may therefore be hunted under certain circumstances.

ROOK (*Corvus frugilegus*)

Resembles carrion crow, but has pale bill with bare patch at its base (adult), and steeper forehead. Belly and thigh feathers tend to be loose, giving trousered effect. Rooks nest colonially, and are found from France to the Black Sea and Baltic, but are absent from most of southern Europe and much of Scandinavia.

Carrion crow (*Corvus corone corone*) alighting

Rooks nest in colonies.
Distribution of carrion crow (left) and of hooded crow (right)
Large photo: rooks at their roost

266

Magpies have increased recently in many areas, to the annoyance of gardeners and huntsmen, who blame them for robbing the nests of songbirds.

The Siberian jay also breeds in Scandinavia. It is rather smaller than the jay. It has a mixed vocabulary of strange mews, screams and whistles.

Jackdaws like to nest in parks, rocks, old buildings and chimneys. They are sociable, like many crows and often associate with starlings and rooks.

▷▷ A pretty bird, but not well liked by hunters as they alert other animals with their raucous alarm calls.

▷ Distribution of jay

▷ Distribution of magpie

▷ Distribution of Siberian jay

▷ Distribution of jackdaw

JAY
(Garrulus glandarius)

Jays, like magpies, often cause losses to other birds by robbing their nests of eggs and young, although the effects of such predation on songbird populations is disputed. They also damage certain crops, such as maize. In woodland, however, jays provide a useful function, hiding acorns and beechnuts by burying them. Not all are recovered, however, so the jay is an unwitting forester, planting future trees to create a mixed natural woodland.

Jays are very conspicuous in flight, with black tail, white rump, and white and blue wing-patches. The body is buff, with black moustache and black bill. They nest in mixed woodland, wooded parks and large gardens.

MAGPIE
(Pica pica)

Magpies are birds of open country with copses, hedges and pasture, but in many areas they have become suburban as well, moving into cities and parks and gardens.

The shiny black and white plumage and long, graduated tail are unmistakable. The call is a chattering 'shak-shak-shak'. The nest is also easy to identify – it is made of twigs, with a domed roof, sited in a thick hedge or tree.

Magpies are sociable birds, often seen in small groups. They feed on a wide range of items, from insects to the eggs and young of other birds.

Hunting is often most successful at the roost, where many birds may congregate.

Cooking with Game

Baroness Sonja von Müffling

In former times, hunting red deer, roe deer, and wild boar was strictly reserved for the aristocracy, so it is not therefore surprising that game cookery is still cloaked in an exclusive aura. Careful preparation of game is vital when serving a special Sunday roast for example. Anyone overcome with desire for a change from their native cookery, should have a peek in our neighbors' cooking pots.

273

Watercolor of two dead gray partridge by Lucas Cranach the elder

Still life with hare and shelduck by Jean Baptiste Oudry

Medieval feast, Breviarium Grimani, around 1500

274

GENERAL ADVICE

Even nowadays, when all delicacies are available in our kitchens at a moment's notice, roast game, whether from feathered or furred animals, is always regarded as central to many a special meal.

Furred game—which in Europe includes all types of deer, chamois, wild boar, rabbit, and hare—is most often prepared for roasting, or the meat is used for ragouts. The most popular roasting joints are saddle (back), leg (haunch), and shin (shank). Neck, breast, head, and belly, and, if desired, heart and liver are perfect cuts for ragouts, and, when chopped small, the raw meat or any left-over cooked meat can be used with the bones to make special sauces and soups.

Cutlets are taken from the haunch, shank, sirloin, or the boned saddle. Larger game animals provide juicy spare rib chops. The sirloin and saddle provide good medallion pieces. Game offal—heart, liver, lungs, kidneys and tongue can all be made into delicious specialty dishes. Game birds—wild goose, wild duck, woodpigeon, pheasant, partridge, and black and red grouse—are generally cooked whole.

Venison is easily digested, low in fat, and very high in protein. It needs to be hung for a long time so that the meat becomes tender, and it should be hung before freezing or being cooked. The meat should not be skinned, but should have been gutted before hanging. Meat that has already been butchered and skinned should be wrapped in thin gauze to protect it from flies, and be hung in a cool, well-aired place.

Venison from older animals should be marinated, or wrapped in a cloth soaked in vinegar. It can be kept in the refrigerator, or another cool place, for two to four days and should be turned occasionally. In hot weather, it is important to check that the soaked cloth does not dry out.

The rule of thumb—never wash game meat—does not apply to wild boar. All other game animals should be wiped inside and out, with a clean non-fibrous cloth, or a piece of paper towel. Wash in clean, cold water but only if the meat has a shot wound. The meat should be rinsed quickly, and dried thoroughly.

Meat that has developed a strong flavor from being hung or marinated for a long time should also not be washed. If, however, the strong flavor of the meat is not desired, then the flavor can be tempered by rinsing the meat in water mixed with potassium permanganate and rubbing the meat all over. The meat should then be rinsed thoroughly in clear water and dried well. The strong flavor is tempered, but the quality of the meat is lowered. Potassium permanganate, available from pharmacies and drugstores, turns the water turn a deep violet color.

Game meat is usually served with plenty of smoked bacon. The bacon slices are wrapped around the meat or used to lard the meat. The meat will never dry out if it is well basted with hot fat. This can be done in a roasting pan, casserole, or on a spit. The basting process seals the meat, preventing the juices from running out. The meat should be placed directly in the oven, under the grill, or on the barbecue after basting.

It is possible to use butter, margarine, or pure olive oil instead of bacon fat, and it is important to remember that game meat is naturally low in fat and to keep this in mind when cooking game. When heating olive oil, add one garlic clove per half pint of oil and remove the garlic before the oil boils. Other types of fat should be avoided, if possible, as they can affect the flavor of the meat.

Game is not only lower in fat than other types of meat, it contains fewer calories, more protein, and more flavor, as well as being nourishing and easy to digest. The animals graze in forests and open fields so the quality of their meat is not destroyed by artificial feeds. Game also contains unsaturated fat, unlike other types of meat which are high in saturated fats. Eating game can help prevent circulatory diseases and heart attacks.

When cooking with game it is important to check that the meat has a pleasant smell, and has not been "heat treated" through bad handling, which causes the meat to become a greenish gray or reddish blue color.

The increased practice of farming deer as a supplement to many farmers' incomes and the necessary supplementary feeding that this farming practice involves does not allow the animals the opportunity to find the necessary nutrients for their diet from nature alone. This has had a negative effect on the quality of the game, and actually increases the fat content of the meat. Less additional fat is therefore required when cooking farmed venison.

Here are a few suggestions for diabetics and slimmers: Game gravy should have all the fat removed and not be thickened. Use yoghurt in place of sour cream. Limit potatoes and cereal products served with the meat, and serve instead with vegetables and salad. Replace sugar with granulated sugar substitute and sprinkle on the meat or use to sweeten game recipes. Game prepared in this way is still a great delicacy.

BARBECUING GAME

Not all cuts of game are suitable for the barbecue. The general rule is: if the meat can be roasted, it can also be barbecued. Barbecue meat should be well hung or marinated, or should be meat from a young animal, and the meat marinated before

cooking. Thin steaks, cutlets, and schnitzel should be tenderized, either with a mallet, or with the palms of the hands. It should be wrapped in thin strips of bacon, and marinated for about one hour. The barbecue should be lit well in advance, and when cooked, the meat should be brown and crispy on the outside, and bright pink (but not bloody) on the inside. Boar meat should always be cooked through. The thinner the cut of meat, the hotter the barbecue should be.

When the meat has been removed from the pickling solution or marinade, it should be dried on a paper towel or non-fibrous cloth, skinned, larded, and oiled. Meat that has been marinated in oil does not require larding, but should simply be lightly dried and barbecued.

Game birds are prepared in much the same way. They should be covered in bacon, larded with bacon fat, or wrapped entirely in bacon slices (small birds only). If necessary, the bird can also be drizzled with oil before being cooked until the meat is tender.

Frozen game thaws out very well in a bowl of buttermilk. Red deer, wild boar, chamois, and mouflon improve in flavor when a few pierced juniper berries are added to the buttermilk marinade, the juniper adding a piquant aroma to the meat. Frozen meat can be thawed in any type of marinade. Boiled marinades should be left to cool completely. Frozen game is particularly good for barbecuing.

FREEZING GAME MEAT

Freezing ensures that the vitamins, nutrients and color of the meat do not deteriorate. Frozen food is easily digested and is suitable for babies, ill people, and convalescents. The freezer should be at a constant temperature of not more than 0° F (–18° C). To reach a low temperature as quickly as possible, many deep freezes have a quick freeze function. This enables food to be preserved for a very long time: the quick freeze section is activated for at least three or four hours, and for not more than twenty-four hours. The freezer returns to "automatic" mode, which keeps the food at a constant temperature. Food which has been "shock frozen" and kept at a constant temperature of 0° to –5° F (–18° to –20° C) will keep for a very long time.

Fresh produce for freezing should be placed close to the walls of the deep freeze. It should not come into contact with food that is already frozen (if necessary, stack the food up in the center of the freezer). When loading the freezer, be sure not to fill it too full, and make sure that the temperature is constant after twenty-four hours. When freezing a whole deer, or a different, large piece of meat, it is recommended to freeze the meat in three stages, about eight hours apart. The meat that is waiting to be frozen should be kept in the refrigerator.

It is important to label food for the freezer, before freezing takes place. The best method is to use adhesive labels on the outside of the meat packaging. The label should have the following information: contents, weight, perhaps age of animal, and "best before" date (the last date the food can be eaten before the flavor deteriorates). It is a good idea to have a chart near the freezer, with a list of the foods which have been frozen.

Once the food has been frozen, the space in the freezer should be organized so that it is being used efficiently, one side of the freezer being left free for new produce. If there is a power cut, do not open the freezer. The insulation should keep the food at the same temperature for about twenty-four hours.

Never refreeze food that has been frozen and thawed out. If the thawed food is cooked, cooled and placed in sealed containers, it can be refrozen.

Valuable old hunting cutlery, 17th century

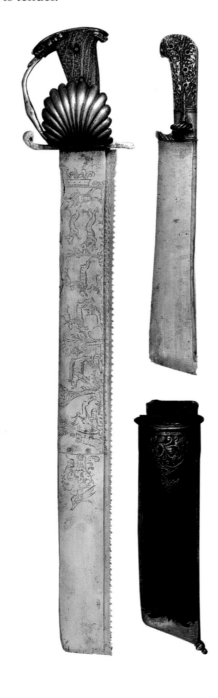

It is important for freezer food to use packaging that will prevent the food from drying out, transferring its flavor to other foods, or changing its own color and flavor. The material used should be durable, not rip or break easily, but be reasonably pliable. Freezer packaging should be kept close at hand. When freezing cooked meals, the freezer container should ideally be heat resistant, so that the meals can be placed directly from the freezer into the oven, without having to transfer the food to another container.

The best containers to use for this purpose are rectangular, made from aluminum foil, and come in different sizes, with lids. These containers adapt easily to changes in temperature, they are light, can be stacked on top of one another, are heat resistant and can be used repeatedly.

Lean game meat, when it has been freshly butchered, prepared in pieces – a roasting joint should not weigh more than 4½ pounds (2 kilos) – will keep in the freezer for about 10 months. Game birds can be frozen for six to eight months.

Larded saddle and haunch of hare, goulash and ragout pieces, game soups, game meat (minced), stuffed game birds, and pre-cooked game dishes can be kept in the freezer for about three months.

The fattier the marinated game, the shorter the time it can be kept without losing its flavor. Fat becomes rancid when cooled; as does the bacon fat often used for larding the meat. Always try and freeze meat that has not been larded and either wrap it in bacon or lard it when it is beginning to defrost. The giblets will keep in the freezer for four months and bones can be kept for six months.

Game broth can be made by boiling chopped bones with tendons and vegetables. This can be thickened to make an extract, sieved and frozen in ice cube trays. When the cubes have frozen they can be removed from the trays and packed in plastic freezer bags. This helps to save space in the freezer. It is best to separate the ice cubes with pieces of aluminum foil so that they do not stick together. The frozen stock cubes should last for about three months.

When frozen food is kept at a constant temperature, it does not spoil after the "best before" date; it does, however, slowly lose its flavor, consistency, and appearance. Fattier game meat should be eaten after three to four months in the freezer.

Hunting to hounds on horseback, engraving, 18th century

Rich game cuisine has long been appreciated.

Artistic French carving tools, early 16th century

Hunting weapons and cutlery belonging to
Augustus the Strong; German, before 1730

PREPARING GAME MEAT FOR THE FREEZER

Seasoned or hung meat that has been divided into two shoulders, two haunches, back, and stewing game (neck, ribs and leg) should be skinned carefully, dried with a non-fibrous cloth, and the tendons removed.

This is how the game should be divided up: Bone sirloin for roasting or chop it into steaks. Leave the shoulder joints whole, and leave small haunches in one piece. Large haunches should have the legs removed and be cut into pieces following the direction of the muscle. These pieces can be chopped into cutlets by cutting across the grain of the meat. Divide up the back meat (the saddle). The front part of the saddle near the shoulder can be divided up into cutlets. The rear part of the saddle, near the tail, should be left whole, as a roasting joint. When freezing cutlets, steaks and chops, place pieces of aluminum foil between the pieces of meat so that they do not freeze into a large block. Place eight to ten individual steaks in one freezer bag, making sure the bag is airtight, and close securely.

Divide stewing meat into goulash and ragout pieces and cut into cubes. Set out the cubes on a

279

plate and fast freeze them. Then divide the cubes into manageable portions, and freeze them in bags.

Cut any small pieces of meat away from the bone and put through the mincer. Freeze in half pound (¼ kg), or pound (½ kg) bags, press the air out of the bags and seal with rubber bands or pieces of sticky tape. Offal should be packed in separate bags. It can be combined if the combination is required for a specific recipe.

To avoid trapping air when freezing meat, using both hands, press the freezer bags firmly over the meat. Press the open end of the bag together and seal with a rubber band to prevent any air reentering the bag. Do not forget to label the freezer bags. When freezing meat that has not been boned, make sure that the bones do not pierce the freezer bag as this will cause the meat to dry out.

PREPARING GAME BIRDS FOR THE FREEZER

All game birds apart from waterfowl are "drawn" and hung in a cool airy place, for a few days. Pluck the birds, starting at the head, and working down towards the tail. Do not scald the feathers first. Some game birds may also be skinned, where the skin and the feathers are stripped away from the flesh. Remove the pharynx and windpipe, and for all birds except snipe and woodcock, remove the head and feet. Remove the innards—look out for the gall bladder—and freeze them separately.

Wipe the bird inside and out with a dry, non-fibrous cloth. Pull the legs up towards the breast and remove the wing tips. Turn the wings backward at the shoulder joint and lay under the back. The giblets can be placed with the skinned neck of the bird, a few stock vegetables and herbs and wrapped up in plastic, or placed in a plastic bag. The giblet package is then inserted into the rear end of the bird. When freezing pigeons make sure that the crop of the bird is removed (as it contains acidic substances) before the bird is taken down after being hung.

Larger game birds can be jointed and frozen in separate pieces. Pack the pieces closely in a freezer bag, squeeze out all the air and seal the bag securely with a rubber band.

Aluminum foil is a good packaging material as it is very smooth. It is vital to ensure that the foil is

Old hunting scene on porcelain

A delicacy for any gourmet: game—with its unique flavor.

not torn, as tears allow air access to the meat, causing the meat to dry out and lose its flavor.

DEFROSTING TIMES

When cooking with game, it is very important to defrost the meat for the right amount of time. Before defrosting, remember to remove the packaging.

Portions of game weighing between one and two pounds (½ to 1 kg) should be defrosted at room temperature for six to eight hours to be properly thawed. Smaller or larger portions require less or more time respectively. Stuffed game birds defrost at a slightly slower rate than birds that have not been stuffed.

Defrosting in the refrigerator takes twice as long. A quicker defrosting process is to place the frozen game or game bird (still in its sealed packaging) into cold water, or under running water. It will be ready for use after one and a half to three hours. Never place the meat in or under hot water; this destroys the flavor.

Larger roasting joints and older game birds must be properly thawed and tenderized. Remember: food that has been frozen and defrosted should not be refrozen. Only cooked food stored in heat- and cold-resistant containers can be refrozen.

What belongs together, goes well together: seasonal field and woodland mushrooms add the final touch to any game recipe.

WILD GOOSE

The term wild goose is used to cover a large number of species, including graylag, Canada, brent, white-fronted and bean goose. All are prepared for cooking in much the same fashion.

A goose that is not fully grown makes a lovely roasting bird, and in fall the meat is particularly flavorsome. Older birds can be made more tender and tasty if they are marinated for a long time and steam cooked. Geese that are actually old are not at all pleasant to eat.

The goose should be drawn fairly soon after it has been killed and the innards removed.

Waterfowl should be eaten soon after they are killed (in contrast to other birds which should be well hung). In summer they should be prepared for eating or put in the freezer by the following day. They can be hung by the neck in a cool place for one or two days, as long as the plumage has been wiped clean.

Waterfowl should always have the oil gland near the tail removed. If this is left in place, it produces a bitter aftertaste. In contrast to tame birds, and like all game birds, wild geese should be plucked from head to tail, and should never be scalded.

ROAST WILD GOOSE WITH WINTER VEGETABLES

1 graylag or Canada goose
freshly ground salt and pepper
dried marjoram
2 apples
butter
1 pint 9 fluid ounces (750 ml) chicken stock
1 bunch finely chopped parsley
1 leek, chopped into rings
2 slices celeriac
7 ounces (200 g) smoked streaky bacon
15 small onions
1 pound 2 ounces (500 g) Brussels sprouts
1 pound 2 ounces (500 g) carrots

Season the goose inside with salt, pepper, and marjoram. Stuff with quarters of apple and close the goose with a small skewer. Baste the outside with melted butter, season with salt and pepper and place in a roasting tin with the back of the goose facing upwards. Pour over two cups of chicken stock, add the leek, celeriac, and parsley and roast the goose for about 45 minutes, until the back has turned a pleasant brown color.

Meanwhile, cut the bacon into strips, pan-fry in a little butter and set aside. Cut the carrots into olive shapes, pan-fry in the skillet used for the bacon and add to the goose in the roasting tin. Turn the goose, and cover with a lid or with some aluminum foil. After another thirty minutes, remove the carrots and set aside. Peel and pan-fry the onions, add to the

Graylag geese feed mainly on grass

goose and remove from the roasting tin after about 20 minutes. Pour another cup of stock into the roasting tin and cook the goose for a further 50 minutes. Remove the cover and cook at a high heat to brown the skin.

Meanwhile, clean the sprouts and pan-fry in a little butter until they are "al dente." Mix with the onions, carrots and bacon and keep warm.

Carve the goose and arrange on a serving plate with the onions, carrots, bacon, and sprouts. Sieve the gravy and skim off the fat; transfer to a gravy boat. Serve with dumplings.

Roast goose, appetizingly presented, is a visual delight.

WILD DUCK

Wild duck is in season when the newly harvested fields offer the birds plenty of corn to eat. Wild duck—like other water birds—should not be hung for a long time, but should simply be hung from the neck, overnight, in a cool place before plucking, cleaning and being cooked or frozen.

Wild duck, like roasting chickens, can be divided into four joints. If they have already been stuffed, the stuffing should be evenly distributed between the portions.

The duck carcass with any remaining cooked meat can be boiled up to make a wonderful soup.

It is possible to distinguish between young and old ducks by looking at their feet. If the skin tears easily, and the toes have pointed claws then the bird is young. A windpipe that yields easily when pressed, is another sign of a young bird, as are feathers that can be pulled out easily.

WILD DUCK WITH LENTILS

2 mallard or 3–4 teal
salt
4 onions
1 bunch fresh marjoram
butter
11 ounces (300 g) smoked, streaky bacon
goose fat
14 ounces (400 g) lentils
2½ pints (1½ l) poultry stock
8 tbs (120 ml) vinegar
4 red chillies

Pluck the ducks, draw them and rub with a non-fibrous cloth. Remove the parson's nose and the oil gland, salt the birds inside and stuff each one with half an onion and some fresh marjoram. Pour melted butter over the birds, add salt, and place in a roasting tin with the back facing upwards. Brown in the oven for about 40 minutes then set aside.

Meanwhile, chop three onions, cut the bacon into strips and braise in a little goose

Wild duck are at their most delicious from the end of September until December. The hunting season ends in January, but meat from the end of the season can be oily.

fat, in a large casserole. Wash the lentils and add to the onion. Pour in the stock and the vinegar, season lightly with salt, and add the chillies.

Pour the lentils into an earthenware casserole dish, place the ducks on top of the lentils with their breasts upwards, cover the dish and simmer for about an hour in the oven.

Remove the lid, skim any fat from the surface, turn the ducks and brown for another 10 minutes. Carve the ducks and serve with the lentils. Serve with noodles and a Brunello di Montalcino wine.

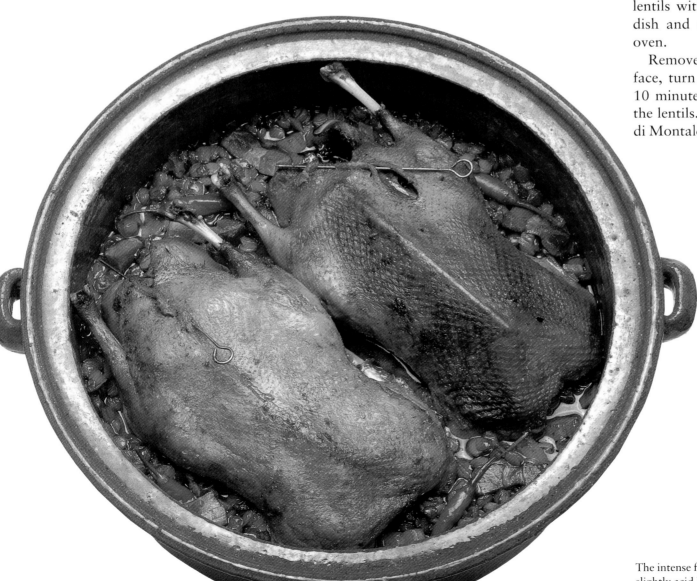

The intense flavor of wild duck is complemented by the slightly acid lentil sauce.

PIGEON

When hunting pigeon, be sure to tear the skin on the neck and remove the crop fairly soon after the bird is caught. This prevents the acid content of the crop from spoiling the overall flavor of the bird. Pluck the bird on the same day from head to tail and hang from the neck, overnight, in a cool and dry place. The following morning, draw the bird, clean it inside and out with a non-fibrous cloth, dry it and singe the bird over a naked flame. Do not wash the bird unless it is an emergency (for example if the intestines have been shot to pieces). In this case, wash it quickly in cold water and dry it well. Game birds should not come in contact with water. The pigeon should now either be seasoned and cooked, or stored in the freezer for use at a later time. When cooking with frozen pigeon, especially with older birds, allow the birds to thaw out thoroughly before they are marinated. Younger birds can be treated in the same way as freshly prepared birds and can be used when lightly thawed. Older pigeons are better for having two to three days in a marinade made from a vinegar or buttermilk base.

For marinating, the food should be placed in a deep bowl made of porcelain, stoneware, or an acid resistant plastic bowl, and the liquid should be poured over the meat until it is covered.

PIGEON BREASTS WITH BEAN SALAD

breasts of three woodpigeons
savory
1 pound 9 ounces (750 g) green beans
half an onion
vinegar (salted), olive oil, mustard
9 ounces (250 g) cherry tomatoes
3½ ounces (100 g) breakfast bacon
butter
freshly ground salt and pepper

Boil the savory in salted water for five minutes, then remove. Clean the beans, blanch in the same water so that they are still crisp, leave to drain and place in a dish.

Chop the onion and sprinkle over the beans. Make a vinaigrette from four tablespoons (60 ml) vinegar, a little mustard, and eight tablespoons (120 ml) olive oil. Pour the vinaigrette over the beans. Quarter the tomatoes and add to the beans. Cut the bacon into strips, pan-fry, and sprinkle over the salad.

Brown the pigeon breasts in the butter, season with salt and pepper, cover and simmer until cooked. Lay the breasts on the beans. Serve this light dish with fresh, white bread, and with a Beaujolais such as a Morgon or St Amour.

Woodpigeon are a little larger than feral pigeons, and are found throughout Europe. Young birds are the best for cooking, but older birds can be used for soups.

PHEASANT

Young pheasant makes a delicious roast, and older birds can also be served as a delicious meal. Young birds can be recognized by their small, stumpy spur and soft breast. The older the bird is, the longer and more pointed the spur.

Shortly after the pheasant is killed it should be drawn (so that it does not get too gamey), and the plumage wiped clean. The bird then needs to be hung for several days with its neck in a noose, in an airy, cool place. Older birds can be hung for up to a week. Then the bird should be plucked and wiped clean with a non-fibrous cloth before being cooked or frozen.

When carving pheasant, cut away the two legs and keep warm. Separate the wings from the bird, leaving a piece of breast attached. Do not be too mean with the breast meat that is served with the wing, pheasant breast has plenty of meat on it, so be generous to make a decent portion of wing and breast meat. The remaing breast meat should be cut away using poultry scissors to make two portions. This yields six portions of pheasant. Later, any meat remaining on the neck, back, and belly can be cut away, finely chopped and, together with a few vegetables, added to a delicious game soup made from the carcass. Any left over gravy and finely chopped, roasted offal can also be added. It is advisable not to use the liver, lungs, and kidneys, as these organs contain a lot of chemicals, partly due to environmental pollution. If the pheasant is very small, it can be divided into four portions.

On special occasions, the pheasant can be presented in a different way. Before plucking the bird, remove the head and neck, the tail with its long spur and both tips of the wings with the long flight feathers attached. Clean the detached parts of the bird carefully inside and out, and dry with a cloth. Impale the head and tail on small wooden kebab skewers and wrap the skewers in pieces of buttered bread or frills made from silver paper. Sharpen the tip of the skewer that is not attached to a part of the bird and put the pieces of pheasant in a cool, well aired place that is protected from flies.

Roast the rest of the pheasant (which has been plucked), divide into portions and place on an upturned, warmed plate, placed in turn on another plate that is longer, but a similar shape. Cover the meat with two wide strips of white paper and surround with a garland of curly parsley. Then place the head and spur through the paper and fix into the cooked meat. Arrange the wings on top of the paper. Sprinkle lemon segments, or finely chopped pieces of lemon in amongst the parsley.

The pheasant, originally from Asia, is often considered king of game birds.

PHEASANT WITH TRUFFLES

1 young pheasant
2 tbs (30 ml) brandy
1 tb (15 ml) dry marsala
1 small black truffle
salt, black pepper
6 slices fatty pork belly
3 tbs (45 ml) olive oil
1 garlic clove
1 sprig rosemary
3½ fluid ounces (100 ml) chicken stock

Prepare the pheasant for cooking. Mix the brandy with the marsala. Slice the truffle finely and marinate in the alcohol for one hour. Remove the slices of truffle and stuff carefully under the skin of the pheasant. Keep the marinade. Cover the pheasant and chill overnight.

Preheat the oven to 350° F (180° C). Season the pheasant with salt and pepper and cover with the pork belly slices. Heat the oil in a casserole. Finely chop the garlic and rosemary and pan-fry in the oil. Do not allow the garlic to discolor. Place the pheasant in the pot, cover, and cook in the oven for 30 minutes. Pour in the truffle marinade and the stock. Baste the pheasant with the frying juices. After 15 minutes, remove the pieces of bacon, increase the oven temperature and allow the pheasant to brown. Remove the pheasant from the pot and keep warm. Sieve the cooking liquid, skim off the fat and reduce until at most six tablespoons of liquid remain. Carve the pheasant and pour the gravy over the meat.

Pheasant: no longer reserved for the nobility.

PARTRIDGE

Partridges should be drawn soon after they have been killed, the plumage should be cleaned and the bird hung from the neck for a few days in a cool and airy place. Pluck the bird and clean it with a non-fibrous cloth before cooking or freezing.

Carving: if the bird is very small, cut it in half lengthways. Otherwise cut away the legs, keeping them whole, then cut across the breastbone so that the breast is divided into two pieces and cut deeply across from the left and right shoulder. Cut away this section, then cut the piece with the wings in half across the breastbone (which can be removed) so that there are two breast portions with wings attached, and one without. This method yields five portions, the partridge can also be cut lengthways and crossways (like a small roasting chicken) to provide four portions.

If a small partridge is stuffed, the stuffing will be equally distributed between the two halves of the bird. If the partridge is divided into four or five portions the stuffing should be carefully removed from the inside of the bird and arranged on the serving plate with the meat.

Young partridges are very tender and particularly delicious for roasting or making pâtés. They can be easily recognized by their yellow feet. Older birds have grey feet. Young birds have pointed wing feathers whilst in older birds the wing feathers have rounded ends.

Older partridges should be marinated for a few days before cooking. The best bases to use for the marinade are buttermilk or sour milk, or a wine vinegar marinade with stock vegetables, four or five pressed juniper berries and a bay leaf. When roasting older birds, use a little of the strained marinade when cooking. This can be seasoned with a little sour or ordinary cream. The bird will not have a sour flavor, despite the sour marinade.

PARTRIDGE WITH RIESLING AND GREEN GRAPES

6 young partridges
salt
1 pound 2 ounces (500 g) green grapes (seedless, if possible)
oil
white pepper
butter
2 glasses Riesling
6 slices mixed grain bread
goose fat
3½ ounces (100 g) bacon slices

Pluck the partridges, draw them and clean thoroughly. Salt the insides of the birds and stuff with a few washed grapes. Tie the feet and the parson's nose together. Brown the backs of the partridges in oil and season with salt and pepper. As soon as the partridges have turned a good color, place them in a roasting pan with their undersides facing upwards. Brush the birds with melted butter and season wih salt and pepper. Pour over two glasses of Riesling and roast in the oven until cooked. In the last fifteen minutes of cooking time, add a few of the grapes to the birds, and pan-fry the remaining grapes in the butter with a little Riesling.

The plumage of the gray partridge is ideally suited to its habitat

After removing the crusts place the slices of bread on a baking sheet greased with goose fat. Pour some of the fat from the partridges over the top of the bread and grill until toasted. Pan- fry the bacon until crisp, and arrange on a warmed serving plate, together with the bread, grapes and partridges. Serve with Bamberg potatoes, green beans, and the roasting juices.

Partridge is a great delicacy, particularly in September and October

NORMAN PARTRIDGE

4 partridges
6 apples
¾ pint (¼ l) calvados
salt, pepper
5½ ounces (150g) fatty sliced bacon
3 tbs (45 g) clarified butter
¾ pint (¼ l) cider
2 tbs (30 g) sugar 1 pint (½ l) cream

Peel and core the apples and cut into eighths. Pour the calvados over the apples, cover and leave to steep for 2 hours. Season the partridges inside and out with salt and pepper. Stuff with a few apple pieces and seal with wooden skewers. Wrap the birds in the bacon and hold in place with cooking thread. Heat the butter in a large pan and brown the birds in the fat for about 5 minutes. Pour in the cider and stew for 30 minutes at a low heat. Cook the remaining pieces of apple with the sugar and a little water over a low heat. They should be soft after about 10 minutes cooking. Remove the partridges from the pan. Take off the cooking thread and arrange on a serving plate with the bacon (which should be cut into strips) around the birds. Deglaze the partridge pan with a little water and mix the cooking juices with the cream. Serve the birds with the apple pieces and the sauce.

PARTRIDGE WITH SAUERKRAUT AND CHAMPAGNE

4 partridges
salt
pepper
6 juniper berries
9 ounces light colored grapes
5½ ounces (150 g) fatty bacon
1 onion
6 tbs (90 g) clarified butter
1 pound 9 ounces (750 g) sauerkraut
¼ pint (⅛ l) meat stock
¼ pint (⅛ l) white wine
¾ pint (¼ l) champagne or good sparkling white wine
1 tbs (15 ml) cognac
7 fluid ounces (200 ml) cream

Pluck the partridges from their heads to their tails, remove the innards, head and feet. Do not wash, but wipe out with a dry cloth.

Season the bird sparingly, both inside and out, with salt and pepper. Pound the juniper berries in a mortar and rub into the skin of the partridges. Wash the grapes thoroughly and remove them from the stalk. Place a few in the stomach cavity of the birds, close, and secure with a wooden skewer.

Cut the bacon into fine slices and wrap around the partridges. Tie in place with cook-ing thread. Finely chop the onion. Heat 3 tablespoons (45 g) clarified butter in a large pan and pan-fry the onion in the butter until transparent. Break up the sauerkraut and add to the onion. Cook for 10 minutes, stirring frequently.

Heat the remaining clarified butter in another pan and carefully place the wrapped partridges into the pan. Pan-fry on all sides for about five minutes, then pour in the stock, cover and simmer for 40 minutes.

Add the wine to the sauerkraut and cook for a further 30 minutes. 10 minutes before the end of the cooking time, add the grapes and stir into the sauerkraut. Then add the champagne or sparkling wine and arrange the sauerkraut on a serving plate.

Remove the partridges from the pan. Take off the cooking thread and the bacon. Arrange the partridges on the sauerkraut.

Mix the partridge juices in the pan with the cognac and cream. Season the sauce with salt, if required, and place in a sauce boat. Serve with black bread, puréed potatoes, or potato croquettes. Goes well with a dry Alsace Riesling.

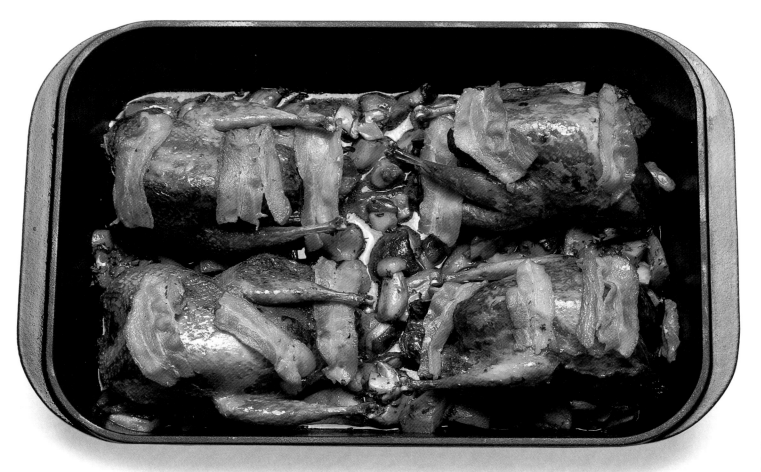

Game bird meat is generally darker than that of domestic poultry. It is very important to wrap the birds in bacon before roasting.

ROE DEER

In its first two years of life, the roe deer produces the most delicious meat; older meat too can make the basis of a delicious dish, as long as it has been well marinated to make the flesh tender.

How to carve the saddle (back cut): Using a large, sharp knife, make a slit down the middle of the roasted saddle up as far as the dorsal vertebra and cut the meat from side to side (for a more attractive shape, cut on a slant) left to right across the central cut and across the grain of the meat. The slices of meat should be as wide as a finger. Ease the meat carefully away from the bone and replace the slices so that the venison joint looks whole. Saddle of venison looks very appetizing on a serving plate with small bunches of parsley and half slices of lemon, and a little sauce poured over the meat itself. The sauce should be served separately in a gravy boat. Saddle of venison can also be presented on a very large platter, with an assortment of vegetables and potatoes all around it. An average saddle of venison will serve about 10 people.

To carve a haunch of venison: Using a large, sharp knife, make a long, deep cut on the upper and underside of the leg. Cut until you feel the bone. Remove the bone carefully, and cut the two halves of the leg into pieces a finger's width thick. Cut across the grain of the meat.

Take a warmed serving plate and place the sliced meat back around the bone so that it looks the same as it did before carving. Garnish appropriately, pour a little sauce over the meat and serve.

Suitable garnishes could be: baked apples stuffed with cowberry sauce, croquettes, mixed vegetables or mushrooms. A haunch of venison can serve up to 12 people.

Slice a shoulder of venison in the same way as a haunch. A shoulder will feed approximately four people.

Roe deer, a graceful inhabitant of our woods and fields, and a vital ingredient in game cookery.

STEAMED SHOULDER OF VENISON

shoulder of roe deer venison
pepper, salt
butter
1 onion
1 carrot
¾ pt (¼ l) meat stock
dash of lemon juice or vinegar
1 bay leaf
1–2 cloves
5–6 peppercorns
2 small parsley roots
1 tbs (15 g) flour

Take the prepared shoulder of venison (either hung or defrosted) without the leg, clean it with a dry, non-fibrous cloth and season with pepper and salt. Brown it quickly in a little butter with some roughly chopped onions and carrots. Pour in the meat stock and the vinegar (or lemon). Add the bay leaf, cloves, peppercorns and cleaned parsley root. Add some more hot water, meat stock or vinegar if required.

Remove the shoulder when cooked, ease the meat away from the bone and cut across the grain of the meat to make slices almost a finger's width thick. Arrange the slices, overlapping one another like roof tiles, in a deep serving dish and keep warm. Stir a little flour, vegetable stock, or juice into the cooking liquid, cook through, season, and strain through a sieve. Pour the sauce over the slices of game.

Serve with bread dumplings or pasta, celeriac or beetroot salad and stewed cranberries.

Well marinated is half-cooked. Older meat (especially roe deer) should always be marinated for a few days, in wine, vinegar, or sour milk.

VENISON NODINI (ROE DEER)
An Italian specialty

1–2 venison cutlets (about a finger's width thick, cut from a haunch of venison, and cut across the grain of the meat) per person
½ medium onion
1 medium bay leaf
½ level tsp fresh or dried chopped thyme
a little basil
1 heaped tbs (20 g) finely chopped parsley
2 pieces of celeriac (about a thumb's thickness) chopped
1 roughly chopped carrot
2 finely chopped sage leaves
1 sprig rosemary
5–6 peppercorns
a good ¾ pint (¼ l) red wine
butter, olive oil
¼ pint (⅛ l) cream

Place the onion, bay leaf and all other spices in a stoneware or porcelain dish, pour over the red wine, stir thoroughly and steep the venison cutlets in this marinade for 12 hours, turning the cutlets frequently. After 12 hours,

remove the cutlets, drain and dry with a non-fibrous cloth or some paper towel. Heat the fat (about half butter and half olive oil) and pan-fry on both sides until crispy. Sprinkle lightly with salt and pepper and pour over about half the marinade (which should be strained). Cook until the wine has evaporated. Remove the cutlets, place in a warmed, deep serving dish, layering them on top of one another like roofing tiles and keep warm.

Stir the remaining marinade into the frying juices, and bring to the boil. Stir in the cream and do not allow to boil any more. Pour the sauce over and around the arranged cutlets. Garnish with sprigs of parsley or rosemary and serve.

This dish is good served with firmly cooked rice, and stewed fruit of any kind. Apricots, peaches, pears, apples, cherries, mirabelles, or plums should be stewed with a little liquid (or half water and half white wine). Sweeten lightly and do not cook for too long. The fruit should still have some "bite" to it and should be served separately from the meat in small bowls.

A good wine for this dish would be a dry red wine from Piedmont.

Cowberries are an excellent addition to all game dishes

Roe deer venison cutlets should be cut carefully from the leg joint, and those from older animals well marinated before cooking.

The best time to pick chanterelles is in the summer, when raspberries and bilberries are in season

A tender back cut of roe deer venison is the embodiment of fine game cookery

SADDLE OF VENISON "BADISCHE ART"

1 saddle of roe deer venison
12 juniper berries
salt, white pepper
3½ ounces (100 g) clarified butter
¾ pint (¼ l) game stock
6 large pears
5½ ounces (150 g) fatty smoked bacon
¾ pint (¼ l) water
½ cinnamon stick
1 pinch lemon peel
3 tbs (45 g) redcurrant jelly
6 shallots
1 pound 6 ounces (600 g) chanterelles
4 tbs (60 ml) oil
2 tbs (30 g) chopped parsley
1½ ounces (40 g) butter
2 tbs (30 g) starch
¼ pint (⅛ l) cream
¼ pint (⅛ l) red wine

Preheat the oven to 475° F (260° C). Pound the juniper berries in a mortar. Skin the saddle of venison and rub the meat with the juniper, some salt, and pepper. Melt the clarified butter in a roasting pan. Place the venison on the butter and put on the middle shelf of the oven for about 10 minutes, basting frequently. Reduce the temperature to 400° F (200° C) and add the stock to the pan. Roast the venison for a further 35 minutes, basting from time to time.

Peel, core, and halve the pears. Cook in the water with the cinnamon stick and lemon peel for about 10 minutes until soft. Remove the pear halves from the pan and leave to cool. When cool, stuff the pears with the redcurrant jelly.

Finely dice the shallots, clean the chanterelles and pan-fry in oil over a high heat for about 1 minute, turning frequently. Add a little butter and keep warm.

Remove the venison from the roasting pan, and keep warm. Deglaze the pan with water and pour into a saucepan. Allow to come to the boil. Mix the starch with the cream and use to bind the sauce. Bring to the boil and add the wine and salt if required. Arrange the pear halves on a platter with the chanterelles. Serve the sauce separately. Good with spätzle or potato croquettes.

Suggested wine: dry Pinot Noir (Spätburgunder) from Baden.

GAME LIVER "GRANDAD HUNTSMAN"

1 roe deer liver (or chamois, red deer, or hare)
2 medium onions
1 large, tender, sweet-sour apple
3 tbs (45 g) butter
pepper
salt

Slice the onions finely. Core the apple and cut into slices ½ inch (1 cm) thick. Wipe the liver with a non-fibrous cloth or paper towel. Using a sharp knife, skin the liver and cut into ½ inch (1 cm) slices. Heat the fat in a large skillet and brown the liver slices for about 2 minutes on each side. Make sure that the fat does not overheat, as this causes the liver to have a bitter taste.

Remove the slices of liver and keep warm. Pan-fry the onion slices in the fat, place the apple pieces on top of the onions and place the liver on top of the apple. Pan-fry until ready.

Put the liver back in the bottom of the skillet with the onion and apple on top, or next to the liver. Season wih salt and pepper. Serve the liver from the skillet (do not cook for too long, or leave to stand for too long, or the liver will become tough).

Best served with fresh, rustic bread, slices of toast, or rolls, and salad. Eat with a cool beer.

GAME OFFAL

Offal must always be fresh. During the summer and on warm days, offal should be eaten at the latest the day after the animal is killed. Since organs contain a lot of blood, they are salted after they have been cooked. This prevents them from becoming tough and leathery.

To prepare liver: Place in lukewarm water after carefully removing the gall bladder. Now the skin can be removed easily. Remove all tubes. Liver from fully grown animals is more tender when it has been soaked in milk thinned with water for a few hours.

NB: Deer have no gall bladder, and neither do pigeons or guinea fowl, the digestive juices flowing directly from the liver into the duodenum.

ROE DEER LIVER WITH BLACKCURRANTS

1 roe deer liver
1 glass red wine
1 glass blackcurrant juice
clarified butter
salt
chilled butter
1½ cups blackcurrants

Place the red wine and blackcurrant juice in a pan and reduce by a half. Skin the liver and cut into ½ inch (1 cm) pieces. Warm the plates. Pan-fry the liver in the clarified butter, for about one and a half to two minutes on each side. Remove from the pan, drain on paper towels and keep warm.

Deglaze the pan with the blackcurrant and wine mixture. Bring to the boil. Using a hand mixer, beat the chilled butter and use to bind the sauce. Pour a circle of sauce onto each plate and place the liver on top of the sauce. Garnish with the blackcurrants and serve at once. Serve with puréed potato and a dry Pinot Noir.

Game offal, in this case roe deer liver, is highly thought of in game cuisine

CHAMOIS AND MOUFLON

Up to two years old, both these types of game animals produce tender venison with a sharp but pleasant flavor. The meat is delicious, but should always be well marinated before cooking, and served hot. Plates should always be warmed, otherwise the flavor of the meat deteriorates. Both chamois and mouflon venison should be served with cowberry sauce or jelly as well as any other special accompaniments.

Venison from chamois, or mouflon young should be skinned and have mustard rubbed into the meat. It should be left overnight. This is known as a mustard marinade.

Young venison (from animals up to two years old) should be marinated in a sour milk marinade. This makes the flesh tender and aromatic. Simply take milk that has "turned" or use lemon juice to sour fresh milk.

Put the venison in a deep, acid-proof dish and pour over the marinade until the meat is completely submerged. Turn the meat frequently, particularly if there is more than one cut of meat in the dish.

Venison from older animals should be steeped in a vinegar marinade for several days. It is also possible to use seasoned sour milk, or buttermilk.

ROAST CHAMOIS
(Styrian recipe)

2–3 pounds (1–1½ kg) chamois venison
½ pint (¼ l) vinegar
1 tsp peppercorns
1 tbs (15 g) juniper berries
2 cloves
2 ounces (60 g) fatty bacon
1 pint (½ l) water
salt, pepper
hot English mustard
1 onion
1 large garlic clove
1 bay leaf
peel of one lemon
1 tbs (15 g) capers
2–3 sardine fillets
1 tbs (15 g) finely chopped parsley
3½ ounces (100 g) butter
meat stock
lemon slices
1 tbs (15 g) flour
½ pint (⅛ l) cream or yogurt
Red wine

Take the hung meat and remove the bones. Clean the meat and hammer to tenderize. Boil the vinegar, peppercorns, juniper berries, cloves, and a little sauce in a saucepan for about 20 minutes. Add the water. Use this as a marinade for the meat and marinate the meat for two to three days. Remove the venison, dry and skin it.

Cut half the bacon into small strips. use to lard the meat and rub the meat all over with mustard, pepper, and salt.

Finely chop the onion, garlic, bay leaf, lemon peel, capers, and sardine fillets. Add one tablesppon (15 g) finely chopped parsley to the mixture and mix with the remaining pork belly (which should be diced) and the butter. Roast in the oven with the venison. Pour over hot meat stock or water, bring to the boil and cook in the oven at 400° F (200° C). Baste from time to time and allow the meat to turn dark brown.

When the meat is soft, remove from the oven, carve and arrange on a warmed serving plate. Garnish with parsley and halved slices of lemon.

Strain the roasting liquid, stir in the flour or sauce thickener and add sour cream or yogurt, and red wine to taste.

Serve with cowberries, boiled potatoes or potato dumplings, with seasonal vegetables.

This dish should ideally be served with a dry, not too heavy red wine, for example a German or Austrian Pinot Noir.

Chamois are mountain dwellers, native to the Alps

Straight from the oven to the table: chamois meat should always be eaten hot

GAME STOCK

3 pounds (1½ kg) game bones, finely chopped
oil
stock vegetables
10 juniper berries
1 bay leaf 2 cloves
2 tbs (30 g) tomato puree
1 pint (½ l) red wine
salt

Pour the oil into a roasting pan and heat in the oven. Put the bones into the pan and heat the oven to 425° F (220° C). Dice the stock vegetables, add to the bones and allow to brown slightly. Add the tomato puree and season lightly with salt. Pour in the red wine, and add enough water to over the bones. Simmer in the oven for 3 hours, adding a little water from time to time. Strain the stock through a sieve and use straight away. Alternatively divide into portions and freeze.

RAGOUT OF YOUNG CHAMOIS VENISON WITH MUSHROOMS
Italian specialty

2–3 pounds (1–1½ kg) chamois fawn stewing venison
2 pints (1 l) sour milk
salt, pepper
1 medium onion
olive oil
flour
1 pint (½ l) game stock
1 sprig fresh rosemary or
1 tsp (5 g) dried rosemary
3½ fluid ounces (100 ml) cream
lemon juice
7 ounces (200 g) fresh mushrooms

Cut the stewing venison into 1 inch (3 cm) cubes and marinate overnight in sour milk. Drain and pat dry with a clean cloth or paper towel. Season the venison with salt and pepper. Finely chop the onion. Heat the olive oil in a saucepan and pan-fry the onion until transparent. Turn up the heat, add the meat and brown on all sides, stirring frequently. Sprinkle the contents of the pan with plenty of flour, and as soon as the flour begins to change color, add the game stock. Then add the rosemary and simmer over a low heat for about 45 minutes until tender. Remove the sprig of rosemary (if used). Add the cream to the meat, warm through, but do not allow to boil. Season with salt and lemon juice to taste.

Roughly chop the mushrooms. Heat the butter in a pan, and pan-fry the mushrooms for about 5 minutes over a medium heat.

Heap the cooked meat in a serving dish. Sprinkle with the fried mushrooms and top with finely chopped, fresh parsley. Carefully pour the sauce around the heaped meat.

Serve with spaghetti and freshly grated Parmesan. A green salad with tomatoes makes a perfect accompaniment.

Marinating is very important to tenderize and season the meat. A properly marinated ragout can be as delicious as a roast game joint.

WILD BOAR

This type of game meat is extremely versatile and can be prepared in many different ways. It can be prepared in much the same way as pork, but should always be larded with either bacon, butter, or margarine.

It is, like all types of game, extremely low in fat.

Wild boar meat is also good salted and smoked. The haunches are sometimes used to make ham, and this is a sought after specialty. Smoked and cured meat is essentially raw, and the stipulated meat inspections have to be properly observed since, like domestic pigs, wild boar are susceptible to trichina.

Wild boar should always be properly cooked through, and cooked fairly slowly to avoid the meat becoming tough. It is advisable to cover the meat when roasting, to prevent toughness. Steaks and chops from young animals are particularly tender. Larger pieces of meat from older animals should always be marinated in red wine, vinegar, or sour milk before cooking. They should be left to marinate for 3–4 days, and the meat should be turned daily. Carve saddle and haunch joints in the same way as for roe venison.

LOIN OF WILD BOAR WITH PEACH HALVES

1 large or 2 small wild boar loins
fatty smoked bacon
butter
lemon or mandarin juice
2 slices white bread
4 peaches, stoned and halved
cowberry jam
almonds
lettuce leaves
salad cream
4 tbs (60 ml) roasting juices
4 tbs (60 ml) peach juice

Lard the well hung, skinned loin of wild boar with the bacon slices. Cutting across the grain of the meat, make slices about three fingers' width thick. Tenderize the slices of meat, season lightly with pepper, and pan-fry in the butter, for about 4 minutes on each side.

Stew the peaches in a little butter with a small amount of sugar. Keep the lid on the saucepan whilst stewing the peaches. Drizzle the peaches with the lemon or mandarin juice. Cut the toasted white bread into quarters, and place a loin slice on each piece of toast. Place a peach half, which has been thickly spread with boiled cowberry jam and chopped or flaked almonds, on top of the meat. Arrange the meat on a bed of lettuce leaves (which can be dressed with salad cream.) Mix the meat and peach juices together and drizzle over the dish. Serve with buttered rice.

Wild boar like to live in moist deciduous woodland, where there is a good supply of acorns or beechmast.

Loin of wild boar, attractively presented, can be the centrepiece of any buffet.

HARE AND WILD RABBIT

Hare produces very good game meat. Half grown and three-quarter grown hares, which have plenty of meat on them but have not yet reached their full adult size, are a great delicacy. To tell if a hare is young, run a spoon along the length of the meat; if the meat tears easily, it is a young animal. Other signs to look out for are: weak and little used claws, and ribs that can be easily broken. The same tests apply to wild rabbit, although the flavor of the meat is not quite as good as that of hare.

Rabbit and hare are generally hung immediately after shooting. After about one to three days in a cool, airy place, the animals are skinned and drawn: the lungs, heart, and liver are set aside, and the intestine removed. The head, neck, ribcage, abdomen and front legs are separated from the back and, together with the giblets, can be used as stewing meat (young hare).

The lungs, liver, and heart can be used to make game dumplings. The back and haunch make a roasting joint, and the shoulders and front legs of fleshier hares can also be used for roasting. Clean these pieces with a cloth, and skin with a sharp knife. Any shot pellets and blue areas caused by shot should be cut out. Flatten the meat with the side of a knife. The meat is now ready for roasting or freezing. To carve a hare, cut the broader areas of the back into pieces 2 inches (6 cm) thick and narrower areas into pieces about 3 inches (8 cm) thick. Cut the meat crossways, using a sharp knife. It is also possible to cut the hare on either side of the spine and to remove the spine. The upper and lower parts of the leg can be carefully eased away from the bone and cut into portions or into pieces about the thickness of a finger. If the slices of back meat are to be reassembled on a hot serving plate, the pieces of leg can be arranged around the back as an attractive way of presenting the meat.

Older hares should be marinated for one to two days before cooking. Alternatively they can be wrapped in a cloth soaked in vinegar and stored in the refrigerator for two to four days. The meat should be turned regularly. Use sour milk, buttermilk, or vinegar as a marinade.

A good marinade for hare can be made from a glass of red wine, half a pint (quarter liter) vinegar, one and a half pints (three quarters of a liter) water, one onion sliced into rings, bay leaves, cloves, a chopped carrot, a few juniper berries and some peppercorns. The hare should be left to marinate for up to two days and turned frequently.

Older rabbits should have hot vinegar marinade poured over them and be left to marinate for one to two days, turning frequently.

PARISIAN HARE SOUP
French specialty

1 pound (½ kg) hare stewing meat (neck, shoulder, front leg, breast, belly)
1 bay leaf
1 small onion, stuck with two cloves
5–6 juniper berries
5 peppercorns
salt
1 tbs (15 g) hot mustard
2 oranges
zest of one whole orange
2 tbs (30 g) redcurrant, raspberry, or blackberry jelly
dry white wine
¾ pint (¼ l) cream
2 pints (1 l) water
halved orange slices without peel
butter

Bring the meat with bones and spices to the boil in a large pan of water. Simmer until tender over a very low heat (for up to an hour). Strain the stock, bone the meat, chop it small and return to the stock together with salt, mustard, orange zest, and fruit jelly. Add white wine to taste. Leave to infuse for a few minutes, and stir in the cream or some condensed milk just before serving. The soup should be served in a terrine and garnished with the orange slices (which should be pan-fried on one side in some butter).

Hares differ, depending on their habitat, be it field, moorland, mountain or woodland. The best meat comes from mountain and woodland hares.

A bowl of hearty hare soup, toasted white bread, and a glass of red wine—could there be a more atmospheric start to a special meal?

BELGIAN ROAST HARE

saddle (and haunch) of hare
a simple red wine
1 onion
2 bay leaves
2–3 cloves
1 carrot
4–5 peppercorns
3½ ounces (100 g) smoked bacon
pepper, salt
1 small glass Mediterranean wine
sour cream or yogurt

The hung hare should be skinned and cleaned. Bring the red wine briefly to the boil, together with one onion, sliced into rings, the bay leaves, cloves, carrots and the peppercorns. Pour over the meat before it is completely cool and leave for 4 days. When marinated, dry the meat. Dice the smoked bacon, roast briefly, then place the hare on top and cook in its own juices in a preheated oven, temperature 350° F (180° C). To keep the meat juicy, baste frequently with spoonfuls of the red wine marinade. The hare should be ready after about 40 minutes in the oven. Remove and keep warm.

To make the gravy, heat up the roasting juices with more of the red wine marinade. Sieve, season with salt and pepper and add a small glass of Mediterranean wine. Stir in the sour cream or yogurt and serve in a preheated sauce boat.

Tastes good with steamed, buttered chestnuts, mashed potato and cowberry jam. A dry Chianti is a suitable wine.

This recipe pleases more than just the eye: roast saddle of hare in a red wine sauce

ANDALUSIAN LEG OF HARE
Spanish delicacy

2 haunches of hare
2 medium garlic cloves
1 pinch salt
freshly milled black pepper
2 large pinches ground thyme
2 tbs (30 ml) liquid soup flavoring
10–20 stoned green olives
3 slices raw smoked ham
smoked bacon slices
½ cup olive oil
1 chopped garlic clove
4–5 tomatoes
1 large glass red wine
cold water
cornstarch (or similar)
3½ fluid ounces (100 ml) cream
lemon juice
black olives
lemon pieces
parsley

Take the hung, skinned haunches of hare and carefully remove the bones. Finely chop the garlic cloves and press with the tip of a knife and a little salt. Mix with thyme, pepper, and the soup flavoring, and rub into the meat.

Stuff the cavity of the meat where the bones were, with the stoned green olives—which themselves should be stuffed with a piece of raw ham and any scraps of meat from the hare bones—packing the olives in tightly. Tie up the meat, and wrap with pieces of smoked bacon, if the meat seems very dry.

Bring the olive oil and the chopped garlic to the boil. Strain it while still hot directly onto the meat and cook the meat to brown it. Cover and simmer over a low heat for about half an hour. Add about four or five skinned and chopped tomatoes.

Allow to cook until the meat is soft. Remove the hare and keep warm.

Deglaze the pan with the red wine and add the starch, dissolved in a little cold water. Bring to the boil. Add the cream and season well with pepper and lemon juice. Serve the sauce separately.

Cut the meat across the hare into slices about as thick as a finger. Drizzle with a little cream and arrange on a warmed plate. Garnish the meat with black olives, lemon pieces, the remains of the smoked ham, and some parsley.

Serve with rice, and if desired, with finely sliced mushrooms.

A hearty red Rioja complements this dish perfectly.

A tasty delicacy from the Iberian peninsula

Hare Pörkölt
Hungarian specialty

4 haunches of hare
1 carrot
1 small leek
1 slice celeriac
1 bay leaf
3 medium onions
3½ ounces (100 g) diced smoked bacon
2 ounces (50 g) clarified butter
1 pinch hot paprika
1 pinch sweet paprika
salt
2–3 tomatoes or some tomato purée
2–3 green, yellow, or red peppers
3 Tbs (45 ml) sour cream or yogurt

Wash and scrub the carrot, leek, and celeriac. Cut the carrot in half lengthways. Cut one onion into quarters. Chop the celeriac and leek into pieces. Put the hare into a large pan together with the stock vegetables and the bay leaf. Fill with salted water. Bring to the boil and cook the haunches over a low heat for about one hour, until soft.

Remove the haunches. Strain the stock and reduce until there is about ¼ pint (⅛ liter) of liquid. Remove the meat from the bones, skin and cut into bite-sized pieces.

Finely chop the remaining onions and brown in the clarified butter with the diced bacon. Sprinkle with the hot and sweet paprika and add the game pieces. Season well with salt, add a little strained stock and stir.

Skin, deseed, and chop the tomatoes. Clean the peppers and cut into fine strips.

Add the tomatoes (or tomato purée) and the peppers to the meat, and cook for 30 minutes. Gradually add the rest of the stock. At the end of the cooking time, when the meat is tender, add the yogurt or sour cream, and arrange in a warmed, deep dish.

Serve with all types of dumplings, small pasta, boiled potatoes, or rice. A heady red wine like Châteauneuf du Pape, Côtes du Rhône, or Chianti goes very well with this dish. May be made hotter by adding chillies, in which case cold beer would be a better choice of drink.

Hare Pörkölt is a Magyar favorite

WILD RABBIT
"LAPIN À LA BIGORRE"
Specialty from the south of France

1 oven ready wild rabbit
3 tbs (45 g) butter
1 ounce (40 g) smoked bacon
2–3 tbs (30–45 g) grated, creamed horseradish
1 egg
3 ounces (100 g) salted potato chips
pepper, salt
liquid soup flavoring
3 tbs (45 g) remoulade
3½ ounces (100 g) low fat yogurt
2 tomatoes
1 bunch curly parsley

Finely dice the bacon. Joint the rabbit and brown on all sides in a casserole, in two tablespoons (30 grams) butter, together with the diced bacon. Set the rabbit pieces aside. Allow to cool slightly and spread all over with the horeseradish. Drain the pan-fried bacon and keep warm. Return the meat and fat to the casserole, cover and cook at a medium heat for about one hour.

Gradually remove the rabbit pieces and place on a lightly greased baking sheet with the rounded sides facing upwards.

Brush the rabbit pieces with beaten egg. Sprinkle with crushed potato chips, dot with pieces of butter and bake in a preheated oven.

Meanwhile, mix the cooking juices of the rabbit with a little warm water or meat stock and cook through. Season the sauce with salt, pepper, liquid soup seasoning, and a little remoulade. Stir in the low fat yogurt and keep warm, but do not allow to boil. Bring the sauce to table in a sauce boat. Arrange the crispy rabbit pieces on a serving plate with the cubes of bacon, skinned slices of tomato and some curly parsley.

Serve with a selection of baby vegetables, boiled parsley, potatoes and slices, two fingers thick, of deseeded canteloupe or honeydew melon. Serve with a dry Pinot Noir.

Wild rabbit, cooked the southern French way, does not look particularly special, but is nevertheless quite outstanding.

HUNTING WITH A CAMERA

HORST NIESTERS

Fortunately people no longer die taking photographs through mixing the explosive photoflash powder incorrectly, and "accidents" in game photography nowadays are trivial by comparison. It is simply a disappointment if a photograph, once developed, does not accurately reflect the photographer's actual experience. In fact, there are relatively few things which must be taken into account to guarantee a photo image which corresponds with reality, and even perhaps exceeds the original impression. Although equipment should not be underestimated, it is not only this which gives fox (above) or ruff (right) the correct exposure. The basic requirements for a good "hunter with a camera" are not of a technical nature, but are qualities such as equanimity, discipline, stamina and care.

Here the camera has successfully captured the interplay of light and shadow on the duck's feathers, and the color highlights, despite the difficult lighting conditions in this riverbank scene.

A hunter should make an ideal wildlife photographer because no one is better qualified to approach timid game. Even the most sophisticated technology does not provide that much. The most important things which the photographic hunter needs to equip himself with are a talent for improvisation, empathy, patience, stamina, a good knowledge of biology, and a passion for hunting.

When I reflect on old literature and the beginnings of game and hunting photography, I recall the names of the pioneers of this form of hunting. Carl Georg Schillings, naturalist and zoologist, was one of the first game and wildlife photographers. Worlds separate his pictures in his 1905 book "With flashlight and sporting gun" from what is now possible with the range of equipment available for photography. Formerly, hunting with a camera was considered a big adventure. Schillings even received letters of encouragement and appreciation from Theodore Roosevelt —even an astronaut has to content himself with less attention nowadays.

When Schillings first set out for Africa in 1897, he was accompanied by more than fifty helpers and carriers. His cameras were large-bore box

cameras (9×12 or 13×18) with an f number of 7. Goertz optical works made him the first long-focus (telephoto lens) camera, which enabled him to capture even distant animals on photographic plate. Image detail recording ability and depth of field of the camera lenses available at the time are no longer comparable with current requirements and technical specifications. Even the preparation of the photoflash powder was a potentially life-threatening undertaking. There was the strict warning instruction to store all the required ingredients separately at all costs, because there were often fatal accidents, even when apparently correct proportions were mixed together. Schillings nevertheless achieved night shots, which showed animals which had been unknown until then. Thus, for example, the hyenas first photographed by him in 1899, appear in natural history articles as *Hyaena schillingsi*.

Other great photographers followed suit, for example, Dr. Arthur Lindgens, who imparted new knowledge to an astonished public in 1937 with his book "Game, Picture and Shot." There had already been solitary hunters with weapons and cameras at the beginning of the 20th century.

Their wish was to capture what had been seen and experienced on film.

Parallel to this, the first professional wildlife photographers began to earn reputations for themselves. Hermann Fischer ("Hunting Animals with a Camera") was granted the task of illustrating the narrative works of Hermann Löns with his pictures. Then came photographers like the Englishman Eric Hosking, an excellent ornithologist, and Walter Wissenbach, who was the first to use a (homemade) remote shutter-release mechanism, and who perfected the technique of the light-box.

Famous scientists like Professor Steiniger, who introduced us to game and wildlife photography in his numerous books, and Julius Behnke von Leitz were the role models for our generation.

I too tried my luck at wildlife and hunting photography almost 40 years ago, and had my photographs published on the front pages of established hunting journals like "Game & Dog", "Deer-stalking" and "Hunter". Years later, in 1970, I founded a charitable organization—in conjunction with Fritz Pölking, one of the most successful wildlife photographers in the world, Professor Steiniger and Walter Wissenbach—which was dedicated exclusively to the photography of wildlife, game and birds. This was the birth of the GDT (Association of German Animal Photographers). None of us realized at the time that this organization, with its total of seven founder members, would one day expand to a membership of 250 internationally active photographers, including some who have achieved world fame. The GDT wildlife photo festival, which has been going for many years, has become an event for wildlife and game photographers throughout Europe.

ANIMAL PHOTOGRAPHY IN PRACTICE

The following explanations are above all intended as suggestions as to how you, the "hunter with a camera" can experience exciting adventures and also acquire a rich bounty of photographs. However, not every photo-hunt is crowned with success—adverse circumstances can thwart your project and it is easy to become disillusioned. Fine weather can change abruptly; the roe buck you have had your eye on for so long may change its habits because lumberjacks have altered its habitat; or a party of hikers wanders through the wood singing merrily and startling the last remaining red deer. The best way is to resign yourself in advance to the fact that although every day may be a hunting day, not every day has to be a successful hunting day.

The most important attribute of all for a successful animal photographer is a love of nature. Equanimity, discipline, stamina and respect are the basic requirements. In addition, he must know his equipment inside out, since the time available to him during the encounter with wild game can

Telephoto lenses can allow eye-contact—as here with this beech marten.

Even atop a scarecrow the kestrel remains on guard.

Caption to pages 304 and 305:
In just a few seconds this chamois could have
been out of sight, as they frequently change
their grazing spots.

◁ The screaming "'ow-'ow-'ow" of the Ural
owl attracts the attention of any photographer.

▷ The white and gray colors of the male
goshawk are a good disguise in the snowy
winter forest.

Caption to pages 310 and 311:
When the cranes swarm across the sky in the evening, the great gray owls also liven up. A photographer has to adapt to such difficult light conditions.

The shot from below is as a rule only appropriate for animals we usually expect to see above us.

Extreme patience is needed to capture the timid marmot on film.

◁ An unfocused background can also be used stylistically. Here it highlights the sharp attentiveness of these European buzzards.

▷ A little owl stares at the camera with an unblinking, knowing gaze.

sometimes amount to only seconds. A matter of moments will prove decisive as to whether you can successfully capture on film what you are seeing and experiencing. The keen wildlife photographer's heart beats faster at the first timid snatch of birdsong or the sound of a swarm of geese and cranes. A little hunting instinct does not go amiss either. The ancient buccaneering instincts of our ancestors are present in each of us, sometimes more marked, sometimes less marked. We must skillfully gather them together and concentrate on the hunt ahead, whether this be in local woods or in the foreign jungle. Every encounter is unique.

CHOOSING THE RIGHT CAMERA
Whether Nikon or Canon, Leica, Minolta or Olympus, every photographer swears by the equipment with which he is successful and which has never let him down.

Irrespective of whether it is standard or medium format, if you are working with a two-camera body kit, you should always use the same make, so that you can handle the camera "with your eyes closed" (all levers, knobs, and locks etc. in the same position). To distinguish quickly between my two completely identical-looking

camera bodies, I have attached different-colored straps to them. The quickest and most practical camera is the standard 35mm single-lens reflex camera (SLR). Its lenses are nowadays of such high quality that the medium format is no longer absolutely necessary, unless you are specializing in landscape photography, calendars and large-sized book illustrations.

CHOOSING THE RIGHT LENS
Basic lenses are the standard lens (50 mm) and a small zoom lens (35–135 mm), which combines wide-angle with telephoto facilities. The lens should allow seamless transition to close-up subjects (macro), so that even a butterfly on a track, or a bee pollinating a flower, can be photographed, filling the frame.

Absolutely essential is the classic 400 mm or 500 mm telephoto lens. Some manufacturers have a telephoto lens in their range which can be adapted for use on nearly all SLR cameras. The pistol grip for sharp focusing permits quick reactions, rather like hunting with a rifle. If image brightness (f number) of 5.6, for example, is not adequate, fast (light-sensitive) film can be of assistance. Faster (brighter) lenses (aperture f4 or

To photograph a yawning snowy owl or a tired hare requires...

...quick reactions on shutter release.

Caption to pages 314 and 315:
Red-throated diver (loon) family on a
Scandinavian lake.

Beech martens are also very photogenic when
stretched to their full height of 16–20 inches
(40–50 cm).

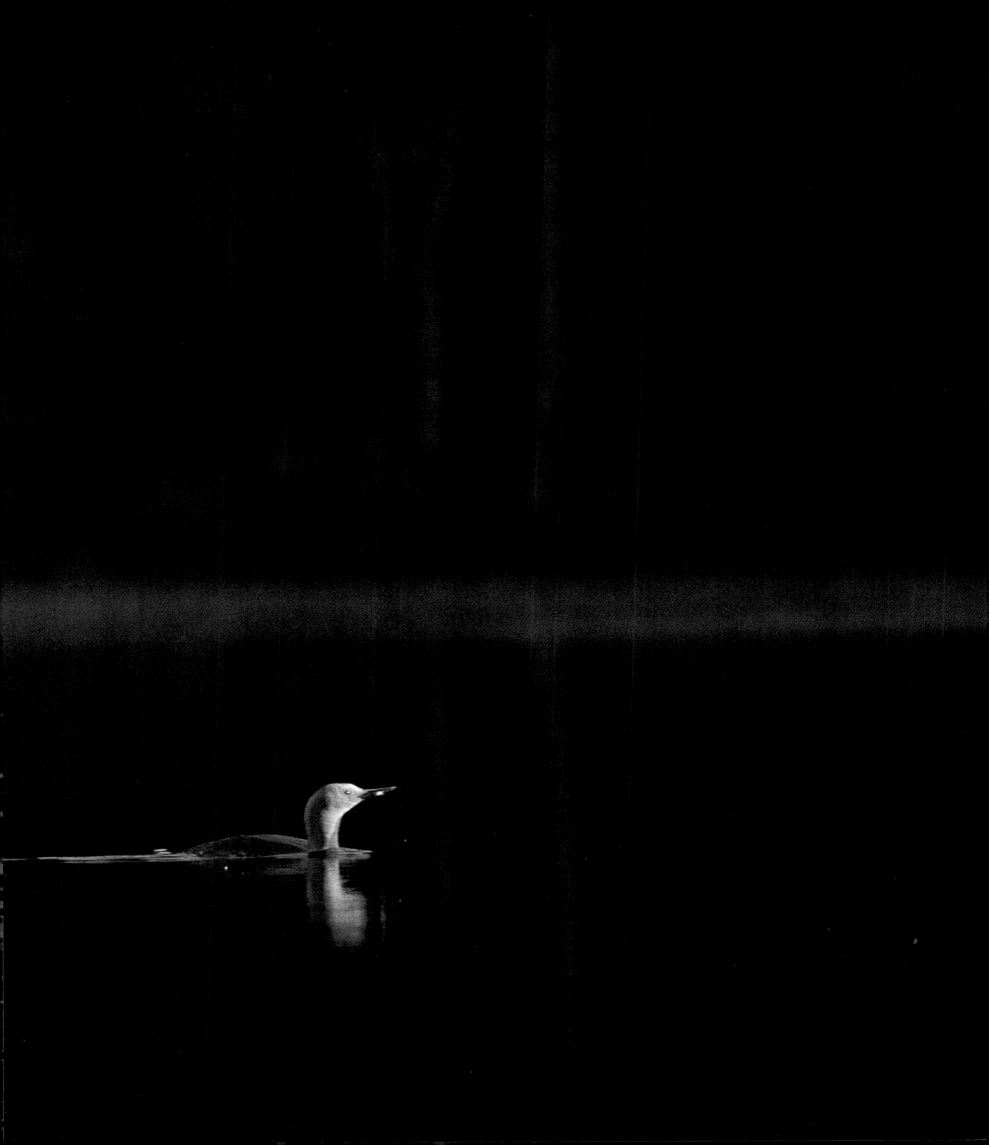

Gregarious marmots make interesting group photographs.

What has eluded this crane has been spotted by the camera—its newly-hatched chick peeps out curiously from the protection of its parent's feathers.

Photographing animals amongst branches can easily cause problems with the foreground.

Often there is only a single opportunity to snap a subject, which means you have to rely on chance.

This photograph and the one on the facing page of two European buzzards won first and second prize in the competition held by the Association of German Animal Photographers.

Colors are a question of the right exposure, which here highlights the russet tones of a red kite.

lower) are almost twice as expensive. Longer lenses are as a rule too unpractical, too difficult and too expensive.

In terms of preparation, a photographer has a distinct advantage over the huntsman with the sporting gun who must comply with strict seasonal restrictions, because for him (the photographer) the whole year is the "hunting season."

It is, however, illegal (and quite rightly so) to photograph, and thereby disturb, species which are threatened with extinction, when they are nesting, at their breeding grounds or at other places of refuge. This similarly applies to threatened plant species. Since the "red lists" of these plants and animals differ from one country to another, and sometimes from region to region within a country, it is vital to obtain the right information before setting out on the hunt with a camera. It is furthermore advisable to consult the owner of the hunting-ground beforehand, because hunting equipment (canopy, raised platform or

screen) ought not to be used without permission. The most promising and successful time of the day for good photographs is either early in the morning or early evening.

A person with a hunting license has an advantage over the layman, as a rule, because he is better informed of the yearly cycle in the hunting-ground, and does not expect to encounter a stag in its prime, for example, in the month of March; it will have discarded its antlers long since. Such a person would also know that the courtship display of black grouse and capercaillie can only be seen in April and May, and that foxes court in January. It is also useful to know that hares produce young up to three times a year on the surface, and that the leverets can see and have a full coat of fur at birth, whereas a rabbit's young are born naked and blind, in underground burrows.

It is important when stalking that you move carefully around the hunting ground, stand still regularly and search the terrain thoroughly through

Although it was "only" awarded second prize, this photograph which shows these two aggressive birds in the air, was far more difficult to take than the one on the ground.

binoculars. Sturdy footwear and clothing which does not rustle (woolen material is best) are advisable.

A good accessory for camera and lens for stalking purposes is a monopod support, because it enables greater flexibility through being able to use relatively long exposures (to 1/50 of a second) when necessary. A telephoto zoom lens is almost like a long-range weapon. The bullet is less effective at a distance of 200 yards than at 100 or 50 yards. This means the longer the exposure and the longer the lens (greater the magnification), the steadier the support must be. In this instance a tripod is even better than a monopod, but is unfortunately less portable, and heavier.

I have wrapped sticky tape around my static supports and lenses (of 300 mm upwards) and sprayed them with camouflage paint. In this way you can avoid the risk of making a noisy disturbance with strange metallic sounds, if you stumble at some point. In addition, the metal parts will not attach themselves to you in extreme heat or extreme cold. Also, use skylight or UV filters on expensive lenses, to protect them from dirt or damage.

If the subject permits it, you should for safety's sake take several photographs of one and the same subject. Aside from the lens aperture and shutter speed combinations given for the camera, it is advisable to take an additional overexposed and underexposed photograph. There are sometimes minute nuances which a camera cannot fathom because of the concise nature of its make-up. It is important in this case that the camera is not set on automatic mode, but instead operated manually. When set on automatic mode, a camera will always select the shutter speed which matches the pre-selected aperture, or vice versa. When operated manually, it is best to select an average setting which if need be can also still take on board any slight movement of the subject.

If the camera has a standard exposure system (and not integral, matrix or spot meters like the newest SLR cameras), and you photograph say a roe buck or red deer stag on a sunny morning in front of a dark forest, then the exposure meter will measure the forest, and the deer in the foreground will be over-exposed by up to 3 aperture "stops". If the camera has a spot meter and you compare the two, you will notice that discrepancies of up to 3 aperture "stops" can occur. It cannot be pointed out often enough to inexperienced photographers how shutter speed and aperture play a decisive part in the resulting picture. Here, therefore, are a few more words of advice:

Film with low sensitivity (e.g. 64 ASA) requires a lot of light (often referred to as slow film), is fine-grained and shows better image detail. The picture produced is therefore richer in contrasts. Film with high sensitivity (e.g. 200 or 400 ASA) requires less

In order to highlight small animals like this muskrat, the photographer must occasionally come down to their level.

Animals which stare directly into the camera can produce exquisite photographs (unless using flash), but they convey the impression they have seen the photographer. Without eye-contact, this polecat seems to have been secretly observed.

Mass scenes hold a fascination, whether on film or in a photograph. There is a graphic quality about the repeating patterns of animals with conspicuous markings, such as the black and white plumage of the male eider.

Animals can also be used to heighten the mood of a landscape shot.

light (often called fast film), but is coarser-grained and does not appear as sharp. It should, therefore, only be used in exceptional cases, such as deer rutting in autumn or courtship of black grouse and capercaillie.

Shutter speed is of similar importance. If you want sharp definition for game which is moving around a lot, you need a "fast" shutter speed, even at the cost of aperture and depth of field. Take, for example, a photograph of a buck pursuing a doe in the rutting season. For this you need 1/500 to 1/1000 of a second. If there is only enough light, however, for 1/125 of a second with wide-open aperture, you must follow the subject with the camera and release the shutter, rather as with a shotgun. By this means

the surrounding areas of the photo will be blurred, but at least it may be possible to get the subject sharp. However, never aim the camera in front (of the subject) as with a shotgun, but always directly at it, and always remember that a wider aperture results in reduced depth of field.

The depth of focus is the distance between the nearest and furthest point from the camera, that which lies in front of and behind the object being photographed, which is in reasonably sharp focus. To photograph a fleeing chamois in the mountains, you need a "fast" shutter speed (1/1000 of a second with aperture set at f4.5 or f5.6), with a 400 mm telephoto lens. This normally means that no more than five or ten yards in front of and

Pictures such as these are sometimes almost "second nature" to a wildlife photographer and may be shot while lying in wait for the real subject.

behind the animal will be sharply focused. However, if the chamois is standing grazing calmly on a slope in the middle of a beautiful mountainous landscape, then, depending on the distance, you can take a photograph at say 1/125 of a second and aperture of f11, thus obtaining a good depth of focus, so that both chamois and landscape appear exquisitely sharp.

A buzzard in the sky would be no more than a dark silhouette under normal exposure. You must, therefore, at least double the aperture (from f11 to f8, or even f5.6), so the feathers appear more sharply defined. Likewise, a single animal in the middle of a snowy landscape will usually be underexposed under normal exposure.

With color negative film it is possible to correct the exposure during development in the laboratory (as with black and white processing), but with slide film (positives) this is not possible. It is wise therefore to run a test film, making a note of all the data so that you become familiar with these points. A beautiful photograph normally requires careful assessment and does not usually result from a snapshot. At this juncture I shall once again repeat a really important point, which is that for a shot with a telephoto lens you require the same steady support as for a long-distance shot with a gun!

Aside from hunting with your camera at the ready, you can also take good photographs from a

323

In time you develop an eye for composition and color associations. What works so well here by chance is the atmospheric empty space in the center of the picture and the striking contrast of the berries.

hide or camouflaged tent. The latter is particularly recommended when you know there is going to be an interesting display close by—fox cubs near their earth, or young rabbits by their burrow, for example, or a group of pheasants or other birds away from the nest.

Those who prefer to use a camouflaged tent should set it up in advance, so that the animals can get used to the "intruder" in peace. A non-glinting dummy lens should be installed with it right at the start; this can later be exchanged for the real telephoto lens. The fewer the disturbances there are which can upset the animals, the sooner the photographer will obtain a decent "shot." If you are hiding next to a lure, on no account photograph the first animal to appear. Magpies, jays and buzzards, in particular, watch the first "scout" closely and wait for his reaction. If this first animal does not feel disturbed at the second visit, at the third visit other species may also venture near. Thus the spell is broken and there is a very good chance of success.

A further tip about a camouflaged tent is, where possible, never go alone to one. If you take someone with you, and this person then leaves the tent again, the animals are more likely to return to their places. It is a well-known fact that animals cannot count.

Beware of reloading previously exposed film—a danger especially on long trips. If a used film is not wound back completely into the cartridge, you can simply cut off the "tip."

If you work with two camera bodies, always take the first shot of a subject with the camera which contains a slide film. You thus have the copy you need for a lecture, printed matter or color print. For subsequent pictures use color negative films because these films are more suitable for large-size print enlargements. Also, slide film requires a perfect exposure, and you must pre-select the detail when visually assessing the shot. Detail in negative films can also be altered in the laboratory, and with different print sizes you can also obtain softer or greater definition in color prints.

Consider the following scene, stalking through a forest. A roe buck suddenly crosses your path—a surprising encounter, and totally unexpected. The camera with the telephoto lens is resting on your shoulder, together with the support. The buck notices the intruder and gazes motionless at the stranger, perhaps for as long as six to eight minutes. Do not remove the static support from your shoulder—not even in slow motion. The buck will in fact immediately see through this action and take flight, baying loudly. Instead, stand perfectly still, as if turned to stone, and with a bit of luck, the buck will start grazing peacefully again. After the first one or two mouthfuls, it will as a rule glance briefly over at the stranger and then leisurely move on. That is the photographer's chance.

Photo-hunting with the car can be extremely successful too. The animal kingdom has adapted to the increase in traffic and hardly regards the car as a threat—at any rate for the most part. When stalking by car take a small sandbag along, so that when you wind the window down, you have a steady rest for your telephoto lens. Even better is a so-called car window static support, to which the camera can be firmly attached.

Stalking by car is particularly rewarding for all small-game photography (e.g. hare, pheasant, deer and wading birds). Take care not to switch off the car engine though, or your quarry will promptly flee.

A good vantage point is a farmer's tractor, which provides excellent camouflage for the wildlife photographer. It will not be seen as a threat in these surroundings, and behind the plough is a good place to capture the great variety of our wildlife. Even a brown hare in its hiding-place will actually let a tractor come astonishingly close.

Although wildlife photography from a camouflaged tent or car is relatively harmless, critical situations can arise. Years ago, I was climbing after a prime chamois in the Alps (fresh snow had fallen the previous day), when suddenly, at almost 5,000 feet (1,500 m), it was as if the animal had been swallowed by an earthquake, and I then realized what sort of terrain I was in. On the climb up I had been able to see precisely what to hold on to and where to put my feet. From the top, however, it all suddenly looked quite different. In addition I was afraid I would break a bone or my camera would be smashed to pieces. After searching unsuccessfully for two hours for a way down, I tried to attract the attention of the people in a passing cable car which was about 50 yards away by calling for help and waving. But the cable car passengers misunderstood my cries for help as a friendly greeting and waved back. Finally, as a last resort, I left my entire camera equipment on the mountain, in order to reach safety before nightfall. My equipment was then brought down safely the following day by a mountain guide.

Another time, a grassy hummock unexpectedly sank beneath me during a black grouse lek in Dutch marshland. I myself sank up to my chest in mud, and only after great difficulty did I

This photograph of a long-eared owl shows how effective backlighting can be if used properly. It also demonstrates that such shots tend not to produce zoologically representative animal portraits.

Shots of animals in the snow provide a challenge for every wildlilfe photographer, because he must largely make do without color contrasts, which in any other season would almost automatically create atmosphere in the picture.

The markings on the feathers of this goshawk make it attractive and are even more sriking in the snow than against a green background. The moose (elk) by contrast (top) relies on a vividly textured background.

This close-up of the face mask of a polecat in the snow imparts an interesting rhythmic sequence of light and dark zones, an effect which would still be there in black and white.

manage to reach terra firma again using rowing movements.

On the Shetland Isles, where I wanted to photograph guillemots, gannets and puffins, I was caught out by a heavy rain shower. For three hours I was not able to move even a yard, because the rain turned the bird droppings (which had accumulated here for decades) into a slippery quagmire, making the rocks totally impassable. It was several hours before the crust was safe enough to walk on, and I was freed from this predicament.

Conditions can also be treacherous at certain seasons and regions. Always be prepared for extreme situations, whether you are in a 120° F (c. 50° C) degree heat in Africa, minus 20° F (minus 30° C) in Alaska, in a hurricane on Norway's sheer coastline, or in the rainforest of Brazil. In extreme heat a cool-bag for films is therefore of great importance. Also, only take along as many films as you will need in a day. Exposed films should also be returned immediately to the cool-bag whenever possible.

At minus 20 degrees in Yellowstone National Park, both my cameras and two films let me down. In other words, a "power pack" (batteries and spare parts) are just as important as thermal clothing and a good pocket warmer—if it is so cold you cannot move your fingers to place a film in the camera or press a button on the camera, then what use are wonderful light and beautiful subjects?

OTHER ITEMS FOR THE CAMERA BAG

- A small set of screwdrivers to tighten up possible loose screws

- A small set of pliers. They can work wonders, especially to remove a surface screw from the static support

- A pair of scissors to deal with torn film

- Sticky tape to hold a camera together if need be, or to seal a partially exposed film in a cartridge to protect it from the light. You can also write notes on sticky tape

- A felt-tipped pen which writes on different materials

- Cleaning cloths and anti-dust spray

- A small torch. In your hide you need to be able to check your camera, put in a film or make notes, even in the dark

Wildlife photography is a science in itself. It has its own "hunting weapons," hunting methods and rules. Animal photography should only be undertaken with extreme care and respect for fauna and flora, because only in this way can we contribute to the conservation of the natural environment.

A series of pictures is always recommended if you want to record the total sequence of a movement or action. It is important that the beginning and end of the series matches the beginning and end of the action. The example here shows that if you ignore this rule, it will alter the impression of the event in question.

327

POSTSCRIPT BY THE SECRETARY GENERAL OF THE CONSEIL INTERNATIONAL DE LA CHASSE ET DE LA CONSERVATION DU GIBIER (CIC) WERNER TRENSE

We should not wonder what sort of devilish occupation hunting really is, like Ortega y Gasset, but rather, like the editor in his Foreword, we should ask what sort of person is a huntsman. The personality of the early hunter cannot be established clearly from prehistoric evidence, but we can make a reasonable guess.

Ancient huntsmen considered killing to be a completely normal activity, and had no moral objections about its legitimacy (the terms moral and legitimate are used here in the sense that we understand them today, even if the prehistoric huntsman would not have understood these concepts in the same way). Eventually, many taboos came into being, and these regulated the activities of hunting people, as indeed we still see amongst communities relying on traditional hunting methods, such as the Inuit, Bushmen, Pygmies and others). It is reasonable to conclude that the huntsmen of ancient times also imposed similar restrictions on the hunting of game. However these may have been motivated, the result was relief for the hunting grounds.

Group hunting would have been the most successful method, but there would probably have been lone huntsmen as well. These types of huntsmen can be found all over the world, whether amongst the Kalahari Bushmen, in the mountains of the Tyrol or Romanian Carpathians, or amongst Norwegian elk hunters. For these huntsmen, hunting is their passion, and such people have to be especially careful not to upset the balance between hunter and game. The truly responsible huntsman would never dispute the right of the animal to its own habitat. The responsible huntsman understands the clear boundaries of hunting, and the point where hunting ends and simple bounty seeking begins.

Whenever large numbers of animals have been wiped out, like the North American herds of buffalo (bison) and the South African springbok, the damage has not been done by true huntsmen, but rather by settlers and adventurers.

With the emergence of society and larger settlements, hunting, once a vital activity, became ritualized as a rite of passage, and communal hunting gave way to society hunting. Large numbers of huntsmen and beaters were required to stage the hunting spectacles, and these people could not be expected to demonstrate the same insight and abilities as skilled individual hunters. Thus the Egyptians organized huge hunts for gazelles, sable antelope, ibexes and elephants inside prepared fences, the Assyrians hunted lions, wild asses and elephants with the help of pits and other traps, and the ancient Persians were already using cloth barriers for hunting fallow deer.

In the Greek and Roman Empires, people could hunt wherever and whenever they wanted, and game was not owned by anyone. People generally hunted in small groups or alone, depending on the type of game, using mainly traps, nets, and throwing spears, and fallow deer were already being kept in game enclosures. In many Roman countries the right to catch game had been in place since antiquity, and this may be a reason why the numbers of game dwindled in these countries, resulting in restrictions being imposed on hunting.

Hunting was affected by another development in central and northern Europe and in England. In central Europe, the hunting privilege of the king was connected with forestry, whereas in each village community, the allocated common land could be hunted by the villagers. By the 14th century, nearly all land was in the hands of the nobility, and only members of the noble classes were allowed to hunt. This privilege affected the hunting of game and clearing of forests, and contributed to an increase in the numbers of game animals. Peasant hunters and farmers were only allowed to catch small game, until even that right was denied them. As a result, the huntsman sought employment from the nobility, or resorted to poaching. This was the time of the hunting guilds and brotherhoods. The great achievements of medieval huntsmen, and their often over-enthusiastic passion, is widely recorded in written and artistic form—as richly illustrated in these two volumes.

Hunting relied on first class, trained professional huntsmen but was misused by the feudal system. Game and the forests in which it was hunted became luxuries, and were tended and treated as status symbols. Game became a means to serve a master who was out of touch with reality and was simply a source of pleasure for him and his estate. In absolutist times, hunting developed into a staged spectacle, and into a misinterpretation of the original principles of hunting presented with the utmost perfection with true hunting inexorably trampled into submission.

In Germany, huntsmen pursued predatory game and large game using hounds, until into the 17th century, and moreover with hounds which follow their prey mainly by sight rather than by smell. A competitive form of hunting developed in the parforce hunt, which reached its height of popularity in France and is still practiced today. In contrast to normal hunting with hounds, in the parforce method huntsmen seek out one particular animal, which the hounds track down using their sense of smell. English huntsmen of this time hunted foxes on horseback, a practice which is still very popular today, and which demands the best performance from rider, horse, and hound.

The French Revolution brought the feudal charade to an end and, with it, the absolute control of the aristocracy over the land. After Napoleonic times huntsmen were set new goals, and peasants and farmers could now hunt freely. In Germany, the farmers especially were so displeased at the rise in the numbers of game which had been reserved for the pleasure of the aristocracy that as soon as the new legal amendment was made in 1848, they immediately set about decimating game animals, both in the areas occupied by France and within the remainder Germany. In 1850 there was an amendment to hunting legislation, and a new hunting law was passed which set out new guidelines.

This new law offered huntsmen a way of reorganizing both hunting and huntsmen alike. They could now create hunting associations, draw up shooting guidelines and return hunting to a more traditional form, with the emphasis again on the lone huntsman.

The development from the original hunter into the huntsman of today has been clearly outlined in these two volumes. Nowadays hunting carries an obligation to show self-discipline and responsibility, being no longer a way of earning one's living, nor a means for selfish pleasure alone.

In our materialistic society, which often shows little awareness of the environment, and at a time when individualism and mistrust is shown towards everything, it is very hard for the solo huntsman. He hunts in the way that solo huntsmen have always hunted; he experiences hunger and thirst, feels cold, sweats, walks, runs, climbs mountains, wades through streams and lakes, sleeps rough or not at all, but above all, he hunts because hunting is his passion. However, most huntsmen do not have a particular passion for hunting, rather they hunt in the way they have learned to hunt with the noble mission to understand more about nature, and to spend their free time in a useful way. Huntsmen are also motivated by thoughts of prestige and admiration.

A great service was done by the French hunting community in 1930, when they decided to found an international hunting federation based in Paris. This federation was named the "Conseil International de la Chasse" (CIC) and represented European countries in all hunting disciplines. Since then, this organisation has opened its doors to many more countries, and nearly all the countries in the world are members of CIC—or as it is now known "Conseil International de la Chasse et du Conservation du Gibier" (the International Hunting Organisation for Game Conservation).

In the rules it states, amongst other things, that political handling of hunting issues is forbidden. There has still been no contravention of this statute, since it alone handles the preservation of hunting and game on behalf of all its members. In conclusion, the principles of the CIC should be followed to provide guidelines for huntsmen throughout the world.

"In an increasingly civilized world, and with more and more people now aware of the effects of industry and agriculture on the natural environment and upon wild animals, the CIC would like to set out its principles for hunting, with conservation very much to the fore.

It wishes hunting to be recognized as the responsible protection and use of wild animals. Game forms an inextricable part of nature and should be maintained for posterity. Only the surplus from game animal populations should be hunted. Game can only thrive when its environment is secure; the conservation and restoration of the environment is therefore also an important matter of concern to huntsmen.

In its infancy, hunting satisfied material needs, but today it must be based, scientifically, upon the sensible use and protection of game species, in atruly modern context.

Through hunting, a human being makes a decision about the life of a game animal and must therefore understand the consequences of his decision. Hunting laws and regulations are based on hunting principles. The huntsman must be able to demonstrate understanding of these principles, before he hunts. He must have excellent self-discipline, observe hunting laws, and when they are adjusted he should alter his own terms in accordance with the law. He should abstain from hunting when changes in the environment or numbers of target species demand it, and refrain from any action which contradicts the precepts of hunting principles, even if regional regulations and customs permit such action.

Only then will the huntsman become a skilled custodian of nature and all her domains. Only when hunting is fully understood and properly executed can it be an important cultural and economic element of society. Hunting also leads to international contacts and associations, which are suitable for establishing hunting ethics, through the exchange of views and knowledge.

The CIC seeks to make these principles known throughout the world. Affiliation to the CIC widens its appreciation and application. The obligation of its members is to represent the CIC by setting a good example to all huntsmen.

The CIC will use all its influence to prevent all actions that contravene hunting principles or which run counter to the conservation of nature."

If the huntsman of today takes full advantage of the experiences of the long and varied history of his craft, we need not be concerned about the conservation of hunting, game, or of the environment.

APPENDIX

ACKNOWLEDGEMENTS

A project of this size can only be completed with the assistance of an experienced team of experts. The publisher and editor would therefore like to thank everyone who has worked on these two volumes.

Our very special thanks to the authors: they are all huntsmen and most of them are members of the International Hunting Organization (CIC). Many people have acted as advisors to the project. First in line is the Director of German Hunting and Fishing museum in Munich, Bernd E. Ergert, also Horst Niesters, Director of the Hellenthal Reserve on the German-Belgian border. Without the specialist knowledge and tireless commitment of Bernd E. Ergert, the compilation of the first volume of this two volume book would have been unthinkable. Horst Niesters, who is known far beyond Germany for his falconry expertise and who has been honored many times by the CIC for his wildlife photography, took an immense amount of care in providing the illustrations for the "Falconry" chapter.

The editor and publisher would like to thank the following four authors for their help: Chief Commissioner for Hunting Ethics in the CIC, Christiane Underberg; expert on game cookery Sonja Freifrau von Müffling; Dr. Susanne K.M. Linn-Kustermann, the only female professional hunter in Germany; and Dr. Sigrid Schwenk, the only hunting scientist in Germany; all of whom gave great support to the publisher.

The aim of this publication, as has been explained, was to make a contribution to the efforts to bring together huntsmen and nature lovers, and to make clear the importance both of hunting and of nature conservation. This goal could only be achieved, in the opinions of both publisher and editor, with contributions from recognized experts. We wish to thank the former secretary of the German Hunting Association (DJV), hunting writer Friedrich Karl von Eggeling, who, together with the Austrian hunting journalist Bruno Hespeler, amongst other things, rendered the sections on game animals more reader-friendly. Sincere thanks also to hunting authors Dr. Egon J. Lechner, Dr. Dietrich Stahl, and Gert G. von Harling, and also to Dr. Johannes Daniel Gerstein and Eduard Paulin, the last two authors in particular who, through their hunting tales, helped to show that hunting has a humorous side too.

We thank Dr. Heribert Kalchreuter, dire of the European Game Research Institute (EWI), for emphasizing the role of practising hunting in maintaining a healthy balance of nature in an intensively cultivated environment.

Our thanks too to Karl Walch, the renowned expert on hunting dogs, and to the biologist Uwe Leiendecker, who shows in his chapter 'Hunter and hunted' that hunting is as old as mankind. The fascinating section about prehistory by Dr. Walter Norden and the informative epilogue from the CIC Secretary General (in office now for more than three decades) lend important perspectives on hunting.

Finally, thanks must be given to the numerous illustrators, artists and wildlife photographers who have given this publication great polish through their talents.

In assembling the high-quality illustrations in these two volumes, many previously unpublished, we had ourselves to become collectors and hunters, so complex and adventure-strewn was the effort to track them all down. One of many examples is the material from the recently discovered Grotte Chauvet in the Ardèche valley: the discoverers of this wonderful cave in the South of France, the owners of the land and the French government are engaged in an on-going legal battle, which made it almost impossible to obtain any visual material. In this context we should like again to thank Jan Thorbecke publishers for their kind help.

We are very fortunate to have been able to include the picture-story by animal photographer Günther Schumann from his book "Mein Jahr mit dem Fuchs" ("My year with the Fox"), published by Wartberg Verlag. In the same context we are very grateful for the excellent specialist analysis by the well-known Wolf researcher Dr. Erik Ziemen, who confirmed that Schumann had broken new scientific ground through his unique experiences with wild foxes in Reinhardswald.

The editor is also fortunate to have joined forces with the Cologne publisher Ludwig Könemann, who made possible the creation of these two rich volumes, on a topic that is not without controversy.

Finally, I would like to offer my respect and personal thanks to a huntsman who paved the way for this book: Joachim Graf von Schönberg-Glauchau. The former secretary of the DJV initiated this project, but was unfortunately prevented by serious illness from a more active editorial involvement.

Kurt G. Blüchel (Editor)

HUNTING ETHICS
Christiane Underberg

To establish ethical values, it is important to distance oneself from the definition of the huntsman and to concentrate on the framework of hunting as applicable to understanding hunting today and in the future.

The key statement of our school of thought is: hunting must serve nature. With this in mind we fulfil the 'principle of responsibility' explained by Hans Jonas. Each ethic makes apparent "the good intentions", and it is only logical that imperatives for conduct ensue.

Principles of hunting ethics are based on:
- solidarity with and responsibility for nature;
- respect for human and cultural values;
- the pleasure of physical and spiritual demands as well as hunting targets and hunting environments;
- commitment to the preservation and use of wild animals, their habitats, and their integration;
- attempting to develop an understanding of hunting in other people.

When hunting, the following points should be remembered:
- All animals and plants have been entrusted to mankind; as huntsmen we should treat them with respect, because hunting carries responsibilities.
- Hunting is closely connected with the history of mankind; thus it is important to maintain traditions, provided that they are regularly reappraised, and to build the foundations for developing traditions.
- The motivation for hunting lies in pleasure for the task, and in aspiration towards results. Hunting without motivation is merely an activity.
- Hunting conduct demonstrates fairness and self control; responsibility for nature and society requires discipline.
- Man, beast, and plant are partners in one mutual concern; this makes it important to understand the connections within ecosystems, and to deepen this understanding, so that the huntsman does nothing which could harm the delicate links in the system.
- The huntsman should strive to preserve and to support the wide variety and diversity of natural life. Hunting should serve nature.
- Activities must not endanger populations of animals or plants. Use of natural resources must be restrained.
- Any hunting activity should aim at regulation, use or harvest, and the hunting catch must be valued.
- Animals should be protected from unnecessary suffering; hunting should be carried out with fairness towards animals in mind.
- Hunting activity requires a high degree of ability, knowledge, information, and education; only those who understand their craft will ever be responsible huntsmen.
- Hunting involves contact and interaction with other people, and the duty of the huntsman is to be open minded when meeting others. Exchanging views and ideas, and cooperation with other people can only be educational.
- Hunting demands constant justification of its actions, exchange of views with other people, and understanding of the beliefs and opinions of others. When involved in third party confrontation, the huntsman should be able to explain his occupation, and clarify its significance.

The CIC expects all huntsmen to:
- Demonstrate an understanding of nature and its context, and to support nature. This requires consideration of current scientific findings, participation in educational seminars, and professional discussion with other huntsmen and people who make use of nature.
- Observe the previously mentioned conditions and the different requirements of nature when hunting; this requires careful observation and appropriate response, regulated intervention, avoiding pain and stress for animals, sustainable culling of all target species, and hunting arrangements that are suitable for the environment and acceptable to society
- Expand their knowledge of their craft; by safe handling of weapons and equipment, checking shooting skills by using equipment in full working order in the correct situation, keeping a good hunting dog and through a good knowledge of game species.
- Treat other huntsmen as he would wish to be treated himself; this involves recognizing the weaknesses of other huntsmen, observance of the interests of others in the same area and concessions for border infringement measures.
- Keep in mind the interests of other people who use natural resources from forest, land and fishing when hunting; this can be shown by being open and friendly, showing consideration for the concerns of third parties and of different interests.
- Be able to discuss knowledgeably the viewpoint of the huntsman with people who have different opinions, and to seek allies; this can only happen through informed public work, thoughtful and open-minded discussion and analysis of customs.
- Approach his enthusiasm for hunting with composure; this can be achieved by regular appraisal of tradition, respect for cultural aspects and through responsible behavior in public.

Our main concern is to persuade people to act in total awareness and in a way that meets these requirements.

THE CODE OF GOOD SHOOTING PRACTICE

The code is reproduced here by kind permission of the British Association for Shooting and Conservation. The differences in types of habitat, in species of game and in conditions make it impossible to be specific on numbers and dates in a code for broad application. The spirit of the code is what is important, and all true sportsmen have a duty to encourage its use and to draw it to the attention of those seeking game shooting.

THE GUIDELINES
1. Managing game and its habitat
This is primarily the concern of the landowner or farmer, and the shooting tenant, and includes the rearing and releasing of game.

(i) **The Law**
It is the duty of every employer to ensure that his employees strictly observe the laws relating to all aspects of game conservation, and understand the reason for them, the importance of observing them and the penalties for breaking them.

(ii) **Wild game**
The ultimate aim of game management is to produce a shootable surplus of wild birds. However, the hand rearing of birds is a valid method of improving or sustaining the game stock where the wild population cannot be realistically managed to produce a reasonable yield. Releasing must not, however, cause harm, directly or indirectly, to wild game populations or to other conserved species.

(iii) **Game husbandry**
Whenever game birds are reared, this shall be done in accordance with the Code of Good Game Rearing Practice with careful attention to the comfort and wellbeing of the birds. Appropriate space, shelter, light, food, water and medication should be provided. Those in charge of the birds must have a good up-to-date knowledge of animal welfare and be prepared to take expert advice. Only good management will result in fit, healthy birds for release.

(iv) **Pheasant release pens**
The size, siting and number of open topped release pens appropriate for a shoot is a function of the nature of the habitat itself, relating to the type and total area of holding cover, the length of woodland edge and so on. The density of birds per release pen cannot be generalised, but the criteria are that the size of pen and numbers released in it should not significantly damage the environment nor endanger the welfare of the birds. One metre of perimeter fence per bird provides a rule of thumb standard for average sized pens, but those in doubt should seek advice from one of the established advisory bodies or an experienced shoot manager who follows the Code. Pens should be sited well away from roads to avoid unnecessary game-bird casualties. The released birds should be encouraged to roost in trees, to leave the vicinity of the pen and to become accustomed to the wild at the earliest opportunity.

(v) **Released partridges**
All partridges reared for shooting should be let out from their release pens before annual shooting on the area has started. Coveys can be held in an area by good management practices. The withdrawal periods for medicated feeds must be strictly observed.

(vi) **Released duck**
Reared duck must always be released onto water, and in numbers which are not excessive for its area. Before shooting they should be wild enough to rise readily from the water.

(vii) **Predator control**
Predator control is usually an essential part of game management. It should be carried out as humanely as possible and with consideration for the sensibilities of others. For example, keepers' gibbets no longer have a place in game conservation.

(viii) **Wild deer management**
This is the responsibility of both landowner and stalker. A detailed code and guidelines are issued by the British Deer Society and have the full support of the organisations which have prepared this Code.

Those managing and participating in deer stalking must be aware that such stalking is carried out with the aim of properly managing a specific population of deer and protecting its habitat. To seek to take only trophy beasts is unsporting. The artificial presentation of deer is unacceptable.

2. Managing the shooting days
This is primarily the concern of the person in charge of the shooting and of his keeper. It is, however, the responsibility of every landowner to ensure that any shoot being run on his land complies with this Code.

(i) **The size of the bag**
If the Four Golden Rules and good management principles are followed, the number of birds will be predetermined, being limited by the nature of the holding cover and of the ground. The shoot manager should decide the likely size of the bag and the number and frequency of days over which the ground will be shot. There should be no competition between the guns which would result in unsportsmanlike behaviour or an inappropriate bag.

The important factor is that the birds should be presented in a way that provides a demanding test of skill compatible with the abilities of the guns.

(ii) **Consideration for others**
Those responsible for organising the season's programme and each day's shooting should ensure that there is

consideration for others who live in, work in, or visit the countryside. Close liaison with tenant farmers and the local hunt is important to avoid any clash of interests. Attention should be paid to the rights and sensibilities of other users of roadways, bridleways and footpaths. Care should be taken to avoid spent shot or shot birds falling onto public places or other people's private property. Others should not be offended unnecessarily by displays of dead game or by inconsiderate behaviour in places such as public houses. Where possible, empty cartridge cases should be picked up.

(iii) **Retrieval and handling of game**
Adequate provision should be made to retrieve game as quickly as possible. When guns have their own dogs they can pick the near birds and the pickers up should then stand well behind the line to pick those that have fallen further back. Guns should indicate clearly where game they have shot has fallen. Wounded game should be hung up to cool so that it is in the best possible condition for ultimate sale and consumption. A separate Code of Good Game Handling Practice is available from the National Game Dealers Association.

(iv) **Cessation of shooting**
The last drive should finish early enough to allow pickers up to complete their task before birds go to roost.

Shooting should be cancelled if conditions such as snowstorms, fog or torrential rain mean that birds cannot be presented in a sporting manner, shot safely and retrieved properly and in marketable condition.

3. Shooting behaviour

This is primarily the concern of the guns on the day, and especially of the leader of the team and, where involved, the sporting agent. It involves especially standards of behaviour and safety; a separate note on shooting safely is included in this Code for the benefit of all concerned.

(i) **Organiser's responsibility**
It is the responsibility of the shoot organiser (landowner or shooting tenant) or his representative (who may be the head keeper), the sporting agent where involved, and the leader of the team of guns to establish the degree of experience and capability of each of the guns in advance of the shooting day. Particular care must be taken with last minute substitutes. All concerned with the organisation should ensure that all the guns fully understand the rules for shooting safely. An experienced representative of the sporting agent should accompany his clients throughout the day and arrangements should be made for any inexperienced guns, or guns for whom

the team leader cannot personally vouchsafe, to be accompanied by an experienced loader or guide while shooting.

(ii) **New and inexperienced guns**
New and inexperienced guns should visit a shooting school prior to taking part in a shooting day, and are advised to ask for a guide or loader on their first day out. Some shoot organisers arrange to start the first day of a team of guns new to them with a briefing session about all aspects of the programme, and sometimes a clay pigeon practice session. Newcomers to game shooting would be well advised to attend their first shoot as a spectator.

(iii) **Rules of safety and rules of the shoot**
It is recommended that the rules of the shoot (e.g. whether ground game may be shot) *and* the safety rules are printed (e.g. on a shoot draw card) and in addition that, whether or not the guns are experienced, both sets of rules are read out at the start of each shooting day. If they can be distributed to the guns in advance of the day as well, so much the better. Experienced shots shooting with strangers will welcome this. It should be made clear both in the terms of the letting of a shooting day, and on the day itself, that in the interests of the safety and enjoyment of the other guns, the beaters and the pickers up, anyone shooting dangerously will be asked to return home immediately.

(iv) **Safety hazards**
The organisers of the day's shooting should be aware of relevant health and safety legislation and of their duty of care. Organisers should give clear information about the conduct of each drive and should ensure that all guns are aware of potential hazards such as stops, flankers, beaters and walking or hidden guns. Each gun has a responsibility to see that he knows of these. Every gun should know the signals for no further shooting forward and for the end of a drive. To avoid confusion with other whistles, and because the sound carries better, a horn rather than a whistle is recommended for these signals.

(v) **Recognition and ranges**
Those new to shooting should ensure that by reading, observation and asking advice they are able to recognise quarry species, pest species and protected species. They should learn to judge ranges and their instructors or guides on a shooting day should make it clear as to when a bird is in shootable range, neither too close nor too far, and when a bird should be left for another gun.

(vi) **Insurance, licences and security**
It is recommended that a condition of letting a day's shooting should be that all providers and guns are fully covered for third party insurance.

The sporting agent or team captain should be asked to make a declaration on this point. All guns should be in possession of a valid shotgun certificate and game licence. Guns and cartridges left in vehicles should be kept out of sight and the vehicles must be locked.

(vii) **Standards of behaviour**
Remember at the end of a shooting day to thank your host (a letter is always appreciated), the keeper (take advice on the customary tipping) and the beaters and pickers up who have contributed to your enjoyment. Everyone involved – shoot owner, shoot organiser, gamekeeper and guns – should at all times remember that they are ambassadors for their sport, and that unsportsmanlike, dangerous or thoughtless behaviour can bring it into disrepute.

4. Non-toxic Shot

Wildfowl are at particular risk from lead poisoning if they eat spent shot when taking in grit to aid digestion. The UK Government has therefore been working with shooting, farming and conservation organisations, along with the gun and ammunition industry, to phase out the use of lead shot over wetlands. The following guidance has been issued:

Lead should not be allowed to fall into coastal and inland wetlands where it may poison waterfowl. Accordingly, any shooting with lead shot from 12-bore guns should not take place over estuaries, salt marshes, foreshore, lakes, reservoirs, gravel pits, ponds, rivers, marshes and seasonally flooded land (river flood plains, water meadows, and grazing marshes), where it would pose a significant threat of poisoning to waterfowl. Since shotgun pellets can travel considerable distances, such shooting should not take place near the edge of the wetland concerned if it would result in the deposition of lead within it.

This means that some people who shoot in or near wetland areas should adjust the way they shoot to avoid lead dropping into areas where it could be picked up by waterfowl. Others who cannot avoid depositing shot in sensitive areas are encouraged to switch to non-toxic alternatives. Landowners particulary concerned about conservation are likely to require this.

FOUR GOLDEN RULES

The Code of Good Shooting Practice is enshrined in the following principle:

Rearing and releasing of game for shooting should only be done in order to provide a sufficient stock of healthy game, fully adapted to the wild, which can be sustained without damage to the environment or to the wild stock.

The Four Golden Rules which follow from this principle are:

1. Game husbandry shall be conducted with all due consideration for the health and welfare of the birds concerned.

2. No more birds shall be released in an area of woodland, game cover, or pond than can be sustained without significantly damaging the environment, including farm crops, or leading to detriment in the health of the birds.

3. No birds shall be released after the start of annual shooting in the area concerned and they shall not be shot until they are fully adult and well adapted to the wild.

4. No bird previously released shall subsequently· be caught up during its shooting season for re-release during that season.

Guidelines for the management of game and game shooting cannot, by definition, be laid down as 'rules'. They embody the spirit of sportsmanship and a fundamental respect for the quarry and its habitat. They are set out in the next section and they cover the three areas of managing game and its habitat; managing the shooting days; and shooting behaviour.

INDEX

REFERENCES TO TEXT AND ILLUSTRATIONS

l = left, r = right, u = upper, b= below